# Business and Human F

Business corporations can and do violate human rights all over the world, and they are often not held to account. Emblematic cases and situations such as the state of the Niger Delta and the collapse of the Rana Plaza factory are examples of corporate human rights abuses which are not adequately prevented and remedied. Business and human rights as a field seeks to enhance the accountability of business – companies and businesspeople – in the human rights area, or, to phrase it differently, to bridge the accountability gap. Bridging the accountability gap is to be understood as both setting standards and holding corporations and businesspeople to account if violations occur.

Adopting a legal perspective, this book presents the ways in which this dual undertaking has been and could be further carried out in the future, and evaluates the extent to which the various initiatives in the field bridge the corporate accountability gap. It looks at the historical background of the field of business and human rights, and examines salient periods, events and cases. The book then goes on to explore the relevance of international human rights law and international criminal law for global business. International soft law and policy initiatives which have blossomed in recent years are evaluated along with private modes of regulation. The book also examines how domestic law, especially the domestic law of multinational companies' home countries, can be used to prevent and redress corporate-related human rights violations.

**Nadia Bernaz** is a senior lecturer at Middlesex University School of Law in London, adjunct lecturer of the Irish Centre for Human Rights at the National University of Ireland, Galway and visiting professor at the Catholic University of Lille (France).

# Human Rights and International Law
Series Editor: Professor Surya P. Subedi, O.B.E.

This series will explore human right law's place within the international legal order, offering much-needed interdisciplinary and global perspectives on human rights' increasingly central role in the development and implementation of international law and policy.

Human Rights and International Law is committed to providing critical and contextual accounts of human rights' relationship with international law theory and practice. To achieve this, volumes in the series will take a thematic approach that focuses on major debates in the field, looking at how human rights impacts on areas as diverse and divisive as security, terrorism, climate change, refugee law, migration, bioethics, natural resources and international trade.

Exploring the interaction, interrelationship and potential conflicts between human rights and other branches of international law, books in the series will address both historical development and contemporary contexts, before outlining the most urgent questions facing scholars and policy makers today

Available titles:

**Human Rights and Charity Law**
*International Perspectives*
Kerry O'Halloran

**Human Rights and Development in International Law**
Tahmina Karimova

**The Emerging Law of Forced Displacement in Africa**
*Development and Implementation of the Kampala Convention on Internal Displacement*
Allehone M. Abebe

**Extracting Accountability from Non-State Actors in International Law**
*Assessing the Scope for Direct Regulation*
Lee McConnell

**Socio-Economic Human Rights in Essential Public Services Provision**
Marlies Hesselman, Antenor Hallo de Wolf and Brigit Toebes

# Business and Human Rights

History, law and policy – bridging the accountability gap

## Nadia Bernaz

Routledge
Taylor & Francis Group

LONDON AND NEW YORK

First published 2017
by Routledge
2 Park Square, Milton Park, Abingdon, Oxon OX14 4RN

and by Routledge
711 Third Avenue, New York, NY 10017

*Routledge is an imprint of the Taylor & Francis Group, an informa business*

*British Library Cataloguing in Publication Data*
A catalogue record for this book is available from the British Library

*Library of Congress Cataloging in Publication Data*
Names: Bernaz, Nadia, author.
Title: Business and human rights : history, law and policy : bridging the accountability gap / Nadia Bernza.
Description: Abingdon, Oxon ; New York, NY : Routlege, 2017. | Series: Human rights and international law | Includes bibliographical references and index.
Identifiers: LCCN 2016022514| ISBN 978-1-138-64902-6 (hbk) | ISBN 978-1-138-68300-6 (pbk) | ISBN 978-1-315-62605-5 (ebk)
Subjects: LCSH: Corporate governance—Law and legislation. | Human rights. |
Social responsibility of business. | Human rights—Economic aspects. | International business enterprises—Law and legislation.
Classification: LCC K1315 .B47 2017 | DDC 341.4/8—dc23
LC record available at https://lccn.loc.gov/2016022514

ISBN: 978-1-138-64902-6 (hbk)
ISBN: 978-1-138-68300-6 (pbk)
ISBN: 978-1-315-62605-5 (ebk)

Typeset in Galliard
by FiSH Books Ltd, Enfield
Printed and bound by CPI Group (UK) Ltd, Croydon, CR0 4YY

# Contents

The twenty-three defendants (...) were among the industrial elite of Germany, not Hitler's black- and brown-shined hooligans. They represented a combination of scientific genius and commercial acumen unique in a private industrial enterprise. They were the executives who made I.G. preeminent in the world of technology and commerce. They served on the boards of directors of the most prestigious corporations in their own country and abroad, where they were treated with awe and admiration. When their government called, they accepted official posts in the spirit of public service. Like their counterparts everywhere, they were among the leading supporters of culture, charity, and religion, donating their names, time, and money. How this group finally arrived at the courtroom at Nuremberg, branded as the 'Devil's Chemists,' charged with unparalleled atrocities, is a profound lesson for the world.

Joseph Borkin, *The Crime and Punishment of I.G. Farben*, London: Andre Deutsch (1978), pp. 3–4.

# Acknowledgements

I would like to thank Katie Carpenter, Joshua Castellino, Anthony Cullen, Shane Darcy, Elvira Dominguez Redondo, Erika George, Tyler Giannini, Jérémie Gilbert, David Keane, Laurent Pech, William Pettigrew, Seb Potter, William Schabas, Tara Van Ho and Aisling Walsh.

A special thank you to the staff of the British Library.

# 1  Introduction

## The impact of business on human rights

Business creates wealth and well-being. By providing jobs, companies ensure that millions of people on all continents remain out of poverty and secure better lives for themselves, fulfilling their right to food, their right to health and their children's right to education. Simply put, the positive impact of business on human rights cannot and should not be ignored. Business and human rights, however, is primarily about the negative impact of business on the enjoyment of human rights. This is not because business is evil; rather, it is because human rights, as a field of study, tends to focus on violations. The typical human rights abuser is the state and it is on this premise that international human rights law has developed after the Second World War. Business and human rights challenges this by looking primarily into human rights violations by non-state actors: private companies.[1]

Business can negatively impact human rights in a variety of ways. The impact can be both internal, affecting people within the company, and external, affecting individuals or communities not directly working for the company. Internal human rights violations include the possible consequences of poor health and safety policies on the right to health. They also include violations of freedom of association when workers are prevented from unionising or discouraged from doing so; violations of the right to privacy when personal information about staff or customers is disclosed or sold; or violations of the right not to be discriminated against when women or people belonging to a specific ethnic or religious group, or caste, are systematically kept in low-ranking jobs or not hired at all. Human rights violations of an external nature are even wider in scope. They range from violations of the right to health and the right to water in instances of land grabbing and pollution to violations of the right not to be subjected to inhuman or degrading treatment when a private security company hired to guard facilities ends up mistreating people living in the area; violations of the right of indigenous

---

1  As discussed throughout the book, business and human rights as a field also looks into the human rights impact of state-owned companies and of individual business people.

peoples not to be subjected to forced assimilation or destruction of their culture when a community is displaced to make room for a mining or other industrial project; and violations of the right to liberty when a bank provides a loan to a criminal regime, giving the government the means to track opponents and imprison them; specifically in conflict zones, violations of the right to life sometimes amounting to war crimes or crimes against humanity, such as when a company manager provides a military officer with vehicles which allow the officer and his unit to get to a village where they kill and rape civilians. In short, the business and human rights field looks into violations of the whole spectrum of human rights, civil and political, as well as economic, social and cultural rights.

'Business and human rights' has grown from a catchy phrase into a scholarly field over the past two decades. It is a field populated by international human rights, corporate, criminal and tort lawyers and business as well as development scholars. Business and human rights encompasses issues ranging from health and safety in Chinese factories, indigenous communities' consent to mining projects in Latin America, consumer protection in France and the status of migrant workers in Dubai to questions of corporate and financial complicity in extrajudicial killings and even the commission of war crimes and crimes against humanity. Business and human rights may refer to changes a company can introduce to minimise its adverse impact on human lives – those of their staff, customers and the wider community – but also to rules a state can introduce to regulate business operations and ensure human rights are respected at all times. Business and human rights is also about corporate and individual liability before courts of law. In sum, it is a diverse field, which is understood differently depending on one's background and field of research and work.

Importantly, business and human rights is a field of study of sometimes insoluble dilemmas. It is about reconciling global and local businesses' constant pressure to succeed and grow with a rich and at times conflicting set of rights. In practice, this means that for a government, a company, an NGO or a group of employees, engaging with business and human rights is not a straightforward process. It requires an understanding of the various stakeholders' positions, the specificities of the company and the industry, the applicable legal framework and the cultural and political contexts. In other words, a business and human rights policy can rarely be limited to creating a checklist. It is necessarily more complex and consequently can lead to frustrations. Although human rights impact assessments are increasingly conducted, human rights protection requires more than ticking boxes. As one corporate participant at a Global Compact Network UK event in June 2014 candidly put it, 'human rights and drilling are not the same thing'. In order to comprehend intricate business and human rights issues, one needs to familiarise oneself with the wider picture.

With this in mind, this book offers a panorama of the field of business and human rights, and the debates associated with it. It is primarily located within the discipline of law, and approaches issues raised by business and human rights from a legal perspective, both international and domestic. It gives an overview of the relevant legal framework and points to remaining challenges and unsolved questions. It also includes historical highlights which provide the background against which business and human rights has developed.

## Business and human rights, corporate social responsibility and related concepts

Business and human rights as a field of study is about how business may negatively impact human rights and the various ways in which such violations can be prevented and addressed, including how business can be held accountable. Corporate social responsibility (CSR) is a related field of study. It rests on the idea that business has responsibilities beyond profit maximisation and towards society at large.[2] It often consists in encouraging companies to adopt and share best practices and it includes notions such as corporate philanthropy.[3] CSR is also about creating value. Hence, the scope of CSR is wider than the scope of business and rights. The point of business and human rights is not to create value but to prevent business from violating human rights or being complicit in violations primarily committed by others, usually governments. Business and human rights is more modest in scope than CSR and has less ambitious goals. Moreover, because it is not based on ethical considerations or 'values', but on identified human rights norms, it is arguably easier to circumscribe, though there is some disagreement on this point.[4]

Although CSR concerns were apparent in the business literature in the United States as early as the 1930s and 1940s, CSR as a field really dates back to the 1950s.[5] In his seminal 1953 book *Social Responsibilities of the Businessman*, Howard Bowen – said to be the 'Father of Corporate Social Responsibility'[6] – wrote:

> The day of plunder, human exploitation, and financial chicanery by private businessmen has largely passed. And the day when profit maximization was the sole criterion of business success is rapidly fading. We

2   Brent D. Beal, *Corporate Social Responsibility, Definition, Core Issues, and Recent Developments*, Los Angeles, London, New Delhi, Singapore, Washington DC: Sage (2014), p. 2.
3   Ibid., p. 13.
4   Michael Santoro notes that '[p]roponents of a legal approach to addressing social justice sometimes view ethical and moral approaches as "soft" and vague, whereas law is said to be "hard" and definite. The feeling from ethicists is, of course, mutual.' Michael A. Santoro, 'Business and Human Rights in Historical Perspective', 14 *Journal of Human Rights* 155, p. 158.
5   Archie B. Carroll, 'Corporate Social Responsibility, Evolution of a Definitional Construct', 38 (3) *Business and Society* 268 (1999), pp. 268–269.
6   Ibid., p. 270.

are entering an era when private business will be judged solely in terms of its demonstrable contribution to the general welfare.[7]

Nobel Prize winner Milton Friedman rejected these ideas and famously argued in 1962 that in a free economy

> there is one and only one social responsibility of business – to use its resources and engage in activities designed to increase its profits so long as it stays within the rules of the game, which is to say, engages in open and free competition, without deception or fraud.[8]

Some still embrace Friedman's ideas. Elaine Sternberg argued in 2000 that 'using business resources for non-business purposes is tantamount to *theft*',[9] while for David Henderson, businesses should not even try to accommodate society's expectations.[10]

Although it has its critics, CSR is now more widely accepted than ever, and among Western-based multinational corporations, CSR policies seem to be the norm rather than the exception, as discussed in Chapter 8.[11] Related concepts, such as 'sustainability', 'corporate citizenship' and the 'social licence to operate', have also emerged. Sustainability, '[i]n its current form (…) is more or less synonymous with CSR, and in certain contexts (…) now appears to be the preferred label for efforts to address the business and society interface'.[12] Corporate citizenship 'is centered around the idea or metaphor of the corporation as a good neighbor or virtuous citizen'.[13] The notion of the social licence to operate

> is often used to refer to the idea that businesses should voluntarily comply with societal expectations in order to preserve their ability (or 'license') to direct their own affairs. In cases in which firms fail to comply

7   Howard R. Bowen, *Social Responsibilities of the Businessman*, Iowa City: University of Iowa Press (reprinted in 2013 from 1953 original), p. 52.
8   Milton Friedman, *Capitalism and Freedom*, Chicago: the University of Chicago Press (2nd edition 2002), p. 133.
9   Elaine Sternberg, *Just Business. Business Ethics in Action*, Oxford: Oxford University Press (2nd edition 2000), p. 41.
10  David Henderson, *Misguided Virtue. False Notions of Corporate Social Responsibility*, London: The Institute of Economic Affairs (2001), p. 63. See also Aneel Karnani, 'The Case against Corporate Social Responsibility', *The Wall Street Journal*, 23 August 2010.
11  CSR practices have developed not only in the West but also in emerging markets, for example in Asia. See Yan Leung Cheung *et al.*, 'Does Corporate Social Responsibility Matter in Asian Emerging Markets?', 92 *Journal of Business Ethics* 401 (2010); and Wendy Chapple and Jeremy Moon, 'Corporate Social Responsibility (CSR) in Asia A Seven-Country Study of CSR Web Site Reporting', 44 *Business and Society* 415.
12  Brent D. Beal, *Corporate Social Responsibility, Definition, Core Issues, and Recent Developments*, Los Angeles, London, New Delhi, Singapore, Washington DC: Sage (2014), p. 12.
13  Ibid., pp. 12–13.

with societal expectations, this freedom (or 'license') may be suspended or revoked. In other words, failure to voluntarily comply with societal expectations may result in firms being forced through regulatory and/or legal means to do so.[14]

Other related concepts include 'conscious capitalism', 'shared value capitalism' and the 'triple bottom line'. Conscious capitalism is a phrase coined by Whole Foods cofounder and co-CEO John Mackey. Conscious capitalism rests on four tenets. First, the point of companies cannot only be about making money; they need a 'higher purpose'.[15] Second, all stakeholders must be satisfied: investors and other stakeholders alike.[16] Stakeholders 'include all the people who impact and are impacted by a business'.[17] These can be 'inner-circle stakeholders'[18] such as customers, team members, investors, suppliers, communities and even the environment; or 'outer-circle stakeholders' such as 'competitors, activists, critics, unions, the media and government'.[19] Third, conscious companies require conscious leadership,[20] and fourth, they need conscious cultures and management.[21]

Harvard professor Michael Porter coined the phrase 'shared value capitalism' in 2006 in an article published in the *Harvard Business Review*.[22] The principle of shared value, it is argued,

> involves creating economic value in a way that *also* creates value for society by addressing its needs and challenges. (...) Shared value is not social responsibility, philanthropy, or even sustainability, but a new way to achieve economic success. It is not on the margin of what companies do but at the center.[23]

Shared value capitalism differs from conscious capitalism in that it focuses on creating economic value for society, but does not prominently feature human values.[24] Both concepts, however, can be said to belong to the CSR (or

---

14   Ibid., p. 29.
15   John Mackey and Raj Sisodia, *Conscious Capitalism*, Boston: Harvard Business School Publishing Corporation (2012), p. 46.
16   Ibid., p. 69.
17   Ibid., p. 72.
18   Ibid., p. 153.
19   Ibid.
20   Ibid., p. 177.
21   Ibid., p. 215.
22   Michael E. Porter and Mark R. Kramer, 'Strategy and Society. The Link between Competitive Advantage and Corporate Social Responsibility', 84 *Harvard Business Review* 78 (2006).
23   Michael E. Porter and Mark R. Kramer, 'Creating Shared Value', 89 *Harvard Business Review* 62 (2011), p. 64.
24   John Mackey and Raj Sisodia, *Conscious Capitalism*, Boston: Harvard Business School Publishing Corporation (2012), p. 294.

sustainability) family, their 'claims of distinctiveness notwithstanding'.[25]

The triple bottom line is a concept first developed in 1997 by businessman John Elkington. He championed the idea of sustainable capitalism, a system in which companies focus not only on the so-called bottom line (i.e. profit maximisation) but on the triple bottom line, which consists in 'the simultaneous pursuit of economic prosperity, environmental quality, and social equity'.[26] In other words, companies ought to embrace a 'people, planet, profit' mindset. The triple bottom line can also be said to be part of the large CSR family.

CSR is therefore a particularly diverse field and, as a result, a notion which is difficult to define.[27] In 2001, the European Commission defined CSR as 'a concept whereby companies integrate social and environmental concerns in their business operations and in their interaction with their stakeholders on a voluntary basis'.[28] In 2011, the European Commission revised the definition to take into account developments in the business and human rights field, and notably the adoption of the 2011 UN Guiding Principles on Business and Human Rights, an initiative discussed in detail in Chapter 7. The new definition moves CSR away from voluntarism and closer to the business and human rights field, where accountability plays a central role. The European Commission now understands CSR as

> the responsibility of enterprises for their impacts on society. Respect for applicable legislation, and for collective agreements between social partners, is a prerequisite for meeting that responsibility. To fully meet their corporate social responsibility, enterprises should have in place a process to integrate social, environmental, ethical, human rights and consumer concerns into their business operations and core strategy in close collaboration with their stakeholders, with the aim of:
> - maximising the creation of shared value for their owners/shareholders and for their other stakeholders and society at large;
> - identifying, preventing and mitigating their possible adverse impacts.[29]

25  Brent D. Beal, *Corporate Social Responsibility, Definition, Core Issues, and Recent Developments*, Los Angeles, London, New Delhi, Singapore, Washington DC: Sage (2014), pp. 76–80.
26  John Elkington, *Cannibalism with Forks. The Triple Bottom Line of 21st Century Business*, Oxford: Capstone (1997), p. 397.
27  As discussed in Archie B. Carroll, 'Corporate Social Responsibility, Evolution of a Definitional Construct', 38 (3) *Business and Society* 268 (1999); and Benedict Sheehy, 'Defining CSR: Problems and Solutions', 131 *Journal of Business Ethics* 625 (2015).
28  EU Commission, Promoting a European Framework for Corporate Social Responsibility, COM(2001)366.
29  EU Commission, A renewed EU Strategy 2011–14 for Corporate Social Responsibility, COM(2011) 681 final.

This definition of CSR, however, is not universally accepted and many companies continue to hold a much less comprehensive view of CSR, viewing it as a distinct area of the business and as an add-on to core operations, as opposed to a concept meant to influence all operations. There is a diversity of views about CSR and, generally speaking, CSR and business and human rights can still be said to be distinct fields.[30]

The micro-blogging website Twitter, where CSR professionals, NGOs, human rights lawyers and academics from the business and legal fields abound, provides an opportunity to observe this diversity at first hand. One particular day illustrated this very well. On 17 April 2013, the United States Supreme Court rendered its decision in a seminal case against the multinational oil and gas company Royal Dutch Shell.[31] Lawyers in the field, who tend to lean towards the human rights rather than the CSR side, were having a busy and exciting day on Twitter. It was almost as if the future of this entire area of study depended on the nine Justices' views regarding whether corporations could be sued before US federal courts for human rights violations committed abroad. Dozens of tweets on the possible outcomes and consequences of this decision were published. At the same time, and seemingly oblivious to this agitation, the sustainable business and CSR professionals and academics continued to post about the latest sustainability reports and the best ways to promote diversity among local managers. This is anecdotal evidence, but the gap between the lawyers' and the CSR professionals' preoccupations that day was manifest. Lawyers are usually called when things have gone wrong. Human rights, criminal and tort law, as fields of study, focus on violations. By contrast, CSR focuses on ways in which business processes can include human rights, environmental and ethical considerations. The work takes place upstream of possible violations. In short, the two groups of professionals work on similar, related questions, but from different angles.

Moreover, and perhaps more importantly, within the CSR field, the idea that one needs to convince corporations to behave responsibly perdures. This is a consequence of the fact that it is viewed as an add-on, as being negotiable and voluntary. For those who believe in voluntarism, there exist a plethora of publications exploring the 'business case' for respecting human rights.[32]

---

30   For an interesting discussion on tension between the two notions, see Andrew Fagan's reflective piece, 'Defending Corporate Social Responsibility: Myanmar and the Lesser Evil', 19 *The International Journal of Human Rights* 867 (2015).
31   *Kiobel v. Royal Dutch Petroleum Co.*, 133 S.Ct. 1659 (2013). This case is looked at in detail in Chapter 10.
32   For a thorough analysis, including a historical perspective on the notion, see Archie B. Carroll and Kareem M. Shabana, 'The Business Case for Corporate Social Responsibility: A Review of Concepts, Research and Practice', 12 *International Journal of Management Reviews* 85 (2010). See also Manuela Weber, 'The Business Case for Corporate Social Responsibility: A Company-Level Measurement Approach for CSR', 26 *European Management Journal* 247 (2008).

However, the premise upon which the business case rests, which is 'that one can promote human rights to earn greater profits – may be attractive for corporations, but is flawed in that it compromises the preemptory nature of human rights'.[33] The Atlantic slave trade, the involvement of corporations in the Holocaust, the ongoing tragedy in Bhopal, the close business relationships of some multinational companies with the white supremacist regime in South Africa – all explored in this book – are testament to the fact that the search for a business case to respect human rights is inappropriate.

## The accountability gap

Emblematic cases and situations such as the state of the Niger Delta and the collapse of the Rana Plaza factory are examples of corporate human rights abuses which are not adequately prevented or remedied. These tragedies uncover powerless victims who lack access to channels that would allow them to raise concerns and bring legal claims. They also reveal a lack of transparency in the operations of global businesses. In sum, the picture is one of limited accountability of business in the human rights area. Business and human rights seeks to enhance the accountability of business – companies and businesspeople – in the human rights area or, to phrase it differently, to bridge the accountability gap.

The notion of accountability is one that is notoriously difficult to define, and is more likely to be considered in the public or political sphere.[34] When someone is elected, or is paid with public money, he or she is expected to act in a way that shows respect for the trust that was placed in them. If they do not do so, it is understood that they might lose their seats, or their jobs. This is how they are being held accountable. The notion of accountability of business is necessarily different from the notion of accountability of public actors. Business executives are not elected, and companies are not set up by popular demand.

In an attempt to define accountability, Bovens distinguishes between, on the one hand, accountability as a virtue and, on the other hand, accountability as a mechanism.[35] When understood as a virtue, accountability is a 'normative concept' or 'a set of standards' for evaluating behaviours, and being accountable is said to be a 'desirable quality'.[36] When understood as a mechanism, accountability is a narrower concept. It refers to 'an institutional

---

33    Surya Deva, 'Human Rights Violations by Multinational Corporations and International Law: Where from Here?', 19 *Connecticut Journal of International Law* 1 (2003–2004), p. 19.

34    Andrew Keay and Joan Loughrey, 'The Framework for Board Accountability in Corporate Governance', 35(2) *Legal Studies* (2015), p. 266.

35    Mark Bovens, 'Two Concepts of Accountability: Accountability as a Virtue and as a Mechanism', 33(5) *West European Politics* (2010), pp. 947–948.

36    Ibid, p. 949.

relation or arrangement in which an agent can be held to account by another agent or institution'.[37] Applying Bovens' framework, business accountability can refer to how businesspeople and corporations should behave, ideally respecting human rights standards and being transparent about their operations. It can also refer to the mechanisms by which they can be held to account after things have gone wrong, by way of direct dialogue with the victims, mediation and, in graver cases, litigation. Hence bridging the accountability gap is to be understood as both setting standards and attempting to change corporate behaviours so that they become respectful of human rights, and holding corporations and businesspeople to account if violations occur. Examples of the former include encouraging companies to adopt human rights policies and conduct human rights impact assessments. Examples of the latter include bringing a civil claim against a company who allegedly violated human rights, prosecuting a business leader for human rights violations amounting to crimes and getting a company to recognize its responsibility in the course of a mediation process. This book covers both aspects.

The accountability gap is clear when it comes to accountability as a virtue and a set of standards. The human rights obligations of companies are unclear, and the way companies operate can lack transparency. The gap is also apparent when it comes to accountability as a mechanism to hold companies to account, especially when the human rights violations occur in developing countries with weaker governance systems. Such lack of accountability is due to the combination of three main factors. First, in cases of grave violations of human rights, transnational corporations and their subsidiaries often become involved in human rights violations as accomplices of the host state.[38] As the host state itself is the main perpetrator of abuse, the courts of the host state are generally not in a position to provide victims with genuine remedies. Moreover, even when governments are not at fault as such, many developing countries have unreliable judicial systems coupled with weak enforcement mechanisms.[39] Second, it is difficult for victims to get access to remedies in the countries of registration of the parent company, as Chapter 10 of this book highlights.[40] Third, there is currently no international mechanism by which corporations can be held accountable for human rights violations.[41]

---

37  Ibid., p. 948.

38  See, for example, African Commission on Human and People's Rights, 155/96: *Social and Economic Rights Action Center (SERAC) and Center for Economic and Social Rights (CESR) v Nigeria*, 27 October 2001.

39  See for example, Ruggie, 'Opening Remarks at Consultation on operationalizing the framework for business and human rights presented by the Special Representative of the Secretary-General on the issue of human rights and transnational corporations and other business enterprises' (2009) at 3.

40  Gwynne Skinner, Robert McCorquodale, Olivier De Schutter and Andie Lambe, *The Third Pillar: Access to Judicial Remedies for Human Rights Violations by Transnational Business*, ICAR, CORE and ECCJ report (2013).

These factors, when taken together, operate to deny victims of corporate human rights violations access to meaningful remedial mechanisms, hence creating an accountability gap.

This book assesses the extent to which the main business and human rights initiatives and accountability mechanisms successfully bridge the accountability gap, by succeeding in changing corporate behaviour so that it is respectful of human rights, and by holding corporations and businesspeople to account if violations occur. These initiatives may be international or domestic and, in the case of private modes of regulation, they may involve a variety of public and private stakeholders.

## Structure of the book

Although business and human rights as a field of research is relatively new, the interplay between business and human rights is not. In the informal words of Professor Ruggie, who was then finishing his mandate as UN Secretary-General Special Representative for Business and Human Rights, 'business and human rights as a substantive issue goes back forever. The slave trade was about business and human rights'.[42] Colonisation and the brutal exploitation of natural resource-rich lands, sometimes directly by European state-owned companies; the Atlantic slave trade; the Industrial Revolution; and the World Wars all gave rise to gross human rights abuses connected to corporate activity. These historical events also generated formidable financial gains for merchants, entrepreneurs and bankers.

Conquest and domination of new territories make for a lucrative enterprise. They allow easier access to natural resources and to cheap labour, and open new markets. But greed alone does not explain all forms of territorial conquests, and particularly the colonial enterprise. As one author explains: 'The list of things which account for the discoveries and colonization is well known: religious zeal, love for adventure, thirst for wealth, revenge by conquest.'[43] Colonisation was undoubtedly motivated by grand dreams of power and religious or ideological domination, and often by a mix of all

41   The implementation of the OECD Guidelines on Multinational Enterprises (OECD (2011), OECD Guidelines for Multinational Enterprises, OECD Publishing), which contain a human rights chapter (Chapter IV, page 31), is monitored by National Contact Points (NCPs) in each OECD country. Although NCPs apply an international text (the Guidelines), may receive complaints against multinational corporations and follow a similar procedure, each of them works separately from the others, and is administered at the domestic level. In other words, they do not constitute an international mechanism as such.

42   John Ruggie, Sir Geoffrey Chandler Speaker Series, 11 January 2011, www.youtube.com/watch?v=__fhV3j4hlE (last accessed 21 March 2016). See also John Elkington, Cannibalism with Forks. The Triple Bottom Line of 21st Century Business, Oxford: Capstone (1997), p. 79: 'The social agenda for business probably has a longer history than the environmental agenda. Think of the early controversies around slavery, child labor, and working conditions.'

43   Marc Ferro, *Colonization: A Global History*, London and New York: Routledge (1997), p. 6.

three. It is also established that, for example, France's latest colonial conquests at the end of the nineteenth century were not motivated so much by economic reasons but rather by a desire to focus French people's attention away from the humiliation of the 1870 defeat against Germany that had left France amputated from the Alsace-Lorraine region. In this context, the quote by French politician Jules Ferry, who famously said that 'colonial policy is the daughter of industrial policy', seems to have served as an *ex post facto* justification for conquest.[44] Hence, the role of business in the colonial process should not be overemphasised. Nevertheless, conquests and colonisation have always been encouraged by those who saw the business opportunities they opened. What is more, in many instances parts of the business community actively supported the invasion of new territories and partly funded it.[45] The human cost of these historical business operations naturally falls under the scholarly field of 'business and human rights'.

The first part of this book, titled 'Historical Highlights', does not aim to be exhaustive and to systematically present a history of corporate human rights abuses. Although fascinating, this could probably fill dozens of history books. Rather, this part focuses on a selection of salient periods, events and cases to illustrate the various ways in which human rights and business have interacted in the past. It provides readers, particularly if they are non-lawyers, with a way into legal questions, by explaining the background against which international human rights and labour law have developed, largely in reaction to human rights violations. It gives an account of egregious violations of rights in which the business sector played a major role, and which led to international responses. On this basis, three different episodes have been selected: the Atlantic slave trade (Chapter 2); the emergence of international labour law as a consequence of the changes brought about by the Industrial Revolution (Chapter 3); and the post-Second World War criminal trials against German industrialists and bankers accused of having done business with the Nazis (Chapter 4).

Part II forms the core of the book. It highlights the challenges posed by the adverse human rights impacts of business and progress made in the area, by focusing on the current international legal and policy frameworks on business and human rights. It is split into four chapters, each of which focuses on one area of law and policy and assesses the extent to which the corporate accountability gap is being bridged within that area.

Chapter 5 is central to the understanding of business and human rights as a field of research. It starts with the idea that international human rights law has developed in a way that technically makes states the only duty-bearers of human rights obligations. Under a conservative reading of the system,

---

44  Mario Levi, book review of Henri Brunschwig, *Mythes et réalités de l'impérialisme colonial français (1871–1914)*, 25(4) *Politique étrangère* (1960), p. 417.

45  Marc Ferro, *Colonization: A Global History*, London and New York: Routledge (1997), p. 7.

corporations, even multinational corporations, are not subjects of international human rights law and therefore are under no legal obligation to abide by human rights treaties. At best, they are under the obligation not to commit violations amounting to international crimes as defined by the Statute of the International Criminal Court. A number of authors, such as Professor Andrew Clapham, have challenged the assertion that corporations have no international human rights obligations.[46] Chapter 5 contributes to this debate and shows how boundaries that were once thought to be immutable are now shifting to allow for greater corporate accountability for human rights abuses.

Chapter 6 focuses on the interplay between human rights and international economic law, an area which is said to have developed in isolation from the overall international legal framework. Chapter 6 'connects the dots' and explains the role of human rights in areas of law which are of crucial importance for business, international investment and international trade law. The chapter highlights the limited role played by human rights considerations in these areas of law, leading to limited corporate accountability.

Chapters 5 and 6 highlight the limitations of the current legal framework, especially in terms of international enforcement. In response, Chapter 7 presents the various international soft law and policy initiatives that attempt to address corporate human rights violations, starting with the United Nations efforts to draft a Code of Conduct for Transnational Corporations in the 1970s. Each of these initiatives aim to bridge the corporate accountability gap. Because they are not binding, these initiatives encourage corporations to respect human rights standards through self-regulation. With this mind, Chapter 8 briefly delves into private modes of regulation as complementary tools to enhance corporate accountability.

Part III, the final part of the book, covers domestic law and policy. It is through legal and political reform at the domestic level and stronger enforcement mechanisms than are provided for at the international level that greater corporate accountability might be achieved. Chapter 9 shows how a business and human rights approach can shape domestic law and policies, resulting for example in the adoption of regulation with extraterritorial implications to induce change in business operations overseas and enhance accountability. Chapter 10 covers the developing business and human rights litigation before domestic courts. It discusses prominent civil and criminal cases and points to the ways in which plaintiffs, and victims in general, have overcome the numerous obstacles that stand in the way of justice and greater corporate accountability.

---

46   Andrew Clapham, *Human Rights Obligations of Non State Actors*, Oxford: Oxford University Press (2006); Surya Deva and David Bilchitz (eds), *Human Rights Obligations of Business: Beyond the Corporate Responsibility to Respect?*, Cambridge: Cambridge University Press (2013); Jernej Letnar Černič and Tara Van Ho (eds), *Human Rights and Business: Direct Corporate Accountability for Human Rights*, Nijmegen: Wolf Legal Publishers (2015).

# Bibliography

*Books*

Beal, Brent D., *Corporate Social Responsibility, Definition, Core Issues, and Recent Developments*, Los Angeles, London, New Delhi, Singapore, Washington DC: Sage (2014).

Bowen, Howard R., *Social Responsibilities of the Businessman*, Iowa City: University of Iowa Press (reprinted in 2013 from 1953 original).

Clapham, Andrew, *Human Rights Obligations of Non State Actors*, Oxford: Oxford University Press (2006).

Deva, Surya and Bilchitz, David (eds), *Human Rights Obligations of Business: Beyond the Corporate Responsibility to Respect?*, Cambridge: Cambridge University Press (2013).

Elkington, John, *Cannibalism with Forks. The Triple Bottom Line of 21st Century Business*, Oxford: Capstone (1997).

Ferro, Marc, *Colonization: A Global History*, London and New York: Routledge (1997).

Friedman, Milton, *Capitalism and Freedom*, Chicago: the University of Chicago Press (2nd edition 2002).

Henderson, David, *Misguided Virtue. False Notions of Corporate Social Responsibility*, London: The Institute of Economic Affairs (2001).

Letnar Černič, Jernej and Van Ho, Tara (eds), *Human Rights and Business: Direct Corporate Accountability for Human Rights*, Nijmegen: Wolf Legal Publishers (2015).

Mackey, John and Sisodia, Raj, *Conscious Capitalism*, Boston: Harvard Business School Publishing Corporation (2012).

Sternberg, Elaine, *Just Business. Business Ethics in Action*, Oxford: Oxford University Press (2nd edition 2000).

*Journal articles*

Bovens, Mark, 'Two Concepts of Accountability: Accountability as a Virtue and as a Mechanism', 33(5) *West European Politics* (2010).

Carroll, Archie B., 'Corporate Social Responsibility, Evolution of a Definitional Construct', 38(3) *Business and Society* 268 (1999).

Carroll, Archie B. and Shabana, Kareem M., 'The Business Case for Corporate Social Responsibility: A Review of Concepts, Research and Practice', 12 *International Journal of Management Reviews* 85 (2010).

Chapple, Wendy and Moon, Jeremy, 'Corporate Social Responsibility (CSR) in Asia A Seven-Country Study of CSR Web Site Reporting', 44 *Business and Society* 415.

Cheung, Yan Leung, Tan, Weiquang, Ahn, Hee-Joon and Zhang, Zheng, 'Does Corporate Social Responsibility Matter in Asian Emerging Markets?', 92 *Journal of Business Ethics* 401 (2010).

Deva, Surya, 'Human Rights Violations by Multinational Corporations and International Law: Where from Here?', 19 *Connecticut Journal of International Law* 1 (2003–2004).

Fagan, Andrew, 'Defending Corporate Social Responsibility: Myanmar and the Lesser Evil', 19 *The International Journal of Human Rights* 867 (2015).

Keay, Andrew and Loughrey, Joan, 'The Framework for Board Accountability in Corporate Governance', 35 (2) *Legal Studies* (2015).
Porter, Michael E. and Kramer, Mark R., 'Strategy and Society. The Link between Competitive Advantage and Corporate Social Responsibility', 84 *Harvard Business Review* 78 (2006).
Porter, Michael E. and Kramer, Mark R., 'Creating Shared Value', 89 *Harvard Business Review* 62 (2011).
Santoro, Michael A., 'Business and Human Rights in Historical Perspective', 14 *Journal of Human Rights* 155.
Sheehy, Benedict, 'Defining CSR: Problems and Solutions', 131 *Journal of Business Ethics* 625 (2015).
Weber, Manuela, 'The Business Case for Corporate Social Responsibility: A Company-Level Measurement Approach for CSR', 26 *European Management Journal* 247 (2008).

## Newspaper article

Karnani, Aneel, 'The Case against Corporate Social Responsibility', *The Wall Street Journal*, 23 August 2010.

## Official documents

EU Commission, Promoting a European Framework for Corporate Social Responsibility, COM(2001)366.
EU Commission, A renewed EU Strategy 2011–14 for Corporate Social Responsibility, COM(2011) 681 final.
OECD Guidelines on Multinational Enterprises (2011).

## Cases

*Kiobel v Royal Dutch Petroleum Co.*, 133 S.Ct. 1659 (2013).
African Commission on Human and People's Rights, 155/96: *Social and Economic Rights Action Center (SERAC) and Center for Economic and Social Rights (CESR) v Nigeria*, 27 October 2001.

## Reports and miscellaneous

Levi, Mario, book review of Henri Brunschwig, *Mythes et réalités de l'impérialisme colonial français (1871–1914)*, 25(4) *Politique étrangère* (1960).
Ruggie, John G., 'Opening Remarks at Consultation on operationalizing the framework for business and human rights presented by the Special Representative of the Secretary-General on the issue of human rights and transnational corporations and other business enterprises' (2009).
Ruggie, John G., Sir Geoffrey Chandler Speaker Series, 11 January 2011, available on YouTube, www.youtube.com/watch?v=__fhV3j4hlE (last accessed 21 March 2016).
Skinner, Gwynne, McCorquodale, Robert, De Schutter, Olivier and Lambe, Andie, *The Third Pillar: Access to Judicial Remedies for Human Rights Violations by Transnational Business*, ICAR, CORE and ECCJ report (2013).

# Part I

# Historical highlights

## Limited accountability

This historical part sheds light on incidences of egregious violations of rights in which the business sector played a major role, and which led to a response at the international level. Using these criteria, three different episodes have been selected: the Atlantic slave trade, the emergence of international labour law and the post-Second World War criminal trials of German industrialists and bankers accused of having done business with the Nazis. They all point to limited, if not non-existent, accountability of business for its implication in human rights violations.

Beyond providing a narrative on these violations, on the implication of business in them and on the international response they triggered, Chapters 2, 3 and 4 offer an entry point into legal issues discussed in the remainder of the book. These issues include whether international law, and specifically international human rights law and international labour law, can directly regulate non-state actors such as private businesses; and the conditions under which an individual, or a company, can be held criminally liable for having entered into business relations with a government engaging in massive human rights violations.

# 2 The Atlantic slave trade

## A business and human rights reading

The Atlantic slave trade and the dependence of the Americas and the Caribbean on slavery from 1500 to 1870 was neither the first nor the last occurrence of slavery. The trade in human beings and their use in all kinds of professions throughout the antiquity and the Middle Ages is well documented, and slavery still exists today. All over the world people have been both enslaved and slave owners or traders.[1] Looking at it with the benefit of hindsight, the condition of serfs in medieval Europe was arguably not much better than the condition of slaves in eighteenth-century Barbados, and both are probably impossible to imagine for a majority of this book's readers.[2] Yet, several factors make the Atlantic slave trade unique.

The slave trade to the Americas was almost exclusively a trade in Africans by European, as well as African, slave merchants. Between 1500 and 1870, an estimated 11 to 12 million Africans were transported from Africa to the New World.[3] Once there, if the enslaved Africans were to have children, those were automatically enslaved, bringing the total number of victims to astronomical levels. As Professor Lauren asserts,

---

1   David Brion Davis, *Inhuman Bondage. The Rise and Fall of Slavery in the New World*, Oxford: Oxford University Press (2006), Chapter 2 on 'The Ancient Foundations of Modern Slavery'.
2   Disease, extreme poverty, high mortality rates, religious fanaticism and appalling lack of hygiene were commonplace in Europe at that time. Thus, the absence of empathy with the fate of Africans on the part of the European masses and even the educated elites is not surprising. As David Brion Davis puts it:

> New World slavery emerged at a time when most people took it for granted that this world was a very cruel, sinful, and brutal place. Until the late eighteenth century (…), the European public was not only insensitive but rushed to witness the most terrible spectacles of torture, dismemberment, and death. In view of this cold-blooded culture, it is perhaps remarkable that the emerging slave trade drew as much courageous fire as it did.

David Brion Davis, *Inhuman Bondage. The Rise and Fall of Slavery in the New World*, Oxford: Oxford University Press (2006), p. 96.
3   Hugh Thomas, *The Slave Trade, The History of the Atlantic Slave Trade 1440–1870*, London: Picador (1997), Appendix 3.

in terms of the total number of millions of human beings, focus on a particular race, creation of an ideology extolling racial superiority and a practice of segregation between masters and slaves, lucrative financial rewards, impact on four continents, and magnitude of tragic brutality, black slavery simply had no parallel in history.[4]

If a representative sample of human rights scholars were to be asked for a list of what they viewed as the worst historical violations of rights, it is likely that the slave trade and the generalised use of slave labour in the Americas would appear high on most lists, along with other historical violations such as the Holocaust. While the great amount of scholarly attention received by slavery in the Americas and the Atlantic slave trade would probably partly explain this, they undoubtedly constitute large-scale, historical human rights violations.

The reasons why the Atlantic slave trade developed and thrived in the ways it did are complex and to some extent still under debate today. One reason often put forward is the widespread belief among European settlers that the formidable resources of the New World could not be exploited without massive imports of enslaved Africans, viewed as the only people physically capable of surviving the harsh conditions of life and labour as well as the diseases associated with the New World.[5] Regardless of whether this assumption was true or whether, as Eric Williams argues, it was *ex post facto* rationalisation,[6] the fact remains that labour was needed if profits were to be made. Hence, although they are not the only factor, business considerations necessarily lie at the heart of the history of the slave trade. It was to generate profits through the trade in slaves, and more importantly through the trade in slave labour's proceeds, that for more than three hundred years millions of people were enslaved and considered chattel.

Yet, greed alone cannot fully explain the development of the Atlantic slave trade. To begin with, the trade was a consequence of prior 'discovery', conquest and desires of colonisation of the New World by powerful European nations. The New World had been 'discovered'. It needed to be conquered, settled and exploited in a way that would enhance the power, prestige and wealth of European monarchies.[7] As historian David Eltis argues,

4    Paul Gordon Lauren, *The Evolution of International Human Rights*, Philadelphia: University of Pennsylvania Press, 2nd edition (2003), pp. 29–30.

5    See, for example, Hugh Thomas, *The Slave Trade, The History of the Atlantic Slave Trade 1440–1870*, London: Picador (1997), p. 97. Some authors disagree with this analysis. Eric Williams, for example, criticises the idea that Africans were brought to the Americas because white labourers could not do the work and shows that 'white servitude' existed for decades prior to the massive imports of enslaved Africans. See Eric Williams, *Capitalism and Slavery* (1944), Chapel Hill: the University of North Carolina Press (1994), pp. 18–22.

6    Eric Williams, *Capitalism and Slavery* (1944), Chapel Hill: the University of North Carolina Press (1994), p. 22.

7    Marc Ferro, *Colonization: A Global History*, London and New York: Routledge (1997), p. 6.

European behavior in the early modern Atlantic was not that of unbridled and profits-maximizing capitalists. An enquiry into deep-seated cultural attitudes on the part of both Europeans and non-Europeans provides just as much insight into the creation of the new Atlantic world as a simple search for the quest for profits.[8]

The reasons for the continuing trade in enslaved Africans over the course of several centuries, which came to include beliefs in the superiority of the 'white race', are outside the scope of this book.[9] Suffice it to say that the 'quest for profits' by states and individuals, and later by companies, at least partially explains the slave trade and the systematic use of slave labour on the American continent. Thus the story of the slave trade and its abolition is also a business and human rights story. The devastating consequences of systematically putting profits before human considerations are precisely what the field of business and human rights intends to study. With this in mind, the aim of this chapter is three-fold. First, it seeks to provide a narrative on some of the greatest human rights violations in history, in which business played a central role. The idea is to show that the involvement of business in human rights abuses is not a new development to be associated with contemporary economic globalization. Quite the contrary, the history of the slave trade shows patterns of exploitation which should feel familiar to the contemporary reader.

Second, the chapter looks at the slave trade as an entry point into issues that are still of relevance today, such as the notion of the 'human rights and business dilemma', the 'business case' to respect human rights and the practice of corporate philanthropy. Third, the chapter acknowledges the almost total lack of accountability for the gross human rights violations the slave trade entailed, but also sheds light on timid international attempts to bridge the accountability gap once the trade had become illegal. These attempts took the form of international courts that adjudicated the search and seizure of ships believed to be used to transport slaves.[10] Briefly mentioned in this chapter, these international courts are explored in more detail in Chapter 5.

The chapter is divided into five sections. The first section describes how and why the Atlantic trade in enslaved Africans started. The second section covers the practicalities of the slave trade, from capture in Africa to sale in the New World. The third section looks at the expansion and the high point of

8   David Eltis, *The Rise of African Slavery in the Americas*, Cambridge: Cambridge University Press (2000), p. 2.

9   See for example the debates between Seymour Drescher, *Capitalism and Antislavery*, London: Macmillan (1986), and Eric Williams, *Capitalism and Slavery* (1944), Chapel Hill: the University of North Carolina Press (1994). See also Richard S. Dunn, *Sugar and Slaves: The Rise of the Planter Class in the English West Indies, 1624–1713*, Chapel Hill: the University of North Carolina Press (1972).

10  On this, see Jenny Martinez, *The Slave Trade and the Origins of International Human Rights Law*, Oxford: Oxford University Press (2012).

the trade in enslaved Africans and sheds light on the operations of, and on one occasion the dilemma faced by, chartered companies involved in the trade, and on philanthropic work by slave traders. The fourth section focuses on British abolition of the slave trade, exploring in particular whether abolitionists successfully made the business case for abolition. The final section explains how states eventually came together to make the slave trade, and later slavery, unlawful under international law. For the first time, large-scale human rights violations implicating the business sector were receiving international attention.

## The early days of the slave trade

In the 1400s, during the century that ended eight years after Columbus's first voyage to the Caribbean, the trade in African slaves was already thriving, though on a more modest scale than was the case in the centuries to come. Historian Hugh Thomas considers that the 'turning point for European journeys to West Africa came in 1415 when the Portuguese mounted a military expedition and took Ceuta', on the Northern coast of Africa, across the strait of Gibraltar. Ceuta had been under Muslim control and was already a place of trade in enslaved Africans, through the Sahara route.[11] The driving force behind the seizure of Ceuta by Portuguese troops was Prince Henry of Portugal, an entrepreneur at heart and 'an important pioneer in the history of the transatlantic slave trade'.[12] In the 1440s, Portuguese sailors began sailing south along the west coast of Africa, starting trade in various goods with the locals, capturing and, later on, buying slaves.

In 1454, Pope Nicholas V issued a bull officially confirming the Portuguese monopoly of trading with West Africa.[13] The 1450s also saw the establishment of the Atlantic island of Madeira as an intensive sugar-producing territory relying on enslaved Africans' work.[14] Another set of islands, the Cape Verde islands, facing today's Senegal and settled by the Portuguese in the 1460s, became 'the biggest slave depot (...) of the sixteenth century'.[15] The peace treaty between Spain and Portugal in 1480 further reinforced the Portuguese domination in the trade of slaves as the treaty gave Portugal full control of Madeira, the Azores, the Cape Verde islands and the parts of mainland Africa facing the latter set of islands. The treaty gave Spain control over the Canary Islands and, similarly, over the parts of mainland Africa facing them.[16] This treaty gave Portugal the opportunity to explore further

11   Hugh Thomas, *The Slave Trade, The History of the Atlantic Slave Trade 1440–1870*, London: Picador (1997), p. 51.
12   Ibid., p. 52.
13   Ibid., p. 65.
14   Ibid., p. 70.
15   Ibid., p. 71.
16   Ibid., p. 76.

south along the coast of Africa. In 1486 the settlement of São Tomé began. In 1487 Bartolomeu Dias was the first European to sail around the Cape of Good Hope and up the coast of East Africa.

From these early days until the end of the eighteenth century, European nations regulated the trade in slaves. Initially, traders had to pay a tax to the Portuguese Crown, which in effect granted the right to trade, and 'was thereby committed to the enterprise'.[17] Bartolommeo Marchionni, of Florence, was one of these traders. He had developed great relations with Spanish and Portuguese monarchs, and he probably financed the expedition of Amerigo Vespucci, who 'discovered' most of Brazil. As Hugh Thomas puts it, 'the career of this extraordinary individual is a reminder that Max Weber and R.H. Tawney were mistaken in thinking that international capitalists were the product of Protestant Northern Europe'.[18]

The practice of shipping slaves to the New World did not start immediately after Christopher Columbus first landed in the Bahamas on 12 October 1492, later claiming Hispaniola and Puerto Rico for the Spanish Crown. The initial idea of the Spanish was to make the native Caribbean islanders work in mines, in particular the gold mines of Hispaniola, for the benefit of the invaders; and, it seems, to sell some of them as slaves in Spain. Diseases and a widespread belief that the natives were not suited to hard work forced the Spanish to change their plans. As the native population was decimated by war, disease and ill-treatment, it soon became clear that more labourers were needed in the colonies. The Atlantic trade in enslaved Africans was the answer to the shortage of labour.

The slave trade to the Americas officially started in 1510 when King Ferdinand of Spain authorised the import of 400 African slaves to the new colonies.[19] The trade was to be regulated and taxed, making it a lucrative business for the state.[20] This was to turn the African slave trade to the Americas into 'a major enterprise'.[21] In 1518, King Charles granted a licence to import 4,000 black slaves into the New World to a Savoyard businessman, Lorenzo de Gorrevod. The licence changed hands several times, which leads Hugh Thomas to note that:

> The first major consignment of slaves for the Americas was thus in every sense a European enterprise: the grant of the Flemish-born Emperor [Charles] was to a Savoyard, who sold his rights, through a Castilian, to Genoese merchants – who, in turn, would (...) have to arrange for the Portuguese to deliver the slaves.[22]

---

17   Ibid., p. 83.
18   Ibid., p. 86.
19   Ibid., p. 93.
20   Ibid., pp. 89–92.
21   Ibid., p. 96.
22   Ibid., p. 99.

Right from its early days, therefore, the Atlantic slave trade was multinational in nature.[23] In the 1530s many more licences were granted to sell slaves from Africa and 'the provision of slaves to the New World was now becoming what it was to be, in ever-increasing dimensions, for the next 350 years: a source of profit for the merchant as well as for the Crown'.[24] Bankers became central figures of the slave trade. Slave trading demanded enormous capital, which had to be raised; insurance, because it was a risky business; and bills of credit and exchange, because the profits would not come until months or even years after the initial investment. Entire families of bankers, especially in Italy, were well versed in this business and naturally came to play a key role in the slave trade.[25]

## The practicalities of the slave trade

Throughout the entire duration of the Atlantic slave trade, from the sixteenth to the nineteenth century, European slave traders obtained African slaves in a variety of ways. The slaves had been made captives after wars of conquest, or had become slaves as a result of punishment under local law, poverty (in the case of parents who had to sell their children to survive) or kidnapping. Most slaves were purchased and not captured by European traders.[26] Although this is a debated point, and it may not have been as widespread as some abolitionists thought, there is evidence that some African rulers entered into war for the main purpose of taking captives and selling them to Europeans, though they surely had their own political motives as well.[27] Few European slave traders engaged in kidnapping. Instead they resorted to buying slaves from African dealers so as not to jeopardise future business.[28]

From capture to arrival at the final destination in the New World, enslaved Africans had to go through different phases, of which the 'Middle Passage' from Africa to the Americas is probably the best known. After capture, usually in the African interior and by African traders, slaves were chained and forced to walk to one of the slave trade cities or depots along the west coast of Africa. Depending on how far in the interior they were taken, this could take weeks or even months. Then they had to wait for a slave ship to come along, and this too could take months. The mortality rate was already high

---

23  David Brion Davis, *Inhuman Bondage. The Rise and Fall of Slavery in the New World*, Oxford: Oxford University Press (2006), p. 87.

24  Hugh Thomas, *The Slave Trade, The History of the Atlantic Slave Trade 1440–1870*, London: Picador (1997), p. 103.

25  David Brion Davis, *Inhuman Bondage. The Rise and Fall of Slavery in the New World*, Oxford: Oxford University Press (2006), p. 87.

26  Hugh Thomas, *The Slave Trade, The History of the Atlantic Slave Trade 1440–1870*, London: Picador (1997), p. 368.

27  Ibid., pp. 371–376.

28  Ibid., p. 377.

at that stage and although there were rebellions, 'many more slaves died during the often long time of waiting for shipment than did so in such rebellions or protests'.[29]

The crossing of the Atlantic lasted a couple of months, with great variations depending on the point of origin and the final destination.[30] Much has been written about the Middle Passage. Eric Williams, writing about the crossing of the Atlantic by white servants in the seventeenth century, remarks: 'the transportation of these white servants shows in its true light the horrors of the Middle Passage – not as something unusual or inhuman but as part of the age.'[31] In other words, the horrifying living conditions of African slaves on board were actually commonplace at the time, and not exclusive to them.[32] They are no less shocking, however.

Enslaved men and women were kept apart and made to lie next and as close as possible to one another in a low-ceilinged, confined space with no consideration for basic hygiene, which led to disease and death. From a business point of view, therefore, it might have made sense not to overcrowd the boats so much, so that fewer of the valuable slaves would die or catch diseases which would in turn decrease their market value in the New World. This was occasionally pointed out to the higher management of the slave trading companies – advice that was largely ignored.[33] In any event, research has shown that 'tight packing' did not have the high impact on mortality one could have expected. However, the fact of having more slaves on board necessarily meant that there was less space to carry food, which in turn, and especially during longer voyages, could lead to higher mortality rates both for slaves and the crew.[34] As David Brion Davis remarks,

> captains of slave ships faced a difficult dilemma. They longed to maximize profits by maximizing the number of slaves taken on each voyage, yet they feared both lethal slave revolts and an increase in slave mortality that would reduce their own share of the total New World sales.[35]

The practicalities of the Middle Passage reflect these contradictory beliefs. On the one hand, enslaved Africans were valuable commodities. On the other, they were treated horribly badly. The fact that they were seen as

29  Ibid., p. 404.
30  Ibid., pp. 408–409.
31  Eric Williams, *Capitalism and Slavery* (1944), Chapel Hill: the University of North Carolina Press (1994), pp. 13 and 34–35.
32  Ibid., p. 14.
33  Hugh Thomas, *The Slave Trade, The History of the Atlantic Slave Trade 1440–1870*, London: Picador (1997), p. 414.
34  Herbert S. Klein, *The Middle Passage*, Princeton: Princeton University Press (1978), pp. 64–65 and 198.
35  David Brion Davis, *Inhuman Bondage. The Rise and Fall of Slavery in the New World*, Oxford: Oxford University Press (2006), p. 93.

valuable can be inferred from the practice of captains, once the coast of Africa was no longer in sight, to allow slaves to go out on the deck at least a few hours a day. This ensured or was meant to ensure that slaves would arrive at their final destination in relative good health, since a dead slave constituted a loss of revenue.[36] This is not to say, however, that abuse was not frequent. Some captains treated slaves with great cruelty and the rape of African women on board was commonplace.[37] Rebellions were frequent and occurred during about 10 per cent of the journeys. Most of them were quelled.[38]

It is also worth mentioning the harsh living conditions of seamen on slave ships. To some extent they too were victims of the trade, albeit indirectly. Poverty drove these very young men into a dangerous life on board, exposed to hurricanes, disease and pirate attacks, and treated with brutality by their officers.[39] There was nothing unusual in their treatment, and this was clearly part of life at the time. Historian Roger Anstey, speaking about seamen's working conditions, remarks that 'what would certainly now be, and possibly then was, regarded as brutal was certainly accepted as necessary. (...) Harsh treatment of sailors was the rule and not only on slave ships.'[40] They were treated so poorly that 'the death rate among the crews of slavers was nearly twice that of the slaves'.[41] Playing an instrumental part in a dirty business, treated like dirt themselves, it is not surprising that the crew did not view the well-being of slaves as an important matter and did not think much about overcrowding the boats.[42] In this brutal context both for the crew and for the enslaved themselves, government regulations about the number of slaves carried on each boat gave the Portuguese a reputation as 'the most humane of the European shippers of slaves',[43] though in fact it seems as though the Dutch had the lowest mortality aboard their slavers.[44]

Upon arrival slaves were gathered, examined, cleaned and fed to make them look better, and the process of finding buyers started. This process could

36   Hugh Thomas, *The Slave Trade, The History of the Atlantic Slave Trade 1440–1870*, London: Picador (1997), p.415.

37   Ibid., p. 416. David Brion Davis points out that one of the reasons for separating the sexes was to facilitate the rape of African women by crew members: David Brion Davis, *Inhuman Bondage. The Rise and Fall of Slavery in the New World*, Oxford: Oxford University Press (2006), p. 93.

38   Hugh Thomas, *The Slave Trade, The History of the Atlantic Slave Trade 1440–1870*, London: Picador (1997), pp. 422–423.

39   Ibid., pp. 308–309.

40   Roger Anstey, *The Atlantic Slave Trade and British Abolition 1760–1810*, London: Macmillan (1975), p. 31.

41   Ibid., p. 32.

42   Hugh Thomas, *The Slave Trade, The History of the Atlantic Slave Trade 1440–1870*, London: Picador (1997), p. 312.

43   Ibid., p. 411.

44   Ibid., p. 421.

take some time and deaths were frequent at this stage as well, despite the better treatment slaves received at this point. Diseases were prevalent and the sick received little or no treatment. Those who were too ill to attract the interest of a buyer were left to die and, from a purely financial point of view, represented a loss.[45] As Hugh Thomas puts it, 'it remains curious that, leaving aside questions of common humanity, merchants who had gone to such trouble and expense to find and transport their captives did not take better care of them'.[46] This is all the more striking because slaves were extremely valuable and became increasingly expensive as the slave trade expanded in volume. Slaves were so expensive that planters put themselves in debt to buy them and could rarely pay the full amount immediately.[47]

## The expansion and high point of the slave trade

In the 1550s the New World became the largest importer of African slaves. Until then most slaves had been sent to Europe or to São Tomé, Cape Verde, Madeira and the Canary Islands.[48] Within the New World, Brazil was the greatest importer of slaves. The Portuguese colony engaged in the industrial production of sugar, relying almost exclusively on African slave labour, and during the second half of the sixteenth century became the world's largest supplier of sugar. The Brazilian model of sugar plantation was later reproduced in the Caribbean islands,[49] and it is not an overstatement to say that the development of the sugar economy changed the world. As David Brion Davis remarks,

> Even in its early stages, the Atlantic Slave System foreshadowed certain features of our modern global economy. One sees international investment of capital in distant colonial regions, where the slave trade resulted in extremely low labor costs to produce goods for a transatlantic market. With respect to consumerism, it is now clear that slave-produced sugar, rum, coffee, tobacco, and chocolate greatly altered the European diet. Apart from their damaging effects, ranging from sugar-induced tooth decay to lung cancer, these luxuries helped to shape by the late eighteenth century a consumer mentality among the masses, especially in England, so that workers became more pliant and willing to accept factory discipline in order to afford their luxury stimulants.[50]

45  Ibid., p. 437.
46  Ibid., p. 432.
47  Ibid., p. 440.
48  Ibid., p. 114.
49  Ibid., p. 135.
50  David Brion Davis, *Inhuman Bondage. The Rise and Fall of Slavery in the New World*, Oxford: Oxford University Press (2006), pp. 87–88.

In 1580, the King of Spain took control of Portugal after the King of Portugal had died without heir. This association was to Spain's great advantage. It already controlled immense territory in South America, and the alliance with Portugal gave the Spanish domination over international trade as well. The Crown contracted Portuguese merchants to supply the New World with African slaves. Towards the end of the sixteenth century, enlightened individuals pleaded against the enslavement of Africans and the slave trade but 'these disparate challenges to the ancient institution [slavery] (…) fell on deaf ears. (…) The age of adventure was over, and that of considerate philanthropy had not arrived.'[51] The second half of the sixteenth century also saw other nations' arrival in the Atlantic slave trade: France, England, the Netherlands, Sweden and Denmark.[52] The Spanish–Portuguese quasi-monopoly in the trading of slaves was brought to an end during the first half of the seventeenth century.

By the 1640s, thanks to conquest both in the Americas and in Africa, the Dutch had become 'the dominant world power, Portugal's successor on both sides of the Atlantic'.[53] They soon lost many territories, however, which reverted back to Portugal. That said, despite these military defeats, in the 1650s the Dutch had remained dominant in the market of slaves for the West Indies.[54] With this in mind, the early days of the Dutch West India Company are of particular interest.

### The Dutch West India Company and the human rights and business dilemma

The operations of the Dutch West India Company, the *West-Indische Compagnie* (WIC), provide an early example – albeit modest – of what could be called today a 'human rights and business dilemma'.[55] Willem Usselinx, the businessman who revived the Company in 1621, seems to have been opposed to slavery. A Calvinist, he believed that the company should be used to support the development of agrarian colonies, as well as the influence of Calvinism in the New World, as opposed to being a mere commercial enterprise.[56] The

---

51   Hugh Thomas, *The Slave Trade, The History of the Atlantic Slave Trade 1440–1870*, London: Picador (1997), p. 147.
52   Ibid., pp. 153–161. See also pp. 222–223.
53   Ibid., p. 183.
54   Ibid., p. 185.
55   The Human Rights and Business dilemmas forum is a website run by the United Nations Global Compact and the private consultancy Maplecroft. It provides case studies and opportunities to discuss 'the dilemmas responsible multi-national companies may face in their efforts to respect and support human rights when operating in emerging economies' (http://human-rights.unglobalcompact.org/, last accessed 15 April 2016).
56   Henk Den Heijer, 'The Dutch West India Company, 1621–1791', *in* Johannes Postma and Victor Enthoven, *Riches from Atlantic Commerce, Dutch Transatlantic Trade and Shipping 1585–1817*, Leiden: Brill (2003), pp. 79–80.

company was thought of primarily as a colonising tool as well as a way to secure domination over the Spanish. Also, 'since the Portuguese were now a part of Spain, their possessions were (…) fair game';[57] hence, 'one major objective of the WIC from its inception was to take Brazil from Portugal'.[58] According to Hugh Thomas, Usselinx's position on slavery was, 'as Adam Smith would [think] a century and a half later, that it was both uneconomical and – most unusually for his time – inhuman'.[59] The thrust of Usselinx's economic argument regarding the desirability of slavery, which he developed in a pamphlet published in 1608, is that in the long run the West Indies 'might, under another economic system, become a much better market for European manufactures than now, with a population of slaves who require nothing'.[60] Views differ on whether Usselinx really thought slavery was inhuman. Goslinga bluntly affirms that Usselinx's antislavery stands had nothing to do with humanitarianism but was simply a side effect of his grand plan, which was to establish sustainable Dutch settlements in the Americas, where protestant Christians would work the land and convert the natives.[61] Writing about Usselinx's pamphlet, Jameson remarks: 'whether slavery is rightful he will not discuss, but if it is thought contrary to the love of our neighbor, its evils can be moderated, and gradual emancipation of body and soul prepared.'[62] This seems to suggest that Usselinx's stand on slavery did not rest solely on economic considerations.

Whatever his true position might have been, others in the company shared Usselinx's doubts about slavery. Shortly after the creation of the company, the directors consulted a group of Calvinist theologians to decide whether or not it was morally acceptable for the company to engage in the slave trade. By this point, and despite the long-term economic arguments Usselinx and others may have put forward, the slave trade and the trade in the proceeds of slave labour were profitable business. Hence, consulting theologians about it resembles the contemporary practice of bringing in consultants or lawyers prior to entering into a potentially lucrative business deal where human rights risks are thought to exist.

Initially, the group of theologians advised the directors to stay away from the trade in human beings, and the directors followed the advice. The company retained this policy for almost a decade but eventually gave in after

---

57 Willie F. Page, *The Dutch Triangle: The Netherlands and the Atlantic Slave Trade 1621–1664*, London: Garland Publishing (1997), p. 22.

58 Ibid.

59 Hugh Thomas, *The Slave Trade, The History of the Atlantic Slave Trade 1440–1870*, London: Picador (1997), p. 162.

60 J. Franklin Jameson, 'Willem Usselinx, Founder of the Dutch and Swedish West India Companies', *Papers of the American Historical Association*, Vol. II No 3 (1887), p. 191.

61 Cornelius Goslinga, *The Dutch in the Caribbean and the Wild Coast, 1580–1680*, Gainsville: University of Florida Press (1971), p. 40.

62 J. Franklin Jameson, 'Willem Usselinx, Founder of the Dutch and Swedish West India Companies', *Papers of the American Historical Association*, Vol. II No 3 (1887), p. 257.

the conquest of Northern Brazil in 1630. Slaves were needed for the colony to be profitable.[63] As Postma puts it, 'no contemporary record is found concerning consultation with theologians; apparently economic incentives were sufficient to brush aside whatever moral scruples might initially have precluded the company from participating in the slave trade'.[64] For Goslinga, 'as is not uncommon, the moral objections which were considered were no match for the tantalizing lure of profits'.[65]

While they changed their minds relatively quickly, the directors' hesitations with regard to a trade they considered morally dubious at best are worth emphasizing. They were faced with a dilemma. The way in which they dealt with their doubts by consulting with those considered to be the experts of the day – theologians – should feel familiar to those currently working in the field of business and human rights.

### *The unevenly successful operations of chartered companies*

All the major slave trading countries, not only the Dutch, created companies to trade with Africa, which included the trade of African slaves. English companies were granted a monopoly over specific trades and with specific territories. Among these companies, the British Royal African Company (RAC) stands out as being the most prominent. It had among its shareholders members of the English royal family as well as the philosopher John Locke.[66] The numerous chartered companies set up in the various countries involved in the slave trade all turned out to be only modestly successful, if not financially unsustainable. McLean argues that the monopolies at least partly explain why these companies were not that profitable in the long run:

> The grant of monopoly status encouraged investors to engage in often highly risky ventures. For the first time, money could be raised in return for shares, profits could be divided among shareholders, and shares could be transferred among members and outsiders. Importantly, new investors among the gentry could be involved in business enterprises alongside the merchants. Profit was the dominant motive of most of these companies and the commercial risk was high.[67]

63  Johannes Postma, *The Dutch in the Atlantic Slave Trade 1600–1815*, Cambridge: Cambridge University Press (1990), pp. 11, 14.
64  Ibid., p. 17.
65  Cornelius Goslinga, *The Dutch in the Caribbean and the Wild Coast, 1580–1680*, Gainsville: University of Florida Press (1971), p. 146.
66  Hugh Thomas, *The Slave Trade, The History of the Atlantic Slave Trade 1440–1870*, London: Picador (1997), p. 201.
67  Janet McLean, 'The Transnational Corporation in History: Lessons for Today?', 79 *Indiana Law Journal* 363 (2004), p. 365.

The slave trade was a risky business indeed, as many things could go wrong, from the death of too many slaves during the Middle Passage to pirate attacks. As a matter of fact, illegal trade, outside any monopoly, occurred on a large scale and supplied the New World with enslaved Africans during the entire time the Atlantic slave trade was carried on.[68] As a result, European governments had to constantly intervene to inject fresh capital into the companies. The idea of regulating the trade through a monopoly contract (such as the *asiento* for trade to the Spanish colonies), which supposedly guaranteed revenue to the state, was showing its limits.[69] In 1713, the Treaty of Utrecht, between France, Spain, Great Britain, Portugal and the United Provinces, granted the much sought-after *asiento* to Britain for a period of thirty years. Britain, in turn, sold this monopoly to the newly established South Sea Company.[70] As Hugh Thomas notes,

> Subscription [to the company] in 1720 reads like a directory of contemporary Britain. Most of the House of Commons (…) and 100 members of the House of Lords (…) were included. So were (…) all the royal family, including the bastards. The Speaker of the House of Commons, Black Rod in the House of Lords, and the Lord Chancellor were also on the list (…) The Swiss canton of Berne had a large holding of South Sea stock (…). So had King's College, Cambridge (…).[71]

In 1720, while the company was only moderately successful in its endeavours in the Americas, the price of its shares collapsed and went from £1,000 to £180 in less than two months. Incredibly, the South Sea Company survived the collapse and continued to trade slaves on a reasonably large scale after that.[72]

In France, John Law, 'a brilliant Scottish adventurer',[73] created the New Company of the Indies (*Nouvelle Compagnie des Indes*) in 1719, which absorbed a number of existing companies such as the French East India Company. In 1720 it further bought the Company of Saint Domingue and the Guinea Company. With this, 'the Nouvelle Compagnie des Indes was by then the largest commercial organisation which the world had yet seen, and even now must be seen as one of the largest undertakings of all time'.[74] It too collapsed due to a bubble effect, and John Law finished his life ruined. While the company survived, this large-scale failure encouraged the French to

---

68  Hugh Thomas, *The Slave Trade, The History of the Atlantic Slave Trade 1440–1870*, London: Picador (1997), p. 229.
69  Ibid., pp. 225 and 227.
70  Ibid., p. 235.
71  Ibid., p. 241.
72  Ibid.
73  Ibid., p. 242.
74  Ibid., p. 243.

abandon the idea of monopolies, instead opening the Atlantic trade to all French merchants who were ready to take part in the business.[75] The liberalisation of the slave trade also occurred in the Netherlands, where the West India Company lost its monopoly in Africa and the West Indies in 1734 and 1738 respectively. In Britain, the Act making commerce entirely free was adopted in 1750.[76]

A significant amount of slavery-related business deals in Britain were concluded in London. Outside of London, Bristol and Liverpool became hubs for slave trading during the eighteenth century, producing dynasties of slave traders.[77] Manchester benefited greatly from Liverpool's position, as goods produced in Manchester, especially cotton goods, were transported to Liverpool and then sold in the Americas and the Caribbean or exchanged for slaves in Africa.[78] British traders also benefited immensely from the increasing imports of slaves in the British colonies of North America, as did North American slave merchants.[79]

### Slave traders as philanthropists

The majority of those engaged in the slave trade were neither exceptional nor abnormally cruel individuals. According to Eric Williams, 'the men most active in this traffic were worthy men, fathers of families and excellent citizens'.[80] Some of them were also committed to charitable causes, 'among the leading humanitarians of their age'[81] and engaged in significant philanthropic projects.[82] The joint-stock company model, where shareholders and directors are distinct, was applied to philanthropic projects via the creation of charitable organisations run by professionals, as opposed to relying solely on individual donations.[83] These new, more efficient charitable techniques, together with merchants' generous donations to charitable causes of their choice, had a significant impact on the lives of the poor in places such as Liverpool, with the building of schools and hospitals to care for the most vulnerable.[84]

75   Ibid., pp. 250, 255.
76   Ibid., p. 265.
77   Ibid., pp. 246, 248.
78   Ibid., p. 249.
79   Ibid., p. 268.
80   Eric Williams, *Capitalism and Slavery* (1944), Chapel Hill: the University of North Carolina Press (1994), p. 46.
81   Ibid., p. 47.
82   Hugh Thomas, *The Slave Trade, The History of the Atlantic Slave Trade 1440–1870*, London: Picador (1997), p. 298.
83   David Owen, *English Philanthropy 1660–1960*, Cambridge: Harvard University Press, (1965), p. 12.
84   For a detailed account of the buildings of Liverpool funded by generous slave trading families, see Laurence Westgaph, 'Built on Slavery', *Context*, Institute of Historic Building Conservation No 108, March 2009, pp. 27–29.

At first glance, it seems contradictory that on the one hand, slave traders' business was to exploit human misery, while on the other many of those individuals were committed to improving the lives of those less fortunate than themselves. There is little contradiction, however, if one considers that by and large the slave trade was not considered immoral at the time. Whereas not all slave traders were at ease with the business,[85] and it 'was certainly not a very honourable branch of English commerce',[86] Bournes noted in 1898:

> very curious is the piety with which these men engaged in their evil work – work not the less evil in itself because the doers saw no harm in it, and because its first and foremost apparent result tended greatly to the naval power and glory of England.[87]

Although they did not see their business in that light, slave traders were active participants in some of the worst human rights violations of all times while, at the same time, dedicated to giving impoverished individuals a better chance in life. To the contemporary observer, and while one must keep a sense of perspective, it is tempting to establish a parallel between these contradictions and some of the contemporary CSR work of multinational companies otherwise perpetrating human rights abuses. Without doubt, the human rights abuses in which companies are engaging today, no matter how serious they may be, do not reach the magnitude of those associated with the slave trade. Moreover, the slave trade was exclusively about the exploitation of individuals, whereas in the vast majority of cases, contemporary abuses are a side effect of the business. However, comparable features can be found, such as public relations considerations, the sincere dedication of some individuals within the business and the fact that sometimes the operational and the philanthropic parts of the business seem to function in isolation from each other.

## The high point of the slave trade

For a variety of reasons, ranging from the building of larger and more reliable ships to the formidable increase in the demand for sugar in Europe, the eighteenth century constituted the apogee of the slave trade.[88] In countries or territories involved in slave trading – along the coast of West Africa and up to Mozambique in East Africa, and in Britain, France, the Netherlands,

85  Hugh Thomas, *The Slave Trade, The History of the Atlantic Slave Trade 1440–1870*, London: Picador (1997), p. 300.
86  Fox Bourne, *English Merchants: Memoirs in Illustration of the Progress of British Commerce*, London: Chatto (1898), p. 201.
87  Ibid., p. 139.
88  See Hugh Thomas, *The Slave Trade, The History of the Atlantic Slave Trade 1440–1870*, London: Picador (1997), Chapter 14.

Spain, Portugal, the newly created United States of America, Saint Domingue, Brazil, Cuba and Barbados, to name the main ones – families of merchants, planters and rulers built fortunes relying directly or indirectly on the trade of slaves and on the trade of slave labour's production, particularly sugar, rice, tobacco, indigo and cotton. Yet the slave trade was a typical high-risk, high-return business. Many things could go wrong and profits were limited accordingly, even after monopolies had ended and free trade had been established. Many ended up losing everything they had due to bad investment decisions, but when things were going according to plan, returns were high. Roger Anstey looked into the profitability of the British slave trade between 1761 and 1807 and found an average return on investment of just under 10 per cent.[89]

During the eighteenth century, the Seven Years' War (French and Indian War), and later in the century the American War of Independence, affected business, but 'these disturbances seemed temporary. The long-term prospects for the slave trade appeared excellent in, say 1780, provided only that the nations could live in peace'.[90] In the 1780s, the slave trade was at its peak.[91] Change, however was underway: 'these years of the greatest level of the Atlantic slave trade also saw the beginning of a discussion whether it was, after all, the right way for civilized men to make a fortune.'[92] Moreover, the trade that had been so profitable in the seventeenth and early eighteenth centuries was starting to become less lucrative, with prices for slaves in Africa rising significantly in the course of the eighteenth century.[93]

## The abolition of the slave trade in British colonies and the business case

The progressive abolition of the trade in enslaved Africans, and of slave labour in the Americas, is a fascinating object of study with a scope much wider than that of this book. The aim of this section is to focus on the British abolition of the slave trade, and within this on an aspect which is of relevance from the point of view of 'business and human rights' as a field of study, namely the question of whether or not abolitionists had to find a 'business case' to ensure the success of their cause. Many contemporary discussions on business and human rights highlight the necessity or at least desirability of finding a business case for respecting human rights. Respecting human rights is good for business, the argument goes, as it helps to build a good

---

89   Roger Anstey, *The Atlantic Slave Trade and British Abolition 1760–1810*, London: Macmillan (1975), pp. 46–47.
90   Hugh Thomas, *The Slave Trade, The History of the Atlantic Slave Trade 1440–1870*, London: Picador (1997), p. 283.
91   Ibid., p. 284.
92   Ibid., p. 286.
93   Ibid., p. 443.

reputation for the company, attracting loyal staff, customers and business partners. In the long run, having a strategy to mitigate human rights risks is more sustainable and more profitable.[94] In the absence of a suitable international legal framework and faced with gaps in domestic law,[95] the business case may be the only argument available in the business and human rights field to try to get companies to take human rights into consideration in the course of their business.

The British Parliament abolished the British slave trade to foreign colonies in 1806,[96] that to its own colonies in 1807[97] and slavery altogether in 1833.[98] It was a pioneer in this respect.[99] The abolition of the slave trade, and then of slavery, occurred after a large-scale successful campaign. Campaigners organised

> early NGOs in the form of abolitionist societies whose dedicated volunteer members published pamphlets and tracts, preached sermons, delivered public speeches, organized meetings and marches, raised funds, gathered signatures on petitions, participated in boycotts, and initiated active campaigns of agitation and protest in order to free the enslaved.[100]

In other words, abolitionists resorted to modern campaigning techniques which in many ways are still used today, especially in the area of human rights. Although it appears highly organised, Christopher Brown has highlighted how, especially in its early days, the antislavery movement in Britain was 'odd rather than inevitable, a peculiar institution rather than the inevitable outcome of moral and cultural progress'.[101] In this context, it is fair to say that abolitionists' success was improbable.

First, British society was far from egalitarian. Quite the contrary, 'inequalities of power had shaped (…) [it] like a vast pyramid',[102] and the living conditions of the working class were poor within Britain itself. It is therefore surprising that British people of different classes united to attack the slave trade and the institution of slavery.

---

94  For a solid discussion on the business case, see Peter T. Muchlinski, 'Human Rights and Multinationals: Is There a Problem?', 77 *International Affairs* 31 (2001), pp. 10–11.
95  See Chapters 5, 9 and 10 in this book.
96  Foreign Slave Trade Act (23 May 1806), 46th Georgii III cap. LII.
97  Slave Trade Act (25 March 1807), 47th Georgii III, Session 1, cap. XXXVI.
98  Slavery Abolition Act (28 August 1833), 3rd & 4th Gulielmi IV, cap. LXXIII.
99  The only other country at the time which had abolished slavery was Haiti.
100  Paul Gordon Lauren, *The Evolution of International Human Rights,* Philadelphia: University of Pennsylvania Press (2003), p. 38.
101  Christopher Leslie Brown, *Moral Capital. Foundations of British Abolitionism,* Chapel Hill: the University of North Carolina Press (2006), p. 30.
102  David Brion Davis, *Inhuman Bondage. The Rise and Fall of Slavery in the New World,* Oxford: Oxford University Press (2006), p. 233.

Second, and perhaps more importantly, at the end of the eighteenth century the British slave trade, although less profitable than it was half a century before, was still successful. Some historians such as Eric Williams have argued that the plantation system in British colonies was declining.[103] To Williams, the abolition of the slave trade in 1807 and the emancipation of enslaved Africans in 1833 were decisions purely motivated by economic interest. The monopoly in the trade of sugar from which the West Indian planters were benefiting was artificial, and the slavery-reliant sugar islands had become a burden for British capitalists.[104] He affirms that

> the humanitarians, in attacking the system in its weakest and most inde-fensible spot, spoke a language that the masses could understand. They could never have succeeded a hundred years before when every impor-tant capitalist interest was on the side of the colonial system.[105]

Williams' assertion that 'the capitalists had first encouraged West Indian slav-ery and then helped to destroy it'[106] has however been strongly criticised since then. Seymour Drescher, in particular, equated the decision to abolish the slave trade to an economic suicide in his seminal book *Econocide*, published in 1977. The triangular trade, he argues, was as profitable as ever in the years preceding abolition.[107] In 1987, David Eltis wrote that the slave trade

> was killed when its significance to the Americas and to a lesser extent to Europe was greater than at any point in its history. For the Americas as well as for Britain at the outset of industrialization, there was a profound incompatibility between economic self-interest and antislavery policy.[108]

Hence one of the main difficulties faced by British abolitionists was that slavery and the slave trade were both common and, as most historians contend, still profitable at the end of the eighteenth century. In those circumstances, convincing politicians and businessmen to part with either was no easy task. In other words, articulating a business case for abolition constituted a challenge.

Several factors explain why the campaign was successful in the end. First, charismatic leaders such as Member of Parliament William Wilberforce made

---

103 Eric Williams, *Capitalism and Slavery* (1944), Chapel Hill: the University of North Carolina Press (1994), p.120.
104 Ibid., pp. 152–153.
105 Ibid., pp. 136.
106 Ibid., p. 169.
107 Seymour Drescher, *Econocide, British Slavery in the Era of Abolition*, Chapel Hill: the University of North Carolina Press, 2nd edition (2010), p. 30.
108 David Eltis, *Economic Growth and the Ending of the Transatlantic Slave Trade*, Oxford: Oxford University Press (1987), p. 15.

the abolition of the trade and of slavery the fight of their lives. Second, thanks to an interesting historical twist, 'Napoleon's restoration of slavery and the slave trade suddenly made abolition compatible with patriotic hostility to the French'.[109] Third, campaigners' tactics were elaborate. They focused on abolishing the slave trade, not slavery, as they knew the latter was going to be much more difficult to obtain.[110] Specifically, they initially focused on the British slave trade to foreign colonies, making the argument that providing enemy nations and business competitors with the workforce they needed was hurting British interests in the long run. Thus the business case seems to have been instrumental to the first abolitionist victory, the adoption of the 1806 Foreign Slave Trade Bill outlawing the slave trade to foreign colonies. During the debates, abolitionists deliberately concealed arguments based on humanity and compassion towards slaves and focused almost exclusively on British self-interest.[111]

Immediately after their first victory in 1806, abolitionists set their eyes on the next step, which was the total abolition of the trade, including to British colonies. After securing a non-binding resolution of intent a few months after the passage of the Act in 1806, the second victory came a year later, in 1807, with the adoption of the Slave Trade Act, 'an Act for the Abolition of the Slave Trade'.[112] To ensure success, however, abolitionists had to change strategy. Indeed, economic and military self-interest arguments – the business case – made no sense with regard to the general abolition of the slave trade, since the trade to British colonies was profitable to Britain. In both Houses, abolitionists passionately defended the Bill on humanitarian grounds, and won.[113] As Roger Anstey puts it:

> The decision to go first for the ending of the British slave trade to foreigners, by an appeal to sound policy, and then to introduce the wavering ranks of independent men to a total abolition, based additionally on justice and humanity, by means of a declaration of intent, was of immense importance.[114]

Authors disagree about the importance of this strategy. For example, Seymour Drescher speaking about the 1806 Act, contends that

109 David Brion Davis, *Inhuman Bondage. The Rise and Fall of Slavery in the New World*, Oxford: Oxford University Press (2006), p. 236.
110 Ibid., p. 235.
111 Roger Anstey, *The Atlantic Slave Trade and British Abolition*, London: Macmillan (1975), pp. 367–376.
112 An Act for the Abolition of the Slave Trade (25 March 1807), 47th Georgii III, Session 1, cap. XXXVI.
113 Roger Anstey, *The Atlantic Slave Trade and British Abolition*, London: Macmillan (1975), pp. 386–387 and 395.
114 Ibid., p. 401.

a close reading of the debates of 1806 reveals that the abolitionists' "mercantilist" strategy became patently and deliberately less necessary before the bill cleared Parliament, and that the abolitionists had gained no more than a superfluous handful of votes by using the mercantilist argument.[115]

Whether the strategy was necessary or not, the fact remains that in parliamentary debates abolitionists initially used this relatively narrow business case, later moved to more humanitarian arguments, and in the end succeeded.

In their campaign to gather public support, abolitionists could also rely on another, more general, business-oriented argument: eighteenth-century economist Adam Smith's contention that free labour was more profitable than slave labour. Adam Smith famously wrote in *The Wealth of Nations*, in 1776, that buying slaves and making them work for free was more expensive than paying wages to free labourers: 'It appears, accordingly, from the experience of all ages and nations, I believe, that the work done by freemen comes cheaper in the end than that performed by slaves.'[116] This is a controversial statement which, in fact, does not systematically hold true. Commenting on it, Seymour Drescher noted that Smith illustrated his argument of the superiority of free labour with a discussion on the productivity of miners in Britain, and that 'it is certainly no accident that he did not choose' to look at sugar production in the West Indies instead, as his argument would probably not have proved true in that context.[117] What is more, '*Wealth of Nations* never directly suggested that West Indian planters would actually increase their higher profit margins still further by emancipating the work force'.[118] On an issue like the slave trade, it appears that even though it may have played a role, the business case had its limits. The slave trade was both profitable and commonplace and to bring about its abolition, other arguments had to be found. Indeed,

> slavery between 1787 and 1807 was not a wasted machine which the British government could phase out like a bankrupt venture, accumulating moral capital in return. The abolitionists were facing a dynamic system. (…) In reality, they had to introduce a fundamental change into the indicators of imperial economic progress. (…) They had to attempt to force the political system to measure the quantum of misery in premature death, forced separation from community and family, and the whole panoply of pain revealed in the handbooks of Caribbean slavery.[119]

115 Seymour Drescher, *Econocide, British Slavery in the Era of Abolition*, Chapel Hill: the University of North Carolina Press, 2nd edition (2010), p. 124.
116 Adam Smith, *The Wealth of Nations*, 1776, London: Penguin Classics (1986), p. 184.
117 Seymour Drescher, *Capitalism and Antislavery*, London: Macmillan (1986), p. 134.
118 Seymour Drescher, *The Mighty Experiment*, Oxford: Oxford University Press (2002), p. 23.
119 Seymour Drescher, *Econocide, British Slavery in the Era of Abolition*, Chapel Hill: the University of North Carolina Press, 2nd edition (2010), p. 165.

British abolitionism is a complex matter and many other factors played a part in the eventual abolition of the trade and of slavery.[120] It is nevertheless of interest to note that at least some abolitionists were of the view that resorting to the business case was going to help their cause, if not guarantee its success. From a strategic point of view, the business case is a powerful tool in the contemporary field of business and human rights. Because of the weak business and human rights legal framework explored further in the book, even when dealing with grave violations which are clearly wrong from a moral point of view, it cannot hurt advocates to work on securing solid business-based arguments and to rely on reputational risks if anything else.

Their 1807 success had made abolitionists feel reasonably optimistic. Indeed, immediately after the adoption of the Slave Trade Act, they thought that stopping the flow of newly enslaved Africans would naturally bring about the abolition of slavery in British colonies. This ideal scenario did not materialise and abolitionists had to fight and win other battles before British Parliament, which lead to the adoption of the Slavery Abolition Act in 1833. This came at an exorbitant cost. Several sections of the Act place compensation of 'the persons hitherto entitled to the services of such slaves' (slave owners and their creditors) for their financial loss at the astronomical sum of 20 million pounds.[121] Unilateral abolition of the slave trade and of slavery in British colonies, however, was not enough to put a permanent end to this lucrative business. Action had to be taken at the international level.

## Outlawing the slave trade and slavery under international law

The Atlantic slave trade was first addressed at the international level at the Congress of Vienna of 1815, during which participating European states signed the non-binding Declaration Relative to the Universal Abolition of the Slave Trade. The Declaration recognised that the slave trade was 'repugnant to the principles of humanity and universal morality' but did not formally outlaw it.[122] However, starting in 1817, the British proceeded to sign bilateral treaties to outlaw the trade in collaboration with their allies.[123]

---

120 On this see Christopher Leslie Brown, *Moral Capital. Foundations of British Abolitionism*, Chapel Hill: the University of North Carolina Press (2006).

121 Slavery Abolition Act (28 August 1833), 3rd & 4th Gulielmi IV, cap. LXXIII.

122 Declaration of the Powers, on the abolition of the Slave Trade (8 February 1815), British and Foreign State Papers, Vol. 3, p. 971.

123 Additional Convention between Great Britain and Portugal, for the Prevention of the Slave Trade (28 July 1817) and Separate Article (11 September 1817), 67 *Consolidated Treaty Series* 398 (1817); *British and Foreign State Papers*, vol. 4, pp. 85 and 115; Treaty between Great Britain and Spain, for the Abolition of the Slave Trade (23 September 1817), 68 *Consolidated Treaty Series* 45 (1817–18); *British and Foreign State Papers*, vol. 4, p. 33; Treaty between his Britannic Majesty and His Majesty the King of the Netherlands, for preventing their Subjects from engaging in any traffic in Slaves (4 May 1818), *British and Foreign State Papers*, vol. 5, p. 125.

Partial abolition of the slave trade through a multilateral treaty came in 1841 with the Treaty for the Suppression of the African Slave Trade signed by Austria, Great Britain, Prussia and Russia.[124] Under Article I, the parties committed to 'prohibit all trade in slaves, either by their respective subjects, or under their respective flags, or by means of capital belonging to their respective subjects; and to declare such traffic piracy'. The remainder of the treaty focused on the right of each party to search vessels, and to detain and try suspected traffickers. Despite the adoption of treaties banning the slave trade largely thanks to British efforts, the illegal trade continued throughout the nineteenth century. In her fascinating book, Jenny Martinez has documented the work of the international courts that adjudicated the search and seizure of ships believed to be used to transport slaves.[125] These proceedings are explored in Chapter 5 as the first instances during which business and human rights issues were examined by international courts, albeit in a limited way.

The next multilateral treaty of importance in this area was the 1890 General Act of the Brussels Conference Relating to the African Slave Trade.[126] This treaty was much more comprehensive than the 1841 Treaty for the Suppression of the African Slave Trade. Signed by seventeen parties, the General Act includes two chapters (I and II) on measures to be taken by colonial powers in Africa in order to prevent the trade, as well as a chapter (IV) requiring parties on the territory of which slavery still existed to prohibit importation, exportation and transit of, as well as trade in, slaves. The General Act of the Brussels Conference's strong stance against slavery and the slave trade reflected the mindset of the day. After having wholeheartedly engaged in the slave trade and encouraged the widespread use of slave labour for business purposes for centuries, European countries then came to believe that slavery was evil and that 'civilised' countries had to abolish it.

The consequences of this stance were two-fold. First, it introduced a sharp distinction between slavery and 'other forms of domination and exploitation'.[127] Slavery was restrictively understood as chattel slavery. This strict approach culminated in the adoption of what eventually became the most widely ratified international treaty on slavery, the 1926 League of Nations

124 Treaty between Austria, Great Britain, Prussia and Russia for the Suppression of the African Slave Trade, signed at London, 20 December 1841, 92 *Consolidated Treaty Searies* 437. France signed the treaty but never ratified it.

125 Jenny Martinez, *The Slave Trade and the Origins of International Human Rights Law*, Oxford: Oxford University Press (2012).

126 General Act of the Brussels Conference Relating to the African Slave Trade between Austria-Hungary, Belgium, Congo, Denmark, France, Germany, Great Britain, Italy, the Netherlands, Persia, Portugal, Russia, Spain, Sweden-Norway, Turkey, the United States and Zanzibar, signed 2 July 1890, 173 *Consolidated Treaty Series* 293.

127 Frederick Cooper, Thomas C. Holt, Rebecca J. Scott, *Beyond Slavery, Explorations of Race, Labor, and Citizenship in Postemancipation Societies*, Chapel Hill and London: the University of North Carolina Press (2000), p. 7.

Slavery Convention.[128] Article 1 of the Slavery Convention defines slavery as 'the status or condition of a person over whom any or all of the powers attaching to the right of ownership are exercised'. Adopting such a narrow definition of slavery had perverse consequences, as 'the evil that was being acknowledged was a precisely bounded evil, marking slavery apart from other modes of controlling labor and other modes of exercising authority'.[129] Indentured labour, a system whereby poor Asian and African workers were contracted to go and work in other parts of the world for the benefit of the colonial state, colonies and private enterprises, is one of the clearest examples of such other modes of controlling labour.

Second, the idea that slavery should be eradicated in all corners of the world provided moral justification to the colonial enterprise in the late nineteenth century, leading to a range of other human rights violations, many of which implicated the business sector.[130] The contradictions inherent in a plan of action whereby people were subjugated, colonised and forced to work for their own good were not apparent at the time. Instead,

> in the 1890s the idea that slavery and colonialism were analogous would have made little sense in concerned circles in Europe. Indeed, heirs to the antislavery tradition were arguing that vigorous intervention into Africa by civilized powers was the only way to stop Africans from enslaving one another.[131]

## Conclusion

This chapter has highlighted the role of business in the historical violation of rights that was the Atlantic slave trade, as well as some of the business and human rights aspects of the trade. As seen, in the 1620s, the directors of the Dutch West India Company were confronted with what we would now call a human rights and business dilemma when they had doubts about the morality of the trade in human beings and wondered whether the company should engage in it or not. British abolitionists initially worked on finding a business case to convince Parliament to abolish the slave trade. Finally, some prominent English slave traders were highly regarded philanthropists, whose generous donations greatly helped those in need in England.

Focus was put on British history and on the abolition of the slave trade under British law. Other countries followed suit and changed their domestic law, but this was not enough to put an end to the trade. International law

128 Convention to Suppress the Slave Trade and Slavery (1926) 60 LNTS 253.
129 Frederick Cooper, Thomas C. Holt and Rebecca J. Scott, *Beyond Slavery, Explorations of Race, Labor, and Citizenship in Postemancipation Societies*, Chapel Hill and London: The University of North Carolina Press (2000), p. 8.
130 Ibid., p. 115.
131 Ibid., p. 108.

had to step in to bring about abolition. As the slave trade and slavery gradually came to be considered evil practices, other practices contrary to human rights in which the business sector played a major role and which also eventually prompted international action developed in European states' colonies. Forced labour in the colonies, and indeed the development of international labour law, are covered in the next chapter.

## Bibliography

### *Books*

Anstey, Roger, *The Atlantic Slave Trade and British Abolition 1760–1810*, London: Macmillan (1975).

Bourne, Fox, *English Merchants: Memoirs in Illustration of the Progress of British Commerce*, London: Chatto (1898).

Brown, Christopher Leslie, *Moral Capital. Foundations of British Abolitionism*, Chapel Hill: The University of North Carolina Press (2006).

Cooper, Frederick, Holt, Thomas C. and Scott, Rebecca J., *Beyond Slavery, Explorations of Race, Labor, and Citizenship in Postemancipation Societies*, Chapel Hill and London: the University of North Carolina Press (2000).

Davis, David Brion, *Inhuman Bondage. The Rise and Fall of Slavery in the New World*, Oxford: Oxford University Press (2006).

Drescher, Seymour, *Capitalism and Antislavery*, London: Macmillan (1986).

Drescher, Seymour, *The Mighty Experiment*, Oxford: Oxford University Press (2002).

Drescher, Seymour, *Econocide, British Slavery in the Era of Abolition*, Chapel Hill: the University of North Carolina Press, 2nd edition (2010).

Dunn, Richard S., *Sugar and Slaves: The Rise of the Planter Class in the English West Indies, 1624–1713*, Chapel Hill: the University of North Carolina Press (1972).

Eltis, David, *The Rise of African Slavery in the Americas*, Cambridge: Cambridge University Press (2000).

Eltis, David, *Economic Growth and the Ending of the Transatlantic Slave Trade*, Oxford: Oxford University Press (1987).

Ferro, Marc, *Colonization: A Global History*, London and New York: Routledge (1997).

Goslinga, Cornelius, *The Dutch in the Caribbean and the Wild Coast, 1580–1680*, Gainsville: University of Florida Press (1971).

Klein, Herbert S., *The Middle Passage*, Princeton: Princeton University Press (1978).

Lauren, Paul Gordon, *The Evolution of International Human Rights*, Philadelphia: University of Pennsylvania Press, 2nd edition (2003).

Martinez, Jenny, *The Slave Trade and the Origins of International Human Rights Law*, Oxford: Oxford University Press (2012).

Owen, David, *English Philanthropy 1660–1960*, Cambridge: Harvard University Press (1965).

Page, Willie F., *The Dutch Triangle: The Netherlands and the Atlantic Slave Trade 1621–1664*, London: Garland Publishing (1997).

Postma, Johannes, *The Dutch in the Atlantic Slave Trade 1600–1815*, Cambridge: Cambridge University Press (1990).

Smith, Adam, *The Wealth of Nations*, 1776, London: Penguin Classics (1986).

Thomas, Hugh, *The Slave Trade, The History of the Atlantic Slave Trade 1440–1870*, London: Picador (1997).
Williams, Eric, *Capitalism and Slavery* (1944), Chapel Hill: the University of North Carolina Press (1994).

## Journal articles

McLean, Janet, 'The Transnational Corporation in History: Lessons for Today?', 79 *Indiana Law Journal* 363 (2004).
Muchlinski, Peter T., 'Human Rights and Multinationals: Is There a Problem?', 77 *International Affairs* 31 (2001).
Westgaph, Laurence, 'Built on Slavery', *Context*, Institute of Historic Building Conservation No 108, March 2009.

## Book chapters

Den Heijer, Henk, 'The Dutch West India Company, 1621–1791', *in* Johannes Postma and Victor Enthoven, *Riches from Atlantic Commerce, Dutch Transatlantic Trade and Shipping 1585–1817*, Leiden: Brill (2003), pp. 77–112.
Jameson, J. Franklin, 'Willem Usselinx, Founder of the Dutch and Swedish West India Companies', *Papers of the American Historical Association*, Vol. II No 3 (1887), pp. 149–382.

## Statutes

Foreign Slave Trade Act (23 May 1806), 46th Georgii III cap. LII.
Slave Trade Act (25 March 1807), 47th Georgii III, Session 1, cap. XXXVI.
Slavery Abolition Act (28 August 1833), 3rd & 4th Gulielmi IV, cap. LXXIII.

## Treaties and declarations

Declaration of the Powers, on the abolition of the Slave Trade (8 February 1815), *British and Foreign State Papers*, Vol. 3, p. 971.
Additional Convention between Great Britain and Portugal, for the Prevention of the Slave Trade (28 July 1817) and Separate Article (11 September 1817), 67 *Consolidated Treaty Series* 398 (1817); *British and Foreign State Papers*, vol. 4, pp. 85 and 115.
Treaty between Great Britain and Spain, for the Abolition of the Slave Trade (23 September 1817), 68 *Consolidated Treaty Series* 45 (1817–18); *British and Foreign State Papers*, vol. 4, p. 33.
Treaty between his Britannic Majesty and His Majesty the King of the Netherlands, for preventing their Subjects from engaging in any traffic in Slaves (4 May 1818), *British and Foreign State Papers*, vol. 5, p. 125.
Treaty between Austria, Great Britain, Prussia and Russia for the Suppression of the African Slave Trade, signed at London, 20 December 1841, 92 *Consolidated Treaty Series* 437.
General Act of the Brussels Conference Relating to the African Slave Trade between Austria-Hungary, Belgium, Congo, Denmark, France, Germany, Great Britain,

Italy, the Netherlands, Persia, Portugal, Russia, Spain, Sweden-Norway, Turkey, the United States and Zanzibar, signed 2 July 1890, 173 *Consolidated Treaty Series* 293.

Convention to Suppress the Slave Trade and Slavery (1926) 60 LNTS 253.

## Miscellaneous

Human Rights and Business dilemmas forum, http://human-rights.unglobalcompact.org/ (last accessed 15 April 2016).

# 3 International labour law

## Early development and contemporary significance for the field of business and human rights

The rise of international labour rights forms an essential chapter in the history of business and human rights. By developing international labour regulation, some states acknowledged and attempted to address at the international level the negative impacts of business, and generally of unbridled capitalism, on human lives. Labour rights were formulated as the Industrial Revolution had provided job opportunities for the growing masses but also generated an impoverished class of workers. Those working in factories remained a small minority largely outnumbered by 'craftsmen and other traditional labourers', despite Karl Marx's influential theories focusing on factory proletariat who were to play the central part in the upcoming revolution.[1] Life was harsh and often short for those working in coal mines in the Cévennes, cotton mills in Manchester and dye factories in Ludwigshafen, and many authors and activists of the nineteenth century argued that the condition of working men, women and children of Europe during and immediately following the Industrial Revolution was comparable to that of slaves in the New World.

Just as the Industrial Revolution was initially an English and later a continental European phenomenon,[2] the initial development of labour standards at the international level may be more accurately described as the development of labour standards in Europe, and to some extent in North America and Japan. As workers' plights were progressively being taken into consideration in Europe at the turn of the twentieth century, colonial policymakers and rulers justified and used forced labour, and subjected 'natives' to appalling working conditions in Africa and Asia. Faced with colonial powers who categorically refused to extend the application of labour standards negotiated in Europe to their colonial possessions, the International Labour Organization (ILO), created after the First World War, was forced to develop

---

1   Lenard R. Berlanstein, 'General Introduction', *in* Lenard R. Berlanstein (ed.), *The Industrial Revolution and Work in Nineteenth Century Europe*, London and New York: Routledge (1992), pp. xiv–xv. See also, in the same book, Christopher H. Johnson, 'Patterns of Proletarianization', pp. 81–101.

2   The Industrial Revolution is said to have started in the second half of the eighteenth century in England. See Kenneth Morgan, *The Birth of Industrial Britain 1750–1850*, Harlow: Pearson, 2nd edition (2011), pp. 3 and 11.

a 'Native Labour Code' alongside the 'International Labour Code', which was meant to apply to 'normal' workers, understood as European workers. Despite its inherent limitations, the ILO has been instrumental in leading states towards the adoption of labour standards, which are systematically negotiated with employers and workers following the principle of tripartism, a distinctive feature of the organisation.

The rise of international labour rights at the beginning of the 1900s predates the rise of international human rights, generally considered to have occurred in the aftermath of the Second World War. Moreover, international labour law is an area of international law mainly aiming at regulating how companies conduct their business so as to limit adverse impacts on workers.[3] It therefore seems logical to include a chapter on the development of international labour law in the present book, which purports to offer a panorama of business and human rights as a field of study. The development of international labour legislation is a clear early attempt by international law to protect rights against abuses committed by business, and it is still of great relevance today. International labour rights, however, may be viewed as distinct from human rights.

With this in mind, the aim of this chapter is three-fold. First, it gives a concise history of the development of international labour rights, so as to provide the historical background against which the contemporary business and human rights debates have evolved. Second, it seeks to clarify terminological questions around the notions of labour rights and human rights, as well as labour standards and labour principles. Setting clear definitions of these notions is important as the book further progresses towards present debates. Third, it contributes to a discussion on the contemporary relevance of international labour law and its relationship with business and human rights.

## International labour law: a concise history

Accounts of working conditions in nineteenth-century Europe often focus on factories, the archetypical 'dark satanic mills' depicted by William Blake in his famous poem.[4] Although, as pointed out above, factory workers actually

---

3   From a strict legal point of view, however, labour standards do not directly bind companies, as states are expected to adopt domestic legislation to give effect to them. For a discussion on the distinction between direct and indirect obligations of business, see Chapter 5.

4   The first two quatrains of the poem read as follows:

And did those feet in ancient times
Walk upon England's mountain green?
And was the holy lamb of God
On England's pleasant pastures seen?
And did the Countenance Divine
Shine forth upon our clouded hills?

constituted a minority, their peculiar fate attracted historians' attention to such an extent that one may get the impression that the vast majority of European wage-earners of the time worked in factories. History books are filled with terrifying accounts of child labour, sixteen-hour-long workdays, pestilential workplaces, poor diet and dire poverty.[5] Moreover, workers were not in a position to demand change, as the law prevented them from doing so in no uncertain terms. As one author notes,

> In the first decades of the Industrial Revolution there was very little the workers could do by themselves to improve their condition. Drawn from agricultural communities they found themselves in unfamiliar surroundings, without friends, and with little leisure. The *laissez-faire* State, guaranteeing the free play of forces, penalised anyone who combined these forces to gain increase in wages or a decrease in hours or who solicited anyone else to leave work, or objected to working with any other employee. Trade unionism therefore was an offence even in the French Revolution.[6]

As workers themselves were silenced, their fate attracted the attention of some progressive individuals – industrialists, politicians and scientists – who actively defended the cause of the working class. Employers who did not necessarily oppose regulation as such and were aware of the working conditions of their employees nevertheless feared that granting better working conditions would put their business at a disadvantage *vis-à-vis* their foreign competitors. Beyond charitable motives, the will to level the playing field thus seems to have constituted a powerful incentive for the development of international regulation.[7] Moreover,

> [a]nother reason for enacting legislation was related to the deteriorating physical strength of a large swathe of the population. It is a little known fact that many young working class men were declared unfit for military

And was Jerusalem builded here
Among these dark satanic mills?

'From Milton' *in Blake. Collected Poems edited by W.B. Yeats*, London and New York: Routledge Classics (2002), p. 211.

5    Lenard R. Berlanstein, 'General Introduction', *in* Lenard R. Berlanstein (ed.), *The Industrial Revolution and Work in Nineteenth Century Europe*, London and New York: Routledge (1992), p. xi. For a first-hand account see for example Louis René Villermé, *Tableau de l'état physique et moral des ouvriers employés dans les Manufactures de Coton, de Laine, et de Soie*, Paris: Jules Renouard et Cie, Vol. II (1840).

6    Antony Alcock, *History of the International Labour Organisation*, London: Macmillan Press Limited (1971), p. 5.

7    Jean-Michel Servais, *International Labour Law*, Third Revised Edition (2011), London: Kluwer Law International, p. 21; John William Follows, *Antecedents of the International Labour Organization*, London: Oxford University Press (1951) pp. v and 10.

service, a sign that their health was rapidly deteriorating because of the conditions in which they worked and lived. The toiling masses were in part becoming so physically worn out that their condition could affect the productive and even strategic capacities of the countries concerned.[8]

British manufacturer Robert Owen is said to have been the first person to publicly call for international regulation in the area of labour. An idealist and a writer, and committed to improving the lives of 'his' workers, he developed a form of utopian socialism and first implemented his ideas in the Scottish village of New Lanark, where he became a mill manager in 1800. At the Congress of Aix-la-Chapelle in 1818 he addressed European nations and tried to convince them of the necessity to improve the fate of the working class.[9]

Later on, Charles Hindley, British industrialist and Member of Parliament from 1835 to 1857, called for international regulation in the area of labour and articulated the idea that such regulation was a necessity to avoid a devastating race to the bottom among European nations and employers with regard to working conditions.[10] Questioned about the risks of introducing legislation to limit the number of working hours (which would drive up production costs) as part of the work of the royal Factories Enquiry Commission in 1833, he dismissed the idea that English cotton spinners would not be able to compete and would eventually be ruined. He then added,

> Should it however unfortunately happen that the excessive competition of foreigners should endanger our trade unless we employed our people longer than was advisable for their comfort and the good of society, I think it would be as proper a subject of treaty with foreign nations as the annihilation of the slave trade.[11]

In 1840, French doctor Louis René Villermé published a study on the 'physical and moral state of workers in cotton, wool and silk factories'. He suggested that to tackle the problem of excessively long working hours, French and foreign manufacturers would have to organise in a 'holy alliance' and decide together to limit the number of working hours – a move he considered very unlikely.[12] Follows pointed to 'the difference between Villermé and Hindley's suggestions (…). Hindley proposed labour legislation by foreign treaty; Villermé suggested an international alliance of

---

8   Ibid., p. 21.
9   John William Follows, *Antecedents of the International Labour Organization*, London: Oxford University Press (1951), p. 6.
10  Ibid., p. 10.
11  Examinations taken by Mr Tufnell, Factories Enquiry Commission, Report from Commissioners, Vol. XXI, 1833, D2, p. 50.
12  Le propriétaire d'une filature de coton ne peut donc rien seul, absolument rien, partout où il existe un établissement semblable au sien. Il faudrait que tous les manufacturiers, non seulement de la localité qu'il habite, mais encore des pays où ses marchandises sont

manufacturers.'[13] Both suggestions have an international element, but the former rests on international law – a treaty binding states – while the latter is a non-legal promise – an 'alliance' – between private actors, however powerful, sincere and determined they might be. As subsequent chapters in this book show, the comparative advantages of public and private modes of regulation still feed contemporary business and human rights discussions.

Intellectural figures such as French political economist Jérôme Adolphe Blanqui, French manufacturer Daniel Legrand and Belgian social reformer and penologist Édouard Ducpétiaux also defended the idea of international regulation as a way to durably improve working conditions.[14] Blanqui and Legrand believed in the involvement of governments to advance the cause, and Ducpétiaux hoped that an alliance of progressive intellectuals would succeed in bringing about change.[15] Both Legrand and Ducpetiaux drew parallels with the international outlawing of the slave trade to justify international action on labour issues.[16]

Alongside those reformist intellectuals, workers themselves began to organise. In 1864, in London, workers, trade unionists and members of various political movements such as anarchists and socialists acted upon Marx and Engels' famous call – 'Proletarians of all countries, unite!' – and created the International Workingmen's Association (IWA), also known as the First International. Karl Marx was among the founders.[17] Their preferred path to change was much different from what reformers had proposed. Many

---

vendues, s'unissent avec lui d'une sainte alliance pour faire cesser le mal qui nous occupe, au lieu de l'exploiter à leur profit. Certes, on ne saurait compter sur un tel désintéressement: aucune classe de la société, jusqu'ici, n'en a donné l'exemple, ni en France, ni ailleurs.

Louis René Villermé, *Tableau de l'état physique et moral des ouvriers employés dans les Manufactures de Coton, de Laine, et de Soie*, Paris: Jules Renouard et Cie, Vol. II (1840), p. 93.

13 John William Follows, *Antecedents of the International Labour Organization*, London: Oxford University Press (1951), p. 24. Follows adds: 'It is probable, however that Villermé derived his 'international' idea from Hindley.'

14 Ibid., p. 26. Jérôme Adolphe Blanqui should not be confused with his younger brother, Louis Auguste Blanqui, a perhaps better known socialist and political activist.

15 Ibid., p. 65.

16 Ibid., p. 34. See also Édouard Ducpétiaux, *De la Condition Physique et Morale des Jeunes Ouvriers et des Moyens de l'améliorer*, Bruxelles: Meline, Cans et Cie (1843), pp. 310–311:

Il importe donc que les nations se concertent et s'entendent sur ce point comme elles se sont entendues naguère pour mettre un terme à la traite. L'ouvrier blanc vaut bien, à tous égards, l'esclave noir, et la condition du premier est même, à certains égards, bien inférieure à celle du second.' Ibid, p. 320: he calls for 'l'avènement d'une politique humaine, généreuse, propre à relier les peuples divisés d'aujourd'hui, et qui conduirait certainement à l'adoption de conventions internationales favorables à l'émancipation des travailleurs blancs comme elles le furent naguère à l'émancipation des nègres'.

17 John William Follows, *Antecedents of the International Labour Organization*, London: Oxford University Press (1951), p. 59.

members of the IWA did not view international legislation as necessary and were oblivious to the business case for it, namely that it could be a way to address unfair competition. Moreover, some members did not believe in engaging in dialogue with governments to demand social reform.[18] Divergences with regard to the best ways to operate led to the eventual schism between the Marxists and the anarchists, led by Bakunin, at the Congress of the Hague in 1872. The First International eventually collapsed in 1876.[19] The reformists of the First International created the Second International in 1889. Although anarchists did not join the Second International, it was far from homogenous and fundamental questions such as 'whether socialists should participate in bourgeois Governments' remained unanswered.[20]

In the final years of the nineteenth century, perhaps encouraged by 'the threat of social unrest and the prompting of individual economists and philanthropists', European governments started to show an interest in the development of international labour legislation.[21] The Swiss government took the lead and in 1897 created a government-backed, yet private, scientific institution, the International Association for the Protection of Workers.[22] This first Association gave way in 1900 to the International Association for Labour Legislation. The International Association for Labour Legislation's main tasks were to undertake research on labour legislation across Europe and to propose international legislation for states to adopt.[23] The Association's strategy was to focus on relatively uncontroversial, narrow topics so as to encourage the quick adoption of international treaties.[24] In 1906, its work led to the convening of an international conference in Berne and the adoption of the first two non-bilateral international labour treaties: the International Convention on the subject of the Prohibition of the Use of White (Yellow) Phosphorus in the Manufacture of Matches and the International Convention respecting the prohibition of night work for

18   Ibid., p. 62.
19   On this see Antony Alcock, *History of the International Labour Organisation*, London: Macmillan Press Limited (1971), p. 7. See also Micheline R. Ishay, *The History of Human Rights. From Ancient Times to the Globalization Era*, Berkeley, Los Angeles, London: University of California Press (2008), pp. 149–150.
20   Antony Alcock, *History of the International Labour Organisation*, London: Macmillan Press Limited (1971), p. 8.
21   Ibid., p. 10.
22   Jean-Michel Servais, *International Labour Law*, Third Revised Edition (2011), London: Kluwer Law International, p. 23.
23   Antony Alcock, *History of the International Labour Organisation*, London: Macmillan Press Limited (1971), p. 11. For more detail on this see Alexandre Millerand, 'Intervention au Congrès International pour la Protection Légale des Travailleurs', Séance d'ouverture – Mercredi 25 juillet 1900 (extract from *Les cahiers du Chatefp* n°7, March 2007).
24   John William Follows, *Antecedents of the International Labour Organization*, London: Oxford University Press (1951), p. 185.

women in industrial employment.[25]

The First World War proved decisive for the rise of international labour rights. Both in Britain and in France, representatives of the labour movement joined governments in 1916. This marked an important step as it showed that the working class was deemed trustworthy enough to be in charge of political affairs during these particularly difficult times.[26] The ideas of the labour movement had become more widely accepted. Yet, while many thought that the future peace treaty should provide protection for workers, ideas diverged with regard to the form such protection would take. In 1917, the United States' entry into the war and the Russian Revolution further complicated the matter. Indeed,

> [t]his meant that at the peace [talks] the right to speak for labour would have no less than three claimants, each with powerful support. The traditional socialists of the Second International and the IFTU [International Federation of Trade Unions, created in 1913], who wanted to do way with capitalism gradually and were prepared to work within the framework of the bourgeois State to that end, were flanked on the left by the communists under Lenin, who had broken with the Second International in November 1914 on the issue of the war and had founded the rival Third International, dedicated to the immediate and violent overthrow of capitalism and the bourgeois State that supported it. On the right, the views of American labour had now to be taken into account. These were, in general, the maintenance of the capitalist system and the gradual accession of the worker to its benefits through legitimate trade-union activity without the intervention of the State.[27]

Discussions on the labour question took place within the labour commission of the peace conference. They led to the inclusion of Part XIII on 'Labour'

---

25  International Convention on the subject of the Prohibition of the Use of White (Yellow) Phosphorus in the Manufacture of Matches (1906). For the text of the Convention, see the ILO Recommendation concerning the Application of the Berne Convention of 1906 on the Prohibition of the Use of White Phosphorus in the Manufacture of Matches (1919). See also International Convention respecting the prohibition of night work for women in industrial employment (1906), reprinted in 4 *American Journal of International Law* 328 (1910), and John William Follows, *Antecedents of the International Labour Organization*, London: Oxford University Press (1951), p. 163. Switzerland is the official depository of both treaties. Before 1906, states had begun to sign bilateral labour treaties. For example, in 1904, France and Italy signed a bilateral treaty on the treatment of Italian workers in France. See John William Follows, *Antecedents of the International Labour Organization*, London: Oxford University Press (1951), pp. 170–171. Alcock notes that by 1915 there were more than twenty similar bilateral treaties. Antony Alcock, *History of the International Labour Organisation*, London: Macmillan Press Limited (1971), p. 13.

26  Antony Alcock, *History of the International Labour Organisation*, London: Macmillan Press Limited (1971), p. 14.

27  Ibid., p. 17.

in the Treaty of Versailles. Section 1 of Part XIII forms the International Labour Organization (ILO) Constitution. Following a British draft, delegates decided that within the future organisation, for each country, the government would hold two votes, while labour and employers' representatives would each hold one vote.[28] This principle of tripartism has survived to this day and constitutes a distinctive feature of the ILO. The establishment of an organisation dedicated to labour issues was a victory for workers, at least European workers. Their demands were finally given international attention. The newly created organisation was to provide a permanent forum for the continuing improvement of labour standards.

Not everyone agreed with the basic premises of the organisation. Some considered that state sovereignty remained too prevalent and revolutionaries disagreed with the consensual, class cooperation focus of the ILO.[29] Despite difficulties, the ILO immediately began its work and at the first ILO Conference, held in Washington at the end of 1919, six conventions were adopted relative to hours of work, unemployment, work of pregnant women and new mothers, night work of women, minimum work age in industry and night work of young people.[30] More than sixty other conventions, the majority of which formed a developing 'International Labour Code', had been adopted by the outbreak of the Second World War in 1939.[31] The ILO also succeeded in adopting four treaties meant to apply in the colonies. These were the Forced Labour Convention (1930), the Recruiting of Indigenous Workers Convention (1936), the Contracts of Employment (Indigenous Workers) Convention (1939) and the Penal Sanctions (indigenous workers) Convention (1939), which together form the Native Labour Code.[32] The Forced Labour Convention remains a key treaty today. It is part of a group

---

28   Ibid., pp. 27–28. See ILO Constitution (Part XIII, Treaty of Peace with Germany (1919) 225 Consol. TS 188), Article 3. The full text of the treaty is available on the website of the Avalon Project (Yale Law School).

29   Antony Alcock, *History of the International Labour Organisation*, London: Macmillan Press Limited (1971), p. 36.

30   C001 – Hours of Work (Industry) Convention, 1919 (No. 1) Convention Limiting the Hours of Work in Industrial Undertakings to Eight in the Day and Forty-eight in the Week; C002 – Unemployment Convention, 1919 (No. 2) Convention concerning Unemployment; C003 – Maternity Protection Convention, 1919 (No. 3) Convention concerning the Employment of Women before and after Childbirth; C004 – Night Work (Women) Convention, 1919 (No. 4) Convention concerning Employment of Women during the Night; C005 – Minimum Age (Industry) Convention, 1919 (No. 5) Convention Fixing the Minimum Age for Admission of Children to Industrial Employment; C006 – Night Work of Young Persons (Industry) Convention, 1919 (No. 6) Convention concerning the Night Work of Young Persons Employed in Industry.

31   For an interesting discussion on the notion of code, see Custos, 'The International Labour Code', 13 *The Political Quarterly* 303 (1942).

32   The Forced Labour Convention, 1930 (No 30), the Recruiting of Indigenous Workers Convention, 1936 (No 50), the Contracts of Employment (indigenous workers) Convention, 1939 (No 64) and the Penal Sanctions (indigenous workers) Convention, 1939 (No 65).

of eight 'core ILO conventions' which apply to all ILO member states, irrespective of whether or not they have ratified them. This is so because the standards they set have been reproduced in the 1998 ILO 'Declaration on Fundamental Principles and Rights at Work'. The Declaration is an important document which spells out the absolute minimum set of labour standards, applicable in all circumstances.[33]

Between 1939 and 1946, no convention was adopted at the ILO due to the Second World War. In 1946, the ILO resumed its standard-setting work and adopted Convention No. 69, the Certification of Ships' Cooks Convention.[34] At the time of writing, there are 189 ILO conventions and 204 ILO recommendations. Alongside these ILO labour standards, in 1977 the organisation adopted the Tripartite Declaration of Principles concerning Multinational Enterprises and Social Policy. The Declaration was updated in 2006.[35] It is of relevance to this book because, unlike labour standards which apply to states, the Declaration is meant to apply to governments but also directly to employers – multinational enterprises themselves – which constitutes an oddity in the international legal landscape. The Declaration covers a range of areas such as collective bargaining, child labour and health and safety. Notably, according to Principle 8, 'all the parties concerned' by the Declaration, including multinational enterprises themselves,

> should respect the Universal Declaration of Human Rights and the corresponding International Covenants adopted by the General Assembly of the United Nations (...). They should contribute to the realization of the ILO Declaration on Fundamental Principles and Rights and Work and its Follow-up, adopted in 1998.

Chapter 5 explores in detail the question of whether multinational companies have human rights obligations under international law. For now suffice it to note that international labour law, through the Tripartite Declaration of Principles, places some responsibilities on multinational companies.[36]

---

33   For a discussion on the significance of the adoption of the Declaration, see Philip Alston, 'Core Human Rights and the Transformation of the International Labour Rights Regime', 15 *European Journal of International Law* 457 (2004), pp. 458–460. See also below.
34   The Certification of Ships' Cooks Convention, 1946 (No. 69).
35   Tripartite Declaration of Principles concerning Multinational Enterprises and Social Policy, adopted by the Governing Body of the International Labour Office at its 204th Session (Geneva, November 1977) as amended at its 279th (November 2000) and 295th Session (March 2006).
36   As discussed in Chapter 7, the Declaration was adopted at a time when other international organisations, notably the United Nations and the Organisation for Economic Cooperation and Development in Europe (OECD), were also in the process of adopting codes of conduct directly applicable to multinational enterprises.

## International labour law and business and human rights

Before the rise of business and human rights as a field of study, discussions about rights in the context of business operations focused on labour rights. This brings questions with regard to the respective boundaries of each field. In order to distinguish between human rights and labour rights one may note that 'while human rights are primarily oriented towards limiting the power of the state, labor rights are primarily oriented towards limiting the power of private actors in the market'.[37] Beyond this difference of focus, some have also argued that there exists a difference in nature between the two sets of rights in the sense that 'while human rights concern individuals and, arguably, achieve outcomes such as better working conditions, labor rights are more collectively orientated, and worker mobilization and negotiations processes take precedence'.[38] Some authors dismiss these differences and contend that labour rights simply are a sub-category of human rights.[39] This section purports to shed some light on this debate, as well as on the various terms international labour law uses to refer to entitlements, namely 'principles', 'standards' and 'rights'.

### *Are labour rights human rights?*

As seen in this chapter, the idea that workers have labour rights and that they should be protected developed progressively in nineteenth-century Europe and received international recognition through the creation of a specialist body in 1919, the International Labour Organization. These advances predate the adoption of the Universal Declaration of Human Rights in 1948. A commonly held opinion is that these two separate developments have given rise to two distinct branches of international law: international labour law and international human rights law. Those who adhere to this opinion contend that labour rights are confined to the workplace and are claimed by workers against their employers, while human rights apply in all other areas of life and are claimed by individuals against the state.[40] However traditional, this distinction rests on unsure grounds. First, under international law, it is states, not businesses, who become parties to labour treaties. Thus although workers expect their employers to respect labour rights, the international obligation to ensure that the said employers respect those rights rests first and foremost on states. In other words, as explained in more detail in Chapter 5 with regard to international law in general, international labour

---

37   Kevin Kolben, 'Labor Rights as Human Rights?', 50 *Virginia Journal of International Law* 449 (2009–2010), p. 452.

38   Ibid.

39   See for example the discussion in Virginia Mantouvalou, 'Are Labour Rights Human Rights?', 3 *European Labour Law Journal* 151 (2012).

40   Kevin Kolben, 'Labor Rights as Human Rights?', 50 *Virginia Journal of International Law* 449 (2009–2010), p. 452.

law binds businesses in an indirect way. Arguably, both international labour law and international human rights law bind states, and states only. Second, leaving international legal considerations aside, it is correct to say that labour rights apply in the workplace only. However, it is incorrect to say that human rights are meant to apply only in non-workplace situations. For example, the Universal Declaration of Human Rights recognises the right to form and join trade unions, and trade unions participated in the drafting process of the Declaration.[41] In other words, human rights claims extend to the workplace, which is not the exclusive domain of labour rights. Conceptually, while the two branches are not identical, they cover similar grounds and overlap a great deal. This led Philip Alston to note that the question of whether labour rights are human rights is to some level a 'non-question'.[42]

Another argument frequently put forward by those who defend the specificity of labour rights is that labour rights are collective in nature, whereas human rights are individualistic and therefore ill-adapted to the labour context.[43] This is debatable. Some labour rights, such as the right to privacy in the workplace, apply in an individualised way, while some human rights, such as the right to freedom of association, or some minority rights, such as indigenous peoples' rights, are clearly collective.[44] The difference of nature between the two sets of rights was bitterly debated in an issue of *New Labor Forum* in 2009. One author, defending the idea that labour rights are not the same as human rights and that labour law ought to retain its specificity, warned that

> [w]hile the motives of those advocating a human rights approach are laudable, the reliance on reframing labor struggles as first and foremost human rights struggles is misplaced. It is not hyperbole to say that the replacement of solidarity and unity as the anchor for labor justice with 'individual human rights' will mean the end of the union movement as we know it. This is true tactically, strategically, and philosophically. Rights discourse individualizes the struggle at work. The union movement, however, was built on and nourished by solidarity and community. The powerless can only progress their work life in concert with each

41 Article 23(4). See for example the letters sent to the UN Secretary-General by the World Federation of Trade Unions and the American Federation of Labor, respectively UN Doc. E/C.2/28 (28 February 1947) and UN Doc. E/C.2/32 (13 March 1947), reprinted in William A. Schabas (ed.), *The Universal Declaration of Human Rights, the Travaux Préparatoires Volume I*, Cambridge: Cambridge University Press (2013) pp. 232 and 237.
42 Philip Alston, 'Labour Rights as Human Rights: The Not So Happy State of the Art', *in* Philip Alston (ed.), *Labour Rights as Human Rights*, Oxford: Oxford University Press (2008), p. 2.
43 As Kevin Kolben put it, 'an ethos of individualism substantially grounds human rights': Kevin Kolben, 'Labor Rights as Human Rights?', 50 *Virginia Journal of International Law* 449 (2009–2010), p. 470.
44 Virginia Mantouvalou, 'Are Labour Rights Human Rights?', 3 *European Labour Law Journal* 151 (2012), p. 162.

other, not alone. Fighting individually, workers lose; fighting together, workers can win.[45]

Another author argued in response that the two frameworks, labour rights and human rights, are 'mutually reinforcing', and that '"Workers' Rights are Human Rights" can join "Solidarity Forever" as leitmotifs for the labor movement'.[46] Specifically, he contended that workers have much to gain in framing their claims as human rights claims and not only as labour claims, as using a human rights discourse may help address criticisms related to partisanship and attract wider support from the public.[47] In other words, it is asserted that '[f]raming labor rights as human rights (…) shifts the labor discourse from economics and special interest politics to ethics and morality'.[48] This is a far-reaching statement, resting on a number of developments that Kevin Kolben documented in a piece published in 2009. He began by acknowledging historical key differences between the labour and human rights movements. First, he noted the dominating role of law in the human rights movement, as opposed to politics in the labour movement.[49] Second, he highlighted the difference of approach between the human rights movement, which seems to rest on charitable values, and the labour movement, which rests on empowerment and direct action by the very groups suffering from oppression.[50] Finally, he observed sociological differences between human rights professionals, characterised as 'elites', and labour professionals, who tend to 'come from the ranks', although this is necessarily oversimplified.[51]

Despite these differences, he argued, some developments have contributed to blurring the distinction between human rights and labour rights. These developments include the rise of non-union labour organisations such as the Fair Labour Association; the focus of human rights organisations such as Amnesty International and Human Rights Watch on labour rights; and the fact that US trade unions increasingly use human rights language.[52] Arguably, labour movements use human rights language to 'more effectively target multinational corporations (MNCs) and engage in corporate campaigning' as 'MNCs have become particularly susceptible, and amenable, to human rights discourse'.[53] Kolben further notes that

45  Jay Youngdahl, 'Solidarity First: Labor Rights Are Not the Same as Human Rights', (2009) 18 *New Labor Forum* 31, p. 31.
46  Lance Compa, 'Solidarity and Human Rights, A Response to Youngdahl', 18 *New Labor Forum* 38 (2009), p. 39.
47  Ibid., p. 42.
48  Kevin Kolben, 'Labor Rights as Human Rights?', 50 *Virginia Journal of International Law* 449 (2009–2010), p. 462.
49  Ibid., pp. 475–476.
50  Ibid., p. 479.
51  Ibid., pp. 480–481.
52  Ibid. pp. 456–460.
53  Ibid., p. 464.

[a]s these companies increasingly link themselves to broader human rights initiatives and labor rights initiatives portrayed as human rights movements, labor movements believe that companies will be more vulnerable and responsive to charges that they have violated human rights and labor rights.[54]

Another development that may have contributed to blurring the distinction between human rights and labour rights was the adoption of ILO Convention 169 on Indigenous and Tribal people, which explicitly refers to the human rights of such people, despite being a labour treaty.[55]

The two categories of rights, therefore, overlap a great deal. This is further reinforced by the fact that the International Labour Organization itself uses human rights language and does not adhere to the idea that the categories of labour rights and human rights are hermetically sealed. What is more, the ILO seems to consider that there exists a hierarchy of rights, where human rights sit at the top. In 1998 the organisation adopted the ILO Declaration on Fundamental Principles and Rights at Work, in which it isolated four core rights – core labour standards – as representing baseline standards which apply irrespective of whether a state has ratified the corresponding labour conventions.[56] In doing so it elevated these rights – freedom of association and the right to collective bargaining, the right not to be subjected to forced or compulsory labour, the right not to be subjected to child labour and the right not to face discrimination in employment – to the level of human rights. In turn this may imply that other, non-selected labour rights are of less value, though this point is strongly debated, as is the question of why these rights and not others made it to the final list.[57]

Beyond the discussions around the ILO Declaration, the reality is that labour rights and human rights cover similar ground and share similar sets of values.[58] As Mantouvalou puts it,

---

54  Ibid., p. 465.

55  C169 – Indigenous and Tribal Peoples Convention, 1989 (No. 169) Convention concerning Indigenous and Tribal Peoples in Independent Countries.

56  Hillary Kellerson, 'The ILO Declaration of 1998 on Fundamental Principles and Rights: A Challenge for the Future', 137 *International Labour Review* 223 (1998). See also Kevin Kolben, 'Labor Rights as Human Rights?', 50 *Virginia Journal of International Law* 449 (2009–2010), p. 454.

57  See the fascinating discussion in the *European Journal of International Law* between professors Philip Alston and Brian Langille: Philip Alston, 'Core Human Rights and the Transformation of the International Labour Rights Regime', 15 *European Journal of International Law* 457 (2004), pp. 485–495; Brian A Langille, 'Core Labour Rights – The True Story (Reply to Alston)', 16 *European Journal of International Law* 409 (2005).

58  For an early opinion on this see C. Wilfred Jenks, *Human Rights and International Labour Standards*, London: Steven and Sons (1960), pp. 127–128. See also Kevin Kolben, 'Labor Rights as Human Rights?', 50 *Virginia Journal of International Law* 449 (2009–2010), p. 450.

the recognition that certain labour rights are human rights (…) does not imply that human rights exhaust labour law as a field of study. What it implies is that some labour rights are stringent normative entitlements, and this should be reflected in law.[59]

This is especially true if one adopts a wide definition of human rights which encompasses civil and political, but also economic, social and cultural, rights.[60] Hence, business and human rights as a field of study is about rights violations by businesses both inside and outside the workplace.

### Principles, standards and rights

The controversial 1998 ILO Declaration on Fundamental Principles and Rights at Work uses the terms 'principles' and 'rights' in its title, and embodies the four core labour standards. This raises questions about the meaning of labour rights, labour principles and labour standards.

To begin with, the term 'right' implies a stronger entitlement than the term 'principle'. Simply put, a principle is 'a normative proposition (…) which falls short of being given the status of a human right'.[61] This idea transpires from the debates relative to the ILO Declaration around the fact that only certain labour standards were considered to warrant the qualification of rights. To distinguish between standards and principles, Mantouvalou suggests that 'some labour rights are human rights on the normative analysis, while there are others that involve the detailed regulation of the employment relation, and these can be called "labour standards"'.[62] Following this reasoning, 'labour rights' should only be used for certain entitlements in the workplace context. The problem with this interpretation is that the list of standards that made it into the Declaration is disputed and many argue that additional standards should have been included.[63] In other words, there is some uncertainty around the ground covered by 'labour rights' as strictly defined.

Going further, the Declaration is about principles and rights, and not simply rights. Alston contends that the distinction was made so as to signify that the standards were 'rights' for the states that had ratified the relevant binding ILO conventions, but mere 'principles' for those that had not. This

59   Virginia Mantouvalou, 'Are Labour Rights Human Rights?', 3 *European Labour Law Journal* 151 (2012), p. 172.
60   See Chapter 5 below on the definition of international human rights law.
61   Philip Alston, 'Core Human Rights and the Transformation of the International Labour Rights Regime', 15 *European Journal of International Law* 457 (2004), p. 477.
62   Virginia Mantouvalou, 'Are Labour Rights Human Rights?', 3 *European Labour Law Journal* 151 (2012), p. 169.
63   Philip Alston, 'Core Human Rights and the Transformation of the International Labour Rights Regime', 15 *European Journal of International Law* 457 (2004), pp. 485–495; Brian A Langille, 'Core Labour Rights – The True Story (Reply to Alston)', 16 *European Journal of International Law* 409 (2005).

distinction, he argues, is unclear, since '[p]hilosophically, a right is a right, even if a government has refused to acknowledge that fact'.[64] To him, the use of the vague term 'principle' in the title of the Declaration is a 'backward step, given that all of the relevant standards have long been recognised as human rights'.[65] For purposes of clarity, the phrase 'labour rights' is used in the remainder of this book to refer to rights applying in the context of the workplace and which have been given international recognition at the ILO through conventions and/or recommendations.

## Conclusion

Business and human rights as a field of study is partly about how businesses treat their employees. Although it seems the phrase 'business and human rights' was only coined at the end of the twentieth century,[66] labour rights gained international recognition and protection much earlier, as exemplified by the creation of the International Labour Organization in 1919. In this context one may legitimately wonder what, if anything, differentiates discussions on historical entitlements such as labour rights from more recent debates around business and human rights. One answer to this interrogation, at least for the purpose of this book, is that labour rights are human rights and that on this basis, business and human rights as a field of study involves looking into whether states, and companies, comply with labour standards. Business and human rights, however, is not only about labour rights; it is about businesses' adverse impacts both within and outside the workplace.

Beyond this, a final point must be made. One characteristic of the contemporary debates on business and human rights at the international level is the minor role played by international trade unions and, overall, the marginal attention paid to labour rights and the work of the ILO. This transpires from the discussions that took place at the time of the elaboration and eventual adoption of the most prominent international standard in the area of business and human rights, the 2011 UN Guiding Principles on Business and Human Rights.[67] The Business and Human Rights Resource Centre, which acts as a repository of documents pertaining to the Guiding Principles, classifies these documents by topic. While labour rights are mentioned in many of these documents, it is telling that they were not deemed important enough to constitute a stand-alone topic.[68] This may seem surprising given

64  Philip Alston, 'Core Human Rights and the Transformation of the International Labour Rights Regime', 15 *European Journal of International Law* 457, p. 476.

65  Ibid., p. 477.

66  Google Books Ngram viewer search for the phrase 'business and human rights'.

67  See Chapter 7 for a detailed account of these discussions.

68  See 'Materials by Topic' on the UN Special Representative's portal of the Business and human Rights Resource Centre's website, http://business-humanrights.org/en/un-secretary-generals-special-representative-on-business-human-rights/materials-by-topic (last accessed 15 June 2016).

that labour law falls neatly within the realm of business and human rights, as shown in this chapter. Analysing the profound reasons for this state of affairs would require conducting research beyond the scope of this book. However, a few points are worth mentioning that may provide some explanation for the marginal attention paid to labour rights in more recent discussions on business and human rights.

For the past few decades, international and domestic trade unions have been steadily declining. Among the various reasons put forward for this are deindustralisation (when the manufacturing sector has traditionally been unionised) in the West and the fact that large manufacturing companies now tend to produce in countries where unionisation rates are much lower, when unionisation is allowed at all.[69] Faced with its own decline, the organised labour movement has remained isolated; some have even said 'sclerotic'.[70] In parallel, at the international level, the 1990s saw a raise in awareness of economic and social rights in the West, for example at the 1993 World Conference on Human Rights in Vienna. The fact that in the early 2000s the prominent London-based NGO Amnesty International – which until then had dealt only with civil and political rights – changed its mandate to incorporate the full range of human rights, including economic and social rights, constitutes an emblematic example of this trend.[71]

In this context, it is perhaps not surprising that in the discussions on business and human rights at the highest level, the 'human rights' side tends to be represented by human rights professionals rather than by the labour movement.[72] It is however an unfortunate situation. Both human rights organisations and the labour movement should be fully engaged in the process, as their end goals are essentially identical: to enhance human dignity. Moreover, in its near century-long existence, the ILO has produced

---

69   On the decline of unions in the West, see Bruce Western and Jake Rosenfeld, 'Workers of the World Divide. The Decline of Labor and the Future of the Middle Class', 91 *Foreign Affairs* 88 (May–June 2012); Cheol-Sung Lee, 'Migration, Deindustrialization and Union Decline in 16 Affluent OECD Countries, 1962–1997', 84 *Social Forces* 71 (2005–2006); Craig Becker, 'The Pattern of Union Decline, Economic and Political Consequences, and the Puzzle of a Legislative Response', 98 *Minnesota Law Review* 1637 (2013–2014); Sharon Rabin Margalioth, 'The Significance of Worker Attitudes: Individualism as a Cause for Labor's Decline', 16 *Hofstra Labor & Employment Law Journal* 133 (1998–1999); John Godard, 'The Exceptional Decline of the American Labor Movement', 63 *Industrial & Labor Relations Review* 82 (2009–2010); Micheline R. Ishay, *The History of Human Rights. From Ancient Times to the Globalization Era*, Berkeley, Los Angeles, London: University of California Press (2008), pp. 294–295.

70   Micheline R. Ishay, *The History of Human Rights. From Ancient Times to the Globalization Era*, Berkeley, Los Angeles, London: University of California Press (2008), p. 263.

71   For an account of how this happened at Amnesty International, see David Petrasek, 'The Indivisibility of Rights and the Affirmation of ESC Rights', *in* Carrie Booth Walling and Susan Waltz (eds), *Human Rights: From Practice to Policy* (2011), pp. 21–25.

72   On the distinction between human rights and labour professionals, see Kevin Kolben, 'Labor Rights as Human Rights?', 50 *Virginia Journal of International Law* 449 (2009–2010), pp. 480–481.

invaluable conventions pertaining to rights in the workplace and has gained considerable experience in these matters. It seems to be a waste of resources and talent to maintain what appears to be an artificial divide between labour rights and business and human rights discussions, as both areas overlap and are mutually reinforcing.

## Bibliography

### Books

Alcock, Antony, *History of the International Labour Organisation*, London: Macmillan Press Limited (1971).

*Blake. Collected Poems edited by W.B. Yeats*, London and New York: Routledge Classics (2002).

Ducpétiaux, Édouard, *De la Condition Physique et Morale des Jeunes Ouvriers et des Moyens de l'améliorer*, Bruxelles: Meline, Cans et Cie (1843).

Follows, John William, *Antecedents of the International Labour Organization*, London: Oxford University Press (1951).

Ishay, Micheline R., *The History of Human Rights. From Ancient Times to the Globalization Era*, Berkeley, Los Angeles, London: University of California Press (2008).

Morgan, Kenneth, *The Birth of Industrial Britain 1750–1850*, Harlow: Pearson, 2nd edition (2011).

Servais, Jean-Michel, *International Labour Law*, London: Kluwer Law International Third Revised Edition (2011).

Villermé, Louis René, *Tableau de l'état physique et moral des ouvriers employés dans les Manufactures de Coton, de Laine, et de Soie*, Paris: Jules Renouard et Cie, Vol. II (1840).


### Journal articles

Alston, Philip, 'Core Human Rights and the Transformation of the International Labour Rights Regime', 15 *European Journal of International Law* 457 (2004).

Becker, Craig, 'The Pattern of Union Decline, Economic and Political Consequences, and the Puzzle of a Legislative Response', 98 *Minnesota Law Review* 1637 (2013–2014).

Compa, Lance, 'Solidarity and Human Rights, A Response to Youngdahl', 18 *New Labor Forum* 38 (2009).

Custos, 'The International Labour Code', 13 *The Political Quarterly* 303 (1942).

Godard, John, 'The Exceptional Decline of the American Labor Movement', 63 *Industrial & Labor Relations Review* 82 (2009–2010).

Jenks, C. Wilfred, *Human Rights and International Labour Standards*, London: Steven and Sons (1960).

Kellerson, Hillary, 'The ILO Declaration of 1998 on Fundamental Principles and Rights: A Challenge for the Future', 137 *International Labour Review* 223 (1998).

Kolben, Kevin, 'Labor Rights as Human Rights?', 50 *Virginia Journal of International Law* 449 (2009–2010).

Langille, Brian A, 'Core Labour Rights – The True Story (Reply to Alston)', 16 *European Journal of International Law* 409 (2005).

Lee, Cheol-Sung, 'Migration, Deindustrialization and Union Decline in 16 Affluent OECD Countries, 1962–1997', 84 *Social Forces* 71 (2005–2006).

Mantouvalou, Virginia, 'Are Labour Rights Human Rights?', 3 *European Labour Law Journal* 151 (2012).

Margalioth, Sharon Rabin, 'The Significance of Worker Attitudes: Individualism as a Cause for Labor's Decline', 16 *Hofstra Labor & Employment Law Journal* 133 (1998–1999).

Western, Bruce and Rosenfeld, Jake, 'Workers of the World Divide. The Decline of Labor and the Future of the Middle Class', 91 *Foreign Affairs* 88 (May–June 2012).

Youngdahl, Jay 'Solidarity First: Labor Rights Are Not the Same as Human Rights' (2009) 18 *New Labor Forum* 31.

## Book chapters

Alston, Philip, 'Labour Rights as Human Rights: The Not So Happy State of the Art', *in* Philip Alston (ed.), *Labour Rights as Human Rights*, Oxford: Oxford University Press (2008), pp. 1–24.

Berlanstein, Lenard R., 'General Introduction', *in* Lenard R. Berlanstein (ed.), *The Industrial Revolution and Work in Nineteenth Century Europe*, London and New York: Routledge (1992), pp. x–xv.

Johnson, Christopher H., 'Patterns of Proletarianization' *in* Lenard R. Berlanstein (ed.), *The Industrial Revolution and Work in Nineteenth Century Europe*, London and New York: Routledge (1992), pp. 84–103.

Petrasek, David, 'The Indivisibility of Rights and the Affirmation of ESC Rights', *in* Carrie Booth Walling and Susan Waltz (eds), *Human Rights: From Practice to Policy* (2011), pp. 21–25.

## Treaties

International Convention on the subject of the Prohibition of the Use of White (Yellow) Phosphorus in the Manufacture of Matches (1906).

International Convention respecting the prohibition of night work for women in industrial employment (1906).

ILO Constitution, Part XIII, Treaty of Peace with Germany (1919) 225 *Consolidated Treaty Series* 188.

C001 – Hours of Work (Industry) Convention (1919).

C002 – Unemployment Convention (1919).

C003 – Maternity Protection Convention (1919).

C004 – Night Work (Women) Convention (1919).

C005 – Minimum Age (Industry) Convention (1919).

C006 – Night Work of Young Persons (Industry) Convention (1919).

C030 – Forced Labour Convention (1930).

C050 – Recruiting of Indigenous Workers Convention (1936).

C064 – Contracts of Employment (indigenous workers) Convention (1939).

C065 – Penal Sanctions (indigenous workers) Convention (1939).

C069 – Certification of Ships' Cooks Convention (1946).
C169 – Indigenous and Tribal Peoples Convention (1989).

## Official documents

UN Doc. E/C.2/28 (28 February 1947).
UN Doc. E/C.2/32 (13 March 1947).
Tripartite Declaration of Principles concerning Multinational Enterprises and Social Policy, adopted by the Governing Body of the International Labour Office at its 204th Session (Geneva, November 1977) as amended at its 279th (November 2000) and 295th Session (March 2006).

## Miscellaneous

Examinations taken by Mr Tufnell, *Factories Enquiry Commission*, Report from Commissioners, Vol. XXI, 1833, D2, p. 50.
Millerand, Alexandre, 'Intervention au Congrès International pour la Protection Légale des Travailleurs', Séance d'ouverture – Mercredi 25 juillet 1900 (extract from *Les cahiers du Chatefp* n°7, March 2007).

# 4  Doing business with the Nazis

## The criminal prosecution of German industrialists after the Second World War

The Second World War and its aftermath mark key moments for the development of international law and principles, particularly in the areas of human rights and humanitarian law. The creation of the United Nations Organization and the adoption of the 1948 Universal Declaration of Human Rights and the four 1949 Geneva Conventions all constitute landmarks in these fields. This period was also the early days of what is now a firmly established area of international law: international criminal law. International criminal law is a branch of law mainly concerned with the criminal responsibility of individuals for atrocity crimes committed during and sometimes outside situations of armed conflict. Contemporary international criminal law focuses on four core crimes: genocide, crimes against humanity, war crimes and aggression.[1] The first international criminal tribunal ever established, the International Military Tribunal (IMT), tried major Nazi war criminals at Nuremberg. The principles embodied in the IMT Charter, further ascertained in the IMT judgment, continue to pervade the field.

The IMT judgment determined the criminal responsibility of high-level figures of the Nazi regime. Moreover, key organisations of the Nazi state; the leadership corps of the Nazi party; and those holding positions of power within the Gestapo, the SD and the Waffen-SS were declared 'criminal', hence giving some early indications about the notion of 'corporate' crimes, in the sense of collective criminal acts.

The IMT indicted a prominent German industrialist, Gustav Krupp, but he did not appear in court due to health reasons. Hence no businessman who did not otherwise hold a high-level political position within the regime was prosecuted at the IMT. After the IMT trial ended, however, the Allies initiated additional criminal proceedings in their respective zones of occupation in Germany. Those targeted a number of German industrialists and bankers. The French, the British and the Soviets also conducted similar trials, but those conducted by the United States' military tribunals are the best

---

1   Statute of the International Criminal Court, 2187 UNTS 90, Article 5.

documented.[2] While these proceedings were not international in nature because they were not held at the IMT but before US military tribunals, the initial plan was to prosecute a number of businessmen at the IMT and the case that the IMT prosecution team put together against those was redirected towards the military tribunals. These subsequent trials result from international collaboration and may thus be considered an 'international response' for the purpose for this book.[3]

These trials have no equivalent in history. They illustrate the circumstances under which businessmen came to be associated with some of the worst human rights violations of all times and shed light on the conditions that need to be fulfilled for criminal liability to arise. Given the dearth of court cases dealing with business crimes of that magnitude, they form an essential chapter in the history of business and human rights.[4] This chapter aims to distil the essential elements of these proceedings from a business and human rights perspective. The first section describes the relationship between the business sector and the Nazi regime. It covers the main aspects of the 'economic case' that the prosecution team put forward at Nuremberg and highlights the legal and political challenges they faced. The second section focuses on two aspects of the judgments which are still of relevance in contemporary business and human rights litigation: the knowledge test for complicity liability and whether necessity may work as a defence.

## The 'economic case' at Nuremberg

At the end of the Second World War, a number of business executives from the chemical and heavy industries were prosecuted for their involvement with the Nazi regime. It was then believed that they had played a key role in bringing Adolf Hitler to power, by providing him with political and financial support. While some German businessmen undoubtedly provided such support, historians have instead highlighted the uneasy relationship between the Nazis and the business world – particularly big business – at least during

2   Grietje Baars, 'Capitalism's Victor's Justice? The Hidden Stories Behind the Prosecution of Industrialists Post-WWII', *in* Kevin Jon Heller and Gerry Simpson (eds), *The Hidden Histories of War Crimes Trials*, Oxford: Oxford University Press (2013), pp. 188–189.

3   Jonathan Bush provides a detailed account of the months leading to the decision that the United States would conduct most trials against industrialists. For a while, the idea of a second international trial focusing on industrialists was also considered. See Jonathan A. Bush, 'The Prehistory of Corporations and Conspiracy in International Criminal Law: What Nuremberg Really Said', 109 *Columbia Law Review* 1094 (2009), pp. 1112–1130.

4   Beyond criminal trials focusing on individual responsibility of businessmen, corporations' liability for their involvement with the Nazi regime formed the basis of a number of civil claims brought in the United States by Holocaust survivors at the end of the 1990s. On those see Michael J. Bazyler, 'The Holocaust Restitution Movement in Comparative Perspective', 20 *Berkeley Journal of International Law* 11 (2002); Steven Whinston, 'Can Lawyers and Judges be Good Historians? A Critical Examination of the Siemens Slave-Labor Cases', 20 *Berkeley Journal of International Law* 160 (2002).

the years prior to Hitler's accession to power.[5] The National Socialist ideology rested on patriotism, a strong government, anti-Semitism and the creation of a new elite which would emerge from lower social classes such as small entrepreneurs, employees and farmers.[6] By contrast, Germany's large firms tended to favour free trade over protectionism; counted many Jews within their workforce, including in the highest levels of management; and were organised in powerful cartels and large conglomerates with very different interests from those of smaller businesses. Moreover, as historian Henry Turner has highlighted, the discourse about the creation of a new elite naturally did not appeal much to those who were already the elite.[7] Hence, the general attitude of big business towards the growing influence of the National Socialist party in the 1920s and early 1930s was at best suspicion, if not outright hostility.[8] The suspicion was mutual, as some Nazi leaders were resolutely anti-capitalist.[9]

Things began to change after Hitler became Chancellor of Germany in 1933. The change gradually emerged out of the realisation that the new regime and big business needed each other.[10] The regime had plans to launch an aggressive war throughout Europe and needed equipment for this. As was the case in most developed countries at the time, the economic crisis of the 1930s was hitting German businesses hard. Thus for the most part the business sector welcomed the opportunities that were to emerge. To begin with, in order to comply with the new racial policies, German business leadership carried out a rigorous 'Aryanisation' process and fired their Jewish

5   Henry Ashby Turner Jr, *German Big Business and the Rise of Hitler*, New York, Oxford: Oxford University Press (1985), pp. 340–341; Joseph Borkin, *The Crime and Punishment of I.G. Farben*, London: Andre Deutsch (1978), p. 2; Gerald D. Feldman, 'Financial Institutions in Nazi Germany: Reluctant or Willing Collaborators?', *in* Francis R. Nicosia and Jonathan Huerner (eds), *Business and Industry in Nazi Germany*, New York, Oxford: Berghahn Books (2004), pp. 18–21; Harold James, 'Banks and Business Politics in Nazi Germany', *in* Francis R. Nicosia and Jonathan Huerner (eds), *Business and Industry in Nazi Germany*, New York, Oxford: Berghahn Books (2004), p. 43; Jonathan Wiesen, *West Germany Industry and the Challenge of the Nazi Past 1945–1955*, Chapel Hill and London: the University of North Carolina Press (2001), pp. 12–13.
6   Henry Ashby Turner Jr, *German Big Business and the Rise of Hitler*, New York, Oxford: Oxford University Press (1985), pp. 342–348.
7   Ibid., p. 348.
8   Joseph Borkin, *The Crime and Punishment of I.G. Farben*, London: Andre Deutsch (1978), p. 2.
9   Harold James, 'Banks and Business Politics in Nazi Germany', *in* Francis R. Nicosia and Jonathan Huerner (eds), *Business and Industry in Nazi Germany*, New York, Oxford: Berghahn Books (2004), p. 43.
10   Henry Ashby Turner Jr, *German Big Business and the Rise of Hitler*, New York, Oxford: Oxford University Press (1985), pp. 349–355; Joseph Borkin, *The Crime and Punishment of I.G. Farben*, London: Andre Deutsch (1978), p. 2; Peter Hayes, 'The Chemistry of Business-State Relations in the Third Reich', *in* Francis R. Nicosia and Jonathan Huerner (eds), *Business and Industry in Nazi Germany*, New York, Oxford: Berghahn Books (2004), p. 73.

employees. Later on, they seized foreign industrial property in countries conquered by the Wehrmacht, and at least benefited from the forced labour programmes. The chemical firm I.G. Farben provides a spectacular example of how big business adapted to the regime. Labelled 'non-Aryan' in the early days of the Nazi regime, I.G. Farben ended up purposely building an industrial complex at Auschwitz, the construction of which cost the lives of more than 25,000 camp inmates.[11] For Turner,

> [m]ost men of big business viewed Nazism myopically and opportunistically. Like many other Germans whose national pride had been wounded by the unexpected loss of the war and humiliating peace treaty, they admired Nazism's defiant nationalism and hoped it could be used to help reassert what they regarded as their country's rightful place among the great powers.
>
> Viewing [the Nazi Party] (…) in terms of narrow self-interest, most failed to perceive the threat it posed to the very foundations of civilized life. Therein lay their heaviest guilt, one they shared, however, with a large part of the German elite.[12]

Gerald Feldman for his part noted that, in the early days of the regime,

> businessmen, especially in the financial sector, continued to believe that they could carry on normal business free of politics. The problem was that the longer the Third Reich lasted, the more it became impossible to distinguish between normal business and criminal business in a wide variety of areas. That is, business opportunities were increasingly defined by the conditions created by the regime, namely, conditions of war, conquest, systematic theft and transfer of assets along racial lines, and mass murder.[13]

On the complex relationship between big business and the Nazi regime, Wiesen concluded that

> [t]he broad picture is one of opportunism, in which companies took advantage of the vagaries of war to keep factories running and profits flowing. But only a combination of factors – outright greed, intimidation, the urge to keep businesses afloat, anti-Semitism, and anti-Slavic

---

11  Joseph Borkin, *The Crime and Punishment of I.G. Farben*, London: Andre Deutsch (1978), pp. 2–3.
12  Henry Ashby Turner Jr, *German Big Business and the Rise of Hitler*, New York, Oxford: Oxford University Press (1985), p. 349.
13  Gerald D. Feldman, 'Financial Institutions in Nazi Germany: Reluctant or Willing Collaborators?', *in* Francis R. Nicosia and Jonathan Huerner (eds), *Business and Industry in Nazi Germany*, New York, Oxford: Berghahn Books (2004), p. 32.

sentiments – can truly account for the overwhelming complicity of German firms in the Nazi economy and the Holocaust.'[14]

This picture contrasts with the core idea behind the economic case put forward by the IMT prosecution team, which was that big business had supported Hitler from the early days and played a key part in the conspiracy to launch an aggressive war. It was believed that their responsibility went beyond having benefited from the circumstances, and that they actually had played an active role in creating them. Despite its inaccuracy, this idea was plausible enough to justify working on an economic case against selected industrialists and bankers who were to face trial for their crimes.

The power of German industries and their organisation in cartels had been the subject of concern since before the end of the war, at least in the United States.[15] In 1944, United States Secretary of the Treasury Henry Morgenthau revealed his controversial post-surrender plan for Germany. One of the key aspects of the plan was 'complete de-militarization of Germany in the shortest possible period of time after surrender'.[16] This was to be achieved through 'the total destruction of the whole Germany armament industry, and the removal or destruction of other key industries which are basic to military strength'.[17] Although not as comprehensive as the Morgenthau plan, the Potsdam Agreement signed by the main Allies in August 1945 included a strict disarmament aspect which aimed to 'eliminate Germany's war potential'.[18] This shows that the Allies saw a clear link between the war and the German industrial sector. In this context, it is unsurprising that the Allies, who had set up the IMT to conduct criminal trials against major war criminals, initially envisaged including industrialists in the list of defendants to be prosecuted at Nuremberg.

The economic case had four main aspects. First, the prosecution believed that some industrialists had played a role in the conspiracy to launch an aggressive war: arguably the most important count at the IMT. Second, most industrialists had been involved in the Aryanisation of industry. Third, many of them had taken advantage of the German occupation of foreign territories to take control of industrial plants and seize equipment. Finally, the most obvious charge against industrialists was 'the recruitment and deployment of

---

14    Jonathan Wiesen, *West Germany Industry and the Challenge of the Nazi Past 1945–1955*, Chapel Hill and London: the University of North Carolina Press (2001), p. 16.

15    Grietje Baars, 'Capitalism's Victor's Justice? The Hidden Stories Behind the Prosecution of Industrialists Post-WWII', *in* Kevin Jon Heller and Gerry Simpson (eds), *The Hidden Histories of War Crimes Trials*, Oxford: Oxford University Press (2013), pp. 165–167.

16    Henry Morgenthau, *Suggested Post-Surrender Program for Germany* (1944), Digitalized and available on the Franklin D. Roosevelt Library and Museum Website, http://docs.fdrlibrary.marist.edu/PSF/BOX31/T297A04.HTML, para. 1. The plan was wide-ranging and included the partitioning of Germany (para. 2) and taking over school and university programmes, as well as the media (para. 5).

17    Ibid.

18    Potsdam Agreement (1945), 145 BFSP 864, Part II(B).

around five million slave labourers, part of whom had been work-to-death labour supplied by the Nazi extermination camps'.[19]

Within the US prosecution team, the economic aspects of the case were handed over to Assistant Attorney General Francis Shea.[20] In July 1945 Shea issued a memorandum addressed to Chief Prosecutor Robert Jackson

> outlining his conception of the 'economic case' and suggesting as defendants Hjalmar Schacht, Fritz Sauckel, Albert Speer, and Walter Funk (all of whom where subsequently named as defendants before the International Military Tribunal), as well as Alfried Krupp and half a dozen leading German industrial and financial leaders.[21]

Jackson supported the idea of an economic case and 'was determined to put the industrial complicity in the planning and waging of aggressive war on display'.[22]

Shea admitted in his memorandum of July 1945 that the economic case rested on unsure evidentiary grounds, and some in the prosecution team had shown little enthusiasm for it.[23] For example, Telford Taylor reports in his memoirs that one team member, John Harlan Amen, declared that 'the task in hand (…) was to convict the major war criminals and then go home', not to 'reform European economics'. Shea's project would 'overload things' and turn a war crimes trial into an 'anti-trust case'.[24] The British Foreign Office also had reservations about prosecuting industrialists at the IMT. Eventually, the four allied delegations met at the end of August 1945 and agreed on a final list of defendants before the IMT. Gustav Krupp was the only industrialist on this list. In November 1945, following a motion presented by his defence lawyer, the IMT declared Gustav Krupp unfit for trial for medical reasons.[25] Chief Prosecutor Jackson then sought to get the indictment modi-

---

19 Grietje Baars, 'Capitalism's Victor's Justice? The Hidden Stories Behind the Prosecution of Industrialists Post-WWII', *in* Kevin Jon Heller and Gerry Simpson (eds), *The Hidden Histories of War Crimes Trials*, Oxford: Oxford University Press (2013), p. 171. See also Kim C. Priemel, 'Tales of Totalitarianism: Conflicting Narratives in the Industrialist Cases at Nuremberg', *in* Kim C. Priemel and Alexa Stiller (eds), *Reassessing the Nuremberg Military Tribunals: Transitional Justice, Trial Narratives, and Historiography*, New York, Oxford: Berghahn Books (2012), p. 164.

20 Telford Taylor, *The Anatomy of the Nuremberg Trials, A Personal Memoir*, London: Bloomsbury (1993), p. 80.

21 Ibid., pp. 80–81.

22 Kim C. Priemel, 'Tales of Totalitarianism: Conflicting Narratives in the Industrialist Cases at Nuremberg', *in* Kim C. Priemel and Alexa Stiller (eds), *Reassessing the Nuremberg Military Tribunals: Transitional Justice, Trial Narratives, and Historiography*, New York, Oxford: Berghahn Books (2012), p. 165.

23 Ibid.

24 Ibid.

25 Gustav Krupp, by this point, was 'bedridden at the Krupp's Austrian villa in Bluhnbach, in an advanced state of senile decay, inarticulate, incontinent, and wholly incapable of standing trial': ibid.

fied to replace Gustav by his son Alfried, a request the tribunal rejected in no uncertain terms.[26]

Industrialists, then, would be tried in subsequent, non-international proceedings.[27] However, by the time the first of the industrialists' trials conducted by the United States opened at Nuremberg in April 1947 (*Flick* case), the context had radically changed. The United States government, determined to contain the spread of communism in Europe, was championing the idea of a prosperous, capitalist Europe. This idea did not fit squarely with the plan to put business leaders on trial. Against this background, it is hardly surprising that the tribunals rejected the prosecution's theories regarding the participation of Germany's big business in the conspiracy to launch wars of aggression.[28] Perhaps these decisions also aimed to reassure American businesses about their own current and future practice. As Baars put it,

> if Krauch's level of knowledge [lead defendant in the *I.G. Farben* case] did not suffice to find him guilty, then du Pont [member of the family who founded leading US chemical company DuPont] and the other US industrialists could rest assured.[29]

## The Nuremberg trials against industrialists and bankers

The United States conducted four subsequent trials against industrialists and bankers. The first was the *Flick* trial – Case No. 5 of the subsequent Nuremberg proceedings – which ran from April to December 1947. The case was against Friedrich Flick himself as well as five directors of the company, whose main line of business was the production of coal and steel. The counts were: (1) slave labour; (2) spoliation; (3) crimes against humanity prior to the war (the *Flick* tribunal eventually held that they had no jurisdiction over this); (4) aiding and abetting criminal activities of the SS; and (5) membership in the SS. Three directors were acquitted, one was found guilty of counts four and five and received a five-year sentence and the last was found guilty of count one and received a two-and-a-half-year sentence. Friedrich Flick was found guilty of counts one, two and four and received a seven-year sentence.[30]

---

26  Ibid., pp. 153–158.
27  For a detailed account of what happened between the dismissal of Gustav Krupp's case and the decision to conduct non-international trials, see Jonathan A. Bush, 'The Prehistory of Corporations and Conspiracy in International Criminal Law: What Nuremberg Really Said', 109 *Columbia Law Review* 1094 (2009), pp. 1112–1130.
28  Grietje Baars, 'Capitalism's Victor's Justice? The Hidden Stories Behind the Prosecution of Industrialists Post-WWII', *in* Kevin Jon Heller and Gerry Simpson (eds), *The Hidden Histories of War Crimes Trials*, Oxford: Oxford University Press (2013), pp. 189–191.
29  Ibid., p. 182.
30  Trials of War Criminals Before the Nuernberg Military Tribunals Under Control Council Law No 10, vol. VI 'The Flick Case', Washington: United States Government Printing Office (1952).

The *I.G. Farben* trial (Case No. 6) lasted almost a year, from August 1947 until July 1948. The case was against twenty-four defendants, all directors of the I.G. Farben conglomerate. The counts were: (1) Planning and waging aggressive war; (2) spoliation; (3) slave labour; (4) membership in the SS; and (5) conspiracy to commit aggressive war. Ten defendants were acquitted. For the others, sentences ranged from mere credit given for the time already spent in prison to eight years. The most severe sentences (six to eight years) were given to the five defendants found guilty of count three, all of whom had been involved in the decision to build the I.G. Farben Buna Werke synthetic rubber plant at Auschwitz with the clear plan to use slave labour from the camp at the plant.[31]

The *Krupp* trial (Case No. 10) took place between December 1947 and July 1948. There were twelve defendants: eleven directors of the Krupp group, as well as Alfried Krupp himself. The counts were: (1) crimes against peace by planning and waging aggressive war; (2) spoliation; (3) slave labour; and (4) conspiracy to commit crimes against peace. As explained below, the *Krupp* tribunal rejected the defence of necessity, which explains the more severe sentences pronounced, ranging between six and twelve years' imprisonment. One defendant received credit for the time he had already spent in prison and was immediately released, while another one was acquitted.[32]

Finally, the *Ministries* trial (Case No. 11) was the longest of all. It ran for over a year between January 1948 and April 1949. The counts were: (1) the planning, initiating and waging of aggressive war; (2) conspiracy to commit crimes against peace; (3) murder and mistreatment of belligerents and prisoners of war; (4) atrocities against German nationals from between 1933 and 1939; (5) atrocities against civilian populations; (6) plunder and spoliation; (7) slave labour; and (8) membership in criminal organisations. Among the twenty-one defendants, two are of interest for the purpose of this book. The first is Emil Puhl, vice-president of the *Reichsbank*, sentenced to five years' imprisonment after having been found guilty of count five. The second is Karl Rasche, director of the Dresdner bank, sentenced to seven years' imprisonment after having been found guilty of counts six and eight.[33]

## Knowledge as the mental element in complicity liability

International crimes tend to be committed by state actors and non-state paramilitary groups, and have a political dimension. Business involvement

31  Trials of War Criminals Before the Nuernberg Military Tribunals Under Control Council Law No 10, vol. VII and VIII 'The I.G. Farben Case', Washington: United States Government Printing Office (1952).
32  Trials of War Criminals Before the Nuernberg Military Tribunals Under Control Council Law No 10, vol. IX 'The Krupp Case', Washington: United States Government Printing Office (1952).
33  Trials of War Criminals Before the Nuernberg Military Tribunals Under Control Council Law No 10, vol. XII, XIII and XIV 'The Ministries Case', Washington: United States Government Printing Office (1952).

with such crimes is often as an accomplice, or aidor and abettor, and not as the main perpetrator. In law, besides the material element (what the company or businessperson has done) and proximity (how close to the abuses, in time and space, the company or businessperson was), the third key element for complicity liability to arise is the mental element, the state of mind of the person when they acted or refrained from acting. These are the main elements of contemporary business and human rights cases, and they were also paramount at Nuremberg. The mental element may be established using three different tests or standards: (1) knowledge (whether the company or businessperson knew or should have known); (2) intent (whether they shared the intent of the main perpetrator); and (3) purpose (whether they have acted purposefully).[34] The purpose standard is meant to be a compromise between mere knowledge and intent.

In the Nuremberg trials against industrialists, knowledge, with no requirement to share the intent of the main perpetrators, was generally deemed sufficient as a mental element for liability to arise.[35] For example, in the *I.G. Farben* case, the prosecution argued that some I.G. Farben directors sat on the board of the company manufacturing Zyklon B gas and that as a result they bore a responsibility in the death of those millions of individuals who perished in gas chambers asphyxiated by that gas. The tribunal held that the said directors had no knowledge of what the gas was used for and dismissed the claim.[36] This implies that, *a contrario*, had the directors known what this insecticide was really used for, their guilt could have been established, thereby making mere knowledge a sufficient mental element for the crime to be constituted. Other post-Second World War tribunals' decisions also lean towards this position.[37] Some have argued that the acquittal of banker Karl Rasche on count five of the indictment in the *Ministries* case (atrocities against civilian populations) constitutes an exception in this respect, as it allegedly embraced the more stringent purpose test.[38] The *Ministries* tribunal found that Rasche funded the SS through donations and loans while knowing perfectly well of the criminal enterprises in which the SS were engaged.

34  For an enlightening description of how corporate complicity arises, see International Commission of Jurists, *Report of the ICJ Expert Legal Panel on Corporate Complicity in International Crimes*, Vol. 1, pp. 8–26.
35  For charges related to crimes against peace, the level of knowledge required was higher than for other charges. On this, see the concurring opinion of Judge Hebert, Trials of War Criminals Before the Nuernberg Military Tribunals Under Control Council Law No 10, vol. VIII 'The I.G. Farben Case', Washington: United States Government Printing Office (1952), Concurring opinion of Judge Hebert on the charges of crimes against peace; Concurring opinion on counts one and five of the indictment, p. 1217.
36  Ibid., pp. 1168–1169.
37  For an analysis of those see Michael J. Kelly, 'Prosecuting Corporations for Genocide under International Law', 6 *Harvard Law and Policy Review* 339 (2012) pp. 351–353.
38  Doug Cassel, 'Corporate Aiding and Abetting of Human Rights Violations: Confusion in the Courts', 6 *Northwestern University Journal of International Human Rights* 304 (2007–2008), p. 309.

Yet they acquitted him. Some have used this decision as precedent for the claim that knowledge is not sufficient as a mental element of the offence and that guilt should only be established when the defendant also shared the criminal intent of the main perpetrators.[39] This interpretation is debatable, however. The relevant part of the decision reads as follows:

> The defendant is a banker and businessman of long experience and is possessed of a keen and active mind. Bankers do not approve or make loans in the number and amount made by the Dresdner Bank without ascertaining, having, or obtaining information or knowledge as to the purpose for which the loan is sought, and how it is to be used. It is inconceivable to us that the defendant did not possess that knowledge, and we find that he did.
>
> The real question is, is it a crime to make a loan, knowing or having good reason to believe that the borrower will use the funds in financing enterprises which are employed in using labor in violation of either national or international law? Does he stand in any different position than one who sells supplies or raw materials to a builder building a house, knowing that the structure will be used for an unlawful purpose? A bank sells money or credit in the same manner as the merchandiser of any other commodity. It does not become a partner in enterprise, and the interest charged is merely the gross profit which the bank realizes from the transaction, out of which it must deduct its business costs, and from which it hopes to realize a net profit. Loans or sale of commodities to be used in an unlawful enterprise may well be condemned from a moral standpoint and reflect no credit on the part of the lender or seller in either case, but the transaction can hardly be said to be a crime. Our duty is to try and punish those guilty of violating international law, and we are not prepared to state that such loans constitute a violation of that law, nor has our attention been drawn to any ruling to the contrary.[40]

As one author suggested, rather than rejecting knowledge as an insufficient mental element, this extract may simply show that the material element of the offence was not present.[41] In other words, Karl Rasche was acquitted of count five not because mere knowledge (which he had) was deemed insufficient as a mental element, but because lending money was not considered to be a satisfactory material element. This case is now authority for the controversial idea that financiers bear a lower level of responsibility than those

39   See United States Court of Appeals for the Second Circuit, *Presbyterian Church of Sudan v. Talisman Energy, Inc.*, 582 F.3d 244, 259 (2d Cir. 2009).
40   Trials of War Criminals Before the Nuernberg Military Tribunals Under Control Council Law No 10, vol. XIV, 'The Ministries Case', Washington: United States Government Printing Office (1952), p. 622.
41   Sabine Michalowski, 'Complicity Liability for Funding Gross Human Rights Violations?', 30 *Berkeley Journal of International Law* 451 (2012), p. 472.

providing goods and services to a criminal regime. Confusion over the Nuremberg precedent on the question of knowledge continues to this day, as also covered in Chapter 10 of this book.

### The defence of necessity

Defendants in the industrialists' trials all attempted to use the defence of necessity with regard to charges related to the use of forced or slave labour. They argued that they could not go against the policies of the Reich, including those regarding labour, and that, in a way, they were forced to make inmates work in their factories and plants.[42] The *Flick* tribunal accepted the defence of necessity for four defendants out of six, arguing that this defence must be available even though Control Council Law No 10 – the legal basis of all subsequent Nuremberg trials – explicitly provided that the defence of superior orders was not available to the defendants. The *Flick* tribunal feared that it 'might be reproached for wreaking vengeance rather than administering justice if it were to declare as unavailable to defendants the defence of necessity here urged in their behalf'.[43] The tribunal considered that defendants Steinbrinck, Burkart, Kaletsch and Terberger could avail themselves of the defence because they were 'under clear and present danger' and could have been in great trouble had they resisted implementing the Reich's forced labour programme. In the tribunal's own words,

> We have already discussed the Reich reign of terror. The defendants lived within the Reich. The Reich, through its hordes of enforcement officials and secret police, was always 'present,' ready to go into instant action and to mete out savage and immediate punishment against anyone doing anything that could be construed as obstructing or hindering the carrying out of governmental regulations or decrees.[44]

However, the *Flick* tribunal considered that defendants Weiss and Flick should be treated differently. These two had done more than passively receive unwilling workers, and instead had shown initiative in requesting more workers. As a result the tribunal deprived them of the complete defence of necessity. The *Flick* trial was the first trial of industrialists and the *Flick* tribunal's position on the defence of necessity was used as precedent in

---

42   For a discussion on this see Kim C. Priemel, 'Tales of Totalitarianism: Conflicting Narratives in the Industrialist Cases at Nuremberg', *in* Kim C. Priemel and Alexa Stiller (eds), *Reassessing the Nuremberg Military Tribunals: Transitional Justice, Trial Narratives, and Historiography*, New York, Oxford: Berghahn Books (2012), p. 177.

43   Trials of War Criminals Before the Nuernberg Military Tribunals Under Control Council Law No 10, vol. VI 'The Flick Case', Washington: United States Government Printing Office (1952), p. 1200.

44   Ibid., p. 1201.

subsequent judgments, particularly in the *I.G. Farben* judgment, in which the tribunal held that they were

> not prepared to say that these defendants did not speak the truth when they asserted that in conforming to the slave-labor program they had no other choice than to comply with the mandates of the Hitler government. There can be but little doubt that the defiant refusal of a Farben executive to carry out the Reich production schedule or to use slave labor to achieve that end would have been treated as treasonous sabotage and would have resulted in prompt and drastic retaliation. Indeed, there was credible evidence that Hitler would have welcomed the opportunity to make an example of a Farben leader.[45]

Judge Hebert disagreed with the majority with regard to the availability of the defence of necessity to the defendants. In a powerful dissent, he wrote:

> Farben's planners, led by defendant Krauch, geared Farben's potentialities to actual war needs. It is totally irrelevant that the defendants might have preferred German workers. That they would have preferred not to commit a crime is no defense to its commission. The important fact is that Farben's Vorstand willingly cooperated in utilizing forced labor. They were not forced to do so. I cannot agree that there was an absence of a moral choice. In utilizing slave labor within Farben the will of the actors coincided with the will of those controlling the government and who had directed or ordered the doing of criminal acts. Under these circumstances the defense of necessity is certainly not admissible.
>
> I am convinced that persons in the positions of power and influence of these defendants might in numberless ways have avoided the widespread participation in the slave-labor utilization that was prevalent throughout the Farben organization. I cannot agree with the assertion that these defendants had no other choice than to comply with the mandates of the Hitler government. Had there been any real will to resist such comprehensive participation in the crime of enslavement, the defendants, possessing superior knowledge in their respective complicated technical fields, could no doubt have avoided such participation through a variety of devices of such imperceptible nature as to avoid the drastic results now portrayed in the posing of this defense. In reality, the defense is an after-thought, the validity of which is belied by Farben's entire course of action. To assert that Hitler would have 'welcomed the opportunity to make an example of a Farben leader' is, in my opinion,

45  Trials of War Criminals Before the Nuernberg Military Tribunals Under Control Council Law No 10, vol. VIII 'The I.G. Farben Case', Washington: United States Government Printing Office (1952), p. 1175.

pure speculation and does not establish the defense of necessity on the facts here involved.[46]

The fact that the *Flick* and *I.G. Farben* tribunals accepted the defence of necessity with regard to the use of forced labour, though neither for all defendants nor with regard to all aspects of the charge, has led to criticism both from academics[47] and from some members of the prosecution teams.[48] In this context, it is worthy of note that the *Krupp* tribunal rejected the defence of necessity in strong and enlightening terms. Speaking of the *Krupp* defendants, they pointed out that with the exception of the lead defendant Alfried Krupp, who owned the firm, 'the most that any of them had at stake was a job'.[49] Therefore,

> the question from the standpoint of the individual defendants resolves itself into this proposition: To avoid losing my job or the control of my property, I am warranted in employing thousands of civilian deportees, prisoners of war, and concentration camp inmates; keeping them in a state of involuntary servitude; exposing them daily to death or great bodily harm, under conditions which did in fact result in the deaths of many of them; and working them in an undernourished condition in the production of armament intended for use against the people who would liberate them and indeed even against the people of their homelands.
>
> If we may assume that as a result of opposition to Reich policies, Krupp would have lost control of his plant and the officials their positions, it is difficult to conclude that the law of necessity justified a choice favorable to themselves and against the unfortunate victims who had no choice at all in the matter. Or, in the language of the rule, that the remedy was not disproportioned to the evil.[50]

46  Trials of War Criminals Before the Nuernberg Military Tribunals Under Control Council Law No 10, vol. VIII 'The I.G. Farben Case', Washington: United States Government Printing Office (1952), Dissenting opinion of Judge Hebert on the charges of slave labour, dissenting opinion on count three of the indictment, pp. 1309–1310.
47  See for example Grietje Baars, 'Capitalism's Victor's Justice? The Hidden Stories Behind the Prosecution of Industrialists Post-WWII', *in* Kevin Jon Heller and Gerry Simpson (eds), *The Hidden Histories of War Crimes Trials*, Oxford: Oxford University Press (2013), pp. 184–185.
48  As reported in Kim C. Priemel, 'Tales of Totalitarianism: Conflicting Narratives in the Industrialist Cases at Nuremberg', *in* Kim C. Priemel and Alexa Stiller (eds), *Reassessing the Nuremberg Military Tribunals: Transitional Justice, Trial Narratives, and Historiography*, New York, Oxford: Berghahn Books (2012), pp. 161–162.
49  Trials of War Criminals Before the Nuernberg Military Tribunals Under Control Council Law No 10, vol. IX 'The Krupp Case', Washington: United States Government Printing Office (1952). p. 1444.
50  Ibid., pp. 1444–1445.

The tribunal went even further and considered the unlikely possibility that the *Krupp* defendants might have been deported to a concentration camp had they refused to cooperate. Even so, the tribunal believed that if the defendants had been sent to such a camp, they

> would not have been in a worse plight than the thousands of helpless victims whom they daily exposed to danger of death, great bodily harm from starvation, and the relentless air raids upon the armament plants; to say nothing of involuntary servitude and the other indignities which they suffered. The disparity in the number of the actual and potential victims is also thought provoking.[51]

The industrialists' trials therefore paint a contrasting picture of the defence of necessity and its possible application with regard to forced labour charges. On the one hand, the *Flick* and *I.G. Farben* tribunals let a number of defendants off the hook by allowing them to rely on the defence. On the other, the *Krupp* tribunal rejected the defence in no uncertain terms, using powerful comparisons between the defendants' privileged condition and the miserable fate of the inmates who were forced to work for the defendants' benefit. Although it remains controversial, necessity is likely to be raised as a defence in business and human rights cases, especially in situations where a government has requested the company or the businessperson to act in a certain way.[52]

## Conclusion

Beyond trials, judgments and dissenting opinions, developments occurring outside the Nuremberg courtroom are also instructive. Historians have documented the public relations campaigns of rehabilitation of German businesses that started at the time of the trials and continued in the subsequent decades.[53] For example, Kim Priemel noted that 'the brunt of the guilt (...) was assigned to the working class',[54] while leading businessmen argued that 'Hitler had risen from the ranks of the proletariat to become its messiah. And against the irresponsible masses a bourgeois business elite had been nothing but

51   Ibid., p. 1446.
52   See International Commission of Jurists, *Report of the ICJ Expert Legal Panel on Corporate Complicity in International Crimes*, Vol. 1, pp. 17–18.
53   S. Jonathan Wiesen, *West Germany Industry and the Challenge of the Nazi Past 1945–1955*, Chapel Hill and London: the University of North Carolina Press (2001), pp. 2–3; Kim C. Priemel, 'Tales of Totalitarianism: Conflicting Narratives in the Industrialist Cases at Nuremberg', *in* Kim C. Priemel and Alexa Stiller (eds), *Reassessing the Nuremberg Military Tribunals: Transitional Justice, Trial Narratives, and Historiography*, New York, Oxford: Berghahn Books (2012), pp. 174–182.
54   Kim C. Priemel, 'Tales of Totalitarianism: Conflicting Narratives in the Industrialist Cases at Nuremberg', *in* Kim C. Priemel and Alexa Stiller (eds), *Reassessing the Nuremberg Military Tribunals: Transitional Justice, Trial Narratives, and Historiography*, New York, Oxford: Berghahn Books (2012), p. 178.

helpless.'[55] In short, they described themselves 'as apolitical professionals who had remained loyal to traditional business ethics'.[56] They also played the anti-communist card with some degree of success, arguing that the trials were anti-capitalistic in essence and that they, as experienced business professionals, were needed to anchor West Germany within the capitalist camp.[57] This position bore fruit to some extent. Part of the US press, as well as individuals such as Senator McCarthy, harshly criticised the very principle of holding war crime trials and accused some members of the US prosecution team of being communists.[58]

The trials of industrialists and bankers for their involvement with the crimes committed by the Nazis are of great relevance to contemporary students and observers of the field of business and human rights. Not only do the judgments constitute an invaluable historical account of this dark period of history, but they also addressed important legal points, as outlined in this chapter. More generally, they provide some elements to tackle one of the most fundamental questions in the field: where to draw the line between 'doing business' and contributing to human rights violations.[59] In the introduction to their book *Business and Industry in Nazi Germany*, Nicosia and Huerner eloquently summarised the uncertainties this question raises. Their words bring this chapter to a close:

> [M]any of the questions raised in this volume are of immediate relevance to contemporary controversies over globalization, the relationship of corporations to the state, corporate labor practices, corporate corruption, and the notion of corporate social responsibility. (...) The most compelling issue emerging from this volume is, of course, the extent to which the experience of business and industry under National Socialism is instructive for the dilemmas we face today. Do the pursuits of profit today, and the social effects of such pursuits, in any way mirror the complicity of some German firms in the expropriation of Jewish-owned businesses, the exploitation of labor, or other assaults on the liberty and dignity of Hitler's victims?[60]

---

55    Ibid.
56    Ibid., p. 179.
57    Ibid., pp. 175–177.
58    Jonathan A. Bush, 'The Prehistory of Corporations and Conspiracy in International Criminal Law: What Nuremberg Really Said' 109 *Columbia Law Review* 1094 (2009), pp. 1197, 1232 and 1239. See also Grietje Baars, 'Capitalism's Victor's Justice? The Hidden Stories Behind the Prosecution of Industrialists Post-WWII', *in* Kevin Jon Heller and Gerry Simpson (eds), *The Hidden Histories of War Crimes Trials*, Oxford: Oxford University Press (2013), p. 189.
59    For a discussion on this see Grietje Baars, 'Capitalism's Victor's Justice? The Hidden Stories Behind the Prosecution of Industrialists Post-WWII', *in* Kevin Jon Heller and Gerry Simpson (eds), *The Hidden Histories of War Crimes Trials*, Oxford: Oxford University Press (2013), p. 178.
60    Francis R. Nicosia and Jonathan Huerner (eds), *Business and Industry in Nazi Germany*, New York, Oxford: Berghahn Books (2004), pp. 11–12.

# Bibliography

## Books

Borkin, Joseph, *The Crime and Punishment of I.G. Farben*, London: Andre Deutsch (1978).

Nicosia, Francis R. and Huerner, Jonathan (eds), *Business and Industry in Nazi Germany*, New York, Oxford: Berghahn Books (2004).

Taylor, Telford, *The Anatomy of the Nuremberg Trials, A Personal Memoir*, London: Bloomsbury (1993).

Turner, Henry Ashby Jr, *German Big Business and the Rise of Hitler*, New York, Oxford: Oxford University Press (1985).

Wiesen, Jonathan, *West Germany Industry and the Challenge of the Nazi Past 1945–1955*, Chapel Hill and London: the University of North Carolina Press (2001).

## Journal articles

Bazyler, Michael J., 'The Holocaust Restitution Movement in Comparative Perspective', 20 *Berkeley Journal of International Law* 11 (2002).

Bush, Jonathan A., 'The Prehistory of Corporations and Conspiracy in International Criminal Law: What Nuremberg Really Said', 109 *Columbia Law Review* 1094 (2009)

Cassel, Doug, 'Corporate Aiding and Abetting of Human Rights Violations: Confusion in the Courts', 6 *Northwestern University Journal of International Human Rights* 304 (2007–2008).

Kelly, Michael J., 'Prosecuting Corporations for Genocide under International Law', 6 *Harvard Law and Policy Review* 339 (2012) pp. 351–353.

Michalowski, Sabine, 'Complicity Liability for Funding Gross Human Rights Violations?', 30 *Berkeley Journal of International Law* 451 (2012).

Whinston, Steven, 'Can Lawyers and Judges be Good Historians? A Critical Examination of the Siemens Slave-Labor Cases', 20 *Berkeley Journal of International Law* 160 (2002).

## Book chapters

Baars, Grietje, 'Capitalism's Victor's Justice? The Hidden Stories Behind the Prosecution of Industrialists Post-WWII', *in* Kevin Jon Heller and Gerry Simpson (eds), *The Hidden Histories of War Crimes Trials*, Oxford: Oxford University Press (2013), pp. 163–192.

Feldman, Gerald D., 'Financial Institutions in Nazi Germany: Reluctant or Willing Collaborators?', *in* Francis R. Nicosia and Jonathan Huerner (eds), *Business and Industry in Nazi Germany*, New York, Oxford: Berghahn Books (2004), pp. 15–42.

Hayes, Peter, 'The Chemistry of Business-State Relations in the Third Reich', *in* Francis R. Nicosia and Jonathan Huerner (eds), *Business and Industry in Nazi Germany*, New York, Oxford: Berghahn Books (2004), pp. 66–80.

James, Harold, 'Banks and Business Politics in Nazi Germany', *in* Francis R. Nicosia and Jonathan Huerner (eds), *Business and Industry in Nazi Germany*, New York, Oxford: Berghahn Books (2004), pp. 43–65.

Priemel, Kim C., 'Tales of Totalitarianism: Conflicting Narratives in the Industrialist Cases at Nuremberg', *in* Kim C. Priemel and Alexa Stiller (eds) *Reassessing the Nuremberg Military Tribunals: Transitional Justice, Trial Narratives, and Historiography*, New York, Oxford: Berghahn Books (2012), pp. 161–193.

## Treaties

Potsdam Agreement, 145 BFSP 864, Part II(B) (1945).
Statute of the International Criminal Court, 2187 UNTS 90 (1998).

## Cases

Trials of War Criminals Before the Nuernberg Military Tribunals Under Control Council Law No 10, vol. VI 'The Flick Case', Washington: United States Government Printing Office (1952).
Trials of War Criminals Before the Nuernberg Military Tribunals Under Control Council Law No 10, vol. VII and VIII 'The I.G. Farben Case', Washington: United States Government Printing Office (1952).
Trials of War Criminals Before the Nuernberg Military Tribunals Under Control Council Law No 10, vol. IX 'The Krupp Case', Washington: United States Government Printing Office (1952).
Trials of War Criminals Before the Nuernberg Military Tribunals Under Control Council Law No 10, vol. XII, XIII and XIV, 'The Ministries Case', Washington: United States Government Printing Office (1952).
United States Court of Appeals for the Second Circuit, *Presbyterian Church of Sudan v. Talisman Energy, Inc.*, 582 F.3d 244; 259 (2d Cir. 2009)

## Reports

International Commission of Jurists, *Report of the ICJ Expert Legal Panel on Corporate Complicity in International Crimes*, Vol. 1 (2008).
Morgenthau, Henry, *Suggested Post-Surrender Program for Germany* (1944), Digitalized and available on the Franklin D. Roosevelt Library and Museum Website, http://docs.fdrlibrary.marist.edu/psf/box31/t297a01.html (last accessed 15 June 2016).

# Part II

# International law and policy
## Limitations and progress

The first part of the book has shown how business can be involved in large-scale human rights violations by focusing on historical violations of rights and how they have been addressed. Leaving history behind, this part focuses on contemporary legal and policy issues and on the limited progress towards greater accountability in the business and human rights field. Chapter 5 explores the relevance of international human rights law and international criminal law for global business. Building on Chapter 5, Chapter 6 looks into the interplay between human rights and other areas of international law which are of crucial importance for business, international investment and international trade law. These two chapters highlight the limitations of the current legal framework, especially in terms of international enforcement. By contrast, Chapter 7 presents the various international soft law and policy initiatives that aim to address corporate human rights violations. Finally, Chapter 8 delves into private modes of regulation as complementary tools to enhance corporate accountability. In these two areas progress is clear, at least when it comes to accountability as a virtue (or a set of standards), and to some extent accountability as a mechanism as well.

# 5 Business, international human rights law and international criminal law

## Shifting boundaries

This chapter explores the relevance of international human rights law and international criminal law for global business. International human rights law has developed in a way that technically makes states the only duty-bearers of human rights obligations. Those obligations derive from treaty law and from customary international law. Under a conservative reading of the system, corporations, even multinational corporations, are not subjects of international human rights law and therefore are under no legal obligation to abide by human rights treaties. At best, they are under the obligation not to commit violations amounting to international crimes as defined by the Statute of the International Criminal Court. Companies have no human rights obligation, the argument goes, and the fact that there is no international court before which victims may claim rights against businesses makes this even clearer.

Yet, while the absence of international enforcement mechanism constitutes a serious limitation, this does not mean that corporations have no human rights responsibilities. This chapter considers the responsibilities of corporations under international human rights law and international criminal law, and shows how boundaries that were once thought to be immutable are now shifting to shape the notion of corporate responsibility and allow for greater accountability in the human rights field. The first section provides a brief introduction to international human rights law. This area of law is traditionally said to apply exclusively to states, as the only subjects of international law. Challenging this assertion, the second section focuses on the question of whether corporations are subjects of international law as well. Beyond this theoretical discussion, the third section explores the contours of corporate human rights responsibilities. The final section brings to light the limitations of international enforcement mechanisms.

## The Universal Declaration of Human Rights and the development of international human rights law

The Universal Declaration of Human Rights, adopted in 1948, represents the first attempt to create a common standard of treatment for human beings across the world, irrespective of their nationality or status.[1] This milestone text recognises that all human beings are equal and that no distinction should be made between them. While the Universal Declaration is mostly focused on civil and political rights, such as the right not to be held in slavery and the right to a fair trial, it also protects economic, social and cultural rights such as the rights to social security and to education. In that sense it attempts to reconcile, though imperfectly, these two main categories of rights.

The use of the term 'universal' is worthy of note. It was deliberately changed from 'international' to shift the focus away from nation states and on to the real addressees, 'the human family'.[2] There is a degree of irony in calling the Universal Declaration of Human Rights 'universal', given that at the time of its adoption a large part of the world was still under colonial domination. For example, only three African states were present during the vote of the UN General Assembly for the adoption of the Universal Declaration. One of them was white supremacist South Africa, hardly a poster child for the universality ideal.[3] It is debatable whether that made the Declaration a truly universal text from the outset. Despite this flaw, it is commonly acknowledged that since the time of its adoption the Universal Declaration has developed what can be called a life of its own, during which its universality has been frequently affirmed.[4] Its simple, non-legalistic language has made it of use beyond courtrooms. More than a piece of legislation, the Universal Declaration of Human Rights has become a text of reference for human rights defenders across the world. It can be used to articulate human rights claims without mention of legal concerns such as jurisdiction, treaty ratification status or exhaustion of local remedies.[5] In short, in the field of human rights, the Universal Declaration of Human Rights holds a unique position, beyond purely legalistic considerations.

Moreover, it is meant to set standards of behaviour not only for states but also, as stated in the preamble, for 'every individual and every organ of society',[6] including businesses. Indeed, this phrasing 'excludes no one, no

*[handwritten margin note: UDHR stds for all legal persons.]*

1    Universal Declaration of Human Rights, GA Res. 217A (III), 10 December 1948.
2    Universal Declaration of Human Rights, Preamble, first paragraph. On the fact that the Declaration is universal and not international, see Johannes Morsink, *Inherent Human Rights. Philosophical Roots of the Universal Declaration*, Philadelphia: University of Pennsylvania Press (2009), pp. 57 and 148–149.
3    The other two countries were Egypt and Ethiopia. South Africa was among the eight countries that abstained. For details on the vote see *Yearbook of the United Nations* 1948–1949, p. 535.
4    William A. Schabas (ed.), *The Universal Declaration of Human Rights, the Travaux Preparatoires Volume I*, Cambridge: Cambridge University Press (2013), p. cxxi.
5    Hurst Hannum, 'The Status of the Universal Declaration of Human Rights in National and International Law', 25 *Georgia Journal of International and Comparative Law* (1995), p. 287.
6    Preamble, Universal Declaration of Human Rights, GA Res. 217A (III), 10 December 1948.

company, no market, no cyberspace'.[7] The idea that the Universal Declaration of Human Rights is not merely addressed to states transpires also from Article 30, which reads as follows: 'Nothing in this Declaration may be interpreted as implying for any State, group or person any right to engage in any activity or to perform any act aimed at the destruction of any of the rights and freedoms set forth herein.' The inclusion of the word 'group' results from a French amendment put forward less than one month before the UN General Assembly adopted the Declaration on 10 December 1948.[8] The French delegation 'considered it essential' to include the word 'group' because 'experience has shown that it was rarely States or individuals that engaged in activities aimed at the destruction of human rights'.[9] During the discussions on the amendment, the Soviet delegate mentioned the business sector as one of the groups covered by the amendment, citing 'high finance' as 'a serious threat to the existence of the United Nations and to peace'.[10] For the Ukrainian delegate, the inclusion of the word 'group' was necessary so as to encompass, for example, 'magnates of high finance and industry, who were largely responsible for the advent of fascism'.[11] Although these comments were made by delegates of Communist countries, who can be said to have been biased against the private sector, the other delegates did not reject that interpretation. Therefore it is safe to infer that in 1948 the drafters of the Universal Declaration of Human Rights intended it to set limits to the behaviour of the business sector. As a matter of fact, companies themselves frequently refer to the Universal Declaration as a standard of behaviour in their human rights policies or codes of conduct.[12]

It is on the basis of the Universal Declaration of Human Rights that international human rights law has developed, both in the form of treaties binding states who have ratified them and as non-written customary law binding all states. Shortly after the adoption of the Universal Declaration of Human Rights in December 1948, the UN Commission on Human Rights resumed its drafting work.[13] The initial idea was to produce a single human rights treaty, encompassing the full scope of human rights: civil, political, economic, social and cultural. The Commission quickly abandoned the idea as the Western bloc and the Soviet bloc had already adopted irreconcilable positions by that point. In a nutshell, the West favoured civil and political

7  Louis Henkin 'The Universal Declaration at 50 and the Challenge of Global Markets', 25 *Brooklyn Journal of International Law* 17 (1999), p. 25.
8  A/C.3/345, 17 November 1948.
9  A/C.3/SR.155, 24 November 1948. This statement is odd because states actually are the main, though not exclusive, human rights violators.
10  A/C.3/SR.156, 25 November 1948.
11  Ibid.
12  See the list of company policy statements on human rights compiled by the Business and Human Rights Resource Centre, http://business-humanrights.org/en/company-policy-statements-on-human-rights (last accessed 21 March 2016).
13  *Yearbook of the United Nations* (1948–1949), p. 538.

rights, while the East favoured economic, social and cultural rights. These ideological dissentions prevented the elaboration of a single treaty and explain why, in the end, the Commission worked on two separate treaties, finally adopted in 1966: the International Covenant on Civil and Political Rights[14] and the International Covenant on Economic, Social and Cultural Rights[15] (hereinafter ICCPR and ICESCR). Together with the Universal Declaration of Human Rights, these treaties form the International Bill of Rights. They are commonly said to represent the minimum rights guaranteed to all human beings. One year earlier, in 1965, the UN General Assembly had adopted the International Convention on the Elimination of All Forms of Racial Discrimination (hereinafter ICERD).[16] Against this firm background, the United Nations has subsequently encouraged the protection of more vulnerable groups (women,[17] children,[18] migrant workers[19] and persons with disabilities[20]) and specific rights (right not to be subjected to torture[21] and to enforced disappearance[22]) through the adoption of six distinct UN treaties between 1979 and 2006.

In parallel, certain regions of the world adopted their own human rights treaties. These treaties include the European Convention on Human Rights,[23] the American Convention on Human Rights[24] and the African Charter on Human and Peoples' Rights.[25] Finally, as discussed in Chapter 3, the numerous conventions elaborated by the International Labour Organization (ILO) may also be said to form part of international human rights law broadly defined. Hence international human rights law encompasses the full range of human rights: labour, civil, political, economic, social and cultural.

These treaties and the various mechanisms of monitoring they have set up, such as the European Court of Human Rights and the UN Committee against Torture, all form part of international human rights law. There also

14   International Covenant on Civil and Political Rights (1966) 999 UNTS 171.
15   International Covenant on Economic, Social and Cultural Rights (1966) 993 UNTS 3.
16   International Convention on the Elimination of All Forms of Racial Discrimination (1965) 660 UNTS 195.
17   Convention on the Elimination of All Forms of Discrimination against Women (1979) 1249 UNTS 13.
18   Convention on the Rights of the Child (1989) 1577 UNTS 3.
19   International Convention on the Protection of the Rights of All Migrant Workers and Members of their Families (1990) 2220 UNTS 3.
20   Convention on the Rights of Persons with Disabilities (2006) 2515 UNTS 3.
21   Convention against Torture and Other Cruel, Inhuman or Degrading Treatment or Punishment (1984) 1465 UNTS 85.
22   International Convention for the Protection of All Persons from Enforced Disappearance (2006) UN Doc. A/61/488.
23   Convention for the Protection of Human Rights and Fundamental Freedoms (1950), CETS No.005.
24   American Convention on Human Rights (1969), OAS TS No 36.
25   African Charter on Human and People's Rights (1981), 21 ILM 58 (1982).

exist mechanisms of monitoring and protection of human rights which are not related to specific treaties. These include, for example, UN Special Procedures and the Universal Periodic Review mechanism. These mechanisms highlight the central role of states as duty-bearers under international human rights law. Typically, international human rights law applies to states in their relationships with individuals or groups falling under their jurisdiction, such as their own nationals or people living on their territories. Because international human rights law has primarily developed in the form of treaties, which are legal agreements into which states enter with each other, it primarily – and some argue exclusively – binds states. Under a strict approach of international human rights law, only states must ensure that they abide by the obligations set out in treaties such as the obligation not to torture (Article 7 ICCPR) and the obligation to ensure the right of everyone to form trade unions (Article 8 ICESCR). This approach is controversial and, while it has merits when it comes to treaties, it is incorrect when it comes to the Universal Declaration of Human Rights, which places duties on a range of actors and not only on states. Speaking of international human rights instruments, Johannes Morsink noted in terms that are worth citing in full:

> This entire system is a man-made one; it therefore has difficulty embracing the inherent character of the human rights that, according to the Declaration, accrue to us automatically at birth without the intervention of anything made or done by humans other than the acts of (natural or artificial) conception that bring us to the world. This new emphasis on the duties of states has deepened the asymmetry between inherent human rights and their correlative duties, for while the rights-holders are still individual human beings, in this new international system the primary duty-bearers are still mostly, though not exclusively, states and their agencies rather than individual human beings. We have a correlation between holders of inherent rights that are not man-made and state duty-bearers that are man-made and therefore contingent. This hybrid of inherent moral rights matched with mostly contingent, man-made states duties has created puzzlement and discomfort among theoreticians of human rights.[26]

The asymmetry between the human rights ideal and the fact that states, because they are sovereign, get to pick and choose the treaties they ratify is an important feature of international human rights law. Moreover, the absence of a compelling enforcement mechanism to ensure compliance blurs the distinction between binding law, such as treaty law and customary international law, and non-binding law, such as the Universal Declaration of Human Rights and, to take an area of particular relevance to the extractive

---

26  Johannes Morsink, *Inherent Human Rights. Philosophical Roots of the Universal Declaration*, Philadelphia: University of Pennsylvania Press (2009), p. 41.

sector, the United Nations Declaration on the Rights of Indigenous Peoples.[27] When a state, during its Universal Periodic Review exercise before the UN Human Rights Council, is found in violation of one of its human rights treaty obligations, it cannot be forced to comply with the obligation and to remedy the violations that may have occurred. There is no international police force similar to the police in a domestic system, which could ensure compliance. In this context, the distinction between binding and non-binding law is not based on whether or not states can be forced to comply, but on whether they must comply, in the case of binding law, or are simply encouraged to do so, in the case of non-binding declarations or documents. In practice, some states comply with most obligations and some comply with very few of them. From a legal perspective, obligations remain, irrespective of whether they are complied with or not.

International human rights law, then, focuses on state obligations and state conduct. This raises questions about the very existence of corporate human rights responsibilities under international law, and more broadly about the status of corporations in the international legal system.

## Are multinational corporations subjects of international law?

According to the traditional view, public international law is the law governing the relationships between states, and states are the only subjects of international law.[28] States have the capacity to create international law for the purpose of regulating their own conduct. They possess an attribute that no other entity possesses, and which lies at the heart of the international legal order: sovereignty. The United Nations Charter edifice is built on the sacrosanct principle of the sovereign equality of states.[29] Other participants in international affairs are negatively described as 'non-state actors'. Their main characteristic is that they are not states.[30] Hence the international legal landscape consists on the one hand of active subjects of law – states – and on the other hand of every other entity – including business entities and individuals – thereby reduced to the status of passive objects of law. This model, however, is disputed.[31]

27   United Nations Declaration on the Rights of Indigenous Peoples (2007), A/RES/61/295.
28   This view is described in the main textbooks in the area. See Antonio Cassese, *International Law*, 2nd edition, Oxford: Oxford University Press (2005), p. 71; Malcolm Shaw, *International Law*, 6th edition, Cambridge: Cambridge University Press (2008), p. 197; Martin Dixon, *Textbook on International Law*, 7th edition, Oxford: Oxford University Press (2013), p. 115; Jan Klabbers, *International Law*, Cambridge: Cambridge University Press (2013), p. 67.
29   Charter of the United Nations (1945), 1 UNTS XVI, Article 2(1).
30   Philip Alston, 'The 'Not-a-Cat' Syndrome: Can the International Human Rights Regime Accommodate Non-State Actors?', *in* Philip Alston (ed.), *Non State Actors and Human Rights*, Oxford: Oxford University Press (2005), p. 7.
31   For an early discussion on this see Philip Jessup, *A Modern Law of Nations*, New York: the MacMillan Company (1948), pp. 19–20.

Some authors favour a complete paradigm shift. For them, the individual, not the state, ought to be put at the centre of a new form of law, global law, that would be better equipped to deal with the challenges of globalisation than is international law.[32] They view the state as obsolete in a globalised world and hope for and predict its end as the centrepoint of international law.[33] Even without adhering to global legal theories, it is undisputable that the twentieth century has seen the emergence of other actors in international law, such as individuals, through the development of international human rights law and international criminal law, and much has been written about the extent to which their more prominent role has affected international law.[34] Drawing in part from the policy-oriented New Haven School, which applies international relations theories to international law, some have criticised the very notion of subjects of law, which is seen as artificially static, and have instead focused on the more dynamic concept of participation.[35] In any event, it appears that subjectivity in international law is a fluctuating notion which renders the task of determining whether corporations can be considered subjects of international law all the more complex.

As early as 1949, examining whether the newly created United Nations Organization was a subject of international law, the International Court of Justice (ICJ) affirmed that 'the subjects of law in any legal system are not necessarily identical in their nature or in the extent of their rights, and their nature depends upon the needs of the community'.[36] The Court concluded that the organisation was a subject of international law, 'capable of possessing international rights and duties' and having 'capacity to maintain its rights by bringing international claims'.[37]

Applying those criteria to individuals (natural persons), it is clear that undisputed international norms provide them with rights they can claim against states, through international human rights law. International law also

32  Rafael Domingo, 'Gaius, Vattel, and the New Global Law Paradigm', *European Journal of International Law* (2011), p. 641.
33  Rafael Domingo, 'The Crisis of International Law', 42 *Vanderbilt Journal of Transnational Law* 1543 (2009), p. 1551. See also Benjamin R Barber, 'Global Democracy or Global Law: Which Comes First', 1 *Indiana Journal of Global Legal Studies* 119 (1993), pp. 119–138; the special issue of *L'Observateur des Nations Unies*, Volume 31, 2011–2012; and the special issue of the *Tilburg Law Review* Vol. 17, Issue 2 (2012).
34  See for example Menno T. Kamminga and Martin Scheinin (eds), *The Impact of Human Rights Law on General International Law*, Oxford: Oxford University Press (2009); Scott Sheeran, 'The Relationship of International Human Rights Law and General International Law: Hermeneutic Constraint, or Pushing the Boundaries?', *in* Scott Sheeran and Sir Nigel Rodley (eds), *Routledge Handbook of International Human Rights Law*, Abingdon and New York: Routledge (2013), p. 79.
35  Jean d'Aspremont, 'Introduction', in Jean d'Aspremont (ed.), *Participants in the International Legal System. Multiple Perspectives on Non-State Actors in International Law*, London and New York: Routledge (2011), p. 2.
36  *Reparation for Injuries Suffered in the Service of the United Nations*, Advisory Opinion: ICJ Reports 1949, p. 178.
37  Ibid. p. 179.

places duties on individuals, albeit limited ones. For example, individuals should refrain from committing genocide and from holding other human beings in slavery. In some instances, they can even be prosecuted at the international level if they breach these duties, which is the central premise of international criminal law. Since they are individuals, international law grants rights and places duties on business managers, and in that sense international law can affect business activities. For example, an individual doing business in a war zone could be guilty of complicity with war crimes as defined in the Rome Statute and prosecuted either by the International Criminal Court or by a domestic court applying international legal principles. Hence, it is uncontroversial to say that under certain circumstances international law places human rights obligations on business actors.

Things get more complex when one looks beyond individuals to focus on business corporations. The question of their status under international law has also attracted some attention.[38] Applying the ICJ criteria – rights, duties and capacity to bring international claims – to corporations, one notes that in a limited way, international law grants them rights. For example, businesses have brought cases against states for violations of their 'human' rights before the European Court of Human Rights.[39] Similarly, bilateral investment treaties grant corporations substantive rights and the right to bring disputes to an arbitral tribunal. In that sense, they can bring claims at the international level. The remaining question, then, is whether international law also places duties on corporations.

Discussions on corporations' possible duties under international law have focused in recent years on the area of human rights. A number of books explore the question and the next section delves into it in detail.[40] Suffice it

38   See for example Jonathan L. Charney, 'Transnational Corporations and Developing Public International Law', 1983 *Duke Law Journal* 748 (1983); Rosalyn Higgins, *Problems and Process: International Law and How We Use It*, Oxford: Oxford University Press (Clarendon), pp. 49–50 (1994); Nicola Jägers, 'The Legal Status of the Multinational Corporation under International Law', *in* Michael K. Addo (ed.), *Human Rights Standards and the Responsibility of Transnational Corporations*, The Hague, London, Boston: Kluwer Law International (1999), pp. 260–270; Peter Muchlinski, 'Multinational Enterprises as Actors in International Law: Creating "Soft Law" Obligations and "Hard Law" Rights', *in* Math Noortmann and Cedric Ryngaert (eds), *Non-State Actor Dynamics in International Law*, Burlington: Ashgate (2010), pp. 10–13.

39   See for example the cases involving the British newspapers *The Guardian* and *The Observer* with regard to Article 10: European Court of Human Rights, *Guardian and Observer v United Kingdom*, 26 November 1991. See also European Court of Human Rights, *Pine Valley Development Ltd and Others v Ireland*, 29 November 1991. On this, see Michael K. Addo, 'The Corporation as a Victim of Human Rights Violations', *in* Michael Addo (ed.), *Human Rights Standards and the Responsibility of Transnational Corporations*, The Hague, London, Boston: Kluwer Law International (1999), pp. 187–196.

40   Among them are: Nicola Jägers, *Corporate Human Rights Obligations: In Search of Accountability*, Antwerpen, Oxford, New York: Intersentia (2002); Jennifer Zerk, *Multinationals and Corporate Social Responsibility Limitations and Opportunities in International Law*, Cambridge: Cambridge University Press (2006); Philip Alston, *Non-*

to say for the moment that if one adopts the three-fold ICJ definition, one must conclude that corporations at least have the duty to refrain from committing genocide and gross violations of international humanitarian law.[41] It would make no sense from a legal point of view if this obligation existed for natural persons, individuals, but not for legal persons, corporations.[42] Beyond legal arguments, and as Weissbrodt and Kruger have noted, even Nobel Prize winner Milton Friedman, who famously wrote that the only social responsibility of business is to make profits, would most likely agree that businesses ought to refrain from committing genocide and using forced labour.[43] Thus, since corporations have rights and duties under international law, and they can bring international claims, they can be considered subjects of law, albeit of a different nature than states.[44]

*State Actors and Human Rights*, Oxford: Oxford University Press (2005); Andrew Clapham, *Human Rights Obligations of Non State Actors*, Oxford: Oxford University Press (2006); Doreen McBarnet, Aurora Voiculescu and Tom Campbell (eds), *The New Corporate Accountability, Corporate Social Responsibility and the Law*, Cambridge: Cambridge University Press (2007); David Kinley (ed.), *Human Rights and Corporations*, Burlington: Ashgate (2009); Jernej Letnar Černič, *Human Rights Law and Business: Corporate Responsibility for Fundamental Human Rights*, Groningen: Europa Law Publishing (2010); Radu Mares, *The UN Guiding Principles on Business and Human Rights*, Leiden: Martinus Nijhoff (2011); Marie-Jose Van der Heijden, *Transnational Corporations and Human Rights Liabilities*, Antwerpen, Oxford, New York: Intersentia (2012); Surya Deva, *Regulating Corporate Human Rights Violations: Humanizing Business*, London: Routledge (2012).

41 They also have duties under the United Nations Convention on the Law of the Sea and, although this has not yet happened, corporations can be sued before the Seabed Dispute Chamber of the Law of the Sea Tribunal. See United Nations Convention on the Law of the Sea (1982), 1833 UNTS 3, Article 187 and 291(2). At the time of writing, the Seabed Dispute Chamber had only issued an advisory opinion and no decision in a contentious case.

42 On this, see Andrew Clapham, *Human Rights Obligations of Non State Actors*, Oxford: Oxford University Press (2006), p. 79: 'As long as we admit that individuals have rights and duties under customary international human rights law and international humanitarian law, we have to admit that legal persons may also possess the international legal personality necessary to enjoy some of these rights, and conversely to be prosecuted for violations of the relevant international duties.'

43 David Weissbrodt and Muria Kruger, 'Human Rights Responsibilities of Businesses as Non-State Actors', *in* Philip Alston (ed.), *Non State Actors and Human Rights*, Oxford: Oxford University Press (2005), p. 337. The original quote is: 'there is one and only one social responsibility of business – to use its resources and engage in activities designed to increase its profits so long as it stays within the rules of the game, which is to say, engages in open and free competition, without deception or fraud'; *in* Milton Friedman, *Capitalism and Freedom*, Chicago: the University of Chicago Press (2nd edition 2002), p. 133.

44 For a similar reasoning as ours, see Nicola Jägers, 'The Legal Status of the Multinational Corporation under International Law', *in* Michael K. Addo (ed.), *Human Rights Standards and the Responsibility of Transnational Corporations*, The Hague, London, Boston: Kluwer Law International (1999), pp. 263–267 ('it has been demonstrated that the statement that these entities are not subjects of international law is no longer valid').

The difference of nature between states and other participants in the international legal system, namely the fact that only states are sovereign, has led one author to create a sub-category of subjects, that of 'secondary limited subjects' as opposed to 'primary full subjects' (states).[45] Other authors have argued that the discussion about whether non-state actors, including corporations, are subjects of international law is in fact sterile. Indeed, the classic theory seems circular in nature: to be a 'full' subject of international law, an entity needs to be sovereign, and since only states are sovereign, they are the only subjects of international law. For example, the former President of the International Court of Justice, Rosalyn Higgins, is critical of the 'subject–object dichotomy' and prefers to talk about 'participants' for every actor, including multinational corporations.[46] Commenting on the so-called impossibility for participants other than states to gain the status of subjects of law, she asserts: 'We have erected an intellectual prison of our own choosing and then declared it to be an unalterable constraint.'[47] Andrew Clapham develops a similar idea: 'International lawyers realize that the role of non-state actors is too important to be ignored, yet feel constrained by the 'rules' on subjectivity to develop a framework to explain the rights and duties of non-state actors under international law.'[48] He therefore suggests leaving the discussion on subjectivity aside and focusing on the capacity of certain actors to acquire rights and duties under international law. He argues:

> We have an international legal order that admits that states are not the only subjects of international law. It is obvious that non-state entities do not enjoy all the competences, privileges, and rights that states enjoy under international law, just as it is also clear that states do not have all the rights that individuals have under international law. A state could not claim to have been subjected to torture under the law of human rights; a state could not claim that she had been denied the right to marry. We need to admit that international rights and duties depend on the capacity of the entity to enjoy those rights and bear those obligations; such rights and obligations do not depend on the mysteries of subjectivity.[49]

He later concludes:

> References to the subjects of international law are obviously misleading. Conflating the question of subjectivity with the concepts of international

45   Surya Deva, 'Human Rights Violations by Multinational Corporations and International Law: Where from Here?', 19 *Connecticut Journal of International Law* 1 (2003–2004), pp. 50–52.
46   Rosalyn Higgins, *Problems and Process: International Law and How We Use It*, Oxford: Oxford University Press (1994), p. 50.
47   Ibid., p. 49.
48   Andrew Clapham, *Human Rights Obligations of Non State Actors*, Oxford: Oxford University Press (2006), p. 60.
49   Ibid., pp. 68–69.

legal personality and international capacity has prevented a clear appreciation of the fact that non-state actors can bear international rights and obligations (even where they have no state-like characteristics or pretensions). Trying to squeeze international actors into the state-like entities box is, at best, like trying to force a round peg into a square hole, and at worst, means overlooking powerful actors on the international stage.[50]

Presenting the positivist perspective on the issue of the legal personality of non-state actors, Jean d'Aspremont notes that while it is not denied that they have rights and duties, as well as a degree of influence on the processes of creation of international law, that still does not confer on them law-making powers.[51] To him, beyond the international capacity to claim rights and to have duties, this is what differentiates states and international organisations from the other actors. He concedes that other actors can have legal personality but they still fall short of being endowed with law-making powers, despite their influence on international affairs.[52] In 1983, Charney criticised corporations' lack of participation in the creation of international legal rules that concern them, arguing that compliance would be higher if they were formally represented and did not have to resort instead to lobbying states for their voices to be heard.[53] This has changed to some extent, if one takes as an example the large consultation process that has accompanied the drafting of the UN Guiding Principles on Business and Human Rights.[54] While it is states, through the UN Human Rights Council, that have adopted the principles and have therefore formally retained (soft) law-making power, the contents of the Guiding Principles reflect the great participation of non-state actors, including corporations, in their elaboration. It is arguable whether that brings them closer to being considered full subjects of international law.

As seen, the question of whether corporations are subjects of international law is much debated. It matters for the purpose of this book because some have argued that since corporations are not subjects of international law, international human rights treaties cannot apply to them. Beyond doctrinal debates, this has had practical implications and contributed to the shelving of the 2003 Draft UN Norms, which attempted to regulate business conduct in the area of human rights by rendering human rights treaties directly applicable to business conduct.[55] As Kinley and Chambers have noted,

50  Ibid., p. 80.
51  Jean d'Aspremont, 'Non-State Actors from the Perspective of Legal Positivism. The Communitarian Semantics for the Secondary Rules of International Law', *in* Jean d'Aspremont (ed.), *Participants in the International Legal System. Multiple Perspectives on Non-State Actors in International Law*, London and New York: Routledge (2011), pp. 25–26.
52  Ibid., pp. 26–27.
53  Jonathan L. Charney, 'Transnational Corporations and Developing Public International Law', 1983 *Duke Law Journal* 748 (1983), pp. 754–755.
54  See Chapter 7.
55  For a discussion on this, see Chapter 7.

a battle cry of the anti-Norms lobby has been that states are the only subjects of international law and that the Norms fly in the face of this legal orthodoxy by attempting to regulate the behaviour of TNCs from an international standpoint.[56]

This regrettable episode shows that the classic model of subjectivity in international law remains influential, if not prevalent.

## The contours of corporate human rights responsibilities

Beyond subjectivity, an important question from a business and human rights perspective is whether corporations have human rights responsibilities under international law. As mentioned in the previous section, the discussion about corporate duties under international law has focused in recent years on human rights duties. There are two main reasons for this. First, it has now become commonplace to say that corporations, in particular multinational corporations, have gained a prominent place on the international stage due to their financial and political weight. In a context of growing influence of large companies, non-governmental organisations have started to document human rights violations committed by these companies or with their complicity, in developing countries. From an advocacy point of view, the argument is that since corporations make large profits, they ought to abide by human rights law. In other words, with power come responsibilities.

Second, and linked to the first reason, severe human rights violations often occur in countries where human rights are also routinely violated by the state, or by non-state actors such as paramilitary groups. Neither states nor rebel groups can be compelled to abide by their international obligations and they may be influenced by advocacy groups only in a limited way. Naming-and-shaming strategies are arguably more efficient with regard to companies than with regard to states. Indeed, public image is directly linked to a company's performance and, ultimately, survival. The argument goes that exposing corporate violations of human rights will make businesses react and change the way they operate.

Discussing whether, from a moral point of view, companies should take human rights into consideration, however, is different from asking whether companies have international human rights obligations under international law and, if so, how they can be enforced through domestic courts or international mechanisms. The latter set of questions is intrinsically linked to the

---

56   David Kinley and Rachel Chambers, 'The UN Human Rights Norms for Corporations: The Private Implications of Public International Law', 6 *Human Rights Law Review* 447 (2006), p. 479. See also Maurice Mendelson, 'In the Matter of the Draft "Norms on the Responsibilities of Transnational Corporations and Other Business Enterprises with Regard to Human Rights"', Appended to the Confederation of British Industry submission to the UN High Commissioner for Human Rights (2004), para. 7.

wider theoretical question discussed in the previous section, which has to do with the status of corporations under international law. International human rights law, as a branch of international law, supposedly only binds states and does not place obligations on other entities such as individuals and corporations. It was primarily designed to address human rights violations by states.

Where, then, do businesses fit in this picture? Businesses, as non-state actors, are first and foremost subjected to the domestic law of the country in which they are legally registered as well as the law of the country in which they are operating, in the case that the company operates in different countries. Domestic law includes the regulation of both areas that are purely commercial in nature and others, such as employment law or environmental regulations, that are related to human rights understood widely. Some states have developed sophisticated legal frameworks applicable to businesses. Others have very few regulations and let businesses regulate themselves to a large extent. States may or may not have legislated or produced regulations to comply with their international human rights law or labour law obligations. For companies, the rationale behind the adoption by the state of the regulation with which they will in turn be required to comply is largely irrelevant. Companies are bound by domestic law, and therefore international human rights law concerns them indirectly. Under a strict understanding of international human rights, therefore, only states are directly bound.

The first sub-section below attempts to shed light on the direct and indirect obligations dichotomy. The second sub-section adds another layer of questions to the discussion. If corporations are said to have direct human rights obligations, is this in relation to the whole range of human rights covered by international human rights law?

### *The direct and indirect obligations dichotomy*

The dichotomy between direct and indirect international human rights obligations is particularly important in the business and human rights field. Under a conservative reading of the law, where non-state actors such as businesses cannot be subjects of law, international law places, at best, indirect obligations on businesses in the area of human rights. This means that international human rights law is only relevant to the extent that states have adopted implementation measures affecting corporations. Placing only indirect obligations on businesses, international law, for all practical purposes, does not regulate them as such. This strict approach needs to be refined. Even if one adheres to the idea that international human rights law does not place direct obligations on businesses, human rights treaties have been interpreted in a way that brings businesses within its scope, albeit in a limited way.

In the European system, a key word in relation to the European Convention on Human Rights' (ECHR's) applicability to businesses is the German legal concept of *Drittwirkung*. *Drittwirkung* is defined as 'the extent to which the Convention is applicable to the behaviour of non-state actors'.[57] Under the Convention system, the question of *private* abuse of human rights arises in a variety of ways,[58] but two are of particular relevance in a discussion on the interplay between business and human rights. First, the Court has interpreted certain articles of the Convention as having created positive obligations for states to act to prevent possible abuses by third parties, including private parties. Second, the Court has had to decide whether a particular entity was a private or a public one for the purpose of applying the Convention.

The first scenario is an example of indirect human rights obligations placed on third parties, an indirect horizontal effect of the treaty. This situation is about a state being held responsible for not having prevented or remedied a private party's abuse towards another private party. Cases from the various human rights systems illustrate this scenario. In *López Ostra v Spain*, for the first time, the European Court of Human Rights (ECtHR) equated pollution with an interference with Article 8 of the Convention on the right to a private and family life. In that instance, the Court concluded that the state had violated the applicant's right to a private and family life by allowing a privately owned waste plant to operate in a certain way.[59] Similarly, in *Tatar v Romania* the Court concluded that the state authorities had failed to take suitable measures in order to protect people's rights to private life and home against the risks that a mining company's activities might entail.[60] In the African system of human rights protection, in a case against Nigeria brought by representatives of the Ogoni population, the African Commission on Human and People's Rights found that the state had failed to protect the Ogoni population from the harm caused by the NNPC Shell Consortium – a public–private venture operating in the region – and had failed to provide or permit studies of potential or actual environmental and health risks caused by the oil operations which were partially undertaken by a privately owned company, a subsidiary of the multinational corporation Royal Dutch Shell. The case also and in fact primarily involved direct abuses by the state, but the state was held liable in part for having failed to control the operations of a private business, which can be said to have violated its indirect obligations under the African Charter in that instance.[61] In the Inter-American system a series of cases deal with state positive obligations to act to protect the rights of indigenous peoples whose ways of life are threatened by oil and logging

57   Andrew Clapham, 'The 'Drittwirkung' of the Convention', *in* R. St. J. Mc Donald *et al.* (eds), *The European System for the Protection of Human Rights*, Deventer: Martinus Nijhoff (1993), p. 163.
58   Ibid.
59   European Court of Human Rights, *López Ostra v Spain*, 9 December 1994.
60   European Court of Human Rights, *Tatar v Romania*, 21 January 2009.
61   African Commission on Human and People's Rights, 155/96: *Social and Economic Rights Action Center (SERAC) and Center for Economic and Social Rights (CESR) v Nigeria*, 27 October 2001.

companies.[62] The UN Human Rights Committee was also faced with a similar case with regard to the Sami, the indigenous peoples of Finland.[63]

In June 2014, the UN Human Rights Council decided to start working on the elaboration of a binding business and human rights treaty.[64] Surely the question of whether the treaty will only bind states, or whether the obligations created will also apply directly to corporations, will feature prominently in the upcoming discussions. A cautious attitude would be to keep the approach adopted by human rights courts and bodies so far and for the treaty to create obligations for states to regulate and control corporations operating on their territories, and possibly corporations registered on their territories but operating overseas. In fact, this latter point could be an interesting addition to the existing international legal landscape. Even without a specific business and human rights treaty, it now seems clear that states have the obligation to ensure that companies do not violate human rights within their jurisdiction, as the caselaw discussed above illustrates. However, there has been debate at the international level as to whether states also have obligations in relation to the foreign activities of companies registered on their territories. Several United Nations treaty bodies, whose function is to monitor state implementation of the UN human rights treaties, have adopted documents that seem to go in that direction. These bodies are the Committee on Economic, Social and Cultural Rights;[65] the Committee on the Elimination of Racial Discrimination;[66] the Committee on the Rights of

---

62 See for example, Inter-American Commission on Human Rights, Report Nº 40/04, Case 12.053, Merits, *Maya Indigenous Communities of the Toledo Districts v Belize*, 12 October 2004. For an update on the situation in Belize see Inter-American Commission on Human Rights, 'IACHR Urges Belize to Guarantee the Rights of Maya Indigenous Communities', Press release No. 32/13, 6 May 2013.

63 Human Rights Committee, *Länsman v. Finland* (511/1992), ICCPR, A/50/40 vol. II (26 October 1994) 66 (CCPR/C/52/D/511/1992) at paras. 9.1–9.8 and 10. No violation of Article 27 of the Covenant was found in this case.

64 UN Human Rights Council, Elaboration of an international legally binding instrument on transnational corporations and other business enterprises with respect to human rights, A/HRC/26/L.22/Rev.1 (25 June 2014).

65 Committee on Economic, Social and Cultural Rights, General Comment No. 14 (2000), The Right to the Highest Attainable Standard of Health (Article 12 of the International Covenant on Economic, Social and Cultural Rights), E/C.12/2000/4, 11 August 2000, Para 39; Committee on Economic, Social and Cultural Rights, General Comment No. 15 (2003), The Right to Water (Articles 11 and 12 of the International Covenant on Economic, Social and Cultural Rights), E/C.12/2002/11, 20 January 2003, para. 33; General Comment No. 17 on the Right of Everyone to Benefit from the Protection of the Moral and Material Interests resulting from any Scientific, Literary or Artistic Production of which He or She is the Author (Article 15, paragraph 1 (c), of the Covenant), E/C.12/GC/17, 12 January 2006, para. 55; and General Comment No. 19 on the Right to Social Security (Article 9 of the Covenant), E/C.12/GC/19, 4 February 2008, para. 54.

66 Concluding observations of the Committee on the Elimination of Racial Discrimination, Canada, CERD/C/CAN/CO/18, 25 May 2007, para. 17; Concluding observations of the Committee on the Elimination of Racial Discrimination, Canada CERD/C/CAN/CO/19-20, 9 March 2012, para. 14; Committee on the Elimination of Racial Discrimination, CERD/C/GBR/CO/18-20, 14 September 2011, para. 29.

the Child;[67] and the Human Rights Committee.[68] This point was strongly debated during the discussions that led to the drafting of the UN Guiding Principles on Business and Human Rights. In the end the Guiding Principles do not require states to regulate the foreign activities of 'their' companies, but they are told that they may do so.[69] In any event, the Guiding Principles do not constitute binding law. With this in mind, the future treaty on business and human rights could go one step further and actually require state parties to regulate the foreign activities of multinational corporations registered on their territories. Chapter 9 provides an overview of the type of measures states have taken to comply with this emerging obligation under international human rights law.

The second scenario that engages the notion of business human rights obligations is when a private or semi-private entity is performing functions that traditionally fall within the category of state functions and violates human rights in the process. At the international level, this would entail state responsibility if the state is in fact in control of the business and the latter's acts could be attributed to the state. Articles 5 to 8 of the International Law Commission Draft Articles on State Responsibility outline the circumstances in which this is possible;[70] for example, when a company is mandated by a state to perform state-like duties such as running a detention centre.[71] At the domestic level, there have been some discussions about the applicability of human rights treaties directly to these otherwise private entities on the ground that they perform state duties. In the United Kingdom, discussions have focused on privately run care homes and prisons and on the extent to which the Human Rights Act, which incorporates the European Convention on Human Rights in the domestic legal system, applies to private companies performing those functions.[72] While interesting for the sake of a discussion on the human rights obligations of businesses, this can be said to be a rather

67  UN Committee on the Rights of the Child, General Comment No 16 on State Obligations Regarding the Impact of the Business Sector on Children's Rights, CRC/C/GC/16, 15 March 2013, para. 43.

68  Human Rights Committee, Concluding observations on the sixth periodic report of Germany, November 2012.

69  Guiding Principles on Business and Human Rights: Implementing the United Nations 'Protect, Respect and Remedy' Framework, A/HRC/17/31, Official Commentary to GP 2. On this subject, see Nadia Bernaz, 'State Obligations with regard to the Extraterritorial Activities of Companies Domiciled on their Territories', *in* Carla Buckley, Alice Donald and Philip Leach (eds), *Towards Coherence in International Human Rights Law: Approaches of Regional and International Systems*, Leiden: Brill, forthcoming 2016.

70  Draft Articles on the Responsibility of States for internationally wrongful acts, A/RES/56/83, 12 December 2001.

71  Example given by Philip Alston in 'The 'Not-a-Cat' Syndrome: Can the International Human Rights Regime Accommodate Non-State Actors?', *in*  Philip Alston (ed.), *Non State Actors and Human Rights*, Oxford: Oxford University Press (2005), p. 10.

72  For a discussion on this see Middlesex University Law Department, *Guidance on Business and Human Rights: A Review*, London: Equality and Human Rights Commission (2011), section 4.1.

classic example of businesses' obligation to abide by domestic law and as such does not constitute an example of international law imposing direct human rights obligations on businesses.

This *tour d'horizon* has highlighted that international human rights law has only recently started to concern itself with business entities and that references to business in that branch of international law remain scarce. This is not the case throughout international law, however, and a variety of treaties in areas as diverse as labour rights, the fight against corruption[73] and terrorism[74] and environmental law[75] mention corporations and intend to regulate their conduct. There is debate as to whether such regulation remains indirect or can in fact be considered direct. The traditional view suggests that while these treaties are a source of regulation for businesses and sometimes seem to be addressed directly to them, in those circumstances international law does not directly regulate business activities.[76] Only when states implement the law, for example by criminalising certain conduct, will businesses become directly affected by it.

Others have argued that 'these developments, while not yet at the level of international liability for (…) [corporations], show the evolution of international regulatory systems towards the creation of norms enforceable on (…) [corporations]'.[77] In other words, they believe that even if they do not constitute conclusive evidence that international law places direct obligations on corporations, these treaties show that international law intends to regulate corporate conduct.

Finally, Ratner believes that environmental treaties, for example, 'impose an international standard of liability on the corporation'.[78] As he puts it, 'the cumulative impact of this lawmaking and application suggests a recognition

---

73  See the OECD Convention on Combating Bribery of Public Officials in International Business Transactions (1997), 37 ILM 1. On this treaty, Steven Ratner notes: 'While adhering to the orthodox distinction between duties of governments under international law and duties of enterprises under domestic law, the treaty nonetheless makes clear that the responsibility of businesses is recognized and may be regulated by international law.' Steven C. Ratner, 'Corporations and Human Rights: A Theory of Legal Responsibility', 111 *Yale Law Journal* 443 (2001–2002), p. 482.

74  UN Convention on the Suppression of the Financing of Terrorism (1999), 2178 UNTS 197.

75  International Convention on Civil Liability for Oil Pollution Damage (1969), 973 UNTS 3; Convention on Civil Liability for Damage Resulting from Activities Dangerous to the Environment (1993), 32 ILM 1228.

76  See for example Sir Nigel Rodley, 'Non State Actors and Human Rights', *in* Scott Sheeran and Sir Nigel Rodley (eds), *Routledge Handbook of International Human Rights Law*, Abingdon and New York: Routledge (2013), p. 540.

77  Menno T. Kamminga, Saman Zia-Zarifi, 'Liability of Multinational Corporations Under International Law: An Introduction', *in* Menno T. Kamminga, Saman Zia-Zarifi (eds), *Liability of Multinational Corporations Under International Law*, The Hague London Boston: Kluwer Law International (2000), p. 10.

78  Steven C. Ratner, 'Corporations and Human Rights: A Theory of Legal Responsibility', 111 *Yale Law Journal* 443 (2001–2002), p. 480.

by many decisionmakers that corporate behavior is a fitting subject for international regulation'.[79] To Ratner these treaties impose direct duties on corporations irrespective of the fact that they call on domestic mechanisms, and not international mechanisms, for implementation and enforcement. Answering those who think the absence of an international enforcement mechanism is proof that the obligations can only be indirect,[80] he maintains that this is beyond the point as it

> confuses the existence of responsibility with the mode of implementing it. It suggests that international law does not itself impose liability on the corporations – even though this is the very language of some of the treaties – because the mechanism for enforcement is through a private lawsuit in one or more states. The treaties do impose responsibility upon the polluters, however; the use of domestic courts to implement this liability does not change this reality, just as the use of such courts to implement international criminal responsibility – through, for example, obligations on states to extradite or prosecute offenders – does not detract from the law's imposition of individual responsibility.[81]

In the same vein, Andrew Clapham notes:

> Lack of international jurisdiction to try a corporation does not mean that the corporation is under no international legal obligations. Nor does it mean that we are somehow precluded from speaking about corporations breaking international law.[82]

Moreover, besides international treaties in the areas of environmental protection, the fight against terrorism and corruption and labour rights, some UN

---

79   Ibid., p. 488. See also David Weissbrodt and Muria Kruger, 'Human Rights Responsibilities of Businesses as Non-State Actors', *in* Philip Alston (ed.), *Non State Actors and Human Rights*, Oxford: Oxford University Press (2005), p. 329.

80   For this point of view see for example Carlos M. Vazquez, 'Direct vs. Indirect Obligations of Corporations under International Law', 43 *Columbia Journal of Transnational Law* 927 (2004–2005), pp. 932–938.

81   Steven C. Ratner, 'Corporations and Human Rights: A Theory of Legal Responsibility', 111 *Yale Law Journal* 443 (2001–2002), p. 481.
    His conclusion appears sound especially given the fact that businesses have been involved in the drafting of these treaties. This is commonplace for ILO Conventions due to the tripartite nature of the organisation where businesses, workers and states are represented, but business was also 'instrumental' in developing international norms on bribery. See Menno T. Kamminga and Saman Zia-Zarifi, 'Liability of Multinational Corporations Under International Law: An Introduction' *in* Menno T. Kamminga and Saman Zia-Zarifi (eds), *Liability of Multinational Corporations Under International Law*, The Hague, London, Boston: Kluwer Law International (2000), p. 8.

82   Andrew Clapham, *Human Rights Obligations of Non State Actors*, Oxford: Oxford University Press (2006), p. 31.

Security Council resolutions have created direct obligations for businesses. Recognising the diamond trade's role in fuelling the conflict in Sierra Leone, the Security Council prohibited the import and export of rough diamonds from Sierra Leone and called upon states to prohibit that trade. The resolution also contained recommendations directly addressed to the diamond industry.[83] The Security Council has also adopted sanctions against non-state actors in relation to the fight against terrorism. The Al-Qaida sanction committee maintains a list of targeted individuals and entities.[84] While these entities currently seem to be more of a charitable rather than a profit-oriented nature, the Security Council has made clear that 'any undertaking or entity owned or controlled, directly or indirectly, by, or otherwise supporting, such an individual, group, undertaking or entity associated with Al-Qaida, Usama bin Laden or the Taliban shall be eligible for designation' to be put on the list.[85] Thus businesses could be added. This is all the more likely because within the framework of sanctions against North Korea, a number of businesses, including banks, have already been listed.[86] The International Court of Justice has confirmed that Security Council resolutions can bind non-state actors. Although the decision was not specifically on corporations, the Court indicated in its Advisory Opinion on *Kosovo* that Security Council resolutions could impose obligations on non-state actors. In doing so, the Court reversed the position it had taken on the matter in its Opinion on the *Israeli Wall*.[87]

Coming back to the area of human rights as such, even firm believers in the indirect international regulation of business, such as Vasquez, contend that there are exceptions to the orthodox view.[88] International human rights law has developed on the premise that human beings are equally worthy of

---

83  S/RES/1306 (2000), paras 1 and 10.

84  Security Council Committee pursuant to Resolutions 1267 (1999) and 1989 (2011) concerning Al-Qaida and associated individuals and entities, 'List established and maintained by the 1267 Committee with respect to individuals, groups, undertaking and other entities associated with Al-Qaida'.

85  S/RES/1904 (2009), para. 3.

86  Security Council Committee established pursuant to Resolution 1718 (2006), 'Consolidated List of Entities and Individuals'.

87  *Accordance with International Law of the Unilateral Declaration of Independence in Respect of Kosovo*, Advisory Opinion, I.C.J. Reports 2010, p. 403, para. 116–117. (Para. 116: 'The Court recalls in this regard that it has not been uncommon for the Security Council to make demands on actors other than United Nations Member States and inter-governmental organizations'); *Legal Consequences of the Construction of a Wall in the Occupied Palestinian Territory*, I.C.J. Reports 2004, p. 136. See also Jean-Marie Kamatali, 'The New Guiding Principles on Business and Human Rights' Contribution in Ending the Divisive Debate over Human Rights Responsibilities of Companies: Is it Time for an ICJ Advisory Opinion?', 20 *Cardozo Journal of International and Comparative Law* 437 (2011–2012), pp. 460–461.

88  Carlos M. Vazquez, 'Direct vs. Indirect Obligations of Corporations under International Law', 43 *Columbia Journal of Transnational Law* 927 (2004–2005), p. 939.

dignity and rights. Human rights represent an ideal whereby everyone is treated with respect, enjoys basic freedoms and sees their basic needs met. Human rights exist irrespective of the technical question of treaty obligations or domestic legislation and formed the subject of discussions of a political and philosophical nature well before the codification of international human rights law. Human rights transcend legal considerations. No one would dare to argue that because the Universal Declaration of Human Rights and human rights treaties did not exist at the time of the Atlantic slave trade, this inhuman enterprise did not constitute a violation of human rights. The difference between then and now is that today we would be able to articulate these violations with reference to texts such as the Universal Declaration and human rights treaties.

International human rights law happens to have developed in a way that makes states the main, if not exclusive, duty-bearers. However, 'to fully address human rights violations, there is a need for other dutyholders than the state. There is no fundamental reason why the emphasis should be on the state only. It is just the way things have developed historically.'[89] While international law has provided standards and tools to phrase human rights concerns, human rights exist outside of international law as well. As has been seen, the Universal Declaration itself is meant to set standards not only for states, but for 'every organ of society'. Moreover, the preambles of both the International Covenant on Civil and Political Rights and the International Covenant on Economic, Social and Cultural Rights state that individuals have 'duties to other individuals and to the community' and are 'under a responsibility to strive for the promotion and observance of the rights recognised' in each of these treaties.[90] While preambles are non-binding, this is an indication that human rights commitments should be a concern to all, and not only states.[91] In sum, 'there is no conceptual barrier to granting

---

89   Steven C. Ratner, 'Corporations and Human Rights: A Theory of Legal Responsibility', 111 *Yale Law Journal* 443 (2001–2002), p. 468.

90   Preambles, International Covenant on Civil and Political Rights (1966) 999 UNTS 171; International Covenant on Economic, Social and Cultural Rights (1966) 993 UNTS 3.

91   On this point, see the position of the Committee on Economic, Social and Cultural Rights, (the body monitoring the implementation of the International Covenant on Economic, Social and Cultural Rights), who asserted that

> while only States are parties to the Covenant and are thus ultimately accountable for compliance with it, all members of society – individuals, families, local communities, non-governmental organizations, civil society organizations, as well as the private business sector – have responsibilities in the realization of the right to adequate food. (...) The private business sector – national and transnational – should pursue its activities within the framework of a code of conduct conducive to respect of the right to adequate food, agreed upon jointly with the Government and civil society.

See Committee on Economic, Social and Cultural Rights, General Comment 12 (The Rights to Adequate Food), E/C.12/1999/5, 12 May 1999, para. 20.

obligations for non-state actors'.[92] It remains to be seen whether the proposed business and human rights treaty will take this route or whether it will adopt a more conservative approach and limit itself to indirect obligations.[93]

### Which rights are relevant?

International human rights law covers a wide range of rights. Some are of a civil or political nature, such as the right to a fair trial and the right to liberty. Others are of an economic, social or cultural nature, such as the right to work and the right to health. Although, for political reasons connected to the Cold War, the law related to both sets of rights developed separately following the adoption of the Universal Declaration of Human Rights in 1948, the UN position is now that human rights are 'indivisible, interrelated and interdependent'.[94] Under certain circumstances, such as an armed conflict or an attack against a civilian population, gross violations of some of these rights – in particular the right to life and the right not to be subjected to torture or held into slavery – may constitute international crimes. These violations are of a different nature from 'simple' violations and they entail individual criminal responsibility under international law.

All these rights are embodied in treaties and soft law instruments, and some are also part of customary international law. As discussed, under a strict reading of international law, states are only bound by the treaties they have ratified and by customary international law; they are not bound by instruments that are strictly speaking non-binding, such as the Universal Declaration of Human Rights or the UN Declaration on the Rights of Indigenous Peoples. In practice, states' international human rights legal obligations vary from state to state, and some states have committed themselves to more than others. Bearing this in mind, determining what the human rights obligations of corporations should be is not straightforward. If one accepts that states are not bound by all human rights law and that, instead, they each have different obligations, it is hard to argue that companies should respect all human rights. From an advocacy point of view adhering to the UN position on indivisibility is tempting, but it may pose difficulties in practice and be seen as unrealistic.

A conservative way to determine which rights businesses should abide by is to say that companies should respect the human rights treaties in force in

---

92  David Weissbrodt and Muria Kruger, 'Human Rights Responsibilities of Businesses as Non-State Actors', *in* Philip Alston (ed.), *Non State Actors and Human Rights*, Oxford: Oxford University Press (2005), p. 331.
93  UN Human Rights Council, Elaboration of an international legally binding instrument on transnational corporations and other business enterprises with respect to human rights, A/HRC/26/L.22/Rev.1 (25 June 2014).
94  Vienna Declaration, A/CONF.157/23, 12 July 1993, para. 5.

the state in which they operate. Perhaps more satisfying from a legal point of view, this approach somewhat misses the point, which is to close a protection gap and to affirm businesses' direct obligations. If a state has ratified few treaties and has poor human rights records, one of the rationales for advocating for corporate human rights responsibility is that corporations may play a role in ensuring that certain rights are respected, though admittedly that may put corporations in untenable positions.[95] By contrast, this approach allows the existence of places where rights-holders can make international claims neither against the state nor against companies. Despite its flaws, this approach was included in the 2000 version of the OECD Guidelines for Multinational Enterprises, but was later abandoned.[96]

Corporations are more likely to violate certain rights and less likely to violate others. From the outset, rights associated with the workplace, such as the right to free assembly or the right to health, seem more relevant than the right to marry. Moreover, violations of some rights are almost always committed in collaboration with another actor, usually the state. For example, a company will rarely violate the right to liberty on its own. However, it can be complicit in a violation, for example by providing state authorities with information leading to the arrest and illegal detention of a trade unionist.[97] Although important to bear in mind, the likelihood of violation cannot serve as a basis to determine which rights businesses should respect.

Another way to address the question is to say that companies should respect human rights that have achieved customary legal status. Scholars and practitioners alike frequently discuss the question of the possible customary legal nature of the Universal Declaration of Human Rights, which would then bind all states irrespective of their treaty commitments.[98] Given the resistance from some states, this position is hard to hold. That said, despite the official UN position on the indivisibility of human rights, it is clear that some rights have achieved customary status while it may not be that evident for others. As Andrew Clapham puts it,

> Although an ongoing debate exists over the extent to which each of the provisions of the [Universal Declaration] (…) have achieved customary law status, the rules prohibiting arbitrary killing, slavery, torture, detention, and systematic racial discrimination – such as apartheid – are

---

95  See for example John Gerard Ruggie, *Just Business*, New York and London: W. W. Norton & Company Inc. (2013), p. xxxii.

96  The 2011 version no longer mentions 'the host government's international obligations and commitments'. OECD, 2011 Update of the OECD Guidelines for Multinational Enterprises Comparative table of changes made to the 2000 text (2012) p. 13. See Chapter 7.

97  On this, see Steven C. Ratner, 'Corporations and Human Rights: A Theory of Legal Responsibility', 111 *Yale Law Journal* 443 (2001–2002), p. 511.

98  William A. Schabas (ed.), *The Universal Declaration of Human Rights, the Travaux Preparatoires Volume I*, Cambridge: Cambridge University Press (2013), p. cxv.

now recognized as rules of customary international law binding on all states.[99]

In other words, there seems to be a set of core human rights obligations that transcend strict legal considerations and indistinctly bind all participants in the international system: states and non-state actors, including corporations. Broadly speaking, gross violations of these rights would fall within the realm of international criminal law. Given that such violations entail individual criminal responsibility under international law, it almost naturally follows that they should also entail corporate responsibility. It would be absurd to contend that corporations are not prohibited from committing genocide, for example.[100] The fact that the International Criminal Court does not have jurisdiction over legal persons does not mean that legal persons cannot commit international crimes, but simply that there is an enforcement gap.[101] As John Ruggie, then UN Secretary-General Special Representative on Business and Human Rights, noted in his report to the Human Rights Council in 2007, 'just as the absence of an international accountability mechanism did not preclude individual responsibility for international crimes in the past, it does not preclude the emergence of corporate responsibility today'.[102]

Corporations do have obligations in relation to gross human rights violations amounting to international crimes. While this is an important point to make, it has limited practical consequences, as such gross violations necessarily occur much less often than 'simple' corporate human rights violations. Arguably, limiting companies' human rights obligations to the area of international criminal law is too narrow and does not cover the bulk of violations.[103] Recourse to international criminal law permits tracing some of the contours of corporate international human rights obligations but it does not settle the matter. The most controversial questions, such as, for example, labour rights and local communities' right to water, are not covered.

The 2011 UN Guiding Principles on Business and Human Rights, the latest UN initiative on business and human rights, have dodged the question

99  Andrew Clapham, *Human Rights Obligations of Non State Actors*, Oxford: Oxford University Press (2006), p. 86.
100 David Weissbrodt and Muria Kruger, 'Human Rights Responsibilities of Businesses as Non-State Actors', *in* Philip Alston (ed.), *Non State Actors and Human Rights*, Oxford: Oxford University Press (2005), p. 337.
101 See below.
102 Report of the Special Representative of the Secretary-General (SRSG) on the issue of human rights and transnational corporations and other business enterprises, A/HRC/4/035, 9 February 2007, para. 21.
103 On this point, see Larissa van den Herik and Jernej Letnar Černič, 'Regulating Corporations under International Law. From Human Rights to International Criminal Law and Back Again', 8 *Journal of International Criminal Justice* 725 (2010). See also Steven C. Ratner, 'Corporations and Human Rights: A Theory of Legal Responsibility', 111 *Yale Law Journal* 443 (2001–2002), p. 495.

of corporate human rights obligations and talk instead of a corporate responsibility to respect human rights, a social expectation rather than a legal obligation.[104] This has allowed the Guiding Principles to include a wide range of human rights. Under Principle 12,

> The responsibility of business enterprises to respect human rights refers to internationally recognized human rights – understood, at a minimum, as those expressed in the International Bill of Human Rights and the principles concerning fundamental rights set out in the International Labour Organization's Declaration on Fundamental Principles and Rights at Work.[105]

This constitutes an important step forward since, as discussed in Chapter 7, the Guiding Principles benefit from a large degree of consensus, but it does not amount to full recognition of corporate human rights obligations. John Ruggie, the architect of the Guiding Principles, noted about the non-legal nature of the corporate responsibility to respect human rights that:

> it was precisely this feature that made it possible for states and businesses to accept linking the content of the responsibility to respect specifically to international human rights instruments – even though not all states have ratified all treaties or voted in favor of all relevant declarations, and even though those instruments generally do not apply legally to companies directly.[106]

## International enforcement

Previous sections have mentioned the absence of international enforcement mechanisms to address corporate human rights violations. So far corporate human rights liability claims have only been brought before domestic courts, and Chapter 10 covers these cases. This section focuses on possible future developments such as the International Criminal Court exercising jurisdiction over corporations, and various proposed international mechanisms to hold corporations to account, including the creation of a World Court of Human Rights. The section begins with a discussion of the international tribunals which enforced the prohibition of the slave trade during the nineteenth century. Although it would be a stretch to call their proceedings 'business and human rights' trials, as they were not adjudicating human rights claims, they nevertheless dealt with cases directed against the business

104 See Chapter 7.
105 UN Guiding Principle 12. The International Bill of Rights is composed of the Universal Declaration of Human Rights, the International Covenant on Civil and Political Rights and the International Covenant on Economic, Social and Cultural Rights.
106 John Gerard Ruggie, *Just Business*, New York and London: W. W. Norton & Company Inc. (2013), p. 101.

of trading in human beings. As such, they provide an interesting reference point to explain contemporary issues of enforcement of corporate human rights obligations at the international level.

### The Mixed Commissions: slave trading on trial

Following the abolition of the slave trade in 1807, the British entered into negotiations with several countries in the hope of putting an end to the trade internationally. In 1817, three separate bilateral treaties were signed with Spain, Portugal and the Netherlands. The treaties outlawed the slave trade, granted rights of reciprocal search and seizure of vessels and created international tribunals ('Mixed Commissions') to give final pronouncements on the legality of searches and seizures to be carried on.[107] Mixed Commissions were initially established in Sierra Leone, Cuba, Brazil and Suriname.[108] Of the total of 600 cases, 500 were heard in Sierra Leone.[109] Later on, treaties were signed with Chile, the Argentine Confederation, Uruguay, Bolivia, Ecuador and finally the United States in 1862, leading to the creation of more commissions in Luanda, Boa Vista (Cape Verde), Spanish Town (Jamaica), Cape Town and New York.

Especially during the early days of the Commissions, under certain circumstances the trade in Africans was still lawful, for example if the slaves had been brought on board the ship within a specific zone on the coast of Africa, agreed on in the treaties. Other limitations were also in place.[110] In other words, the trade was only partially abolished, and many of the cases revolved around determining the nationality of the ship.[111] Initially, if the ship

---

107 Article 8 of the Anglo-Portuguese Treaty and Article 12 of the Anglo-Spanish Treaty provided that: 'In order to bring to Adjudication, with the least Delay and Inconvenience, the Vessels which may be detained for having been engaged in an illicit Traffic of Slaves, there shall be established, within the Space of a Year at furthest from the Exchange of the Ratifications of the present Convention, Two Mixed Commissions, formed of an equal Number of Individuals of the Two Nations, named for this Purpose by their respective Sovereigns.' See Additional Convention between Great Britain and Portugal, for the Prevention of the Slave Trade (28 July 1817) and Separate Article (11 September 1817), 67 Consolidated Treaty Series 398 (1817); British and Foreign State Papers, vol. 4, pp. 85 and 115; Treaty between Great Britain and Spain, for the Abolition of the Slave Trade (23 September 1817), 68 Consolidated Treaty Series 45 (1817–18); British and Foreign State Papers, vol. 4, p. 33.

  Article 7 of the Anglo-Dutch treaty is similarly phrased but refers to 'Mixed Courts of Justice' as opposed to 'Mixed Commissions'. See Treaty between his Britannic Majesty and His Majesty the King of the Netherlands, for preventing their Subjects from engaging in any traffic in Slaves (4 May 1818), British and Foreign State Papers, vol. 5, p. 125.

108 Jenny Martinez, *The Slave Trade and the Origins of International Human Rights Law*, Oxford: Oxford University Press (2012), p. 69.

109 Ibid., p. 79.

110 Ibid., p. 75.

111 Moreover, until 1862 all British attempts to sign a similar agreement with the United States failed even though the United States had outlawed the slave trade as well. See Jenny Martinez, *The Slave Trade and the Origins of International Human Rights Law*, Oxford: Oxford University Press (2012), Chapter 3.

was not British, Spanish, Portuguese or Dutch, and even if it was transporting slaves, then the search and seizure were unlawful and the ship eventually returned to its owner, with its cargo of slaves. The use of forged registration papers to make the ship appear French, for example, was commonplace.[112]

If the Commission decided that the ship had indeed engaged in illegal slave trading, it was sold at auction and the proceeds shared between governments. Captains of the patrolling ships who had done the initial search and seizure were entitled to a financial reward. The slaves were freed and, pursuant to the treaties, given a certificate of freedom.[113] The Commissions had no criminal jurisdiction over the slaver's crew.[114] Despite their limitations – the most obvious being the non-participation of France and the late participation of the United States – the Commissions changed the lives of thousands of Africans. As Martinez highlights,

> These were real people, and their lives were made at least a little bit better because of the efforts to enforce the international treaties against the slave trade. In sheer human impact, no other international court has directly affected so many individuals. Indeed, regardless of whether or not the mixed courts were 'successful' in terms of their impact on the overall transatlantic slave trade, they were successful in their impact on the nearly 80,000 individuals who were granted their legal freedom by the courts.[115]

These mechanisms were not like the judicial or quasi-judicial human rights enforcement mechanisms of today, whereby rights-holders claim rights against duty-bearers. Slaves rarely appeared before the Mixed Commission and they were considered secondary in the process, 'beneficiaries of the system, to be sure, but hardly active participants in it'.[116] Martinez argues, however, that the Mixed Commissions were international human rights mechanisms. She compares their proceedings to the various ways in which contemporary human rights violations are addressed not as direct claims before international judicial or quasi-judicial bodies, but as broader issues tackled through, for example, the investigations of UN Special Procedures.

---

112  Ibid., p. 74.
113  Many of those individuals, especially those who were already in the New World, eventually ended up living as slaves or quasi-slaves because of the absence of follow-up mechanisms to the decisions and the absence of funds to send them back to Africa. See Jenny Martinez, *The Slave Trade and the Origins of International Human Rights Law*, Oxford: Oxford University Press (2012), Chapter 5.
114  Ibid., pp. 76–77. Many criticised the absence of criminal jurisdiction over the crew but this was never changed. That said, some of them were actually tried before domestic courts (ibid. pp. 92–93).
115  Ibid., p. 85. Not only unprecedented, the number of people impacted by the decisions is also unmatched. See Ibid., pp. 94–95.
116  Ibid., p. 99.

Victims still often do not play a central role today.[117]

Of central importance to this book is Martinez's contention that international human rights law is not an invention of the period following the Second World War. Instead, it can be traced back to the antislavery movement and in turn to the Mixed Commissions. While post-Second World War international human rights law rests on the idea that only states violate human rights, one of the consequences of this shift of perspective is a 'much greater emphasis on nonstate actors'.[118] Martinez argues that

> [r]eviving the centrality of private transnational actors to the history of international human rights law's origins highlights the possibility of making international legal mechanisms a more central tool for addressing human rights violations by private actors today. What about non-state terrorist organisations that commit war crimes and crimes against humanity, or individual and businesses engaged in contemporary forms of forced labor trafficking? This would represent a dramatic shift in the focus of international human rights law and activism.[119]

As shown earlier in this chapter, there is no fundamental reason why states should be the only duty-bearers in the field of human rights. Individuals and corporations can be duty-bearers as well. In that context, the history of the Mixed Commissions draws the contemporary observer's attention to the fact that, additionally, there is no conceptual impossibility regarding the creation of international mechanisms to deal with corporations' wrongdoings in the area of human rights. It may only be a matter of time before such mechanisms are set up.

## The International Criminal Court and corporate crimes

The International Criminal Court, the permanent tribunal created in 1998 by the Statute of Rome, has jurisdiction over the crime of aggression, genocide, crimes against humanity and war crimes committed by individuals only. It does not have jurisdiction over crimes committed by legal persons such as corporations. The exclusion of legal persons as entities who may be prosecuted by the International Criminal Court, however, does not rest on solid theoretical grounds.[120] It is not a simple omission either; rather, it is the result of a negotiating process which could have brought about a different outcome. Article 23 of the final Draft Statute produced by the Preparatory

---

117 Ibid., pp. 150–151.
118 Ibid., p. 162.
119 Ibid., p. 163.
120 On this see Jonathan A. Bush, 'The Prehistory of Corporations and Conspiracy in International Criminal Law: What Nuremberg Really Said', 109 *Columbia Law Review* 1094 (2009).

Committee before the start of the Rome Conference in 1998 contained these two bracketed paragraphs:

> [5. The Court shall also have jurisdiction over legal persons, with the exception of States, when the crimes committed were committed on behalf of such legal persons or by their agencies or representatives.
> 6. The criminal responsibility of legal persons shall not exclude the criminal responsibility of natural persons who are perpetrators or accomplices in the same crimes.][121]

The commentary to the Draft Statute pointed to the 'deep divergence of views as to the advisability of including criminal responsibility of legal persons in the Statute. Many delegations [were] (...) strongly opposed, whereas some strongly favour[ed] its inclusion. Others [had] (...) an open mind'.[122] Tanzania was among the supporters. The Tanzanian delegate highlighted that

> one of the allegations concerning the genocide in Rwanda was that there had been companies in whose warehouses arms bought with the profits of those companies had been stored and from which they had been distributed, with the full knowledge of the representatives of those companies.

He considered that legal persons, such as companies, 'should be held criminally liable, if only by paying fines or by being liquidated'.[123]

In the end no consensus in favour of the inclusion of corporate liability emerged and Article 23 of the Statute only grants the Court jurisdiction over individuals. These individuals may be corporate officials. Thus in theory the Court may examine business and human rights cases;[124] in practice, however, this is unlikely to happen. The International Criminal Court was created to deal with the worst offenders who bear the greatest responsibility in the commission of crimes, and, as seen, business officials' involvement in crimes tends to be as aidors and abettors, not as main perpetrators.

The result of the negotiations in Rome is that in order for the Court to exercise jurisdiction over corporations, the Statute would have to be amended. Although this is an unlikely prospect, it is worth noting that the

---

121 UN Doc. A/CONF.183/2/Add.1, p. 49.
122 Ibid., note 3.
123 UN Doc. A/CONF.183/C.1/SR.1, p. 8.
124 On this see Reinhold Gallmetzer, 'Prosecuting Persons Doing Business with Armed Groups in Conflict Areas', 8 *Journal of International Criminal Justice* 947 (2010). Some organisations have tried to alert the attention of the prosecutor to situations involving businesspeople, unsuccessfully for the moment. See Nadia Bernaz, 'Complaint to the International Criminal Court against the CEO of Chevron', *Rights as Usual* (2014), http://rightsasusual.com/?p=895 (last accessed 21 March 2016).

Statute was amended in 2010 to include a definition of the crime of aggression, which proves that when political will is present international law can be adapted to take into account a new consensus among states. Granting the Court jurisdiction over corporate crimes would send a strong signal that certain behaviours are unacceptable. It would make clear that corporations are not excluded from the reach of international law as duty-bearers and could foster a most welcome sense of accountability, even if no prosecution is ever initiated. The amendment of the ICC statute is part of a wider discussion on corporate accountability for international human rights violations, and features in the debates over the adoption of a future business and human rights treaty.[125]

## Monitoring mechanisms and the World Court of Human Rights

The current business and human rights legal landscape does not include any international monitoring mechanism. It is one of the reasons behind civil society's support of a business and human rights treaty, as it is hoped that the treaty will include such a mechanism. In 2007 Manfred Nowak suggested the creation of a World Court of Human Rights in the context of a reform of the UN human rights mechanisms which had just led to the UN Commission on Human Rights' replacement with the UN Human Rights Council.[126] The World Court would be created by a treaty, to which states would voluntarily adhere, along the same model as the Statute of Rome establishing the International Criminal Court. More importantly for our purposes, the statute would be open for 'ratification' by non-state actors, including businesses. Hence,

> transnational corporations (...) might be invited and encouraged to accept the binding jurisdiction of the World Court in relation to selected human rights in the sphere of their respective influence, such as the prohibition of forced or child labour; the right to form and join trade unions; the right to collective bargaining; and the prohibition of discrimination. The World Court would not only be in a position to decide in a binding judgment whether or not a business corporation subject to its jurisdiction has violated any human right of an employee, a client or any other person affected, but it might also provide proper reparation to the victim concerned.[127]

---

125 See also developments at the Special Tribunal for Lebanon with regard to corporate criminal liability before international courts: Nadia Bernaz, 'Corporate Criminal Liability under International Law: The *New TV S.A.L.* and *Akhbar Beirut S.A.L.* Cases at the Special Tribunal for Lebanon', 13 *Journal of International Criminal Justice* 313–330 (2015).

126 Manfred Nowak, 'The Need for a World Court of Human Rights', 7 *Human Rights Law Review* 251 (2007).

127 Ibid., pp. 256–257. See also Manfred Nowak, 'On the Creation of World Court of Human Rights', 7 *National Taiwan University Law Review* 257 (2012), p. 269.

Article 51(1) of the Draft Statute for a World Court of Human Rights, entitled 'Declaration by Entities', sets up an opt-in mechanism whereby

> Any Entity may at any time declare (...) that it recognizes the competence of the Court to receive and examine complaints from any person, non-governmental organization or group of individuals claiming to be the victim of a violation by the respective Entity of any human right provided for in any human rights treaty listed in Article 5 (1).[128]

The idea of a World Court of Human Rights which could receive claims against corporations is probably far from materialising, for two main reasons. First, there seems to be limited state support for its establishment for the moment. Second, it is debatable whether companies would be comfortable joining such a system. They have voluntarily joined other systems, such as the UN Global Compact, and on the whole there seems to be at least some endorsement of the UN Guiding Principles on Business and Human Rights.[129] But submitting themselves to a proper Court's jurisdiction is an entirely different matter. To overcome this difficulty, one can imagine a system whereby, in a way similar to the International Criminal Court system, state ratification would entail the World Court's jurisdiction over companies registered in the territory of that state, whether or not companies agree with this. This idea was put forward in one of the earlier drafts.[130] The problem with this approach is that unlike individuals, who are unlikely to change nationality to escape the jurisdiction of the International Criminal Court, companies are used to playing around with their place of registration and could incorporate themselves in a state that has not joined the Court in order to shield themselves from its jurisdiction. The fear of losing prominent businesses and the jobs and tax revenue they bring could be a deterrent for states. Despite this flaw, it is an option which might still be worth exploring. The presence of an international court to hear claims from victims against corporations for human rights violations would be a major step in the business and human rights field, and one that would unmistakably indicate that boundaries have indeed shifted. Perhaps a similar court system, focused on

128 Julia Kozma, Manfred Nowak and Martin Scheinin, 'A World Court of Human Rights: Consolidated Statute and Commentary' *in* Swiss Federal Department of Foreign Affairs and Geneva Academy of International Humanitarian Law and Human Rights, *Protecting Dignity: An Agenda for Human Rights* (2011). Under Article 4(1), 'The term 'Entity' refers to any inter-governmental organization or non-State actor, including any business corporation, which has recognized the jurisdiction of the Court in accordance with Article 51'. See also Martin Scheinin, 'International Organizations and Transnational Corporations at a World Court of Human Rights', 3 *Global Policy* 488 (2012).
129 See Chapter 7.
130 Swiss Federal Department of Foreign Affairs and Geneva Academy of International Humanitarian Law and Human Rights, *Protecting Dignity: An Agenda for Human Rights* (2011), p. 62.

corporate defendants, will be included in the future treaty on business and human rights.

## Conclusion

This chapter has highlighted some of the complexities of the business and human rights debate at the international level. It has shown how we may now look beyond the traditional model which sees states as the only duty-bearers in international human rights law and how largely self-imposed boundaries are shifting, leading to greater corporate accountability.

This, however, is only part of the picture. As discussions about the human rights obligations of corporations are intensifying, other branches of international law directly affecting business operations have developed with little consideration for human rights. The next chapter focuses on international economic law, and on its relationship with international human rights law. Moreover, as mentioned in this chapter, international soft law instruments have also been developed in the area of business and human rights and the picture can only be complete after a discussion of those as well; this takes place in Chapter 7.

## Bibliography

### Books

Alston, Philip, *Non-State Actors and Human Rights*, Oxford: Oxford University Press (2005).

Cassese, Antonio, *International Law*, 2nd edition, Oxford: Oxford University Press (2005).

Clapham, Andrew, *Human Rights Obligations of Non State Actors*, Oxford: Oxford University Press (2006).

Deva, Surya, *Regulating Corporate Human Rights Violations: Humanizing Business*, London: Routledge (2012).

Dixon, Martin, *Textbook on International Law*, 7th edition, Oxford: Oxford University Press (2013).

Friedman, Milton, *Capitalism and Freedom*, Chicago: the University of Chicago Press (2nd edition 2002).

Jägers, Nicola, *Corporate Human Rights Obligations: In Search of Accountability*, Antwerpen, Oxford, New York: Intersentia (2002).

Jessup, Philip, *A Modern Law of Nations*, New York: the MacMillan Company (1948).

Kamminga, T. and Scheinin, Martin (eds), *The Impact of Human Rights Law on General International Law*, Oxford: Oxford University Press (2009).

Kinley, David, (ed.), *Human Rights and Corporations*, Burlington: Ashgate (2009).

Klabbers, Jan, *International Law*, Cambridge: Cambridge University Press (2013).

Kozma, Julia, Nowak, Manfred and Scheinin, Martin/Swiss Federal Department of Foreign Affairs and Geneva Academy of International Humanitarian Law and Human Rights, *A World Court of Human Rights: Consolidated Statute and Commentary* (2011).

Letnar Černič, Jernej, *Human Rights Law and Business: Corporate Responsibility for Fundamental Human Rights*, Groningen: Europa Law Publishing (2010).

Mares, Radu, *The UN Guiding Principles on Business and Human Rights*, Leiden: Martinus Nijhoff (2011).

Martinez, Jenny, *The Slave Trade and the Origins of International Human Rights Law*, Oxford: Oxford University Press (2012).

McBarnet, Doreen, Voiculescu, Aurora and Campbell, Tom (eds), *The New Corporate Accountability, Corporate Social Responsibility and the Law*, Cambridge: Cambridge University Press (2007).

Morsink, Johannes, *Inherent Human Rights. Philosophical Roots of the Universal Declaration*, Philadelphia: University of Pennsylvania Press (2009).

Ruggie, John Gerard, *Just Business*, New York and London: W. W. Norton & Company Inc. (2013)

Schabas, William A. (ed.), *The Universal Declaration of Human Rights, the Travaux Preparatoires Volume I*, Cambridge: Cambridge University Press (2013).

Shaw, Malcolm, *International Law*, 6th edition, Cambridge: Cambridge University Press (2008).

Van der Heijden, Marie-Jose, *Transnational Corporations and Human Rights Liabilities*, Antwerpen, Oxford, New York: Intersentia (2012).

Zerk, Jennifer, *Multinationals and Corporate Social Responsibility Limitations and Opportunities in International Law*, Cambridge: Cambridge University Press (2006).

## *Journal articles*

Barber, 'Benjamin R., Global Democracy or Global Law: Which Comes First', 1 *Indiana Journal of Global Legal Studies* 119 (1993).

Bernaz, Nadia, 'Corporate Criminal Liability under International Law: The *New TV S.A.L.* and *Akhbar Beirut S.A.L.* Cases at the Special Tribunal for Lebanon', 13 *Journal of International Criminal Justice* 313–330 (2015).

Bush, Jonathan A., 'The Prehistory of Corporations and Conspiracy in International Criminal Law: What Nuremberg Really Said', 109 *Columbia Law Review* 1094 (2009).

Charney, Jonathan L., 'Transnational Corporations and Developing Public International Law', 1983 *Duke Law Journal* 748 (1983).

Deva, Surya, 'Human Rights Violations by Multinational Corporations and International Law: Where from Here?', 19 *Connecticut Journal of International Law* 1 (2003–2004).

Domingo, Rafael, 'The Crisis of International Law', 42 *Vanderbilt Journal of Transnational Law* 1543 (2009).

Domingo, Rafael, 'Gaius, Vattel, and the New Global Law Paradigm', *European Journal of International Law* (2011), p. 641.

Gallmetzer, Reinhold, 'Prosecuting Persons Doing Business with Armed Groups in Conflict Areas', 8 *Journal of International Criminal Justice* 947 (2010).

Hannum, Hurst, 'The Status of the Universal Declaration of Human Rights in National and International Law', 25 *Georgia Journal of International and Comparative Law* (1995).

Henkin, Louis, 'The Universal Declaration at 50 and the Challenge of Global Markets', 25 *Brooklyn Journal of International Law* 17 (1999).

Kamatali, Jean-Marie, 'The New Guiding Principles on Business and Human Rights' Contribution in Ending the Divisive Debate over Human Rights Responsibilities of Companies: Is It Time for an ICJ Advisory Opinion?', 20 *Cardozo Journal of International and Comparative Law* 437 (2011–2012).

Kinley, David, and Chambers, Rachel, 'The UN Human Rights Norms for Corporations: The Private Implications of Public International Law', 6 *Human Rights Law Review* 447 (2006).

Nowak, Manfred, 'The Need for a World Court of Human Rights', 7 *Human Rights Law Review* 251 (2007).

Nowak, Manfred, 'On the Creation of World Court of Human Rights', 7 *National Taiwan University Law Review* 257 (2012).

Ratner, Steven C., 'Corporations and Human Rights: A Theory of Legal Responsibility', 111 *Yale Law Journal* 443 (2001–2002).

Scheinin, Martin, 'International Organizations and Transnational Corporations at a World Court of Human Rights', 3 *Global Policy* 488 (2012).

van den Herik, Larissa and Letnar Černič, Jernej, 'Regulating Corporations under International Law. From Human Rights to International Criminal Law and Back Again', 8 *Journal of International Criminal Justice* 725 (2010).

Vazquez, Carlos M., 'Direct vs. Indirect Obligations of Corporations under International Law', 43 *Columbia Journal of Transnational Law* 927 (2004–2005).

## Book chapters

Addo, Michael K., 'The Corporation as a Victim of Human Rights Violations', *in* Michael Addo (ed.), *Human Rights Standards and the Responsibility of Transnational Corporations*, The Hague, London, Boston: Kluwer Law International (1999), pp. 187–196.

Alston, Philip, 'The 'Not-a-Cat' Syndrome: Can the International Human Rights Regime Accommodate Non-State Actors?', *in* Philip Alston (ed.), *Non State Actors and Human Rights,* Oxford: Oxford University Press (2005), pp. 3–36.

Bernaz, Nadia, 'State Obligations with regard to the Extraterritorial Activities of Companies Domiciled on their Territories', *in* Carla Buckley, Alice Donald and Philip Leach (eds), *Towards Coherence in International Human Rights Law: Approaches of Regional and International Systems*, Leiden: Brill, forthcoming 2016.

Clapham, Andrew, 'The 'Drittwirkung' of the Convention' *in* R. St. J. MacDonald, F. Matscher and H. Petzold (eds), *The European System for the Protection of Human Rights*, Deventer: Martinus Nijhoff (1993), pp. 163–206.

d'Aspremont, Jean, 'Introduction', in Jean d'Aspremont (ed.), *Participants in the International Legal System. Multiple Perspectives on Non-State Actors in International Law*, London and New York: Routledge (2011), pp. 1–21.

d'Aspremont, Jean, 'Non-State Actors from the Perspective of Legal Positivism. The Communitarian Semantics for the Secondary Rules of International Law', *in* Jean d'Aspremont (ed.), *Participants in the International Legal System. Multiple Perspectives on Non-State Actors in International Law*, London and New York: Routledge (2011), pp. 23–40.

Jägers, Nicola, 'The Legal Status of the Multinational Corporation under International Law', *in* Michael K. Addo (ed.), *Human Rights Standards and the Responsibility of Transnational Corporations*, The Hague, London, Boston: Kluwer Law International (1999), pp. 259–270.

Kamminga, Menno T. and Zia-Zarifi, Saman, 'Liability of Multinational Corporations Under International Law: An Introduction' *in* Menno T. Kamminga and Saman Zia-Zarifi (eds), *Liability of Multinational Corporations Under International Law*, The Hague, London, Boston: Kluwer Law International (2000), pp. 1–13.

Muchlinski, Peter, 'Multinational Enterprises as Actors in International Law: Creating "Soft Law" Obligations and "Hard Law" Rights', *in* Math Noortmann and Cedric Ryngaert (eds), *Non-State Actor Dynamics in International Law*, Burlington: Ashgate (2010), pp. 9–39.

Rodley, Sir Nigel, 'Non State Actors and Human Rights', *in* Scott Sheeran and Sir Nigel Rodley (eds), *Routledge Handbook of International Human Rights Law*, Abingdon and New York: Routledge (2013), pp. 523–544.

Sheeran, Scott, 'The Relationship of International Human Rights Law and General International Law: Hermeneutic Constraint, or Pushing the Boundaries?', *in* Scott Sheeran and Sir Nigel Rodley (eds), *Routledge Handbook of International Human Rights Law*, Abingdon and New York: Routledge (2013), pp. 79–108.

Weissbrodt, David and Kruger, Muria, 'Human Rights Responsibilities of Businesses as Non-State Actors', *in* Philip Alston (ed.), *Non State Actors and Human Rights*, Oxford: Oxford University Press (2005), pp. 315–350.

## Special issues

Special issue of *L'Observateur des Nations Unies*, Volume 31, 2011–2012.
Special issue of the *Tilburg Law Review* Vol. 17, Issue 2 (2012).

## Treaties

Additional Convention between Great Britain and Portugal, for the Prevention of the Slave Trade (28 July 1817) and Separate Article (11 September 1817), 67 Consolidated Treaty Series 398 (1817); British and Foreign State Papers, vol. 4, pp. 85 and 115.

Treaty between Great Britain and Spain, for the Abolition of the Slave Trade (23 September 1817), 68 Consolidated Treaty Series 45 (1817–18); British and Foreign State Papers, vol. 4, p. 33.

Treaty between his Britannic Majesty and His Majesty the King of the Netherlands, for preventing their Subjects from engaging in any traffic in Slaves (4 May 1818), British and Foreign State Papers, vol. 5, p. 125.

Charter of the United Nations (1945), 1 UNTS XVI.

Convention for the Protection of Human Rights and Fundamental Freedoms (1950), CETS No.005.

International Convention on the Elimination of All Forms of Racial Discrimination (1965), 660 UNTS 195.

International Covenant on Civil and Political Rights (1966), 999 UNTS 171.

International Covenant on Economic, Social and Cultural Rights (1966), 993 UNTS 3.

American Convention on Human Rights (1969), OAS TS No 36.

International Convention on Civil Liability for Oil Pollution Damage (1969), 973 UNTS 3.

Convention on the Elimination of All Forms of Discrimination against Women (1979), 1249 UNTS 13.
African Charter on Human and People's Rights (1981), 21 ILM 58 (1982).
United Nations Convention on the Law of the Sea (1982), 1833 UNTS 3.
Convention against Torture and Other Cruel, Inhuman or Degrading Treatment or Punishment (1984), 1465 UNTS 85.
Convention on the Rights of the Child (1989), 1577 UNTS 3.
International Convention on the Protection of the Rights of All Migrant Workers and Members of their Families (1990), 2220 UNTS 3.
Convention on Civil Liability for Damage Resulting from Activities Dangerous to the Environment (1993), 32 ILM 1228.
OECD Convention on Combating Bribery of Public Officials in International Business Transactions (1997), 37 ILM 1.
UN Convention on the Suppression of the Financing of Terrorism (1999), 2178 UNTS 197.
Convention on the Rights of Persons with Disabilities (2006), 2515 UNTS 3.
International Convention for the Protection of All Persons from Enforced Disappearance (2006), UN Doc. A/61/488.

## *Official documents*

A/C.3/345, 17 November 1948.
A/C.3/SR.155, 24 November 1948.
A/C.3/SR.156, 25 November 1948.
Universal Declaration of Human Rights (1948), GA Res. 217A (III).
Vienna Declaration (1993), A/CONF.157/23.
Draft Statute for the International Criminal Court and Draft Final Act (1998), UN Doc. A/CONF.183/2/Add.1.
United Nations Diplomatic Conference of Plenipotentiaries on the Establishment of an International Criminal Court (1998), UN Doc. A/CONF.183/C.1/SR.1.
Resolution on the Situation in Sierra Leone (2000), S/RES/1306.
Draft Articles on the Responsibility of States for Internationally Wrongful Acts (2001), A/RES/56/83.
United Nations Declaration on the Rights of Indigenous Peoples (2007), A/RES/61/295.
S/RES/1904 (2009).
Report of the Special Representative of the Secretary-General (SRSG) on the issue of human rights and transnational corporations and other business enterprises (2007), A/HRC/4/035.
Guiding Principles on Business and Human Rights: Implementing the United Nations 'Protect, Respect and Remedy' Framework (2011), A/HRC/17/31.
Elaboration of an international legally binding instrument on transnational corporations and other business enterprises with respect to human rights (2014), A/HRC/26/L.22/Rev.1.

## *United Nations Treaty Bodies' General Comments*

UN Committee on the Rights of the Child, General Comment No 16 (2013), State

Obligations Regarding the Impact of the Business Sector on Children's Rights, CRC/C/GC/16.

COMMITTEE ON ECONOMIC, SOCIAL AND CULTURAL RIGHTS

General Comment No. 12 (1999), The Right to Adequate Food, E/C.12/1999/5, 12 May 1999.
General Comment No. 14 (2000), The Right to the Highest Attainable Standard of Health (Article 12 of the International Covenant on Economic, Social and Cultural Rights), E/C.12/2000/4, 11 August 2000.
General Comment No. 15 (2003), The Right to Water (Articles 11 and 12 of the International Covenant on Economic, Social and Cultural Rights), E/C.12/2002/11, 20 January 2003.
General Comment No. 17 on the Right of Everyone to Benefit from the Protection of the Moral and Material Interests resulting from any Scientific, Literary or Artistic Production of which He or She is the Author (Article 15, paragraph 1 (c), of the Covenant), E/C.12/GC/17, 12 January 2006.
General Comment No. 19 on the Right to Social Security (Article 9 of the Covenant), E/C.12/GC/19, 4 February 2008.

*United Nations Treaty Bodies' Concluding Observations*

Committee on the Elimination of Racial Discrimination, Canada, CERD/C/CAN/CO/18, 25 May 2007.
Committee on the Elimination of Racial Discrimination, United Kingdom, CERD/C/GBR/CO/18-20, 14 September 2011.
Committee on the Elimination of Racial Discrimination, Canada CERD/C/CAN/CO/19-20, 9 March 2012.
Human Rights Committee, Germany, CCPR/C/DEU/6, November 2012.

**Cases and advisory opinions**

*Reparation for Injuries Suffered in the Service of the United Nations*, Advisory Opinion: ICJ Reports 1949, p. 178.
*Guardian and Observer v United Kingdom*, [1991] 14 EHRR 153.
*Pine Valley Development Ltd and Others v Ireland*, [1992] 14 EHRR 319.
*Länsman v Finland* [1992] CCPR/C/52/D/511/1992.
*López Ostra v Spain*, [1995] 20 EHRR 277.
African Commission on Human and People's Rights, 155/96: *Social and Economic Rights Action Center (SERAC) and Center for Economic and Social Rights (CESR) v Nigeria*, 27 October 2001.
Inter-American Commission on Human Rights, Report Nº 40/04, Case 12.053, Merits, *Maya Indigenous Communities of the Toledo Districts v Belize*, 12 October 2004.
*Legal Consequences of the Construction of a Wall in the Occupied Palestinian Territory*, Advisory opinion: ICJ. Reports 2004, p. 136.
European Court of Human Rights, *Tatar v Romania* [2009], Application No 67021/01.

*Accordance with International Law of the Unilateral Declaration of Independence in Respect of Kosovo*, Advisory Opinion, ICJ Reports 2010, p. 403.

## Miscellaneous

Nadia Bernaz, 'Complaint to the International Criminal Court against the CEO of Chevron', *Rights as Usual* (2014), http://rightsasusual.com/?p=895 (last accessed 21 March 2016).

Inter-American Commission on Human Rights, 'IACHR Urges Belize to Guarantee the Rights of Maya Indigenous Communities', Press release No. 32/13, 6 May 2013.

List of company policy statements on human rights compiled by the Business and Human Rights Resource Centre, http://business-humanrights.org/en/company-policy-statements-on-human-rights (last accessed 21 March 2016).

Maurice Mendelson, 'In the Matter of the Draft "Norms on the Responsibilities of Transnational Corporations and Other Business Enterprises with Regard to Human Rights"', Appended to the Confederation of British Industry submission to the UN High Commissioner for Human Rights (2004).

Middlesex University Law Department, *Guidance on Business and Human Rights: A Review*, London: Equality and Human Rights Commission (2011)

OECD, 2011, Update of the OECD Guidelines for Multinational Enterprises Comparative table of changes made to the 2000 text (2012).

Security Council Committee pursuant to Resolutions 1267 (1999) and 1989 (2011) concerning Al-Qaida and associated individuals and entities, 'List established and maintained by the 1267 Committee with respect to individuals, groups, undertaking and other entities associated with Al-Qaida'.

Security Council Committee established pursuant to Resolution 1718 (2006), 'Consolidated List of Entities and Individuals'.

Swiss Federal Department of Foreign Affairs and Geneva Academy of International Humanitarian Law and Human Rights, *Protecting Dignity: An Agenda for Human Rights* (2011). *Yearbook of the United Nations* 1948–1949.

# 6 Human rights and international economic law

## Connecting the dots

The rise of business and human rights as a field of study has renewed the spotlight on corporations' global operations. In the 1960s and 1970s, discussions regarding corporations at the international level tended to focus on their complex relationships with capital-importing developing states in the context of debates on the so-called New International Economic Order, and not on their human rights impact as such.[1] Nationalisations and expropriations of foreign investors, and sovereignty of host states over their natural resources, were the key concerns of the time. Then came the 1980s and the 1990s, periods characterised by the spread of the economic liberalisation ideology. In practical terms, this has resulted in an exponential development of foreign direct investment, arguably fostered by the signature of hundreds of bilateral investment treaties (BITs), as well as in the purported destruction of all obstacles to international trade and the creation of a sophisticated organisation to help reach that goal, the World Trade Organization (WTO). Deregulation but also technological advances and new financial instruments have increasingly facilitated capital flow. As one author remarks,

> because of these developments, investors, companies and financial services professionals enjoy more choices than ever as to where to set up their operations, and can participate in far-flung markets virtually anywhere, instantly, regardless of national origin and boundaries.[2]

The dearth of regulation is identified as a source of adverse human rights impacts,[3] and international financial institutions such as the World Bank and the International Monetary Fund (IMF), as well as the WTO, have received

---

1 Philip Alston, 'The 'Not-a-Cat' Syndrome: Can the International Human Rights Regime Accommodate Non-State Actors?', *in* Philip Alston (ed.), *Non State Actors and Human Rights*, Oxford: Oxford University Press (2005), p. 7. See also Chapter 7 of this book on the early work of the United Nations on transnational corporations.
2 Chris Brummer, *Soft Law and the Global Financial System. Rule Making in the 21st Century*, Cambridge: Cambridge University Press (2012), p. 11.
3 Mary Dowell-Jones and David Kinley, 'Minding the Gap: Global Finance and Human Rights', 25 *Ethics & International Affairs* 183 (2011), p. 184.

their share of criticism for being too opaque and for putting financial considerations before human ones.[4]

International economic law is composed of a patchwork of rules divided into distinct areas of law. Core areas of international economic law are international trade law and international investment law. While discussing the interplay between human rights law and other branches of international law, it is commonplace to point to the fragmentation of international law. The argument goes that these sub-categories of international law form 'self-contained regimes'.[5] As the International Law Commission puts it:

> 'Trade law' develops as an instrument to regulate international economic relations. 'Human rights law' aims to protect the interests of individuals (…). Each rule-complex or 'regime' comes with its own principles, its own form of expertise and its own 'ethos', not necessarily identical to the ethos of neighbouring specialization. 'Trade law' and 'environmental law', for example, have highly specific objectives and rely on principles that may often point in different directions. In order for the new law to be efficient, it often includes new types of treaty clauses or practices that may not be compatible with old general law or the law of some other specialized branch. Very often new rules or regimes develop precisely in order to deviate from what was earlier provided by the general law. When such deviations become general and frequent, the unity of the law suffers.[6]

While international trade law, international investment law and international human rights law have largely developed independently from one another, these areas are not sealed and they all operate under the umbrella of international law. The purpose of this chapter is to connect the dots and to show how international investment and international trade law and practice have been and could be further reconciled with human rights law, which would in turn contribute to bridging the corporate accountability gap. The first section presents both areas and their interplay with human rights. It highlights the points of tension between international economic law and human

---

4   See for example Adam McBeth, *International Economic Actors and Human Rights*, London and New York: Routledge (2010).
5   Report of the Study Group of the International Law Commission, 'Difficulties arising from the diversification and expansion of international law', UN Doc. A/CN.4/L.682 (2006) Para. 15.
6   Report of the Study Group of the International Law Commission, 'Difficulties arising from the diversification and expansion of international law', UN Doc. A/CN.4/L.682 (2006) Para. 15. The conclusions of the final report of the ILC on this question, however, are more nuanced. For example, the report points out that 'International law is a legal system. Its rules and principles (i.e. its norms) act in relation to and should be interpreted against the background of other rules and principles. As a legal system, international law is not a random collection of such norms. There are meaningful relationships between them' (p. 7).

rights considerations. The second section explains the place of human rights within dispute settlement in international investment and international trade law. The third section is forward-looking and examines the changes which could be introduced to further harmonization between, on the one hand, the different legal regimes in the field of international economic law and, on the other, international human rights law. These changes include, for example, the negotiation of investment treaties where the human rights duties of states and investors are clearly spelled out from the outset, and the inclusion of a labour rights clause in trade agreements. The final section looks into the human rights obligations of the key international organisations in the area of international economic law and the accountability mechanisms they have set up. These mechanisms also enhance corporate accountability, albeit in an indirect way.

## International economic law: main features and interplay with human rights

### *International trade law*

International trade law refers to the set of rules governing the transboundary trade of goods and services. Although of great relevance for private actors such as corporations, international trade law is about inter-state relationships. The main sources of international trade law are trade agreements such as the General Agreement on Tariffs and Trade (GATT) and related agreements, which aim to remove obstacles to transboundary free trade such as tariffs, quotas and subsidies. The World Trade Organization provides a forum for states to negotiate further, and a dispute settlement mechanism. International trade law is of primary concern for corporations as it dictates whether and how they can import and export goods and services. However, international trade law concerns corporations indirectly, as states retain the power to regulate transboundary trade. Corporations cannot sue or be sued under international trade law. A typical dispute involves a state suing another state if the former believes that international trade law has been violated, for example when the latter has unlawfully subsidised a branch of domestic industry, hence granting that branch an unfair advantage on the international market compared to its foreign competitors. Although corporations are not direct participants in them, trade disputes are relevant for corporations and their outcome can have a profound impact on business. As a matter of fact, industry lobbies often lie behind inter-state disputes before the WTO dispute settlement bodies.[7]

---

7   Cornelia Woll, 'Global Companies as Agenda Setters in the World Trade Organization', *in* John Mikler (ed.), *The Handbook of Global Companies*, Chichester: John Wiley and Sons Ltd (2013), p. 265. See also Sorcha Macleod and Douglas Lewis, 'Transnational Corporations: Power, Influence and Responsibility', 4 *Global Social Policy* 77 (2004), p. 82.

International trade rules can interfere with human rights in a variety of ways.[8] The WTO aims to create growth and economic well-being, both of which are clearly positive from a human rights perspective. At the theoretical level, the promises of free trade fit squarely with the promises of human rights.[9] However, the free trade ideology is said to have its limits and world trade law can negatively affect the realisation of human rights, especially in poorer countries. Taking the right to health as an example, the impact of the Agreement on Trade Related Intellectual Property Rights (TRIPS) on access to generic HIV/AIDS drugs in poorer parts of the world is well documented.[10] Similarly, some have highlighted that the rules on trade in agricultural products may endanger the right to food of the poorest.[11] While the rules are negotiated by states and are primarily addressed to states, their impact, albeit indirect, on the operations of privately owned business is clear. For example, when a pharmaceutical company has invested millions of dollars in the development of a drug and has successfully protected it with a patent, they reasonably expect profits from selling the drug, perhaps even if this translates into depriving the poorest of life-saving medication.

Fundamental questions lie at the heart of these debates. Is trade liberalisation 'inherently antithetical to the development goals of human rights'?[12] Or, rather, 'can it be argued that the promotion of economic efficiency is a useful precondition to the ultimate advancement of human rights via increased world welfare?'[13] Tackling these questions in detail would be beyond the scope of the present book, but it is important to phrase them, if only to contextualise the remainder of this chapter.

## *International investment law*

International investment law grants corporations a more active role than international trade law. The main international legal instruments of that

8   See Sheldon Leader, 'Human Rights and International Trade', *in* Scott Sheeran and Sir Nigel Rodley (eds), *Routledge Handbook of International Human Rights Law*, Abingdon and New York: Routledge (2013), p. 246. It is worth noting that sometimes states give priority to human rights considerations and voluntarily create obstacles to trade, such as outright bans on the trade of certain products. This is the case of the EU Council Regulation (EC) No 1236/2005 of 27 June 2005 concerning trade in certain goods which could be used for capital punishment, torture or other cruel, inhuman or degrading treatment or punishment.

9   Philip M. Nichols, 'Trade Without Values', 90 *Northwestern University Law Review* 658 (1995–1996), pp. 661–667.

10  See for example Holger Hestermeyer, *Human Rights and the WTO. The Case of Patents and Access to Medicine*, Oxford: Oxford University Press (2007).

11  Report of the Special Rapporteur on the Right to Food, UN Doc. E/CN.4/2006/44, 16 March 2006, para. 40.

12  Jeff Waincymer, 'The Trade and Human Rights Debate: Introduction to an Interdisciplinary Analysis', *in* Sarah Joseph, David Kinley and Jeff Waincymer (eds), *The World Trade Organization and Human Rights. Interdisciplinary Perspectives*, Cheltenham: Edward Elgar (2009), p. 3.

13  Ibid.

branch of law are International Investment Agreements (IAAs), the vast majority of which are bilateral investment treaties (BITs), in which states agree to treat investors (individuals or corporations) of the other party in a certain (friendly) way.[14] The aim of these agreements is to foster economic growth by providing a stable and predictable legal environment for foreign investors in given countries. Indeed, although economic considerations are decisive in an investment decision, legal security is also important.[15]

Unlike trade, which involves minimal interaction between corporations and the foreign country, investment is necessarily longer-term and corporations or private investors have a direct interest in the development of clear rules. Investment contracts between investors and states are the other main source of international investment law, and are of a mixed nature (public/private and international/domestic).[16] Dispute settlement in that area of law is through international arbitration, which can involve two states but usually involves a corporation suing a state for not having respected the terms of the BIT or the investment contract.

Just like international trade law, the promise of investment law is a win–win situation whereby the host state benefits from the investment through tax revenue, the creation of employment for local people and technology transfers, while the investor makes a profit. In practice, international investment law has attracted fierce criticism for being too business-friendly, at the expense of human rights.[17] The interaction between that branch of law and human rights is three-fold. First, investors may bring human rights claims, for example related to their right to a fair trial or their right to property, against the states where they have invested.[18] Second, investment law can become an obstacle to the full realisation of human rights if it prevents a host state from adopting protective domestic legislation that could have an impact on the investment. For example, if a state decides to strengthen the health and safety requirements in the mining industry, that might entail additional costs for investors, who can in turn challenge the measure as being contrary to the initial investment contract. Third, investors may themselves interfere

14   In 2015, there were 3,271 IIAs in force, including 2,926 BITs. See United Nations Conference on Trade and Development, *World Investment Report*, July 2015, p. 106.
15   Rudolf Dolzer and Christoph Schreuer, *Principles of International Investment Law*, Oxford: Oxford University Press (2008), p. 8.
16   Sheldon Leader, 'Human Rights, Risks, and New Strategies for Global Investment', 9 *Journal of International Economic Law* 657 (2006), p. 666.
17   For useful documents on investment and human rights see the London School of Economics Investment & Human Rights Learning Hub, http://blogs.lse.ac.uk/invest-ment-and-human-rights/ (last accessed 21 March 2016).
18   For a discussion on the parallels between the human right to property and the investor's right against expropriation see Pierre-Marie Dupuy, 'Unification Rather than Fragmentation of International Law? The Case of International Investment Law and Human Rights Law', *in* Pierre-Marie Dupuy, Francesco Francioni and Ernst-Ulrich Petersmann (eds), *Human Rights in International Investment Law and Arbitration*, Oxford: Oxford University Press (2009), p. 52.

with human rights, such as the right to water or indigenous peoples' rights, with or without the complicity of the state.[19] These three scenarios will be looked at in detail in the next section on dispute resolution.

For now suffice it to say that human rights considerations do not appear to be a priority for arbitral tribunals, who on the contrary seem to have an 'ingrained inclination to overlook public policy issues' and a tendency 'to avoid highly controversial issues regarding international human rights law'.[20] This may be due to the fact that corporate lawyers and not public lawyers populate the investment litigation world, both as judges and counsels, although this point is disputed.[21] What is certain, as one author noted, is that these tribunals 'have not sought to develop a consistent body of rules regarding the relationships between human rights and investment instruments' and that 'their jurisprudence is still in a formative period'.[22] In a number of cases against Argentina the respondent state attempted to put forward human rights considerations based on its international human rights obligations, or on circumstances of necessity due to the financial crisis it was facing, so as to justify the measures it had taken against some foreign investors. Argentina's strategy systematically failed. In *Azurix*, Argentina had argued that in the case of an incompatibility between human rights law and the BIT, the former should prevail. The tribunal dismissed the argument by noting that 'the matter [had] (...) not been fully argued' and that, in any event, it '[failed] (...) to understand the incompatibility in the specifics of the instant case'.[23] In a similar vein, the award in *Siemens* reads as follows:

> [T]he Tribunal notes the reference made by Argentina to international human rights law ranking at the level of the Constitution after the 1994 constitutional reform and implying that property rights claimed in this arbitration, if upheld, would constitute a breach of international human rights law. This argument has not been developed by Argentina. The

19 On this see Jan Wouters and Nicolas Hachez, 'When Rules and Values Collide: How Can a Balanced Application of Investor Protection Provisions and Human Rights Be Insured?', 3 *Human Rights and International Legal Discourse* 301 (2009).

20 Moshe Hirsch, 'Investment Tribunals and Human Rights: Divergent Paths', *in* Pierre-Marie Dupuy, Francesco Francioni and Ernst-Ulrich Petersmann (eds), *Human Rights in International Investment Law and Arbitration*, Oxford: Oxford University Press (2009), pp. 112–113.

21 See Stephen Schwebel, 'The Overwhelming Merits of Bilateral Investment Treaties', 32 *Suffolk Transnational Law Review* 263 (2008–2009), p. 268.

22 Moshe Hirsch, 'Investment Tribunals and Human Rights: Divergent Paths', *in* Pierre-Marie Dupuy, Francesco Francioni and Ernst-Ulrich Petersmann (eds), *Human Rights in International Investment Law and Arbitration*, Oxford: Oxford University Press (2009), p. 107.

23 International Centre for the Settlement of Investment Disputes, *Azurix Corp. v the Argentine Republic*, No. ARB/01/12 (2006), para 261. The International Centre for Settlement of Investment Disputes is a dispute-settlement institution and is part of the World Bank Group.

Tribunal considers that, without the benefit of further elaboration and substantiation by the parties, it is not an argument that, prima facie, bears any relationship to the merits of this case.[24]

Finally, in *Sempra*, Argentina argued that because of the crisis its constitutional order was on the verge of collapse, and that therefore it rightfully disregarded the BIT and the investment contract. The Tribunal noted that 'even if emergency legislation became necessary in this context, legitimately acquired rights could still have been accommodated by means of temporary measures and renegotiation'.[25]

This series of cases against Argentina highlight the difficulties associated with reconciling the necessity to preserve a predictable investment environment and environmental and human rights considerations. This is not to say that all host states pursue human rights goals while all foreign investors prevent them from doing so;[26] conversely, the vulnerable position of investors in host states, one of the key reasons for the development of a set of protective principles under international investment law, is at times exaggerated.

## Human rights considerations in investment and trade disputes

This section provides examples of cases where human rights considerations have arisen in investment and trade disputes. It highlights the difficulties associated with reconciling human rights obligations of states and companies with international investment and trade law. One issue common to both areas of law has to do with the 'policy space' of states, in other words the extent to which states retain the possibility to adopt human rights-inspired legislation despite their obligations under international trade and investment law. Two other issues are specific to international investment law and concern potential human rights claims by and against investors.

### Policy space in investment and trade disputes

As discussed above, international investment law and international trade law have the effect of granting certain advantages to international business. For

24  International Centre for the Settlement of Investment Disputes, *Siemens A.G. v The Argentine Republic*, No. ARB/02/8 (2007), para 79.
25  International Centre for the Settlement of Investment Disputes, *Sempra Energy International v. The Argentine Republic*, ARB/02/16 (2007), para. 332. See also the discussion on necessity in International Centre for the Settlement of Investment Disputes, *CMS Gas Transmission Company v. The Argentine Republic*, ARB/01/8 (2005), paras. 304–394.
26  Stephen Schwebel, 'The Overwhelming Merits of Bilateral Investment Treaties', 32 *Suffolk Transnational Law Review* 263 (2008–2009), p. 268. See also James D. Fry, 'International Human Rights Law in Investment Arbitration: Evidence of International Law's Unity', 18 *Duke Journal of Comparative & International Law* 77 (2007–2008).

example, BITs usually provide that future disputes will be settled by an arbitral tribunal. This is better for foreign investors than having to rely on the domestic courts of the host state, which may be less favourable to them, if not downright unreliable due to poor infrastructure and unclear processes – or even corruption. Similarly, by encouraging the openness of domestic markets to foreign goods, international trade law is of great relevance to those seeking to export such goods. Issues may arise when states, despite their obligations under investment treaties, investment contracts and trade agreements, decide to adopt measures disrupting this otherwise favourable situation for business in order to further the protection of human rights, or use human rights as an excuse. If the disruption is deemed too important, the alleged injured parties can bring the dispute to a judicial body who will have to answer questions as to whether states retain the right to legislate and the extent of their 'policy space'. The injured parties bringing claims may be either the investors themselves, in the case of investment law, or the states whose businesses suffer from the measures, in the case of trade law, where – as seen – disputes are formally of an inter-state nature. In both situations, the state that has taken the measures is likely to justify them by its human rights obligations, hence using the policy space argument as a counterclaim or a defence.

The first issue that arises out of the above scenario is that of the jurisdiction of arbitral tribunals or dispute settlement bodies of the WTO to even consider defences of a human rights nature. In the WTO system, things are relatively settled. Dispute Settlement Panels and the Appellate Body can make decisions on matters that are not strictly trade-related, but only if the human rights arguments are raised as defences:

> So, for instance, a claim could not be brought before a WTO panel by Country A alleging that Country B was utilising slave labour in the production of goods to export. Nor would a WTO panel have the jurisdiction to rule on a claim by Country A that Country B was failing to utilise compulsory licences in order to provide access to affordable medicines. In neither of the above cases is the claim trade-based. Rather they are both claims by one country about the protection of human rights in another country, albeit the claims do involve trade issues. (...) But, human rights measures may be raised as a defence within WTO dispute settlement proceedings. So, if Country A were to bring a case against Country B alleging that [Country B] was breaching non-discrimination provisions of the GATT in barring products made by slave labour, then WTO panels could potentially rule on a defence by Country (...) [B] (if raised) that discrimination was justified on human rights grounds. Similarly, if Country A alleged a breach of the TRIPS Agreement by Country B in its use of compulsory licences, then it would be within the jurisdiction of a WTO panel to rule on a defence raised by Country B that it was utilising compulsory licences in order to protect the right to health of its population.

> So it appears to be within the jurisdiction of WTO dispute settlement panels to rule on human rights issues which are raised as defences by countries accused of breaching their WTO obligations.[27]

Things are not that clear-cut when it comes to international investment law. Undoubtedly, the fact that there is no centralised dispute settlement mechanism but that, on the contrary, each dispute arises out of a specific BIT and/or investment contract, and is dealt with by a specific arbitral tribunal which may have its own views about jurisdiction, plays a role in that state of affairs. The jurisdiction of an arbitral tribunal depends on the contents of the compromissory clause of the BIT or the investment contract and by which jurisdiction is triggered. If the clause is narrowly worded so as to include only disputes about the investment *per se*, which is often the case, then the tribunal may declare itself incompetent to address human rights defences and counterclaims.

This, however, does not end the discussion. The issue is not only one of jurisdiction, for a tribunal may look at human rights arguments in the process of determining whether the state has breached its obligations under the BIT or the investment contract. In other words, despite a narrowly worded jurisdictional basis to do so, the tribunal may still examine human rights defences as part of its evaluation of whether or not a breach has occurred. The tribunal's ability to do this depends on the law applicable to the dispute, as agreed by the parties. For example, the International Centre for Settlement of Investment Disputes (ICSID) Convention provides that in the case that the parties disagree about the applicable law, the tribunal can be asked to 'apply the law of the Contracting State party to the dispute (...) and such rules of international law as may be applicable'.[28] This indicates an openness of the parties to see the investment put into its wider context, which includes at least human rights treaties to which the state is a party and customary international human rights law. In short, while 'the present role of human rights in the context of investment arbitration is peripheral at best',[29] human

---

27  James Harrison, *The Human Rights Impact of the World Trade Organisation*, Oxford and Portland: Hart Publishing (2007), pp. 188–189. The original quote mistakenly mentions a defence raised by Country A. Presumably this is a typographical error, which I have taken the liberty of correcting.

28  Convention of the International Centre for Settlement of Investment Disputes (1965), 575 UNTS 159, Article 42. On the question of applicable law see Pierre-Marie Dupuy, 'Unification Rather than Fragmentation of International Law? The Case of International Investment Law and Human Rights Law', *in* Pierre-Marie Dupuy, Francesco Francioni and Ernst-Ulrich Petersmann (eds), *Human Rights in International Investment Law and Arbitration*, Oxford: Oxford University Press (2009), p. 56 and, in the same book, Clara Reiner and Christoph Schreuer, 'Human Rights and International Investment Arbitration', p. 85.

29  Clara Reiner and Christoph Schreuer, 'Human Rights and International Investment Arbitration', *in* Pierre-Marie Dupuy, Francesco Francioni and Ernst-Ulrich Petersmann (eds), *Human Rights in International Investment Law and Arbitration*, Oxford: Oxford University Press (2009), p. 83.

rights considerations may still play a role in arbitral tribunals' reasoning.

Moreover, even if the compromissory clause does not refer to international law, it is still possible for human rights law to be considered. First, if the Constitution of the host state gives primacy to international law, international human rights law may become applicable to the dispute.[30] Second, human rights can be encompassed in wider considerations of transnational or international public policy (*ordre public*). The recourse to transnational or international public policy considerations in arbitration decisions is not a new practice. In an article published in 1986, Pierre Lalive refers to an 1854 arbitral award in the case of the ship *Creole* and sees in it the burgeoning notion of transnational public policy. In that case arbitrators faced the following question: was it correct to recognise the right to property over enslaved individuals that 'owners' had transported in a ship which did not arrive at its destination due to a slave rebellion? In the award, while in the end recognising the loss of property in favour of slave-owners, the arbitrator referred to slavery as being 'odious and contrary to the principles of justice and humanity'.[31] According to Lalive, there is no doubt that the arbitrator had what would now be called considerations of transnational public policy in mind while writing this, and that the use of terms of that nature would lead to a different result in contemporary arbitration practice.[32] Closer to us, in a famous 1963 award the arbitrator highlighted that 'corruption is an international evil; it is contrary to good morals and to an international public policy common to the community of nations',[33] and that 'contracts which seriously violate *bonos mores* or international public policy are invalid or at least unenforceable'.[34] To Lalive, regardless of what one wants to call these considerations – general principles of law recognised by civilised nations, rule of immediate applicability, transnational public policy – it is the same notion which is at stake.[35]

In sum,

> arbitrators can, on their own initiative, invoke an issue of blatant violation of fundamental human rights deemed to be incompatible with (...) 'transnational public policy'. One can note, furthermore, that, unsurprisingly, the prohibitions that are thus identified coincide generally if

30  Pierre-Marie Dupuy, 'Unification Rather than Fragmentation of International Law? The Case of International Investment Law and Human Rights Law', *in* Pierre-Marie Dupuy, Francesco Francioni and Ernst-Ulrich Petersmann (eds), *Human Rights in International Investment Law and Arbitration*, Oxford: Oxford University Press (2009), p. 59.

31  Reports of International Arbitral Awards, *The Creole v. Great Britain*, Volume XXIX, p. 52.

32  Pierre Lalive, 'Ordre public transnational (ou réellement international) et arbitrage international', *Revue de l'arbitrage* (1986) No. 3, p. 336.

33  ICC Award No. 1110 of 1963, *Yearbook of Commercial Arbitration*, 1996, p. 52.

34  Ibid., p. 51.

35  Pierre Lalive, 'Ordre public transnational (ou reellement international) et arbitrage international', *Revue de l'arbitrage*, 1986, No. 3, p. 337.

not all with that part of fundamental human rights which is currently acknowledged, this time on the basis of *public* international law, as belonging to *jus cogens*, namely customary peremptory international law.[36]

Although arbitrators, as well as dispute settlement panel members within the WTO, can refer to human rights law, or considerations, in their assessment of the scope of policy space retained by states in particular disputes, in practice the balancing exercise between obligations has rarely turned to the advantage of human rights protection – when it has occurred at all.

Under investment law, investors have brought claims against states that had adopted measures based on two main arguments. Investors have argued that the state's measures were incompatible with the fair and equitable treatment (FET) of foreign investment. Incidentally, and outside human rights considerations, FET is the most commonly invoked standard in investment disputes.[37] Investors have also argued that the state's measures amounted to indirect expropriation.

The fair and equitable treatment of foreign investment (or foreigners in general) is a well-established principle of international law, but its contours are the subject of much discussion. In the classic *Neer* case of 1926 it was held that

> the treatment of an alien, in order to constitute an international delinquency, should amount to an outrage, to bad faith, to wilful neglect of duty, or to an insufficiency of governmental action so far short of international standards that every reasonable and impartial man would readily recognize its insufficiency. Whether the insufficiency proceeds from deficient execution of an intelligent law or from the fact that the laws of the country do not empower the authorities to measure up to international standards is immaterial.[38]

This interpretation of the principle of fair and equitable treatment allows states comfortable policy space. For example, if a state decides to adopt stricter health and safety standards applicable to the mining sector, and this entails additional costs for foreign investors, the treatment of foreign investors would be deemed fair and equitable, unless the regulation is clearly

---

36  Pierre-Marie Dupuy, 'Unification Rather than Fragmentation of International Law? The Case of International Investment Law and Human Rights Law', *in* Pierre-Marie Dupuy, Francesco Francioni and Ernst-Ulrich Petersmann (eds), *Human Rights in International Investment Law and Arbitration*, Oxford: Oxford University Press (2009), pp. 60–61.

37  Rudolf Dolzer and Christoph Schreuer, *Principles of International Investment Law*, Oxford: Oxford University Press (2008), p. 119.

38  Mexico-USA Claims Commissions, *L. F. H. Neer and Pauline Neer (U.S.A.) v. United Mexican States*, 15 October 1926, Reports of International Arbitral Awards, Vol. IV, pp. 61–62.

meant to punish them and entails outrageous costs for no clear reason. In more recent times, however, arbitral tribunals have expanded the scope of the principle to a considerable extent. For example, the arbitral tribunal in the 2003 *Tecmed* case decided that the FET provision of the bilateral treaty between Spain and Mexico requires

> the Contracting Parties to provide to international investments treatment that does not affect the basic expectations that were taken into account by the foreign investor to make the investment. The foreign investor expects the host State to act in a consistent manner, free from ambiguity and totally transparently in its relations with the foreign investor, so that it may know beforehand any and all rules and regulations that will govern its investments (...) to be able to plan its investment and comply with such regulations.[39]

This interpretation amounts to saying that any change in the law will be considered unfair and inequitable, a standard which incidentally 'would be difficult for even the most developed countries to meet', and effectively creates a wholly unreasonable 'full-fledged stabilization clause'.[40] Stabilisation clauses are common in investment treaties and aim to 'freeze' the law at a certain point in time so as to avoid the negative implications of future legal and regulatory changes in the host state. While they are common features of international investment law, their contours can vary a great deal and there is disagreement on how to interpret them.[41] For example, what the tribunal intended by the 'basic expectations' of investors is open to interpretation. Surely, the fact that a state has human rights obligations cannot be said to be a surprise for investors. As Wouters and Hachez put it, in words that are worth citing in full:

> [W]ith regard to human rights we submit that it would be quite difficult for an investor to defend the idea that its basic expectations were that the host state would put on hold its obligation progressively to realise international human rights for the sake of the investor's business profits. Can an investor reasonably expect a host state to refrain from taking human rights measures warranted under the applicable international human rights framework every time this risks hurting investors' business interests?

39  ICSID, *Tecnicas Medioambientales Tecmed S.A. v The United Mexican States*, Case No. ARB (AF)/00/2 (2003), para. 154.
40  Jan Wouters and Nicolas Hachez, 'When Rules and Values Collide: How Can a Balanced Application of Investor Protection Provisions and Human Rights Be Insured?', 3 *Human Rights and International Legal Discourse* 301 (2009), p. 328.
41  Rudolf Dolzer and Christoph Schreuer, *Principles of International Investment Law*, Oxford: Oxford University Press (2008), p. 75.

Investors may not base their investments upon the assumption that the regulatory framework, whether in the environmental field or in the area of human rights, will forever remain still. Investors should on the contrary factor in that regulation is by definition bound to evolve with economic, social and environmental changes as much as it is bound to be brought in line with the host state's international obligations. This appears all the more true when the investor makes its investment in a country which it knows applies low human rights standards and is being pressed by the international community to take steps to strengthen their application in accordance with its human rights-related international commitments.

(…)

In other words, the only expectation that the investor may have is that the regulatory framework applicable to it will evolve in a reasonably fair and equitable way, and not that it will not evolve. It is only in this sense that the legitimate expectations element of fair and equitable treatment should be construed, and arbitral tribunals should refrain from stretching it to the point where it applies to public interest-oriented measures taken in good faith.[42]

The *Saluka* arbitral tribunal followed that line of reasoning and emphasised that

No investor may reasonably expect that the circumstances prevailing at the time the investment is made remain totally unchanged. In order to determine whether frustration of the foreign investor's expectations was justified and reasonable, the host State's legitimate right subsequently to regulate domestic matters in the public interest must be taken into consideration as well.[43]

Another common claim before investment tribunals is that the state has acted in a way that amounts to (indirect) expropriation. Expropriation is a central notion in investment law. While the right to expropriate is a logical consequence of the territorial sovereignty of states, most treaties contain requirements that must be fulfilled for an expropriation to be considered lawful. Four requirements may be considered part of customary international law. First, the measure that leads to expropriation of the foreign investor

---

42  Jan Wouters and Nicolas Hachez, 'When Rules and Values Collide: How Can a Balanced Application of Investor Protection Provisions and Human Rights Be Insured?', 3 *Human Rights and International Legal Discourse* 301 (2009), pp. 329–330. Pierre-Marie Dupuy, 'Unification Rather than Fragmentation of International Law? The Case of International Investment Law and Human Rights Law', *in* Pierre-Marie Dupuy, Francesco Francioni and Ernst-Ulrich Petersmann (eds), *Human Rights in International Investment Law and Arbitration*, Oxford: Oxford University Press (2009), p. 54.

43  UNCITRAL, Saluka Investments BV v The Czech Republic, para. 305.

must serve a public purpose. Second, it must not be arbitrary and discriminatory. Third, principles of due process (such as fair and equitable treatment) must be adhered to. Finally, the measure must come with prompt, adequate and effective compensation. This final requirement is the one that gives rise to the highest number of disputes.[44] For the purpose of this book, this requirement is particularly important, especially in tandem with the first one, which concerns the reasons given as justification for the measures.

Discussions revolve around whether arbitral tribunals ought to look only at the effects of a measure (is it an expropriation or not?) or whether they can look at the wider picture and the motives of the measure to decide on its legality and, crucially, on the level of compensation entailed. Cases have concerned the protection of the environment and not human rights as such, but the reasoning can easily apply to both areas. A key case in this respect is *Metalclad*. In that case, the tribunal concluded that it needed not 'decide or consider the motivation or intent of the adoption' of the contested measure which prevented the company from completing the construction of a hazardous waste landfill that it was to operate.[45] In a similar vein, in *Santa Elena*, the tribunal noted that

> Expropriatory environmental measures—no matter how laudable and beneficial to society as a whole—are, in this respect, similar to any other expropriatory measures that a state may take in order to implement its policies: where property is expropriated, even for environmental purposes, (…) the state's obligation to pay compensation remains.[46]

It is not disputed here that compensation should follow measures that amount to expropriation. It is an essential feature of investment law and one that investors legitimately want to protect. This does not mean that the state should be the only party concerned with environmental or human rights protection. We can imagine a system whereby expropriation would be lawful if it is accompanied by a legitimate public motive. In such case, compensation would be paid but the amount reduced. In sum, investors whose property was expropriated would 'share the burden of the human rights-inspired measures'.[47] This is not a mere academic hypothesis. In 2012, in *Occidental v Ecuador II*, an arbitral tribunal found that due to the contributory negligence of the claimant company, the award for damages should be

44   Rudolf Dolzer and Christoph Schreuer, *Principles of International Investment Law*, Oxford: Oxford University Press (2008), p. 91.
45   ICSID, *Metalclad Corporation v United Mexican States*, Case No. ARB(AF)/97/1 (2000), para. 111.
46   ICSID, *Compañía del Desarrollo de Santa Elena S.A. v The Republic of Costa Rica*, Case No. ARB/96/1 (2000), para. 72.
47   Jan Wouters and Nicolas Hachez, 'When Rules and Values Collide: How Can a Balanced Application of Investor Protection Provisions and Human Rights Be Insured?', 3 *Human Rights and International Legal Discourse* 301 (2009), p. 325.

reduced by 25 per cent.[48] While this case had nothing to do with human rights-inspired measures, it goes to show that the principle of sharing the burden between the claimant and the respondent state has gained some acceptance under international investment law.[49]

Interpreting fair and equitable treatment and the right to full compensation in case of expropriation too widely, irrespective of the state's motives, is damaging for the protection of human rights. Not only can arbitral tribunals rule out legitimate measures in specific instances, but the over-protection of investors interests can lead to what Wouters and Hachez have called 'regulatory chill'.[50] In other words, states may refrain from addressing human rights issues, thereby putting themselves in violation of their human rights obligations, so as to avoid upsetting investors or potential investors and continue to be seen as open to foreign investment. As seen in Chapter 5, enforcement mechanisms in international human rights law, even against states, are rather limited. By contrast, international investment law benefits from sophisticated and efficient dispute settlement mechanisms, which can lead to the payment of comfortable compensation packages to wronged investors. With this in mind, states, especially developing states, that are faced with a choice between the two are likely to adhere to investment rules rather than to human rights rules.[51] This is all the more regrettable because 'those countries which are in the greatest need of affirmative legislation pertaining to human rights or, more broadly, development issues often also happen to be the ones which commit to the most stringent protections in favour of foreign investors'.[52]

States may also hesitate to legislate in the human rights area due to their obligations under international trade law. In that area, discussions about the scope of the state's policy space are also ongoing. First, it must be noted that so far the WTO dispute settlement bodies have not had to deal with any case in which a clear conflict between a norm of international human rights law and an international trade rule was phrased. That said, cases that have come before WTO panels have been related to the environment, public health and

---

48    ICSID, Occidental Petroleum Corporation Occidental Exploration and Production Company v The Republic of Ecuador, Case No. ARB/06/11 (2012), para. 687.

49    This principle is not only valid under international investment law, but under general international law as well. In reaching their conclusion, the *Occidental* tribunal relied on Articles 31 and 39 of the International Law Commission Draft Articles on the Responsibility of States for International Wrongful Acts (paras 665–668).

50    Jan Wouters and Nicolas Hachez, 'When Rules and Values Collide: How Can a Balanced Application of Investor Protection Provisions and Human Rights Be Insured?', 3 *Human Rights and International Legal Discourse* 301 (2009), p. 310, note 35.

51    On this see Sheldon Leader, 'Human Rights, Risks, and New Strategies for Global Investment', 9 *Journal of International Economic Law* 657 (2006), p. 690.

52    Jan Wouters and Nicolas Hachez, 'When Rules and Values Collide: How Can a Balanced Application of Investor Protection Provisions and Human Rights Be Insured?', 3 *Human Rights and International Legal Discourse* 301 (2009), p. 310.

food safety, which are all relevant in a wider discussion on human rights.[53] Beyond those areas, an interesting case discussed below was about selective procurement based on human rights criteria, but the claim was withdrawn.

A clear example of possible conflict between WTO rules and human rights considerations would be the adoption by a state of measures aiming to ban imports of certain products due to human rights concerns associated with that product.[54] These measures could be 'inward', aiming to protect that state's own population against the dangers of the product, or 'outward', aiming to protect human rights abroad. The latter are more problematic because while states have human rights obligations towards their own population, it is still debated whether they have obligations towards individuals who fall outside their jurisdiction.[55]

One of the key principles under international trade law is that there should be no discrimination between 'like' products produced domestically and those which are imported. They should all be treated equally in a given market. In 1989 the United States introduced a regulation to ban the sale of shrimp that had not been caught with a 'turtle excluder device'. The aim of the measure was to ensure that sea turtles, an endangered species, were not being killed in the process of catching shrimp. This had the effect of preventing the fishermen of certain developing countries from selling their shrimp in the United States, and as a result indirectly favoured shrimp fished in the United States. Importantly, the regulation was discriminatory because it gave Caribbean countries more time to comply with the measure, as well as technical help to do so. India, Malaysia, Pakistan and Thailand brought a case against the United States. Faced with the question of whether the shrimp caught with or without the use of the device were like products, the Appellate Body answered that they were and that therefore the United States had breached its obligations by treating them differently. The United States was in violation of Article XI GATT prohibiting import restrictions.

Article XX GATT provides for exceptions allowing states to depart from their obligations in order to pursue non-trade objectives such as public morals, and human, animal or plant life or health. This article is the closest to a human rights provision the GATT contains.[56] However, the measure

---

53　Sarah Joseph, *Blame It on the WTO*, Oxford: Oxford University Press (2011), p. 51.

54　See for example EU Council Regulation (EC) No 1236/2005 of 27 June 2005 concerning trade in certain goods which could be used for capital punishment, torture or other cruel, inhuman or degrading treatment or punishment.

55　Sarah Joseph, *Blame It on the WTO*, Oxford: Oxford University Press (2011), pp. 96–97. On the dangers of outward measures, see Sheldon Leader, 'Human Rights and International Trade', *in* Scott Sheeran and Sir Nigel Rodley (eds), *Routledge Handbook of International Human Rights Law*, Abingdon and New York: Routledge (2013), pp. 250–252.

56　Some authors argue that it should be used as such. See Salman Bal, 'International Free Trade Agreements and Human Rights: Reinterpreting Article XX of the GATT', 10 *Minnesota Journal of Global Trade* 62 (2001).

could not be 'saved' by Article XX because one of the requirements for Article XX's applicability, as detailed in its *chapeau*, is that the measures 'are not applied in a manner which would constitute a means of arbitrary, or unjustifiable discrimination between countries where the same conditions prevail, or a disguised restriction to trade'. Because the measure favoured certain countries over others, it was deemed in violation of international trade law.

Discriminating against products based on how they were produced is of relevance to a discussion on international trade and human rights. If instead of protecting turtles, the United States had sought to protect workers against unsafe workplaces, the dispute settlement body would have found itself with a business and human rights case at hand. What would it decide then? Article XX sets up a 'three-step test before a measure will be saved from WTO illegality'.[57] First, the measure has to be of a nature described in Article XX, such as a measure for the protection of public morals or human health. Second, the measure must be necessary. As Sarah Joseph has noted,

> Inward measures, especially those designed to protect health, seem likely to pass the necessity test so long as they are reasonably effective in achieving a goal within Article XX. Outward measures would rarely satisfy the necessity criterion. Indeed, outward measures would rarely satisfy the test given that unilateral economic sanctions are often ineffective (or even counterproductive) in restoring human rights compliance in the target state.[58]

Third, as seen in the *US-Shrimp* case, the measure must satisfy the requirements of the *chapeau*. States therefore have limited policy space to adopt human rights oriented legislation.

One case could have provided the dispute settlement body with a good opportunity to address these issues first-hand. Although the case concerned an alleged violation of the *Government Procurement Agreement* (GPA) and not the GATT, the GPA contains an exceptions clause which is similar to Article XX GATT. Therefore, the three-step test outlined above was relevant in that context as well.[59] The case originated from a law adopted in the US

---

57   Sarah Joseph, *Blame It on the WTO*, Oxford: Oxford University Press (2011), p. 107.
58   Ibid., pp. 113–114.
59   Government Procurement Agreement, Article XXIII(2):

> Subject to the requirement that such measures are not applied in a manner which would constitute a means of arbitrary or unjustifiable discrimination between countries where the same conditions prevail or a disguised restriction on international trade, nothing in this Agreement shall be construed to prevent any Party from imposing or enforcing measures: necessary to protect public morals, order or safety, human, animal or plant life or health or intellectual property; or relating to the products or services of handicapped persons, of philanthropic institutions or of prison labour.

State of Massachusetts in 1996, the *Act Regulating State Contracts with Companies Doing Business with or in Burma (Myanmar)*.[60] 'Doing business with Burma' was widely defined and simply operating in the country was enough to be targeted.[61] Essentially, the Act provided that companies falling into that category were to be listed, and public authorities in Massachusetts prohibited from purchasing goods or services from them, unless the purchase was deemed 'essential'. The Act was human rights-inspired and aimed at ensuring that public money was not spent on companies benefiting, even loosely, from the Burmese dictatorship. The rationale for and efficacy of this boycott-type legislation is discussed in some detail in Chapter 9. For now, the idea is to focus on the relationship between this Act and WTO law.

The Act was in force for two years before the US Supreme Court struck it down on constitutional grounds.[62] Before that, several prominent companies such as Apple and Hewlett Packard ended their operations in Burma in order to avoid appearing on the list. Other companies who were not concerned by the Act nevertheless pulled out of Burma to avoid bad publicity.[63] In 1997, when the Act was still in force, Japan and the European Union brought a claim against the United States before the WTO dispute settlement mechanism, asking for the Act to be withdrawn on the grounds that it violated United States obligations under international trade law.[64] Specifically, they alleged a violation of Article VIII(b) of the *Government Procurement Agreement* which, after having established the principle of non-discrimination among suppliers, provides that 'any conditions for participation in tendering procedures shall be limited to those which are essential to ensure the firm's capability to fulfil the contract in question'. The Act adversely affected Japanese and EU companies to the point that Japan and the EU initiated proceedings. The fact that around that time similar selective purchasing laws had been adopted in other states and cities around the United States probably also played a role.[65] Had this practice spread throughout the country, and not remained active only in Massachusetts, the consequences could have been even more serious for a number of companies. Unfortunately, since the US Supreme Court struck down the Act, the proceedings at the WTO were ended and no panel was given the opportunity to look into the compatibility of this human rights-oriented legislation

---

60  1996 Mass. Acts 239, ch. 130.
61  Ibid. 240.
62  United States Supreme Court, *Crosby, Secretary of Administration and Finance of Massachusetts, et al. v. National Foreign Trade Council* 530 U.S. 363.
63  Mark B. Baker, 'Flying over the Judicial Hump: A Human Rights Drama featuring Burma, the Commonwealth of Massachusetts, the WTO and the Federal Courts', 32 *Law and Policy in International Business* 51, pp. 93–94.
64  United States—Measure Affecting Government Procurement, WT/DS 88 and DS 95, terminated on 11 February 2000.
65  Christopher Avery, *Business and Human Rights at a Time of Change* (1999), chapter 2.8, http://198.170.85.29/Chapter2.htm#2.8 (last accessed 15 June 2016).

with one of the WTO agreements. Without attempting to guess what a WTO panel would have concluded,[66] and irrespective of issues related to the legitimacy of the Act, the fact that some WTO members spent time and resources on challenging the Act is telling and raises questions about policy space for WTO member states. WTO member states who have similar legislation in mind may hesitate before adopting it – an example of regulatory chill, as discussed above with regard to investment law.

### Human rights claims by investors

A discussion on the interplay between human rights and investment law necessitates a review of human rights claims against, but also by, investors themselves. Although there is a lot less to say about the latter than about the former, it should be noted at the outset that a better integration of human rights considerations in investment arbitration practice could first and foremost benefit investors. It is all the more important because investors generally see themselves as the weaker parties in investment disputes with states, although this is a debatable point.[67] Access to justice, fair treatment by the courts and the right to property appear to be the most relevant of those rights.

Interestingly, alien investors benefited from the protection of international law before the development of modern international human rights law post-Second World War. In other words, 'the history of modern international law shows that the *alien* preceded chronologically the *individual*, understood as the human being, a fact which can easily be explained by the structure of the classical Westphalian international legal framework',[68] which posits that states

---

66    For the sake of argument, the fact that the Act was clearly outward-looking means that it would probably not have passed the three-step test.

67    Moshe Hirsch, 'Investment Tribunals and Human Rights: Divergent Paths', *in* Pierre-Marie Dupuy, Francesco Francioni and Ernst-Ulrich Petersmann (eds), *Human Rights in International Investment Law and Arbitration*, Oxford: Oxford University Press (2009), p. 112. On this Stephen Schwebel wrote:

> the international arbitral process, placed in context, is not asymmetrical. The host state may be able to bring a counter-claim against the investor. But much more than that, the government of a state has many means, legal and not, for bringing pressure to bear upon the foreign investor. The government has not only the police power; it has the police. It can bring the weight of its bureaucracy, and its politicians, to bear. It can prescribe, delay, decree, tax, incite, and strangle. For the foreign investor to be able to require international arbitration of disputes goes only some way to right a balance that usually inclines in favor of the host government.

Stephen Schwebel, 'The Overwhelming Merits of Bilateral Investment Treaties', 32 *Suffolk Transnational aw. Review* 263 (2008–2009), p. 268.

68    Pierre-Marie Dupuy, 'Unification Rather than Fragmentation of International Law? The Case of International Investment Law and Human Rights Law', *in* Pierre-Marie Dupuy, Francesco Francioni and Ernst-Ulrich Petersmann (eds), *Human Rights in International Investment Law and Arbitration*, Oxford: Oxford University Press (2009), p. 47.

are the only subjects of international law. In that context, individuals are defined by their nationality, as nationals or aliens depending on the jurisdiction to which they are subject, as opposed to their human condition. The development of access to justice as an investor's right under international investment law is significant because it allows the investor to stand as an individual (or a company), not as an alien (company) – a shift which leads to overlaps between aliens' rights and human rights.[69]

Investors rarely invoke human rights in investment disputes, presumably because most investors are corporate investors, and the idea that companies can have 'human' rights still feels odd to some.[70] Another factor is that the protection granted by human rights instruments is generally lower than that granted in investment treaties and contracts.[71] Thus the incentive for investors to use human rights treaties is low.

A handful of arbitral tribunals have addressed issues related to the human rights of investors. In *Tecmed* the arbitral tribunal emphasised the vulnerable position of the foreign investor who

> has a reduced or nil participation in the taking of the decisions that affect it, partly because the investors are not entitle [sic] to exercise political rights reserved to the nationals of the State, such as voting for the authorities that will issue the decisions that affect such investors.[72]

69 Francesco Francioni, 'Access to Justice, Denial of Justice and International Investment Law', *in* Pierre-Marie Dupuy, Francesco Francioni and Ernst-Ulrich Petersmann (eds), *Human Rights in International Investment Law and Arbitration*, Oxford: Oxford University Press (2009), p. 65.

70 Although rare, human rights claims by companies are possible under certain international human rights instruments. See Protocol 1 to the European Convention on Human Rights on the right to property; European Court of Human Rights, *Guardian and Observer v United Kingdom*, 26 November 1991; *Pine Valley Development Ltd and Others v Ireland*, 29 November 1991; Inter-American Court of Human Rights, *Cantos v Argentina*, 7 September 2001 (Preliminary Objections). In parallel, there have been interesting developments in the United States, with the Supreme Court holding that the First Amendment to the US Constitution protects corporations (*Citizens United v Federal Election Commission*, 558 U.S. 310). By contrast, the Optional Protocol to the International Covenant on Civil and Political Rights makes it clear that only individual and not body corporates can bring claims against states before the UN Human Rights Committee. The UN Human Rights Committee reiterated this point in a number of cases: see for example *S.M. v Barbados*, Communication No. 502/1992 (decision on inadmissibility), 31 March 1994; *Lamagna v Australia*, Communication No. 737/1997 (decision on inadmissibility), 7 April 1999.

71 Clara Reiner and Christoph Schreuer, 'Human Rights and International Investment Arbitration', *in* Pierre-Marie Dupuy, Francesco Francioni and Ernst-Ulrich Petersmann (eds), *Human Rights in International Investment Law and Arbitration*, Oxford: Oxford University Press (2009), p. 88. For an example of the contrary, see Paula F. Henin, 'The Jurisdiction of Investment Treaty Tribunals over Investors' Human Rights Claims: The Case Against Roussalis v. Romania', 51 *Columbia Journal of Transnational Law* 224 (2012–2013).

72 ICSID, Tecnicas Medioambientales Tecmed S.A. v The United Mexican States, Case No. ARB (AF)/00/2 (2003), para. 122.

In doing so they cited the *James v UK* judgement of the European Court of Human Rights as an authority.[73]

In *Mondez*, another decision by an arbitral tribunal, the Canadian company claimed that it had been denied the right to access to court in the United States. The tribunal examined caselaw from the European Court of Human Rights and noted that since the decisions 'emanate[d] from a different region', they could at best 'provide guidance by analogy'.[74] In the end the claim was dismissed. This makes sense since European Court of Human Rights caselaw has little to do with a dispute between a Canadian company and the United States. The tribunal did not have much of a choice and ended up disregarding this caselaw altogether. If, however, Article 14 of the International Covenant on Civil and Political Rights, ratified by both Canada and the United States, had been invoked, the result may have been different.

Finally, in *Lauder*, the arbitral tribunal cited a European Court of Human Rights judgement to clarify the distinction between direct and indirect expropriation in relation to the right to property.[75] The claimant company also lost its case.

Although the practice highlighted above does not seem to reveal successful reliance on human rights instruments on the part of claimants before investment tribunals, it is worth mentioning that the possibility for investors to bring claims, some of them of a human rights nature, in these forums constitutes a considerable advantage. Whereas victims of human rights abuses by states have to exhaust local remedies before accessing international human rights courts of bodies, this requirement is absent in investment arbitration which investors can access directly. Moreover, investment awards benefit from more efficient enforcement than human rights bodies' decisions.[76]

## Human rights claims against investors

Investment arbitration is primarily meant to allow foreign investors to bring claims against host states for not having respected their obligations, mainly emanating from bilateral investment treaties and investment contracts and, to some extent, from customary international law. Host states are not

---

73   European Court of Human Rights, *James and Others v United Kingdom* (1986), para. 63.
74   ICSID, Mondev International Limited v United States of America, Case No. ARB (AF)/99/2 (2002), para. 144.
75   UNCITRAL, *Lauder v The Czech Republic* (2001), para. 200.
76   Jan Wouters and Nicolas Hachez, 'When Rules and Values Collide: How Can a Balanced Application of Investor Protection Provisions and Human Rights Be Insured?', 3 *Human Rights and International Legal Discourse* 301 (2009), p. 308. See also Todd Weiler, 'Balancing Human Rights and Investor Protection: A New Approach for a Different Legal Order' (2004) 27 *Boston College International and Comparative Law Review* 429, pp. 430–431.

entitled to bring claims against investors, whether of a human rights nature or otherwise.[77] In the context of an existing arbitration claim against a state, if that state has concerns about the behaviour of the investors, it may bring a counterclaim. It is however difficult for states to do this due to strict jurisdictional constraints. As seen above with regard to the policy space left to states, compromissory clauses usually limit the jurisdiction of arbitration tribunals to the investment *per se*, leaving little room for other aspects, including human rights counterclaims. Moreover, while states have little room for counterclaims, the direct victims of human rights violations cannot bring any claim at all. In short, investors have access to justice through arbitration but those adversely impacted by the investors' activities typically cannot bring claims either before the courts of the host state,[78] which are often prevented from dealing with cases related to the investment, or before the arbitral tribunal.[79] How, then, can human rights violations by investors be addressed? The answer to this question is four-fold.

First, as already mentioned, the state may raise counterclaims in the context of an ongoing investment dispute before an arbitral tribunal. This is difficult as tribunals may not have jurisdiction over those claims, as they are considered unrelated to the investment *per se*. This constitutes a serious obstacle. Moreover, the reality of corporate human rights violations, especially the ones committed against individuals not working for the company (that is, not labour-related), is that companies are accomplices, not principal perpetrators. More often than not, especially in grave violations amounting to international crimes, the principal perpetrator is the state. With regard to less serious violations, it is common for states to simply not view their population's claims as valid or important, and to turn a blind eye to, or in the worst cases encourage, the violations. In that context, it is unlikely that the state will raise counterclaims in the course of an investment dispute.[80] On a more fundamental level, a state bringing claims on behalf of individuals or groups is disempowering for these individuals or groups. The real victims are not the ones bringing the claim: it is a system that 'reproduces the

77 Jan Wouters and Nicolas Hachez, 'When Rules and Values Collide: How Can a Balanced Application of Investor Protection Provisions and Human Rights Be Insured?', 3 *Human Rights and International Legal Discourse* 301 (2009), p. 313.
78 There are exceptions to this. See for example the ongoing judicial saga over allegations of pollution against Texaco/Chevron in Ecuador, discussed in Chapter 10.
79 Francesco Francioni, 'Access to Justice, Denial of Justice and International Investment Law', *in* Pierre-Marie Dupuy, Francesco Francioni and Ernst-Ulrich Petersmann (eds), *Human Rights in International Investment Law and Arbitration*, Oxford: Oxford University Press (2009), pp. 71–72.
80 Clara Reiner and Christoph Schreuer, 'Human Rights and International Investment Arbitration', *in* Pierre-Marie Dupuy, Francesco Francioni and Ernst-Ulrich Petersmann (eds), *Human Rights in International Investment Law and Arbitration*, Oxford: Oxford University Press (2009), p. 89.

paternalistic model of governmental espousal of private claims'[81] characteristic of the mechanism of diplomatic protection, and which human rights law seeks to challenge.

Second, victims can decide to bring a claim before international human rights bodies, when those are available. These claims are brought against the state for not having prevented abuses by third parties, in that case investors. Such cases were discussed in Chapter 5.[82] Not only is this a limited avenue, since many states have not accepted the jurisdiction of human rights courts and bodies, but these claims are also not targeting investors themselves. Moreover, because the state often has committed violations as well, less attention is given to the adverse impact of the investors' operations. This is one of the downsides of the state-centred nature of international human rights law.

Third, victims of human rights violations can be allowed to present an *amicus curiae* brief to the arbitral tribunal who has jurisdiction over the investment dispute. *Amicus curiae* means 'friend of the court'. Presenting an *amicus curiae* brief is a way for organisations, governments,[83] international organisations[84] and even in one instance an Indian Nation (indigenous community) in the United States[85] to provide the tribunal with their views about, and expertise on, the case. It is a way to bring the attention of the tribunal to the wider, non-strictly investment-related issues surrounding a dispute. These can include concerns about the environment, human health and human rights in general. The participation of third parties, hence potential victims of human rights abuses, in investment arbitration is a relatively recent trend. In a controversial ruling in *Aguas del Tunari SA* in 2005, the arbitral tribunal rejected the petition of an environmental non-governmental organisation requesting permission to intervene in the proceedings. In a letter sent to the organisation, the president of the tribunal asserted that the requests of the organisation were 'beyond the power or the authority of the Tribunal to grant', that 'the consensual nature of arbitration place[d] the control of the issues (...) [they] raise[d] with the parties, not the Tribunal'

---

81　Francesco Francioni, 'Access to Justice, Denial of Justice and International Investment Law', *in* Pierre-Marie Dupuy, Francesco Francioni and Ernst-Ulrich Petersmann (eds), *Human Rights in International Investment Law and Arbitration*, Oxford: Oxford University Press (2009), p. 72.

82　See for example African Commission on Human and People's Rights, 155/96: *Social and Economic Rights Action Center (SERAC) and Center for Economic and Social Rights (CESR) v Nigeria*, 27 October 2001.

83　See for example Supplemental Brief for the United States as Amicus Curiae in Partial Support of Affirmance, *Kiobel v Royal Dutch Petroleum Co.*, 133 S.Ct. 1659 (2013) (No. 10-1491).

84　ICSID, AES Summit Generation Ltd. and AES-Tisza Erömü Kft. v. Republic of Hungary, Case No. ARB/07/22 (2010), para. 3.22.

85　UNCITRAL, *Glamis Gold v United States*, Decision on Application and Submission by Quechan Indian Nation, 16 September 2005.

and that 'the consent required of the Parties to grant the request (...) [was] not present'.[86]

The winds of change, however, have been blowing. As early as 2003, parties to the North American Free Trade Agreement (NAFTA) had allowed tribunals to accept third parties' participation in arbitral proceedings.[87] Moreover, in 2006 the rules of the ICSID were amended so as to allow ICSID tribunals to consider the submission of third party briefs. Crucially, while the parties should be consulted, new Rule 37(2) provides that the submission of third parties' briefs does not depend on their consent.[88]

*Amicus curiae* briefs have been submitted in a number of arbitration disputes and this is now an established trend.[89] The 2001 NAFTA dispute *Methanex* was the first case in which this was allowed,[90] followed by the *UPS* case that same year.[91] Before the ICSID, new Rule 37(2) was applied for the first time in *Biwater*.[92] It was also considered in *Suez*, although it was not strictly applicable to the dispute.[93] In *Suez* the tribunal noted that

> the investment dispute centers around the water distribution and sewage systems of a large metropolitan area, the city of Buenos Aires and surrounding municipalities. Those systems provide basic public services to millions of people and as a result may raise a variety of complex public and international law questions, including human rights considerations. Any decision rendered in this case, whether in favor of the Claimants or the Respondent, has the potential to affect the operation of those systems and thereby the public they serve.[94]

What these cases have in common is the tribunal's insistence that the 'rights' granted to the intervening parties were procedural only and not substantive,

---

86 ICSID, *Aguas del Tunari SA v Republic of Bolivia*, Case No. ARB/02/3 (2005), para. 17.

87 NAFTA Free Trade Commission, Statement of the Free Trade Commission on Non-Disputing Party Participation (2003).

88 ICSID Convention, Regulation and Rules, Rule 37(2).

89 Eugenia Levine, 'Amicus Curiae in International Investment Arbitration: The Implications of an Increase in Third-Party Participation', 29 *Berkeley Journal of International Law* 200 (2011), p. 208.

90 UNCITRAL, *Methanex Corp. v United States*, Decision of the Tribunal on Petitions from Third Persons to Intervene as Amici Curiae, 15 January 2001.

91 UNCITRAL, *United Parcel Service of America v Canada*, Decision of the Tribunal on Petitions for Intervention and Participation as Amici Curiae, 17 October 2001.

92 ICSID, *Biwater Gauff (Tanzania) Ltd. v United Republic of Tanzania*, Case No. ARB/05/22, Procedural Order No. 5 (2 February 2007).

93 See Andrew de Lotbinière McDougall and Ank Santens, 'ICSID Tribunals Apply New Rules on Amicus Curiae', White and Case LLP, March 2007.

94 *Aguas Argentinas, S.A., Suez, Sociedad General de Aguas de Barcelona, S.A. and Vivendi Universal, S.A. v The Argentine Republic*, ICSID Case No. ARB/03/19, Order in Response to a Petition for Transparency and Participation as Amicus Curiae (19 May 2005), para. 19.

and were limited to the submission of briefs, hence did not include participation in the oral proceedings, for instance.[95] In other words, the submission
of *amicus* briefs is far from constituting a proper remedy for victims. At best
briefs can alert the tribunal to the possible negative effects of an investment,
and it is debatable whether they may influence the final outcome of the
case.[96] Perhaps *amicus* briefs' most important role is that they contribute to
raising public awareness of arbitration proceedings which traditionally lack
transparency, to some extent enhancing these proceedings' legitimacy.[97]
Although limited, this new role for third parties has attracted waves of criticism, with some arguing that investors may feel threatened by what is viewed
as a politicisation of investment disputes, and that allowing even wider participation will increase costs and lengthen proceedings.[98]

The fourth and final potential avenue to adjudicate human rights claims
against investors is the use of the domestic courts of the investor's state of
nationality. The obstacles associated with this type of remedy are numerous
and are examined in detail in Chapter 10. For now, suffice it to say that this
does not constitute a reliable form of remedy for victims of human rights
violations by investors in host states.

## Towards a greater emphasis on human rights in international economic law

So far, this chapter has highlighted the main features of the interplay between
human rights considerations and international trade and investment law,
focusing on existing caselaw. While it is possible for arbitrators and WTO
panel members to better integrate human rights considerations into international economic law, for example by interpreting the treaties in a way that
leaves a certain amount of policy space to states, changes in treaty law (and
investment contracts) may be more reliable in the long run. This holds true
especially in investment law, where there is no centralised dispute settlement
mechanism, and where as a result conflicting or at least incoherent caselaw
may have developed. The first subsection below focuses on the development

95   Eugenia Levine, 'Amicus Curiae in International Investment Arbitration: The Implications
     of an Increase in Third-Party Participation', 29 *Berkeley Journal of International Law* 200
     (2011), pp. 210–212.
96   Francesco Francioni, 'Access to Justice, Denial of Justice and International Investment
     Law', *in* Pierre-Marie Dupuy, Francesco Francioni and Ernst-Ulrich Petersmann (eds),
     *Human Rights in International Investment Law and Arbitration*, Oxford: Oxford
     University Press (2009), pp. 74–75.
97   Eugenia Levine, 'Amicus Curiae in International Investment Arbitration: The Implications
     of an Increase in Third-Party Participation', 29 *Berkeley Journal of International Law* 200
     (2011), p. 217. See also M. Orellana *et al.*, *Bringing Community Perspectives to Investor-
     State Arbitration: The Pac Rim Case*, London: IIED (2015).
98   For a useful summary of the critics see Eugenia Levine, 'Amicus Curiae in International
     Investment Arbitration: The Implications of an Increase in Third-Party Participation', 29
     *Berkeley Journal of International Law* 200 (2011), pp. 219–221.

of investment agreements and investment contracts that would integrate human rights principles. The second subsection introduces the idea of including labour rights clauses within international trade agreements.

### Mainstreaming human rights considerations in investment law

Commentators have proposed several different ways to mainstream human rights considerations in investment law. One option would be to revive the idea of a multilateral agreement, which was abandoned at the end of the 1990s after the negotiations for the creation of the Multilateral Agreement on Investment (MAI) failed. States' official positions vary a great deal on the expediency of simply creating such a treaty, let alone including human rights considerations in it, though some argue that many of these disagreements are exaggerated.[99] Moreover, NGOs would have high expectations regarding the inclusion of human rights in the text and could significantly delay negotiations, as they have done in the context of the MAI.[100] In sum, it seems unreasonable to rely on a hypothetical multilateral agreement to mainstream human rights in international investment law.[101] One author suggests that the ICSID Convention could be amended to include a general exceptions clause similar to Article XX in the GATT agreement. This would allow arbitral tribunals following ICSID rules of procedure to consider human rights and environmental issues and to balance them with investment-related considerations.[102] The obstacles to this are many, which leads Patrick Dumberry to portray this route as 'rather illusionary'.[103] In the end, change is most likely to occur through the introduction of modifications within the main source of investment law, BITs. Guiding Principle 9 of the UN Guiding Principles

99 See Stephen Schwebel, 'The Overwhelming Merits of Bilateral Investment Treaties', 32 *Suffolk Transnational Law Review* 263 (2008–2009), pp. 265–266.
100 On the role of NGOs in the 1990s MAI saga, see Stephen J. Kobrin, ' The MAI and the Clash of Globalizations', *Foreign Policy* (Fall 1998), p. 97. The ongoing discussions about the Transatlantic Trade and Investment Partnership, though limited to Canada, the United States and the EU and not global in nature, reveal a less than central role for human rights considerations. For a compilation of opinions on this, see the dedicated page of the Business and Human Rights Resource Centre, http://business-humanrights.org/en/transatlantic-trade-and-investment-partnership-ttip-background-commentaries-on-social-environmental-impacts-0 (last accessed 21 March 2016).
101 Patrick Dumberry, 'Corporate Investors' International Legal Personality and their Accountability for Human Rights Violations under International Investment Agreements', *in* Armand de Mestral and Céline Lévesque (eds), *Improving International Investment Agreements*, Abingdon: Routledge (2013), p. 191.
102 Kate M. Supnik, 'Making Amends: Amending the ICSID Convention to Reconcile Competing Interests in International Investment Law', 59 *Duke Law Journal* 343 (2009–2010), pp. 365–366.
103 Patrick Dumberry, 'Corporate Investors' International Legal Personality and their Accountability for Human Rights Violations under International Investment Agreements', *in* Armand de Mestral and Céline Lévesque (eds), *Improving International Investment Agreements*, Abingdon: Routledge (2013), p. 191.

on Business and Human Rights, endorsed by the UN Human Rights Council in 2011, recognises this. It reads as follows: 'States should maintain adequate domestic policy space to meet their human rights obligations when pursuing business-related policy objectives with other States or business enterprises, for instance through investment treaties or contracts.'[104]

Integrating human rights considerations in BITs may take two mutually reinforcing forms. First, there can be specific mentions of human rights within the treaty. Second, the treaty can introduce ways for victims to bring human rights claims against investors. Referring to human rights in an investment treaty is more complicated than it looks at first glance. A soft way to do it is to refer to states' human rights obligations in the preamble of the treaty. For example, the preamble of the 2012 Model US BIT provides that the parties are 'desiring to achieve these objectives in a manner consistent with the protection of health, safety, and the environment, and the promotion of internationally recognized labor rights'.[105] Article 31 of the Vienna Convention on the Law of Treaties provides that a treaty should be interpreted in its context, which includes its preamble.[106] Thus mentioning environmental protection and labour rights may result in arbitral tribunals taking them into consideration when interpreting the treaty in the course of a given dispute, for example when the extent of policy space left to the host state is being discussed. Similar mentions of internationally recognised human rights could have been made, and may make their way into future preambles.

A more robust way is to include a tailor-made human rights clause in the treaty, which lists the rights which state parties as well as investors must respect. Since only states are parties to BITs, these obligations only bind investors in an indirect way.[107] On the positive side, this ensures that human rights law is not entirely forgotten. That said, a human rights clause listing specific rights is not ideal, because human rights are hard to reconcile with such a 'pick and choose approach'.[108] Also, it can be argued that it is not particularly time-efficient for states to have to decide which rights to include in each BIT, and their exact contours.

---

104 Guiding Principle 9, see Chapter 7 below. See also 'Principles for Responsible Contracts: Integrating the Management of Human Rights Risks into State-Investor Contract Negotiations: Guidance for Negotiators', UN Document A/HRC/17/31/Add.3 (25 May 2011). This document was submitted to the UN Human Rights Council by the UN Secretary-General Special Representative on Business and Human Rights at the same time as the UN Guiding Principles.

105 US Model Bilateral Investment Treaty (2012), available on the United States Department of State website at www.state.gov/documents/organization/188371.pdf (last accessed 21 March 2016), preamble.

106 Vienna Convention on the Law of Treaties, 1155 UNTS 331, Articles 31(1) and (2).

107 See discussion on the direct and indirect obligations dichotomy in Chapter 5.

108 Patrick Dumberry, 'Corporate Investors' International Legal Personality and their Accountability for Human Rights Violations under International Investment Agreements', *in* Armand de Mestral and Céline Lévesque (eds), *Improving International Investment Agreements*, Abingdon: Routledge (2013), p. 191.

An easier and more efficient route would be to include in the BIT that the parties commit to protecting the rights listed in the International Bill of Rights and the core International Labour Organisation Conventions, and that investors must respect these rights. This is in line with the UN Guiding Principles on Business and Human Rights, which outline state duties and corporate responsibility in the area of human rights.[109] Having such a clause in the BIT could lead to the negotiation of investment contracts in which human rights protection would be better integrated. For example, an investment contract could include a stabilisation clause in which the state would commit to not modifying the regulatory landscape, so as to protect the investor, but which would make clear that reasonable measures aimed at advancing human rights could be adopted. In the case of conflict, it would be for an arbitral tribunal to decide whether the measures were reasonable, not looking only at whether they harmed the investor, but also looking at whether they were necessary to enhance the protection of human rights.

In practice, the language used in the rare BITs that do mention rights is much softer, and the obligations much fewer. Article 13 of the 2012 US Model BIT, entitled 'investment and labor', reads as follows:

> 1. The Parties reaffirm their respective obligations as members of the International Labor Organization ('ILO') and their commitments under the ILO Declaration on Fundamental Principles and Rights at Work and its Follow-Up.
> 2. The Parties recognize that it is inappropriate to encourage investment by weakening or reducing the protections afforded in domestic labor laws. Accordingly, each Party shall ensure that it does not waive or otherwise derogate from or offer to waive or otherwise derogate from its labor laws where the waiver or derogation would be inconsistent with the labor rights referred to in [subsequent] subparagraphs (…), or fail to effectively enforce its labor laws through a sustained or recurring course of action or inaction, as an encouragement for the establishment, acquisition, expansion, or retention of an investment in its territory.

International obligations are mentioned, but only in the area of labour rights, and there is no mention of investors' responsibility. A similar provision refers to environmental agreements.[110] Moreover, both provisions are outside the scope of arbitration.[111] Article 16 of the Canadian 2012 Model BIT, entitled 'Corporate Social Responsibility', vaguely mentions investors' responsibilities in those terms:

---

109 For an in-depth discussion of the Guiding Principles, see Chapter 7.
110 US Model Bilateral Investment Treaty (2012), available on the United States Department of State website at www.state.gov/documents/organization/188371.pdf (last accessed 21 March 2016), Article 12.
111 Ibid., Article 24.

Each Party should encourage enterprises operating within its territory or subject to its jurisdiction to voluntarily incorporate internationally recognized standards of corporate social responsibility in their practices and internal policies, such as statements of principle that have been endorsed or are supported by the Parties. These principles address issues such as labour, the environment, human rights, community relations and anti-corruption.[112]

To be clear, encouraging investors to voluntarily incorporate standards is far from recognising that investors have human rights obligations, but it is a good start. Unfortunately, as their names suggest, model BITs are just model treaties. They form a starting point for negotiations but the adoption of a slightly more human rights-friendly model BIT does not mean that the actual BITs signed will incorporate these aspects. For example, the Canada–Tanzania BIT – signed in 2013, hence after the introduction of Article 16 to the model BIT – does not mention the corporate social responsibility of enterprises.[113]

The model BIT that went the furthest in incorporating human rights and human rights-related considerations was the Norwegian 2007 Draft Model BIT, shelved in 2009 due to opposition from NGOs and businesses alike.[114] The preamble mentioned corporate social responsibility, labour rights, human rights, the United Nations Charter and the Universal Declaration of Human Rights. Draft Article 11, just like Article 13(1) of the 2012 US Model BIT, provided that states should not lower their labour standards so as to attract foreign investment. Draft Article 12 established the state's 'right to regulate' to ensure investment is undertaken in a manner sensitive to 'health, safety or environmental concerns'. Draft Article 24, modelled after Article XX of the GATT, provided that unless measures were of a discriminatory nature, nothing in the BIT should be interpreted in a way that would prevent states from enforcing measures necessary, among other goals, to protect human health and the environment. Draft Article 32, entitled 'Corporate Social Responsibility', provided that the Parties were to 'encourage investors to conduct their investment activities in compliance with the OECD Guidelines for multinational enterprises and to participate in the United Nations Global Compact'.

---

112 On this see Catharine Titi, 'The Evolving BIT: A Commentary on Canada's Model Agreement', (26 June 2013), International Institute for Sustainable Development, www.iisd.org/itn/2013/06/26/the-evolving-bit-a-commentary-on-canadas-model-agreement/ (last accessed 21 March 2016).

113 Agreement between the Government of Canada and the Government of the United Republic of Tanzania for the Promotion and Reciprocal Protection of Investments, available on the Government of Canada's website, www.international.gc.ca/trade-agreements-accords-commerciaux/agr-acc/fipa-apie/tanzania-text-tanzanie.aspx?lang=eng (last accessed 21 March 2016).

114 Damon Vis-Dunbar, 'Norway Shelves its Draft Model Bilateral Investment Treaty', 8 June 2009, International Institute For Sustainable Development.

Mainstreaming human rights in investment law is fraught with difficulties and is likely to face opposition from investors who may view the protection of human rights as a threat to their rights and interests. Yet it is telling that the 2012 Model Treaty of the United States, a significant capital-exporting state, mentions labour rights and the protection of the environment. As some authors have noted, this inclusion is partly due to the fact that in the years preceding the adoption of the 2012 Model BIT, the United States ran into trouble when certain existing BITs essentially prevented it from legislating, notably in the area of environmental protection. Hence they decided to protect their policy space when drafting a new model BIT.[115]

Beyond mentioning human rights and allowing states to retain the policy space necessary to protect human rights, BITs could include provisions on the enforcement of investors' human rights obligations. This would be significant given the tendency of international investment law to favour investors. One way to enforce investors' human rights obligations is to allow states to bring human rights counterclaims, as highlighted above. A more radical way would be to allow states, and victims, to bring claims against investors.[116] This is unlikely to materialise, not least because arbitration is based on the consent of the parties.[117]

From a policy perspective, John Ruggie identified the fragmentation within governments – that is, the fact that human rights and investment issues are dealt with by distinct government agencies with no or little communication between them – as one of the obstacles for the successful inclusion of human rights-friendly provisions in investment agreements.[118]

### Including a labour rights clause in trade agreements

Some have argued that human rights considerations should be placed at the heart of international trade law. As Ernst-Ulrich Petersmann puts it,

> in order to remain democratically acceptable, global integration law (e.g. in the WTO) must pursue not only 'economic efficiency' but also

---

115 Jan Wouters, Sanderijn Duquet and Nicolas Hachez, 'International Investment Law: The Perpetual Search for Consensus', *in* Olivier De Schutter, Johan Swinnen and Jan Wouters (eds), *Foreign Direct Investment and Human Development. The Law and Economics of International Investment Agreements*, Abingdon: Routledge (2013), p. 49. See also ibid, p. 57.

116 On this, see this inspiring article: T Weiler, 'Balancing Human Rights and Investor Protection: A New Approach for a Different Legal Order', 27 *Boston College International and Comparative Law Review* 429 (2004).

117 Patrick Dumberry, 'Corporate Investors' International Legal Personality and their Accountability for Humans Rights Violations under International Investment Agreements', *in* Armand de Mestral and Céline Lévesque (eds), *Improving International Investment Agreements*, Abingdon: Routledge (2013), p. 193.

118 John Gerard Ruggie, *Just Business*, New York and London: W. W. Norton and Company Ltd (2013), p. 87. See also ibid., p. 182.

'democratic legitimacy' and 'social justice' as defined by human rights. Otherwise, citizens will rightly challenge the democratic and social legitimacy of integration law if it pursues economic welfare without regard to social human rights.[119]

The inclusion of a labour rights clause in trade agreements is an oft-cited proposed reform that would encourage a greater emphasis on human rights in international trade law. The rationale for this inclusion is that unbridled free trade is said to encourage

> a 'race to the bottom' in that States will (...) depress labour conditions to maintain trade competitiveness. If the 'race to the bottom' thesis is true, the progressive realization of labour rights is being undermined, and free trade is acting as a catalyst for human rights abuses. In such a case, it would be appropriate for WTO rules to alleviate that impact by safeguarding labour rights in some way.[120]

The idea that international trade law in its current form encourages a race to the bottom is controversial in itself, with extreme positions on either end of the spectrum and a range of different shades in the middle.[121] This divisive discussion is beyond the scope of the present book, but it is worth mentioning it, if only to understand the context in which proposals for a labour rights clause have developed.[122]

The clause could take two main forms. First, it could introduce minimum standards similar to the minimum standards of protection states must guarantee under the Trade Agreement on Intellectual Property (TRIPS). Second, labour rights could be mentioned as a justification for certain measures under Article XX of the GATT and similar articles in other agreements, such as the above-mentioned Article XXIII(2) in the Government Procurement Agreement. If a clause of the second type was to be adopted, a state which introduces measures aimed at guaranteeing that imported products are produced following minimum labour standards, hence disturbing the free flow of goods by preventing the circulation of products not produced according to these standards, would not be in violation of its obligations under the GATT and other trade agreements. The clause would play the role of a human rights exception, allowing for human rights-inspired trade

---

119 Ernst-Ulrich Petersmann, 'Time for a United Nations "Global Compact" for Integrating Human Rights into the Law of Worldwide Organizations: Lessons from European Integration', 13 *European Journal of International Law* 621 (2002), p. 624.
120 Sarah Joseph, *Blame It on the WTO*, Oxford: Oxford University Press (2011), p. 131.
121 James Harrison, *The Human Rights Impact of the World Trade Organisation*, Oxford and Portland: Hart Publishing (2007), pp. 77–80.
122 Philip Alston, 'Core Human Rights and the Transformation of the International Labour Rights Regime', 15 *European Journal of International Law* 457 (2004), pp. 471–474.

sanctions. Adam McBeth notes that such an amendment, if it were possible to introduce it,

> maintains the approach of having human rights and social concerns as an add-on to the trade system, rather than a central goal. It would also be located beneath the existing chapeau, subjugated to the prohibitions on arbitrary or unjustified discrimination.[123]

The expediency of this clause is also a controversial matter, with some authors arguing that the proposed clause really aims at protecting developed countries from competition from developing countries, while others maintain that it should be adopted as a matter of social urgency.[124]

In 1996 the Ministerial Conference, the plenary body at the WTO, rejected the idea of a labour rights clause in no uncertain terms:

> We renew our commitment to the observance of internationally recognized core labour standards. The International Labour Organization (ILO) is the competent body to set and deal with these standards, and we affirm our support for its work in promoting them. We believe that economic growth and development fostered by increased trade and further trade liberalization contribute to the promotion of these standards. We reject the use of labour standards for protectionist purposes, and agree that the comparative advantage of countries, particularly low-wage developing countries, must in no way be put into question.[125]

The adoption of a labour rights clause, which would require amending at least the GATT, appears particularly unlikely, and discussions on this do not seem to be on the WTO's agenda at the moment.[126]

## The human rights obligations of international organisations

As subjects of international law, international organisations have certain human rights obligations. Although they have not become parties to human

---

123 Adam McBeth, *International Economic Actors and Human Rights*, Abingdon and New York: Routledge (2010), p. 161.

124 Kaushik Basu, 'Compacts, Conventions and Codes: Initiatives for Higher International Labor Standards', 34 *Cornell International Law Journal* 487 (2001), pp. 492–494; Jagdish Bhagwati, 'The Boundaries of the WTO. Afterword: The Question of Linkage', 96 *American Journal of International Law* 126 (2002), pp. 131–134; Adelle Blackett, 'Whither Social Clause? Human Rights, Trade Theory and Treaty Interpretation', 31 *Columbia Human Rights Law Review* 1 (1999).

125 Singapore Declaration (1996), WT/MIN(96)/DEC.

126 Sarah Joseph, *Blame It on the WTO*, Oxford: Oxford University Press (2011), p. 271.

rights treaties,[127] they are arguably bound by customary international law. A number of authors support this position.[128] Others have put forward a different argument which gives a more prominent role to the obligations of states as members of international organisations. For example, Adam McBeth contends that by virtue of their international personality, 'international organisations must have a duty not to frustrate the human rights obligations of their member States'.[129] He further argues that since states have human rights obligations, they must abide by them also 'while engaged in the business of an international economic institution of which they are members',[130] as the Committee on Economic, Social and Cultural Rights made clear in some General Comments.[131] Some have resisted the idea that international organisations have human rights obligations;[132] such blunt rejection, however, is no longer the norm. The establishment of accountability mechanisms in organisations such as the World Bank and the International Finance Corporation constitutes an important development in this respect, and one that also enhances corporate accountability, albeit indirectly.[133]

127  In 2014, the Court of Justice of the European Union gave an opinion against the ratification of the European Convention on Human Rights by the European Union: Opinion 2/13 of the Court of Justice of the European Union, 18 December 2014.

128  See for example Sigrun Skogly, *Human Rights Obligations of the World Bank and the International Monerary Fund*, London and Sydney: Cavendish Publishing (2001), pp. 19–23.

129  Adam McBeth, *International Economic Actors and Human Rights*, Abingdon and New York: Routledge (2010), p. 67.

130  Ibid, p. 65. See also Peter T. Muchlinski, 'International Finance and Investment and Human Rights', *in* Scott Sheeran and Sir Nigel Rodley (eds), *Routledge Handbook of International Human Rights Law*, Abingdon and New York: Routledge (2013), pp. 265–275.

131  See General Comment 15 para. 36 and General Comment No. 19: UN Doc. E/C.12/GC/19 (4 February 2008), para. 58. See also Philip Alston, 'The 'Not-a-Cat' Syndrome: Can the International Human Rights Regime Accommodate Non-State Actors?', *in* Philip Alston (ed.), *Non State Actors and Human Rights*, Oxford University Press (2005), p. 29.

132  For example, François Gianviti, former General Counsel of the IMF, argued in 2005 that the IMF was not bound by the International Covenant on Economic, Social and Cultural Rights because this treaty had not achieved customary legal status. François Gianviti, 'Economic, Social, and Cultural Human Rights and the International Monetary Fund', *in* Philip Alston (ed.), *Non State Actors and Human Rights*, Oxford: Oxford University Press (2005), pp. 120–122.

133  Other, less prominent mechanisms exist in other institutions and work in ways similar to the Inspection Panel and the IFC Ombudsman. These are: the Independent Consultation and Investigation Mechanism (ICIM) of the Inter-American Development Bank; the Accountability Mechanism (AM) of the Asian Development Bank; the Project Complaint Mechanism (PCM) of the European Bank for Reconstruction and Development; and the Independent Review Mechanism (IRM) of the African Development Bank. On those mechanisms see generally Arnaud Poitevin, 'Des 'prérequis' pour la levée de fonds sur les marchés internationaux: les normes environnementales et sociales des institutions financières internationales et leurs sanctions', 142 *Journal du droit international* 527 (2015).

The World Bank Inspection Panel and the International Financial Corporation (IFC) Compliance Advisor Ombudsman (CAO) are accountability mechanisms in the area of project finance in which human rights considerations play an important role.[134] They are non-judicial mechanisms and they do not provide reparations for victims of corporate abuse. However, they can lead to significant changes in projects which the IFC and the World Bank are considering funding or are already funding so that they better integrate human rights considerations. By inducing change in the way institutions lend money, these mechanisms aim to prompt changes in the way corporations spend it.

The World Bank established the Inspection Panel in 1993, following sharp criticism from civil society organisations with regard to a number of projects it had funded, such as the Sardar Sarovar Dam and Canal projects in India, which had adverse social and environmental impacts. On several occasions the Bank had not complied with its own policies on such impacts, with devastating consequences for local populations.[135] In this context, the main function of the Panel is to ascertain whether the Bank is following its own policies, and to break the 'culture of approval' that existed within the organisation and which was 'driven by a promotion incentive structure that rewarded staff for moving through as many projects as possible without paying adequate attention to potential social and environmental impacts or effectiveness of implementation'.[136] The most relevant Bank policies with regard to human rights are the Safeguard Policies, which include, for example, an operational policy on indigenous peoples.[137]

The Inspection Panel has three members and although it is part of the Bank structure, it works as an independent institution. Project-affected

---

134 The World Bank Group consists in five different institutions: the International Bank for Reconstruction and Development (IBRD), the International Development Association (IDA), the International Finance Corporation (IFC), the Multilateral Investment Guarantee Agency (MIGA) and the International Centre for the Settlement of Investment Disputes (ICSID). The term 'World Bank' refers to the first two institutions, the IBRD (focused on developing and emerging countries) and the IDA (focused on the poorest countries), which provide loans to developing countries to fund development projects in areas such as health, education or infrastructure. The IFC provides financial products and services such as loans to the private sector for projects in developing countries. MIGA provides private investors and lenders with various guarantees to mitigate risks associated with their investment, such as war or expropriation. The World Bank Inspection Panel deals with complaints related to projects funded by the World Bank as defined. The IFC Compliance Advisor Ombudsman (CAO) deals with complaints related to projects which the IFC finances and/or MIGA supports. On the topic of project finance and human rights generally, see Sheldon Leader, 'Project Finance and Human Rights', *in* Juan Pablo Bohoslavsky and Jernej Letnar Černič (eds), *Making Sovereign Financing and Human Rights Work*, Oxford: Hart Publishing, (2014), p. 199.
135 World Bank, Accountability at the World Bank. The Inspection Panel at 15 Years (2009), p. 3.
136 Ibid., pp. 3–5.
137 World Bank, OP 4.10 – Indigenous Peoples (2005).

people can complain to the Panel alleging harm resulting from a World Bank-financed project. The Panel investigates the complaint (formally called the Request for Inspection or the Request) but will only look at whether the Bank has complied with its own policies. While in this process it may look at other actors' actions, such as the private sector's or those of a state, it does not make determinations with regard to them.[138] Once the Request is deemed eligible, the panel needs to get approval to investigate the case from the Bank's Board of Executive Directors, which is generally obtained.[139] At the end of the investigation, the Panel writes a publicly available final report (the Investigation Report), which determines whether the Bank has complied with its own policies or not, but crucially not whether the Requesters' human rights were violated. Treakle, Fox and Clark give the example of a Request that the panel had to dismiss because 'the claimants had not made a link between the conditions they complained of and specific bank policy violations'.[140] The Bank's Management is under an obligation to respond to the Investigation Report. This response 'generally includes' an Action Plan.[141]

The Inspection Panel was a great improvement in the Bank's work when it was established and it has positively affected the lives of many. Its powers, however, are limited. Since it cannot 'issue an injunction, stop a project, or award financial compensation for harm suffered', the Requesters are often disappointed with the outcome, as they expected more.[142] The Panel is also unable to follow through with the Action Plan, which is left in the hands of the Bank's management. This has led to concrete problems in a number of projects.[143] Other critics have pointed to the Panel's lack of independence and general lack of powers. Ultimately, 'because the Panel has no power to remedy the problems that it uncovers, any resolution that the Panel (…) helps a community achieve must have also been within the desires of the Bank'.[144] Another significant point is that the Inspection Panel can only

---

138 World Bank, Accountability at the World Bank. The Inspection Panel at 15 Years (2009), p. 17.

139 Ibid. p. 30.

140 Kay Treakle, Jonathan Fox and Dana Clark, 'Lessons Learned', *in* Dana Clark, Jonathan Fox and Kay Treakle (eds), *Demanding Accountability. Civil Society Claims and the World Bank Inspection Panel*, Lanham, Boulder, New York, Oxford: Rowman & Littlefield Publishers (2003), pp. 267–268.

141 World Bank, Accountability at the World Bank. The Inspection Panel at 15 Years (2009), p. 41.

142 Kay Treakle, Jonathan Fox and Dana Clark, 'Lessons Learned', *in* Dana Clark, Jonathan Fox and Kay Treakle (eds), *Demanding Accountability. Civil Society Claims and the World Bank Inspection Panel*, Lanham, Boulder, New York, Oxford: Rowman & Littlefield Publishers (2003), p. 258.

143 Enrique R. Carrascott and Alison K. Guernsey, 'The World Bank's Inspection Panel: Promoting True Accountability Through Arbitration', 41 *Cornell International Law Journal* 577 (2008), pp. 598–599.

144 Ibid, p. 599.

investigate if the project is not 'closed or substantially disbursed'.[145] This is a major constraint since 'many problems with projects don't show up until years after funds are disbursed. (…) For those affected people, there simply is no official response.'[146] The logic behind this rule is that the bank 'loses its leverage to influence government implementation once it no longer controls the finances'.[147] Finally, as mentioned above, the Panel's mandate is narrow as it is only limited to a determination of whether or not the Bank's internal policies were violated. It does not rule on whether the Bank itself or those who have received money from the Bank have violated human rights.

The IFC Compliance Advisor Ombudsman (CAO) was established in 1999 for reasons similar to those behind the establishment of the Inspection Panel.[148] The CAO has three separate roles. The CAO Advisor's role is to advise the higher management of the World Bank Group and the IFC and MIGA on issues of social and environmental nature. The CAO Ombudsman deals with complaints from people affected by a project funded by the IFC or that the IFC is considering funding.[149] Just like the World Bank Inspection Panel, if the project has ended, the CAO provides no solution. The approach is problem-solving, as opposed to the Inspection Panel's more fault-finding approach.[150] The CAO Ombudsman gathers information and engages in a dialogue with communities and the IFC/MIGA private client in order to bring the dispute to an end. In that process the CAO may make recommendations directly to a company.[151] Some have argued that if a concerted solution is found – one to which all parties, including the investors, have agreed – 'such written compromise may give rise to contractual obligations enforceable in local courts or arbitration'.[152] If, however, a concerted solution is not found, the case is transferred to the CAO Compliance branch.

---

145 Panel Resolution, Resolution IBRD 93–1 (1993), para. 14(c).

146 Kay Treakle, Jonathan Fox and Dana Clark, 'Lessons Learned', *in* Dana Clark, Jonathan Fox and Kay Treakle (eds), *Demanding Accountability. Civil Society Claims and the World Bank Inspection Panel*, Lanham, Boulder, New York, Oxford: Rowman & Littlefield Publishers (2003), p. 267.

147 Ibid.

148 Benjamin M. Saper, 'The International Finance Corporation's Compliance Advisor/Ombudsman (CAO): An Examination of Accountability and Effectiveness from a Global Administrative Law Perspective', 44 *New York University Journal of International Law and Policy* 1279 (2011–2012), p. 1290.

149 CAO Operational Guidelines 2.2.1.

150 Benjamin M. Saper, 'The International Finance Corporation's Compliance Advisor/Ombudsman (CAO): An Examination of Accountability and Effectiveness from a Global Administrative Law Perspective', 44 *New York University Journal of International Law and Policy* 1279 (2011–2012), p. 1291.

151 Elisa Morgera, 'Human Rights Dimensions of Corporate Environmental Accountability', *in* Pierre-Marie Dupuy, Francesco Francioni and Ernst-Ulrich Petersmann (eds), *Human Rights in International Investment Law and Arbitration*, Oxford: Oxford University Press (2009), p. 519.

152 Ibid., p. 520.

CAO Compliance conducts audits of the IFC and MIGA and checks whether they have adhered to their own policies, for example the policy requiring IFC and MIGA clients to ensure that their project is in line with eight IFC Performance Standards, most of which are of relevance from a human rights perspective, before they can be eligible for funding.[153] Audits can be triggered in three different ways. First, an audit can be requested by the President of the World Bank Group or senior management of the IFC and MIGA. Second, it can be requested by the CAO Vice-President. Third, and more importantly for our purpose, it is triggered when, following a complaint to the CAO Ombudsman, the issues raised before the Ombudsman have not been solved. In that case, if the CAO Compliance audit concludes that relevant policies were adhered to, the case is closed, irrespective of whether the project actually adversely impacted or continues to impact the local population. In that sense, it is in the complainants' interests that the dispute is solved at the first stage, that of the CAO Ombudsman. That first stage is therefore important. It permits the conclusion that the IFC CAO mechanism is more effective than the World Bank Inspection Panel mechanism. As seen, the only option for the Panel is to check whether policies were adhered to. In the case that they were, the process ends. The CAO will also end the process if it finds that policies were adhered to, but will do so only in the second stage, if the conciliation phase has failed. In other words, prior to being dealt with by CAO Compliance, the CAO Ombudsman must have heard the grievances and attempted to address them in some way, even if no specific policies were violated. Following the audit, if CAO Compliance finds that policies were not followed, it

> will keep the compliance investigation open and monitor the situation until actions taken by IFC/MIGA assure CAO that IFC/MIGA is addressing the noncompliance. CAO will then close the compliance investigation. CAO makes public the current status of all compliance cases.[154]

At this point, the system reaches its limit. Besides leaving the case open, the CAO cannot do anything. For example, in the case of the Mozal project in

153 The Performance Standards are as follows: Performance Standard 1: Assessment and Management of Environmental and Social Risks and Impacts; Performance Standard 2: Labor and Working Conditions; Performance Standard 3: Resource Efficiency and Pollution Prevention; Performance Standard 4: Community Health, Safety, and Security; Performance Standard 5: Land Acquisition and Involuntary Resettlement; Performance Standard 6: Biodiversity Conservation and Sustainable Management of Living Natural Resources; Performance Standard 7: Indigenous Peoples; Performance Standard 8: Cultural Heritage. See *IFC Performance Standards on Environmental and Social Sustainability*, 1 January 2012, www.ifc.org/wps/wcm/connect/115482804a0255 db96fbffd1a5d13d27/PS_English_2012_Full-Document.pdf?MOD=AJPERES (last accessed 15 June 2016).
154 CAO Operational Guidelines, 4.4.6.

Mozambique, NGOs had complained to the CAO Ombudsman about the repercussions on human health of an aluminium smelter operated by the global mining company BHP Billiton. No agreement was reached in the first phase and the case went before CAO Compliance. In the audit, CAO Compliance concluded that the IFC had violated some of its policies. The IFC's response to the audit reads as follows: 'IFC acknowledges the CAO's view' but 'believes that staff took reasonable and timely actions consistent with policies and procedures',[155] which seems to have ended the discussion. Beyond keeping the case open, and since the IFC disagrees with its conclusion, the CAO cannot proceed further. This is not to say that such negative outcomes are systematic. In another case related to investments in the palm oil industry in Indonesia, a finding that the IFC had not complied with its own policies prompted a positive outcome. After officially acknowledging shortcomings,[156] the IFC changed its strategy regarding the palm oil industry and is now actively committed to finding solutions that will satisfy both the industry and the local populations. While this remains a controversial topic, the positive attitude of the IFC has prompted CAO Compliance to close the case.[157]

While far from constituting mechanisms to establish whether the World Bank and the IFC have complied with their human rights obligations under international law, the Inspection Panel and the CAO mechanism nevertheless contribute to the integration of human rights considerations in the work of these organisations.[158] These mechanisms fit into a discussion on the corporate accountability gap and international efforts to bridge it because they shed light on some human rights violations arising out of business operations and may contribute to preventing some of them.

## Conclusion

This chapter has highlighted the various points of tension between human rights and international investment and international trade law. These areas of law are at times said to have developed in isolation from other areas of international law, including international human rights law. Things have started to change, with human rights being integrated into model BITs or

---

155 IFC Response to CAO Audit of IFC investments in Mozal, Mozambique (C-I-R4-YI2-F156), 13 March 2013, p. 1.

156 Final IFC Management Group Response to CAO's Audit Report on Wilmar, 4 August 2009, p. 1.

157 Monitoring and Closure Report: IFC's response to the CAO Audit of IFC's Investments in Wilmar Trading (IFC No. 20348), Delta-Wilmar CIS (IFC No. 24644), Wilmar WCap (IFC No. 25532) and Delta-Wilmar CIS Expansion (IFC No. 26271), 27 March 2013.

158 For an early commentary on this see Dinah Shelton, 'Protecting Human Rights in a Globalized World', 25 *Boston College International and Comparative Law Review* 273 (2002), p. 290. For a detailed analysis of these accountability mechanisms, see Caitlin Daniel, Kristen Genovese, Mariëtte van Huijstee and Sarah Singh (eds), *Glass Half Full? The State of Accountability in Development Finance*, Amsterdam: SOMO (January 2016).

considered by relevant organisations' accountability mechanisms. Much more remains to be done, however, to give human rights a more prominent role within investment and trade law and policies, and to enhance corporate accountability in those areas. Soft law initiatives developed in recent years encourage states to work harder on this, as well as other areas of business and human rights. These developments are analysed in detail in Chapter 7.

## Bibliography

### *Books*

Brummer, Chris, *Soft Law and the Global Financial System. Rule Making in the 21st Century*, Cambridge: Cambridge University Press (2012).

Dolzer, Rudolf and Schreuer, Christoph, *Principles of International Investment Law*, Oxford: Oxford University Press (2008).

Harrison, James, *The Human Rights Impact of the World Trade Organisation*, Oxford and Portland: Hart Publishing (2007).

Hestermeyer, Holger, *Human Rights and the WTO. The Case of Patents and Access to Medicine*, Oxford: Oxford University Press (2007).

Joseph, Sarah, *Blame It on the WTO*, Oxford: Oxford University Press (2011).

McBeth, Adam, *International Economic Actors and Human Rights*, London and New York: Routledge (2010).

Ruggie, John Gerard, *Just Business*, New York and London: W. W. Norton and Company Ltd (2013).

Skogly, Sigrun, *Human Rights Obligations of the World Bank and the International Monetary Fund*, London and Sydney: Cavendish Publishing (2001).

### *Journal articles*

Alston, Philip, 'Core Human Rights and the Transformation of the International Labour Rights Regime', 15 *European Journal of International Law* 457 (2004).

Baker, Mark B. 'Flying over the Judicial Hump: A Human Rights Drama featuring Burma, the Commonwealth of Massachusetts, the WTO and the Federal Courts', 32 *Law and Policy in International Business* 51.

Bal, Salman, 'International Free Trade Agreements and Human Rights: Reinterpreting Article XX of the GATT', 10 *Minnesota Journal of Global Trade* 62 (2001).

Basu, Kaushik, 'Compacts, Conventions and Codes: Initiatives for Higher International Labor Standards', 34 *Cornell International Law Journal* 487 (2001).

Bhagwati, Jagdish, 'The Boundaries of the WTO. Afterword: The Question of Linkage', 96 *American Journal of International Law* 126 (2002).

Blackett, Adelle, 'Whither Social Clause? Human Rights, Trade Theory and Treaty Interpretation', 31 *Columbia Human Rights Law Review* 1 (1999).

Carrascott, Enrique R. and Guernsey, Alison K., 'The World Bank's Inspection Panel: Promoting True Accountability Through Arbitration', 41 *Cornell International Law Journal* 577 (2008).

Dowell-Jones, Mary and Kinley, David, 'Minding the Gap: Global Finance and Human Rights', 25 *Ethics & International Affairs* 183 (2011).

Fry, James D., 'International Human Rights Law in Investment Arbitration: Evidence of International Law's Unity', 18 *Duke Journal of Comparative & International Law* 77 (2007–2008).

Henin, Paula F., 'The Jurisdiction of Investment Treaty Tribunals over Investors' Human Rights Claims: The Case Against Roussalis v. Romania', 51 *Columbia Journal of Transnational Law* 224 (2012–2013).

Kobrin, Stephen J., 'The MAI and the Clash of Globalizations', *Foreign Policy* (Fall 1998).

Lalive, Pierre, 'Ordre public transnational (ou réellement international) et arbitrage international', *Revue de l'arbitrage* (1986) No. 3, p. 329.

Leader, Sheldon, 'Human Rights, Risks, and New Strategies for Global Investment', 9 *Journal of International Economic Law* 657 (2006).

Levine, Eugenia, 'Amicus Curiae in International Investment Arbitration: The Implications of an Increase in Third-Party Participation', 29 *Berkeley Journal of International Law* 200 (2011).

Macleod, Sorcha and Lewis, Douglas, 'Transnational Corporations: Power, Influence and Responsibility', 4 *Global Social Policy* 77 (2004).

Nichols, Philip M., 'Trade Without Values', 90 *Northwestern University Law Review* 658 (1995–1996).

Petersmann, Ernst-Ulrich, 'Time for a United Nations "Global Compact" for Integrating Human Rights into the Law of Worldwide Organizations: Lessons from European Integration', 13 *European Journal of International Law* 621 (2002).

Poitevin, Arnaud, 'Des "prérequis" pour la levée de fonds sur les marchés internationaux: les normes environnementales et sociales des institutions financières internationales et leurs sanctions', 142 *Journal du droit international* 527 (2015).

Saper, Benjamin M., 'The International Finance Corporation's Compliance Advisor/Ombudsman (CAO): an Examination of Accountability and Effectiveness from a Global Administrative Law Perspective', 44 *New York University Journal of International Law and Policy* 1279 (2011–2012).

Schwebel, Stephen, 'The Overwhelming Merits of Bilateral Investment Treaties', 32 *Suffolk Transnational Law Review* 263 (2008–2009).

Shelton, Dinah, 'Protecting Human Rights in a Globalized World', 25 *Boston College International and Comparative Law Review* 273 (2002).

Supnik, Kate M., 'Making Amends: Amending the ICSID Convention to Reconcile Competing Interests in International Investment Law' 59 *Duke Law Journal* 343 (2009–2010).

Weiler, Todd, 'Balancing Human Rights and Investor Protection: A New Approach for a Different Legal Order', 27 *Boston College International and Comparative Law Review* 429 (2004).

Wouters, Jan and Hachez, Nicolas, 'When Rules and Values Collide: How can a Balanced Application of Investor Protection Provisions and Human Rights be Insured?', 3 *Human Rights and International Legal Discourse* 301 (2009).

**Book chapters**

Alston, Philip, 'The 'Not-a-Cat' Syndrome: Can the International Human Rights Regime Accommodate Non-State Actors?', *in* Philip Alston (ed.), *Non State Actors and Human Rights*, Oxford: Oxford University Press (2005), pp. 3–36.

Dumberry, Patrick, 'Corporate Investors' International Legal Personality and their Accountability for Human Rights Violations under International Investment Agreements', *in* Armand de Mestral and Céline Lévesque (eds), *Improving International Investment Agreements*, Abington: Routledge (2013), pp. 179–194.

Dupuy, Pierre-Marie, 'Unification Rather than Fragmentation of International Law? The Case of International Investment Law and Human Rights Law', *in* Pierre-Marie Dupuy, Francesco Francioni and Ernst-Ulrich Petersmann (eds), *Human Rights in International Investment Law and Arbitration*, Oxford: Oxford University Press (2009), pp. 45–62.

Francioni, Francesco, 'Access to Justice, Denial of Justice and International Investment Law', *in* Pierre-Marie Dupuy, Francesco Francioni and Ernst-Ulrich Petersmann (eds), *Human Rights in International Investment Law and Arbitration*, Oxford: Oxford University Press (2009), pp. 63–81.

Gianviti, François, 'Economic, Social, and Cultural Human Rights and the International Monetary Fund', *in* Philip Alston (ed.), *Non State Actors and Human Rights*, Oxford: Oxford University Press (2005), pp. 113–138.

Hirsch, Moshe, 'Investment Tribunals and Human Rights: Divergent Paths', *in* Pierre-Marie Dupuy, Francesco Francioni and Ernst-Ulrich Petersmann (eds), *Human Rights in International Investment Law and Arbitration*, Oxford: Oxford University Press (2009), pp. 97–114.

Leader, Sheldon, 'Human Rights and International Trade', *in* Scott Sheeran and Sir Nigel Rodley (eds), *Routledge Handbook of International Human Rights Law*, Abingdon and New York: Routledge (2013), pp. 245–262.

Leader, Sheldon, 'Project Finance and Human Rights', *in* Juan Pablo Bohoslavsky and Jernej Letnar Černič (eds), *Making Sovereign Financing and Human Rights Work*, Oxford: Hart Publishing, (2014), pp. 199–212.

Morgera, Elisa, 'Human Rights Dimensions of Corporate Environmental Accountability', *in* Pierre-Marie Dupuy, Francesco Francioni and Ernst-Ulrich Petersmann (eds), *Human Rights in International Investment Law and Arbitration*, Oxford: Oxford University Press (2009), pp. 511–524.

Muchlinski, Peter T., 'International Finance and Investment and Human Rights', *in* Scott Sheeran and Sir Nigel Rodley (eds), *Routledge Handbook of International Human Rights Law*, Abingdon and New York: Routledge (2013), pp. 263–284.

Reiner, Clara, and Schreuer, Christoph, 'Human Rights and International Investment Arbitration', in Pierre-Marie Dupuy, Francesco Francioni and Ernst-Ulrich Petersmann (eds), *Human Rights in International Investment Law and Arbitration*, Oxford: Oxford University Press (2009), pp. 82–96.

Treakle, Kay, Fox, Jonathan and Clark, Dana, 'Lessons Learned', *in* Dana Clark, Jonathan Fox and Kay Treakle (eds), *Demanding Accountability. Civil Society Claims and the World Bank Inspection Panel*, Lanham, Boulder, New York, Oxford: Rowman & Littlefield Publishers (2003), pp. 247–277.

Waincymer, Jeff, 'The Trade and Human Rights Debate: Introduction to an Interdisciplinary Analysis', *in* Sarah Joseph, David Kinley and Jeff Waincymer (eds), *The World Trade Organization and Human Rights. Interdisciplinary Perspectives*, Cheltenham: Edward Elgar (2009), pp. 1–38.

Woll, Cornelia 'Global Companies as Agenda Setters in the World Trade Organization', *in* John Mikler (ed.), *The Handbook of Global Companies*, Chichester: John Wiley and Sons Ltd (2013), pp. 257–271.

Wouters, Jan, Duquet, Sanderijn and Hachez, Nicolas, 'International Investment Law: The Perpetual Search for Consensus', *in* Olivier De Schutter, Johan Swinnen and Jan Wouters (eds), *Foreign Direct Investment and Human Development. The Law and Economics of International Investment Agreements*, Routledge (2013), pp. 25–69.

## Statutes

1996 Mass. Acts 239, ch. 130.

## Treaties

Convention of the International Centre for Settlement of Investment Disputes (1965), 575 UNTS 159.

Vienna Convention on the Law of Treaties (1969), 1155 UNTS 331.

Agreement on Government Procurement (1994), 1915 UNTS. 103.

## Official documents

Panel Resolution, Resolution IBRD 93–1 (1993).

Singapore Declaration (1996), WT/MIN(96)/DEC.

NAFTA Free Trade Commission, Statement of the Free Trade Commission on Non-Disputing Party Participation (2003).

Committee on Economic, Social and Cultural Rights, General Comment No. 15 (2003), The Right to Water (Articles 11 and 12 of the International Covenant on Economic, Social and Cultural Rights), E/C.12/2002/11, 20 January 2003.

EU Council Regulation (EC) No 1236/2005 of 27 June 2005 concerning trade in certain goods which could be used for capital punishment, torture or other cruel, inhuman or degrading treatment or punishment.

World Bank, OP 4.10 – Indigenous Peoples (2005).

Report of the Special Rapporteur on the Right to Food, UN Doc. E/CN.4/2006/44, 16 March 2006.

Report of the Study Group of the International Law Commission, 'Difficulties arising from the diversification and expansion of international law', UN Doc. A/CN.4/L.682 (2006).

ICSID Convention, Regulation and Rules, ICSID/15 (2006).

Committee on Economic, Social and Cultural Rights, General Comment No. 19 on the Right to Social Security (Article 9 of the Covenant), E/C.12/GC/19, 4 February 2008.

Final IFC Management Group Response to CAO's Audit Report on Wilmar, 4 August 2009.

'Principles for Responsible Contracts: Integrating the Management of Human Rights Risks into State-Investor Contract Negotiations: Guidance for Negotiators', UN Document A/HRC/17/31/Add.3 (25 May 2011).

*IFC Performance Standards on Environmental and Social Sustainability*, 1 January 2012, www.ifc.org/wps/wcm/connect/115482804a0255db96fbffd1a5d13d27/PS_English_2012_Full-Document.pdf?MOD=AJPERES (last accessed 15 June 2016).

US Model Bilateral Investment Treaty (2012), available on the United States Department of State website at www.state.gov/documents/organization/188371.pdf (last accessed 21 March 2016).

Supplemental Brief for the United States as Amicus Curiae in Partial Support of Affirmance, *Kiobel v. Royal Dutch Petroleum Co.*, 133 S.Ct. 1659 (2013) (No. 10-1491).

CAO Operational Guidelines (2013).

IFC Response to CAO Audit of IFC investments in Mozal, Mozambique (C-I-R4-YI2-F156), 13 March 2013.

Monitoring and Closure Report: IFC's response to the CAO Audit of IFC's Investments in Wilmar Trading (IFC No. 20348), Delta-Wilmar CIS (IFC No. 24644), Wilmar WCap (IFC No. 25532) and Delta-Wilmar CIS Expansion (IFC No. 26271), 27 March 2013.

United Nations Conference on Trade and Development, *World Investment Report*, July 2015.

Agreement between the Government of Canada and the Government of the United Republic of Tanzania for the Promotion and Reciprocal Protection of Investments, available on the Government of Canada's website, www.international.gc.ca/trade-agreements-accords-commerciaux/agr-acc/fipa-apie/tanzania-text-tanzanie.aspx?lang=eng (last accessed 21 March 2016).

## Cases and opinions

*The Creole v Great Britain* (1853), Reports of International Arbitral Awards, Volume XXIX, p. 26.

*L. F. H. Neer and Pauline Neer (U.S.A.) v United Mexican States* (1926), Reports of International Arbitral Awards, Vol. IV, p. 60.

*James and Others v United Kingdom*, [1986] 8 EHRR 123.

*Guardian and Observer v United Kingdom*, [1991] 14 EHRR 153.

*Pine Valley Development Ltd and Others v Ireland*, [1992] 14 EHRR 319.

*Citizens United v Federal Election Commission*, 558 U.S. 310 (2010).

*S.M. v Barbados* [1994], CCPR/C/50/D/502/1992.

*ICC Award No. 1110 of 1963, Yearbook of Commercial Arbitration*, 1996, p. 52.

*Lamagna v Australia* [1997], CCPR/C/65/D/737/1997.

*Crosby, Secretary of Administration and Finance of Massachusetts, et al. v National Foreign Trade Council* 530 U.S. 363 (2000).

WTO Panel Report, United States—Measure Affecting Government Procurement, WT/DS 88 and DS 95, terminated on 11 February 2000.

*Metalclad Corporation v United Mexican States*, International Centre for the Settlement of Investment Disputes, No. ARB(AF)/97/1 (2000).

*Compañía del Desarrollo de Santa Elena S.A. v The Republic of Costa Rica*, International Centre for the Settlement of Investment Disputes, Case No. ARB/96/1 (2000).

*Lauder v The Czech Republic* (2001), UNCITRAL.

African Commission on Human and People's Rights, 155/96: *Social and Economic Rights Action Center (SERAC) and Center for Economic and Social Rights (CESR) v Nigeria*, 27 October 2001.

*Cantos v Argentina*, Preliminary objections, IACHR Series C no 85, [2001] IACHR 15.

*Methanex Corp. v United States*, Decision of the Tribunal on Petitions from Third Persons to Intervene as Amici Curiae (2001), UNCITRAL.

*United Parcel Service of America v Canada*, Decision of the Tribunal on Petitions for Intervention and Participation as Amici Curiae (2001), UNCITRAL.

*Mondev International Limited v United States of America*, International Centre for the Settlement of Investment Disputes, ARB (AF)/99/2 (2002).

*Tecnicas Medioambientales Tecmed S.A. v The United Mexican States*, International Centre for the Settlement of Investment Disputes, ARB (AF)/00/2 (2003).

*CMS Gas Transmission Company v The Argentine Republic*, International Centre for the Settlement of Investment Disputes, ARB/01/8 (2005).

*Glamis Gold v United States*, Decision on Application and Submission by Quechan Indian Nation, (2005), UNCITRAL.

*Aguas del Tunari SA v Republic of Bolivia*, International Centre for the Settlement of Investment Disputes, ARB/02/3 (2005).

*Aguas Argentinas, S.A., Suez, Sociedad General de Aguas de Barcelona, S.A. and Vivendi Universal, S.A. v The Argentine Republic*, International Centre for the Settlement of Investment Disputes, ARB/03/19, Order in Response to a Petition for Transparency and Participation as Amicus Curiae (2005).

*Saluka Investments BV v The Czech Republic* (2006), UNCITRAL.

*Azurix Corp. v the Argentine Republic*, International Centre for the Settlement of Investment Disputes, ARB/01/12 (2006).

*Siemens A.G. v The Argentine Republic*, International Centre for the Settlement of Investment Disputes, ARB/02/8 (2007).

*Sempra Energy International v The Argentine Republic*, International Centre for the Settlement of Investment Disputes, ARB/02/16 (2007).

*Biwater Gauff (Tanzania) Ltd. v United Republic of Tanzania*, International Centre for the Settlement of Investment Disputes, ARB/05/22, Procedural Order No. 5 (2007).

*AES Summit Generation Ltd. and AES-Tisza Erömü Kft. v Republic of Hungary*, International Centre for the Settlement of Investment Disputes, ARB/07/22 (2010).

*Occidental Petroleum Corporation Occidental Exploration and Production Company v The Republic of Ecuador*, International Centre for the Settlement of Investment Disputes, ARB/06/11 (2012).

Opinion 2/13 of the Court of Justice of the European Union, 18 December 2014.

## Miscellaneous

Avery, Christopher, *Business and Human Rights at a Time of Change* (1999), chapter 2.8, http://198.170.85.29/Chapter2.htm#2.8 (last accessed 15 June 2016).

Daniel, Caitlin, Genovese, Kristen, van Huijstee, Mariëtte and Singh, Sarah (eds), *Glass Half Full? The State of Accountability in Development Finance*, Amsterdam: SOMO (January 2016).

de Lotbinière McDougall, Andrew and Santens, Ank, 'ICSID Tribunals Apply New Rules on Amicus Curiae', White and Case LLP, March 2007.

London School of Economics Investment & Human Rights Learning Hub, http://blogs.lse.ac.uk/investment-and-human-rights/ (last accessed 21 March 2016).

Orellana, M., Baños, S. and Berger, T., *Bringing Community Perspectives to Investor-State Arbitration: the Pac Rim Case*, London: IIED (2015).

Titi, Catharine, 'The Evolving BIT: A Commentary on Canada's Model Agreement', (26 June 2013), International Institute for Sustainable Development, www.iisd.org/itn/2013/06/26/the-evolving-bit-a-commentary-on-canadas-model-agreement/ (last accessed 21 March 2016).

Transatlantic Trade and Investment Partnership, Business and Human Rights Resource Centre, http://business-humanrights.org/en/transatlantic-trade-and-investment-partnership-ttip-background-commentaries-on-social-environmental-impacts-0 (last accessed 21 March 2016).

Vis-Dunbar, Damon, 'Norway Shelves its Draft Model Bilateral Investment Treaty', 8 June 2009, International Institute For Sustainable Development.

World Bank, *Accountability at the World Bank. The Inspection Panel at 15 Years* (2009).

# 7 International soft law initiatives on business and human rights

The two previous chapters have highlighted the limitations of the current international legal framework regarding business and human rights. This chapter leaves international law strictly speaking to the side and focuses on soft law initiatives which have blossomed in this field in the past few decades. Because of their non-binding, recommendatory nature, these initiatives go hand in hand with self-regulation, which is covered in the next chapter on private modes of regulation.

When the United Nations began developing standards of behaviour for multinational corporations in the 1970s, business and human rights was not a discrete field of study. Instead, the UN focused on the regulation of foreign direct investment, which included the regulation of multinational corporations, in human rights and other fields, as well as host states' obligations regarding the treatment of foreign investors. The scope was therefore wider than simply 'business and human rights'. By contrast, current business and human rights initiatives are narrow in scope. Nowadays, the treatment of foreign investors and corporations' human rights responsibilities tend to be considered separately, and have led to the development of distinct regulatory frameworks. This is perhaps for the best given that, as seen in this chapter, the former was always more problematic. On the negative side, while it is possible to separate the two questions, this leads to a somewhat artificial divide. Although they overlap considerably, international investment law and the international regulation of multinational corporations in the human rights field have evolved separately. By looking at investment law and the international regulation of multinational corporations in two different chapters, the structure of this book reflects the divide – as artificial as it may be.[1]

International regulation of business in the human rights field is growing and this chapter cannot give an exhaustive list of all the existing initiatives in the area. Rather, it aims to present the main features of the global

---

1  A large part of Chapter 6 was on international investment law, while this chapter is on business and human rights regulation. On the divide, see Seymour J. Rubin, 'Harmonization of Rules: A Perspective on the UN Commission on Transnational Corporations', 8 *Law and Policy International in Business* 875 (1976), p. 882.

governance of business in the area of human rights, to place them in their historical context and to discuss the extent to which they are bridging the corporate accountability gap at the international level.

## Drafting codes of conduct in the 1970s: confrontation and the New International Economic Order

The 1970s constitute a turning point in the business and human rights field. Before that, and although corporate human rights violations were far from uncommon, there was little awareness of public opinions in the developed world about the adverse impacts of Western corporations in the developing world. The 1970s were a time of great change marked by a series of crises, scandals and conflicts which had a profound influence in the West: the oil crisis; the ensuing economic crisis; the wave of expropriation of Western foreign capital from developing countries; the end of the fixed exchange rates system; the Watergate scandal; the coup against the democratically elected President of Chile, Salvador Allende; the Arab–Israeli War; and the eventual retreat of US troops from Vietnam, to name but a few. In the United States, US multinational company ITT's role in the Chilean coup that led to the dictatorship of Augusto Pinochet prompted the creation of a committee, chaired by Senator Church, within the US Senate Foreign Relations Committee. During its three years of existence the Church Committee documented dozens of accounts of corruption and ill-behaviour of US multinationals around the world. At the same time the US Securities and Exchange Commission also investigated corporate misconduct abroad. All this led to a legislative response in the United States, with the adoption of the controversial Foreign Corrupt Practices Act, and also to an embryonic change in corporate culture. This change was limited and most of its corporate advocates favoured self-regulation rather than legislation. Despite these limitations, the 1970s mark the beginning of discussions on corporate social responsibility as a concept of relevance to modern global business.[2]

In parallel the United Nations intensified its work on the adverse impacts of multinational corporations and on issues of business and human rights, although they were not named as such at the time. In the 1960s the UN had focused its attention on foreign direct investment, on its role in development and on the concept of permanent sovereignty over natural resources.[3] This was a time when the global corporation, as we now know it, was starting to thrive.[4] The feeling among newly independent states, organised in the Group

2   For a fascinating account of these changes and developments, see Tagi Sagafi-Nejad and John Dunning, *The UN and Transnational Corporations. From Code of Conduct to Global Compact*, Bloomington and Indianapolis: Indiana University Press (2008), pp. 41–49.
3   UN General Assembly Resolution 1803 (XVII) Permanent Sovereignty over natural resources.
4   See an early analysis of multinational corporations by George W. Ball, 'Cosmocorp: The Importance of Being Stateless', 2 *Columbia Journal of World Business* 25 (1967).

of 77, which by then were forming a majority in the UN General Assembly and could often count on the support of the Socialist bloc, was that while they had gained political independence, they were still under the economic domination of former colonial powers. The growing presence of foreign multinationals constituted a visible illustration of the situation and there was particular concern among host countries about home countries' extraterritorial regulation of the corporations domiciled in their territories.[5] The goal of newly independent developing countries was therefore to achieve true independence that would encompass economic aspects, and they sought to achieve this through the adoption of UN General Assembly resolutions calling for the creation of a New International Economic Order[6] and the adoption of a Charter of Economic Rights and Duties of States.[7] These landmark resolutions challenge, and propose ways to address, economic inequalities between developing and developed countries. The tone of the day was confrontational, and developing countries' claims included for example their absolute right to control the investment activities of multinational corporations on their territories.[8]

It is in this context that the UN work on multinational corporations became more specific, especially after the UN Economic and Social Council (hereinafter ECOSOC) adopted a 'pivotal'[9] resolution in 1972, in which they cited the following extract on multinational corporations from the 1971 UN World Economic Survey:

> While these corporations are frequently effective agents for the transfer of technology as well as capital to developing countries, their role is sometimes viewed with awe, since their size and power surpass the host country's entire economy. The international community has yet to formulate a positive policy and establish machinery for dealing with the issues raised by the activities of these corporations.[10]

Having noted the dearth of guidance in this area, the ECOSOC requested the Secretary-General to appoint 'from the public and private sectors (...) a study group of eminent persons (...) to study the role of multinational corporations and their impact on the process of development (...) and also

---

5   Stephan Coonrod, 'The United Nations Code of Conduct for Transnational Corporations', 18 *Harvard International Law Journal* 273 (1977), pp. 282–285.
6   UN General Assembly Resolutions 3201 (S-VI) and 3202 (S-VI), 1 May 1974.
7   UN General Assembly Resolution 3281 (XXIX) Charter of Economic Rights and Duties of States, 12 December 1974.
8   Ibid., Article 2(2)(a).
9   Tagi Sagafi-Nejad and John Dunning, *The UN and Transnational Corporations. From Code of Conduct to Global Compact*, Bloomington and Indianapolis: Indiana University Press (2008), p. 52.
10  UN Department of Economic and Social Affairs, *World Economic Survey 1971, Current Economic Developments*, UN Doc. E/5144 (1972), p. 10.

their implications for international relations'.[11] The Group of Eminent Persons met several times in 1973 and 1974 and used a UN Department of Economic and Social Affairs (hereinafter DESA) report on Multinational Corporations in World Development as a background document for their discussions.[12] The report was groundbreaking in a variety of ways.[13] For the purpose of this book, two aspects deserve closer attention. First, the report points to what is still one of the key issues in the business and human rights field:

> Despite the considerable and transnational power which multinational corporations possess they, unlike governments, are not directly accountable for their policies and actions to a broadly based electorate. Nor, unlike purely national firms, are the multinational corporations subject to control and regulation by a single authority which can aim at ensuring a maximum degree of harmony between their operations and the public interest. The question at issue, therefore, is whether a set of institutions and devices can be worked out which will guide the multinational corporations' exercise of power and *introduce some form of accountability to the international community* into their activities.[14]

Although the report is several decades old, this should still feel familiar to the contemporary observer. As further discussed in this chapter, interrogations of how to 'introduce some form of accountability' for multinational corporations at the international level remain a common feature of business and human rights as a field.

Second, the report suggests the elaboration of a 'broad international code of conduct'[15] for multinational corporations, a task that occupied the United Nations for decades, until the adoption of the UN Guiding Principles in 2011. At the time the report was written, only one document fitting into the

11   ECOSOC Resolution 1721 (LIII), 1972 in UN Doc. E/5209, p. 4. Resolution 1721's title is 'The impact of multinational corporations on the development process and on international relations'.

12   This is described in the Group of Eminent Persons' final report, *The Impact of Multinational Corporations on the Development Process and on International Relations*, UN Doc. E/5500/Add.1 (Part I) (24 May 1974) 13 ILM. 800 (1974), pp. 801–802. The report's reference is: UN DESA, *Multinational Corporations in World Development*, UN Doc. ST/ECA/190 (1973).

13   For a useful summary of the report's main points, see Tagi Sagafi-Nejad and John Dunning, *The UN and Transnational Corporations. From Code of Conduct to Global Compact*, Bloomington and Indianapolis: Indiana University Press (2008), pp. 59–64.

14   UN DESA, *Multinational Corporations in World Development* UN Doc. ST/ECA/190 (1973), p. 2. Emphasis added. The report also states: 'Many will agree that some measure of accountability of multinational corporations to the international community should be introduced' (p. 3).

15   UN DESA, Multinational Corporations in World Development UN Doc. ST/ECA/190 (1973), p. 102.

category of a code of conduct for multinational corporations existed: the International Chamber of Commerce's Guidelines for International Investment.[16] The International Confederation of Free Trade Unions had approved the idea of a code in 1969 but had not made progress on its actual development.[17]

In the course of their work, and not unlike the actions of the UN Secretary-General Special Representative on Business and Human Rights during his six-year mandate (2005–2011) that led to the adoption of the UN Guiding Principles, the Group of Eminent Persons held a series of hearings and called for statements from academics, representatives of the business sector, NGOs and governments from all over the world. Senior business executives of companies such as Fiat, Exxon, IBM, Nestlé, Pfizer, Rio Tinto, Royal Dutch Petroleum, Siemens and Unilever testified before the group.[18] The majority of these executives supported the idea of a code of conduct.[19]

Following consultations, the Group of Eminent Persons produced a report entitled *The Impact of Multinational Corporations on the Development Process and on International Relations.* The report suggests developing a code of conduct for multinationals, explaining that such codes, 'although they are not compulsory in character, (...) act as an instrument of moral persuasion, strengthened by the authority of international organizations and the support of public opinion'.[20]

The report was not limited to a discussion on a code and the Group of Eminent Persons embraced a holistic approach. In the report the Group analysed the role of multinational corporations, their relationships with home and host states, how they fit into the international economic system, how they impacted host states' economies and communities and how they could better contribute to development. The report also pointed to the limits of corporate self-regulation and to the need for government regulation.[21] Although the phrase 'human rights' is barely mentioned in their report, the protection of human rights as well as social justice seems to have informed the Group's approach.[22]

16 The labour policies of the Guidelines are reprinted in David H. Blake, 'International Labor and the Regulation of Multinational Corporations: Proposals and Prospects', 11 *San Diego Law Review* 179 (1973–1974), p. 203.
17 On this see ibid., pp. 195–197.
18 DESA, Summary of the Hearings Before the Group of Eminent Persons to Study the Impact of Multinational Corporations on Development and on International Relations, UN Doc. ST/ESA/15, pp. iii–iv.
19 Ibid., pp. 34–35, 37; 42, 59, 69, 117, 122, 150, 155, 186, 283, 299–300, 308, 384, 416, 443, 445, 455.
20 Group of Eminent Persons' final report, The Impact of Multinational Corporations on the Development Process and on International Relations, UN Doc. E/5500/Add.1 (Part I) (24 May 1974) 13 ILM 800 1974, p. 833.
21 Ibid, pp. 810–812.
22 See ibid. p. 816.

The Group of Eminent Persons also recommended the creation of institutions to deal with these questions within the UN. This led to the creation of the inter-governmental Commission on Transnational Corporations (CTNC) and the Centre on Transnational Corporations, whose task was to carry out research and gather information on TNCs.[23] Both institutions were set up in 1974.[24] At its first session in March 1975, the Commission on Transnational Corporations decided to make the drafting of a code of conduct its priority for the years to come.[25] The Commission started to work on this within the above-mentioned context of tensions between developing and developed states on economic matters. These tensions had surfaced on various occasions before, as other organisations had also been drafting similar instruments.

At the regional level, two initiatives stood out: the OECD Guidelines for Multinational Enterprises and Decision 24 of the Commission of the Cartagena Agreement. The Organisation for Economic Cooperation and Development (OECD), whose membership was developed, home countries, adopted the first version of the OECD Guidelines on Multinational Enterprises in 1976 after several years of work.[26] The current version of the Guidelines is much more sophisticated than the 1976 version and, as shown in detail below, remains one of the main instruments in the business and human rights field. For now suffice it to note, as one author did shortly after the adoption of the Guidelines, that 'the fact that even the relatively homogeneous OECD was unwilling or unable to develop a legally-binding document suggests the difficulties proponents of a mandatory U.N. code (…) [were going to] face within the more heterogeneous'[27] Commission on Transnational Corporations.

Another regional development was the adoption by the Commission of the Cartagena Agreement of a Common Regime of Treatment of Foreign Capital and of Trademarks, Patents, Licenses, and Royalties, also known as Decision 24.[28] Decision 24, adopted in 1970, aimed to ensure that foreign direct investment in Latin America would be authorised only if the proposed investment was to further development goals. This Code did play a role in channelling investment but was never a complete success.[29]

23   Ibid. pp. 830–832.
24   ECOSOC Resolution 1913 (LVII), December 1974; ECOSOC Resolution 1908 (LVII), December 1974.
25   Commission on Transnational Corporations, Report on the First Session, E/5655 and Corr. 1; E/C.10/6 and Corr.1 and Add.1.
26   Daniel J. Plaine, 'The OECD Guidelines for Multinational Enterprises', 11 *International Lawyer* 339 (1977), p. 340.
27   Stephan Coonrod, 'The United Nations Code of Conduct for Transnational Corporations', 18 *Harvard International Law Journal* 273 (1977), p. 289.
28   Translated and reprinted in 10 *International Legal Materials* 152 (1971). At the time the Andean Pact (which came into existence with the signing of the Cartagena Agreement in 1969) had five member states: Bolivia, Chile, Colombia, Ecuador and Peru.
29   Stephan Coonrod, 'The United Nations Code of Conduct for Transnational Corporations', 18 *Harvard International Law Journal* 273 (1977), p. 292.

Some organisations developed narrow codes of conduct focusing on certain areas only, as opposed to comprehensive codes covering all aspects of multinational corporations' activities. For example, the UN Conference on Trade and Development (UNCTAD) focused on transfer of technology and restrictive business practices.[30] In 1977 the International Labour Organisation adopted the Tripartite Declaration of Principles Concerning Multinational Enterprises and Social Policy, which focuses on areas of relevance to the ILO such as working conditions and industrial relations.[31]

When the UN Commission on Transnational Corporations initiated its work on the Code of Conduct, it was therefore in a position to draw upon a considerable amount of work that had been conducted beforehand in other fora. This did not necessarily facilitate the work of the Commission as past efforts in the area had revealed tensions and points of disagreement, especially between capital-exporting and capital-importing countries. The Commission summarised the task at hand in a document entitled 'Issues Involved in the Formulation of a Code of Conduct':[32]

> [a] primary decision concerns the code's precise purposes; a second concerns the actors to be covered, whether TNCs only or Governments and TNCs; a third concerns the code's comprehensiveness, the substantive issues that will be included within its provisions; and the fourth involves the approach or the stringency and method of implementing its provisions, in other words, its legal nature and the means of surveillance and the possible penalties to be imposed.[33]

With regard to the first point, the Commission wanted the future code to serve two main purposes: encouraging development in host countries; and preventing costly disputes between host and home states, and between host states and companies, by levelling the playing field for all.[34]

Second, the Commission had to decide whether the code would be addressed to multinational corporations only, or to companies and governments. Developing countries favoured the first option, as they felt threatened by what they saw as powerful multinational corporations that needed to be constrained; capital-exporting countries favoured the second option, hoping that the code would also help clarify points of contention, discussed in Chapter 6 of this book, about the treatment of foreign investors by host

---

30  Transnational Corporations: Issues Involved in the Formulation of a Code of Conduct, UN Doc. E/C.10/17, 20 July 1976, para. 19. Despite its name, UNCTAD is an organisation and not a conference.
31  See Chapter 3 in this book.
32  Transnational Corporations: Issues Involved in the Formulation of a Code of Conduct, UN Doc. E/C.10/17, 20 July 1976.
33  Ibid., para. 22.
34  Transnational Corporations: Issues Involved in the Formulation of a Code of Conduct, UN Doc. E/C.10/17, 20 July 1976, para. 27–32.

countries. The Commission rightly observed that the first option was not realistic. Indeed, it noted that

> any effort to harmonize rules of behaviour for TNCs will similarly limit the freedom of Governments to set their own constraints. It is, therefore, not strictly possible to adopt a code for TNC behaviour without at the same time altering governmental policies.[35]

Hence, from the start, the Commission saw the code of conduct as covering both corporate and government activities.

The substantive issues that the code would cover, and over which disagreement existed, were numerous and the Commission discussed them at length in its report. They included *inter alia* the adherence of multinational corporations to social and economic goals and objectives of the countries in which they operate. While it was highlighted that such adherence should generally be encouraged so as to favour development goals, the Commission also pointed to the difficulties arising when government policies were in clear contravention of international law, for example by being overtly racist and/or in contravention of human rights.[36] This question remains one of the key dilemmas in the business and human rights field. There is still no clear-cut answer when it comes to determining the appropriate behaviour that a multinational corporation should adopt when dealing with a government violating human rights.[37] The challenge of drafting guidance on this was immense at the end of the 1970s, and it remains so several decades later.

Another point of contention concerned corruption, its definition and whether home countries, host countries, or both should tackle it.[38] The Commission also listed a range of controversial, potentially explosive, commercial and economic issues. They included the question of ownership or control by multinational corporations over sectors of the economy, which may contravene the principle of sovereignty over natural resources; the practice of transfer pricing, defined as 'fixing of prices of goods and services which are traded between various affiliates – or between parent and affiliate – located in different countries';[39] taxation; competition; transfer of technology; consumer and environmental protection; and employment and labour issues.[40] With regard to employment and labour, the Commission highlighted the extent of

---

35  Ibid., para. 54.
36  Ibid., para. 72–73.
37  Some institutions, such as the South African Truth and Reconciliation Commission, have noted the moral wrongfulness associated with businesses simply benefiting from the racist Apartheid regime: South African Truth and Reconciliation Commission Report, Vol IV, Chapter 2, para. 161.
38  Transnational Corporations: Issues Involved in the Formulation of a Code of Conduct, UN Doc. E/C.10/17, 20 July 1976, para. 77–78.
39  Ibid., para. 98.
40  Ibid., para. 87–123.

the problem by noting for example the practice of host countries offering 'anti-union measures to transnational corporations as incentives'.[41]

The Commission delved into the question of disclosure of information on the activities of multinational corporations and government policies regarding these activities, a key aspect if one was to monitor the effectiveness of the future code. Disclosure is a complex matter raising difficulties related to issues such as the type of data that should be disclosed, the frequency with which it should be disclosed and, if it is not made public, the authority entitled to receive the information.[42] Adhering to its choice to draft not only a code of conduct for multinational corporations but also a code of conduct on multinational corporations' activities addressed to both corporations and governments, the Commission also listed the main issues regarding home and host government policies such as extraterritorial legislation, the principle of national treatment and expropriations.[43]

Besides its contents, the Commission also discussed the appropriate approach that the code should adopt and noted that 'a code concerning TNCs may range from general to specific, from voluntary to mandatory. Likewise, the measures for its implementation may range from national to international action.'[44] It added:

> Possible mixes of these approaches are many. Take, for example, general / specific formulation, voluntary / mandatory compliance and national / international implementation. The minimum approach would be a general, voluntary, nationally-implemented code. This would give the greatest leeway both to Governments and transnational corporations. Generality allows for a variety of interpretations; voluntary compliance allows TNCs considerable freedom of action; implementation through national action permits Governments a great amount of discretion. The maximum approach, namely, a specific, mandatory, internationally-implemented code, would constrain not only TNCs but also Governments as it would reduce their alternatives; it would, in fact, be the closest to international law.
>
> Between the minimum and maximum approaches there is a continuum.[45]

Commenting on the Commission's document, one author highlights that

> To some extent (…) the emphasis on the formal legal nature of a possible code is misplaced. A sense of formality may be important to the

41   Ibid., para. 116.
42   Ibid., para. 124–125.
43   Ibid., para. 130–141.
44   Ibid,. para. 56.
45   Ibid., para. 58–59.

persuasiveness of an international agreement as a norm-creator. But of perhaps greater importance is the international consensus which lies behind the instrument and the concomitant respect that concerned actors would accord it as a legal norm; an agreement need not be binding to be recognized as an authoritative guide to behavior.[46]

This author then immediately points to one of the practical difficulties in gaining multinational corporations' approval, that of some states' opposition to the presence of multinational corporations at international meetings, as these states did not want the private sector to be put on equal footing with sovereign states.[47] On the necessity to include the private sector in the discussions, he warns that 'a blatantly hostile instrument developed without adequate involvement by business leaders may only serve to reduce levels of TNC investments and modify the form they take to the detriment of host countries'.[48] Another author insists that all relevant private stakeholders, trade unions, consumer groups and NGOs – and not only multinational corporations – ought to be part of the process and proposes ways in which this could work in practice.[49] To this author, 'it is the knowledge of the insider, the feel of the actors themselves, their approach and viewpoint, and the feedback from their own activities and their constituencies that are most valuable'.[50]

In the end, the Commission asserted that 'the effectiveness of a code of conduct on transnational corporations will depend then on three major factors: (1) the formal legal character of the instrument in which it is embodies; (2) the precise language of its provisions; (3) the machinery for its implementation'.[51] Regarding its legal character, the code could take the form of 'a multilateral convention; a declaration of principles adopted by sovereign states or a resolution of an organ of an international organisation'.[52] Regarding language, the Commission noted that the code could have a greater impact, even if formally non-binding, if its provisions were drafted in a specific rather than a general way. It also introduced the idea of the code providing for differentiated obligations depending for example on the sector in which the corporation operated.[53] Regarding the machinery for implementation, the Commission seemed to favour an international, non-judicial

---

46  Stephan Coonrod, 'The United Nations Code of Conduct for Transnational Corporations', 18 *Harvard International Law Journal* 273 (1977), p. 297.

47  Ibid., pp. 298–299.

48  Ibid., p. 304.

49  Nian Tzu Wang, 'The Design of an International Code of Conduct for Transnational Corporations', 10 *Journal of International Law and Economics* 319 (1975), pp. 322–327.

50  Ibid., p. 325.

51  Transnational Corporations: Issues Involved in the Formulation of a Code of Conduct, UN Doc. E/C.10/17, 20 July 1976, para. 151.

52  Ibid., para. 153.

53  Transnational Corporations: Issues Involved in the Formulation of a Code of Conduct, UN Doc. E/C.10/17, 20 July 1976, para. 159.

and conciliatory mechanism of dispute settlement. The idea was to give an international institution the power to supervise the code's application while continuing to work on the question of the activities of multinational corporations so as to continuously adapt the code. The Commission stated that 'in the absence of a formal judicial decision-making and enforcement mechanism, the imaginative utilization of working parties, fact-finding panels, exchange of information procedures, and even of technical assistance, could be of considerable effect'.[54]

As a final point, it is worth noting that the Commission envisaged not only for the code to impose obligations on governments to make corporations abide by the code's provisions, but also the possibility for the code to impose obligations directly on corporations – a controversial point given the traditional position which denies multinational corporations the status of subjects of international law, as discussed in Chapter 5. The Commission itself described this option as 'less usual'.[55] This point led to major criticism of one of the other UN initiatives on business and human rights, the Draft Norms, covered further in this chapter.

Within the Commission on Transnational Corporations, the Working Group on the Code presented a draft Code at the eighth session of the Commission in 1982.[56] The document contains many bracketed provisions, which shows that states could not agree on their precise wording. It contains a part on 'activities of transnational corporations', which is addressed to multinational corporations themselves, and a part on 'treatment of transnational corporations', which is addressed to states. The part addressed to states, which includes sections on the general treatment of multinational corporations in countries in which they operate, nationalization and compensation and jurisdiction is almost entirely bracketed, indicating that no consensus had been found. Clearly issues relating to the treatment of foreign investors had proved to be most problematic, which is unsurprising given the opposition on this matter between capital-importing and capital-exporting countries at the time. While there seems to have been a higher degree of consensus with regard to the activities of transnational corporations, there were many unsolved issues as well.

Draft Article 9 dealt with multinational corporations' 'adherence with economic goals and development objectives, policies and priorities', and draft Article 12 with 'adherence to socio-cultural objectives and values'. Draft Article 13, entitled 'Respect for Human Rights and Fundamental Freedoms', read as follows:

Transnational corporations should/shall respect human rights and fundamental freedoms in the countries in which they operate. In their

---

54  Ibid., para. 165–166.
55  Ibid., para. 147.
56  U.N. Document E/C.10/1982/6, 5 June 1982, reprinted in 22 ILM 192 (1983).

social and industrial relations, transnational corporations should/shall not discriminate on the basis of race, colour, sex, religion, language, social, national and ethnic origin or political or other opinion. Transnational corporations should/shall conform to government policies designed to extend equality of opportunity and treatment.

Draft Article 14, entitled 'Non-collaboration by transnational corporations with racist minority regimes in southern Africa', was entirely bracketed and sought to encourage multinational corporations to disinvest from South Africa and Namibia as well as for multinational corporations still operating there to 'engage in appropriate activities with a view to contributing to the elimination of racial discrimination practices under the system of apartheid'.

On the whole, the draft Code appears extremely ambitious. First, it attempted to tackle the most controversial questions regarding states' treatment of foreign investors. This point probably led to the eventual collapse of the Code.[57] Second, it was designed to fit into an existing legal framework. Indeed, draft Article 1 stated that the ILO Tripartite Declaration of Principles concerning Multinational Enterprises and Social Policy 'should apply in the field of employment, training, conditions of work and life and industrial relations'. Draft Article 20 indicated that 'the International Agreement on Illicit Payments adopted by the United Nations should apply in the area of abstention from corrupt practices'. In other words, drafters were conscious of other initiatives and tried to avoid duplication. While this is a laudable strategy, it surely complicated an already difficult drafting process. Third, the draft Code did not shy away from the other controversial questions of the day, such as the concept of permanent sovereignty over natural resources (draft Article 6) and foreign corporate collaboration with Apartheid South Africa (draft Article 14). Finally, the draft Code included an 'international institutional machinery'. It envisaged a monitoring role for the Commission on Transnational Corporations based on state reports, a common feature of UN mechanisms, and one which is still not in place today when it comes to business and human rights.

Within the Commission, discussions on the draft Code lasted for over a decade and eventually came to an end in 1992.[58] Several reasons can be put forward to explain this. In the 1980s the world economy underwent substantial changes, with ever increasing competition among developing states to attract foreign direct investment. As seen in Chapter 6, developed states secured the signing of numerous bilateral investment treaties to protect foreign investors' interests in developing countries. Transition

57   Peter Muchlinski, 'Attempts to Extend the Accountability of Transnational Corporations: The Role of UNCTAD', in Menno T Kamminga and Saman Zia-Zarifi (eds), *Liability of Multinational Corporations under International Law*, The Hague, London, Boston: Kluwer Law International (2000), p. 102.

58   Ibid., p. 101.

towards a market economy was already underway in many socialist states. The coming to power of the prominent Reagan administration in the United States and the Thatcher administration in the United Kingdom, both of whom championed unbridled deregulation, illustrates the shift away from the ideological underpinning of the Code of Conduct for Transnational Corporations.[59]

In 1993, the UN work on these issues was transferred to UNCTAD and the Commission on Transnational Corporations was dissolved. As Muchlinski puts it, there has been a

> shift from a negotiating process aimed primarily at the conclusion of a Code of Conduct addressed to TNCs and governments, to a more detached and analytical approach aimed at ensuring further and better knowledge concerning the activities of TNCs and their effect on the development process, and on ensuring that developing countries are themselves better aware of, and able to deal to their benefit with, the principal issues arising out of a possible emerging global framework of investment rules.
>
> It is possible to describe this shift as one towards a new 'consensus' in international investment policy, one which may view TNCs in a less hostile manner than before and which places investor protection along-side development concerns. However, that is to assume that the original UN position was different. The Group of Experts vision in the 1970s was precisely that of consensus around the basic assumption that FDI by TNCs is good for development but that it may need a degree of regulation to ensure that this is the case.[60]

The story of the failed draft Code of Conduct for multinational enterprises shows the limitations of approaching the question from an ideological perspective. Although the Code was abandoned, states, and to some extent corporations, were far from hostile to the idea of introducing some regulation at the international level. A number of questions that had been discussed in the context of the Code quickly resurfaced after 1992. Initiatives such as the UN Global Compact, the UN Draft Norms and the UN Guiding Principles on Business and Human Rights flow from the work done around

---

59   Ibid., p. 103. For a detailed discussion of the reasons behind the Code's failure see Karl P. Sauvant, 'The Negotiations of the United Nations Code of Conduct on Transnational Corporations Experience and Lessons Learned', 16 *The Journal of World Investment & Trade* 11 (2015), pp. 56–62. See also Tagi Sagafi-Nejad and John Dunning, *The UN and Transnational Corporations. From Code of Conduct to Global Compact*, Bloomington and Indianapolis: Indiana University Press (2008), pp. 110–111.

60   Peter Muchlinski, 'Attempts to Extend the Accountability of Transnational Corporations: The Role of UNCTAD', in Menno T Kamminga and Saman Zia-Zarifi (eds), *Liability of Multinational Corporations under International Law*, The Hague, London, Boston: Kluwer Law International (2000), pp. 114–115.

the draft Code and the efforts of the Commission on Transnational Corporations to bridge the corporate accountability gap.

## The UN Global Compact

On 31 January 1999, speaking at the World Economic Forum of Davos, UN Secretary-General Kofi Annan declared: 'I propose that you, the business leaders gathered in Davos, and we, the United Nations, initiate a global compact of shared values and principles, which will give a human face to the global market.'[61] Although the association between the private sector and the United Nations organisation, the political inter-governmental organisation *par excellence*, was not unheard of at the time, as a number of UN agencies had already partnered with the private sector,[62] the idea of the Global Compact was groundbreaking in that it aimed at making this association global and across sectors. On a more fundamental level, the United Nations extending a hand to the private sector was significant because it represented a break from what some have described as the hostility of the UN towards business from the early days of the organisation and throughout the Cold War.[63] The Global Compact initiative differs from the work the United Nations had previously done on multinational corporations – and specifically from the efforts to draft a Code of Conduct, which took place in a climate of 'mutual suspicion',[64] as described in the previous section. The Code was meant to regulate business operations. Similarly, the Global Compact seeks to encourage corporations to abide by a short set of principles. However, unlike the draft Code, one of the Global Compact's main features is that it aims to foster dialogue among corporations and between corporations and other stakeholders. In that sense, it is more a platform to facilitate corporate engagement with the principles than a regulatory tool, a key point to attract support from the private sector.

Kofi Annan's proposal at Davos must be put in its context. At the beginning of the 1990s, as the Cold War was coming to an end – and as illustrated for example by the, admittedly timid, participation of businesses in the United Nations Rio Summit in 1992 – the United Nations' attitude towards

---

61   Press Release, Secretary-General, 'Secretary-General Proposes Global Compact on Human Rights, Labour, Environment, in Address to World Economic Forum in Davos', UN Doc. SG/SM/6881, 1 February 1999.

62   Betty King, 'The U.N. Global Compact: Responsibility for Human Rights, Labor Relations, and the Environment in Developing Nations', 34 *Cornell International Law Journal* 481 (2001), p. 482.

63   Jean-Philippe Thérien and Vincent Pouliot, 'The Global Compact: Shifting the Politics of International Development?', 2 *Global Governance* 55 (2006), pp. 56–59; Georg Kell, 'The Global Compact: Selected Experiences and Reflections', 59 *Journal of Business Ethics* 69 (2005), p. 70.

64   Georg Kell, 'The Global Compact: Selected Experiences and Reflections', 59 *Journal of Business Ethics* 69 (2005), p. 70.

the private sector was changing. After his election as UN Secretary-General in 1996, Kofi Annan initiated a *rapprochement* with the business community.[65] At its inception, the Global Compact was therefore part of an emerging trend towards a better relationship between the business world and the United Nations.[66] While the relationship between the United Nations and the private sector was thawing, the challenges ahead were, and still are, numerous and complex. George Kell, former executive Director of the Global Compact, noted in 2005 that:

> High expectations created by the speech and subsequent pronouncements created enormous pressure to deliver. The Global Compact 'Office,' consisting of only John Ruggie, Denise O'Brien and myself, had to invent solutions and scramble for operational tools to 'give globalization a human face' and to juggle the conflicting interests of the initiative's participants. This was a challenging proposition given a lack of funding and the absence of in-house expertise, and it left indelible marks on the not-so-halcyon early days of the Compact.[67]

Kofi Annan officially launched the Global Compact in July 2000. Initially it rested on nine principles. A tenth one on corruption was added in 2004. The principles derive from key international texts in the areas of human rights, labour, the environment and anti-corruption, namely the Universal Declaration of Human Rights, the International Labour Organization's Declaration on Fundamental Principles and Rights at Work, the Rio Declaration on Environment and Development and the United Nations Convention Against Corruption. They currently read as follows:

*Human Rights*
Principle 1: Businesses should support and respect the protection of internationally proclaimed human rights; and
Principle 2: make sure that they are not complicit in human rights abuse.

*Labour*
Principle 3: Businesses should uphold the freedom of association and the effective recognition of the right to collective bargaining;
Principle 4: the elimination of all forms of forced and compulsory labour;
Principle 5: the effective abolition of child labour; and
Principle 6: the elimination of discrimination in respect of employment and occupation.

---

65  Ibid., p. 71.
66  Jean-Philippe Thérien and Vincent Pouliot, 'The Global Compact: Shifting the Politics of International Development?', 2 *Global Governance* 55 (2006), p. 60.
67  Georg Kell, 'The Global Compact: Selected Experiences and Reflections', 59 *Journal of Business Ethics* 69 (2005), p. 69.

*Environment*
Principle 7: Businesses should support a precautionary approach to environmental challenges;
Principle 8: undertake initiatives to promote greater environmental responsibility; and
Principle 9: encourage the development and diffusion of environmentally friendly technologies.

*Anti-Corruption*
Principle 10: Businesses should work against corruption in all its forms, including extortion and bribery.

For a company to join the Global Compact, the CEO of that company must write a letter to the Secretary-General of the United Nations 'expressing commitment to (i) the UN Global Compact and its ten principles; (ii) engagement in partnerships to advance broad UN goals; and (iii) the annual submission of a Communication on Progress (COP)'.[68] Participating companies are expected to:

1. Make the Global Compact and its principles an integral part of business strategy, day-to-day operations and organizational culture;
2. Incorporate the Global Compact and its principles in the decision-making processes of the highest-level governance body (i.e. Board);
3. Contribute to broad development objectives (including the Millennium Development Goals) through core business activities, advocacy, philanthropy and partnerships;
4. Communicate publicly (through its annual report or other public document such as a sustainability report) the ways in which it implements the principles and supports broader development objectives – also known as the Communication on Progress; and
5. Advance the Global Compact and the case for responsible business practices through advocacy and active outreach to peers, partners, clients, consumers and the public at large.[69]

The submission of an annual Communication on Progress (COP) is the only firm commitment given by participating companies. This requirement was introduced in 2003.[70] The COP is a report in which the company discloses its efforts to implement the ten principles of the Global Compact. The Global Compact website provides guidance on how to prepare a COP. Once drafted, the COP must be posted on that website. Failure to prepare a COP

---

68   Global Compact Website, Apply Now section.
69   Global Compact Website, Business Participation section.
70   Surya Deva, 'Global Compact: A Critique of the UN's "Public–Private" Partnership for Promoting Corporate Citizenship', 34 *Syracuse Journal of International Law and Commerce* 107 (2006–2007), p. 120.

may result in the company's being listed as 'non-communicating', and can lead to expulsion from the Global Compact. The COP team maintains searchable lists of participants as well as of non-communicating and expelled companies.[71] In exchange for abiding by their obligation to produce a COP, participating companies may communicate on their participation in the Compact and, under strict conditions, use one of the official Global Compact logos.[72]

Besides the commitment made by the company to respect the principles, and the light monitoring mechanism described above, the main point of the Global Compact is to provide a platform for companies to exchange good practices. The website lists a number of engagement opportunities for willing companies on themes such as women's empowerment, climate, water, responsible investing, child labour and supply chain management.[73]

The Global Compact also includes an embryonic complaint mechanism in cases of systematic or egregious abuse. Upon receiving a complaint against a company, and unless it considers it to be *prima facie* frivolous, the Global Compact Office may facilitate a resolution of the dispute either directly by contacting the company, or by referring the dispute to the local Global Compact network, or by suggesting the use of other mechanisms such as an OECD National Contact Point.[74] If the company does not respond to the Office, it may be listed as non-communicating and treated in the same way as a company which has not submitted its COP. If the Office is not satisfied by the company's response to the allegations to the extent that

> the continued listing of the participating company on the Global Compact website is considered to be detrimental to the reputation and integrity of the Global Compact, the Global Compact Office reserves the right to remove that company from the list of participants and to so indicate on the Global Compact website.[75]

It is not an overstatement to say that the Global Compact as an initiative stands out in the inter-governmental arena that is the United Nations organisation. The Global Compact functions without much state involvement; as such it has prompted suspicion from states. In the year the Compact was launched, the Group of 77 – the coalition of developing states at the UN – called for more governmental control over it, and for the development of rules of engagement of the private sector with the United Nations.[76] George

---

71  Global Compact Website, Communication on Progress Section.
72  Global Compact Website, Policy on the Use of the Global Compact Name and Logos.
73  Global Compact Website, Engagement Opportunities Section.
74  See below.
75  Global Compact Website, Integrity Measures section.
76  Ministerial Statement adopted by the Twenty-Fourth Annual Meeting of the Ministers of Foreign Affairs of the Group of 77, 15 September 2000, para. 13.

Kell describes how the Global Compact ignited developing countries' fears that it was 'a disguised form of protectionism, introducing social conditions through the back door of the realm of economic transactions', and how European governments had to manoeuvre to rescue the Compact from threats of governmental control.[77] Commenting in July 2000 on the launch of the Compact, Betty King, then US Representative to the UN Economic and Social Council, harshly noted that

> the presence of the upper echelons of major multinational corporations was as notable as the absence of representatives of UN member states, particularly those in the developing world. The latter's absence was an obvious demonstration of their disdain for globalization, their deep distrust of the corporate world, their suspicion of the enthusiasm with which these titans had embraced the Global Compact, and their outdated beliefs about the purity of the intergovernmental system.[78]

Without necessarily adhering to her analysis, the truth remains that it probably took the Global Compact to restore the private sector's trust in the United Nations that years of discussions on the Code of Conduct had eroded. This is arguably one of the main achievements with which the Global Compact may be credited, together with global business' enhanced awareness of the social and environmental impacts of their operations, especially those in the developing world.[79] It represents a first attempt to develop a relationship between the world's main international organisation and the private sector. It has succeeded in engaging in dialogue with the private sector on human rights and environmental and corruption issues. The work around the Compact also feeds into the ongoing discussion, recounted in Chapter 5, regarding corporations as potential subjects of international law. The Compact stands as proof that the UN and the private sector may talk to each other with minimal governmental intervention and that the traditional boundaries of international law may indeed be shifting.[80]

Despite what is suggested by the ten principles upon which it rests, the Global Compact is not meant to be a regulatory instrument. Instead, it is primarily a learning forum.[81] As such, it can do nothing to address human

77  Georg Kell, 'The Global Compact: Selected Experiences and Reflections', 59 *Journal of Business Ethics* 69 (2005), p. 76.
78  Betty King, 'The U.N. Global Compact: Responsibility for Human Rights, Labor Relations, and the Environment in Developing Nations', 34 *Cornell International Law Journal* 481 (2001), pp. 482–483.
79  Ibid.
80  Surya Deva, 'Global Compact: A Critique of the UN's "Public–Private" Partnership for Promoting Corporate Citizenship', 34 *Syracuse Journal of International Law and Commerce* 107 (2006–2007), pp. 149–150.
81  John Ruggie, 'The Global Compact as a Learning Network', 7 *Journal of Corporate Citizenship* 371 (2001), p. 372.

rights violations by companies operating in developing countries with no or little regard for the impact they may have on local populations' rights. All the Compact can do is facilitate discussions on issues that companies want to tackle. This leads Oshionebo to note that

> the GC's focus on learning and governance, rather than on regulation of corporate conduct, appears to miss the point (...).
>
> It assumes that the social irresponsibility of TNCs in the developing world stems from lack of proper governance or from lack of knowledge about good business practices. This is rarely the case. While it is true that the irresponsible behavior of TNCs is encouraged by several factors including the regulatory incapacity of, and corruption in, developing countries, the problem is equally attributable to the selective and discriminatory observances of good practices by TNCs.
>
> TNCs' choice of where to apply good business ethics and where to disregard them appears curiously to be dependent on the geographical location of their operations. TNCs generally behave well, or at least better, when operating in developed countries. This does not mean that incidences of bad behavior by TNCs have not occurred, or are not occurring, in developed countries.
>
> The unsavory activities of Enron, Worldcom, and most recently, Merck's marketing of Vioxx allegedly after knowing its adverse effects on human health, are prime examples. But such bad behaviors, it appears, are the exception and not the rule. Quite contrary, these same TNCs, aided and abetted by host governments, often resort to irresponsible practices in the execution of their business activities in developing countries. How else do we explain Shell's apparent observance of good corporate governance practices in its operations in the United States, Canada, and other parts of the developed world while it wilfully disregards these practices in its operations in places like Nigeria? This is indeed a worrisome trend which, in all respects, should not be alluded to lightly or en passant.[82]

For critics of the Global Compact, the 'archetype of voluntarism',[83] its lack of teeth is an irremediable flaw. However, as John Ruggie notes, 'the GC's critics wish it were something that it is *not:* a regulatory arrangement, specifically a legally binding code of conduct with explicit performance criteria and independent monitoring and enforcement of company compliance.'[84]

---

82   Evaristus Oshionebo, 'The UN Global Compact and Accountability of Transnational Corporations: Separating Myth from Realities', 19 *Florida Journal of International Law* 1 2007, pp. 20–21.

83   John Gerard Ruggie, *Just Business*, New York and London: W. W. Norton and Company Ltd (2013), pp. xxvii–xxviii.

84   John Ruggie, 'The Global Compact as a Learning Network', 7 *Journal of Corporate Citizenship* 371 (2001), p. 372.

Defending the Compact, George Kell highlights that it 'was simply not what some wanted it to be', and that 'explanations to the contrary were ignored'.[85] Indeed, the Global Compact does not address the question of corporate human rights responsibility in a way that can be satisfactory for victims of corporate abuse and their defenders. Neither the COP nor the complaint mechanism are strong enough to be able to do that, and the risk of 'blue-washing', or companies' participation in the UN Global Compact to clean up bad human rights and environmental records, remains real. Since the Global Compact does not properly regulate business, the question, then, is whether it is worth investing time and effort into it.

Many authors have underlined the advantages of the Global Compact as a soft law instrument. First, some have argued that there was no other option at the time and that therefore the Global Compact is the child of pragmatic necessity. As John Ruggie put it in 2001,

> the probability of the General Assembly's adopting a meaningful code anytime soon approximates zero. The only countries eager to launch such an effort at this time are equally unfriendly to the private sector, human rights, labor standards, and the environment.[86]

Moreover, the United Nations does not have the capacity to monitor the operations of multinational corporations around the world. Finally, the private sector would have strongly resisted the idea of the United Nations developing a binding code of conduct.[87] Ruggie's latter argument, which implies that the private sector has to agree to being regulated, is only relevant if states do not support the idea of regulation. If states agreed to impose obligations on corporations, of a human rights nature or otherwise, there would be no need to seek corporate approval of the initiative. Corporate approval, however, becomes necessary when, due to the unwillingness of states, the best that can be achieved is a voluntary mechanism such as the Global Compact.

Second, beyond pragmatic reasons, some have also argued that in the long run the Global Compact may prove more successful at addressing corporate human rights violations than a binding regulatory mechanism. John Ruggie noted for example that at the time the Compact was set up, a number of concepts – such as complicity in human rights abuses – could not yet be defined with the degree of precision that would be necessary for their inclusion in a binding code of conduct. In that context he hoped that 'accumulated experience – through trial, error, and social vetting – (...) [would] gradually fill in the blanks'.[88] Other authors decidedly supported the Global Compact as a soft law initiative and opposed the idea that it was a second-best option.[89] They viewed the ten vague principles of the Global Compact as a clever and innovative way to acquaint the private sector with human rights and other issues and concluded as follows:

The low 'precision' score of the Compact's ten principles encourages widespread corporate participation in the initiative. Rather than alienate companies by scaring them away with detailed rules, the Compact gives them the autonomy to implement its principles in different ways, according to what works best in their industry and in the jurisdiction in which they operate. Comparisons can be made with the Open Method of Coordination governance system (OMC) operating within the European Union, which also allows for the flexible adaptation of policy initiatives (...).[90]

Supporters of the Global Compact insist on the advantages of progressively strengthening and enriching the system. The short history of the Compact proves them right in the sense that the 'integrity measures', such as for example the risk of being publicly expelled from the Global Compact, were only introduced in 2005. In other words, they were introduced after a relatively large number of companies had already joined.[91]

Surya Deva disagrees with the idea that the lack of precision of the ten principles is an advantage, and that the Global Compact is not a regulatory framework:

The generality-cum-vagueness of the Compact principles is counter-productive from the perspective of both sincere and insincere corporate citizens. The language of these principles is so general that insincere corporations can easily circumvent or comply with them without doing anything to promote human rights or labor standards. On the other hand, even a sincere corporate citizen like Novartis finds the language too general to be implemented.[92]

Deva contends that despite claims to the contrary, the Global Compact tries to regulate corporate behaviour but without clearly saying so, which to him leads to a 'directional crisis', or at least uncertainty. In this context, one of the

85  Georg Kell, 'The Global Compact: Selected Experiences and Reflections', 59 *Journal of Business Ethics* 69 (2005), p. 72.
86  John Ruggie, 'The Global Compact as a Learning Network', 7 *Journal of Corporate Citizenship* 371 (2001), p. 373.
87  Ibid.
88  Ibid.
89  Roya Ghafele and Angus Mercer, '"Not Starting in Sixth Gear": An Assessment of the UN Global Compact's Use of Soft Law as a Global Governance Structure for Corporate Social Responsibility', 17 *University of California Davis Journal of International Law and Policy* 41 (2010–2011), pp. 48–49.
90  Ibid., p. 54.
91  Ibid., pp. 51–53.
92  Surya Deva, 'Global Compact: A Critique of the UN's "Public–Private" Partnership for Promoting Corporate Citizenship', 34 *Syracuse Journal of International Law and Commerce* 107 (2006–2007), p. 129.

risks is the 'philanthropisation' of the Global Compact, that is, a strengthened focus on philanthropy instead of positive change in core corporate practices.[93] Companies' attempts to offset their poor human rights records by engaging in charity work are a regrettable feature of the business and human rights world. Fortunately, the directional uncertainty of the Global Compact has not resulted in its dilution to the extent that philanthropy actions could be said to be dominating discussions. If we accept as a starting point that the idea behind the Global Compact was to build a relationship of trust between the United Nations and the private sector, and to raise awareness of the private sector's possible adverse impact on human rights and the environment, then the fact that the Global Compact clearly falls neither within the regulatory nor within the learning forum category is beyond the point.

Another of Deva's points of criticism of the Compact was that companies from Europe were disproportionately represented, accounting for 49 per cent of the total number of participating companies, or 2,902 in 2005.[94] Although diversity has improved, the uneven participation in the Compact remains an issue. In September 2014, the Compact claimed over 8,000 business participants from 145 countries. Among these, 2,169 – 27 per cent – were from one of the G8 countries, and 852 – about 10 per cent – from one of the BRICS.[95]

As seen, the Global Compact is a purely 'voluntary corporate citizenship initiative',[96] which has its flaws and inherent limitations. Importantly, however, the Global Compact is only one of the existing international initiatives in the business and human rights area. As such it can be seen as only one aspect of the international governance of corporations, especially multinational corporations. Ursula A. Wynhoven has shown how the 2011 UN Guiding Principles (see below), which have a clearer regulatory approach, and the UN Global Compact complement each other. To take one example, UN Guiding Principles 15 and 16 require companies to adopt a human rights policy, and the Global Compact has developed guidance on how to go about this.[97] While the Guiding Principles are not the answer to the challenges of the business and human rights field, they and the Global Compact

---

93   Evaristus Oshionebo, 'The UN Global Compact and Accountability of Transnational Corporations: Separating Myth from Realities', 19 *Florida Journal of International Law* 1 2007, p. 29.

94   Surya Deva, 'Global Compact: A Critique of the UN's "Public–Private" Partnership for Promoting Corporate Citizenship', 34 *Syracuse Journal of International Law and Commerce* 107 (2006–2007), p. 136.

95   G8 Countries: US, 307 (Active: 230); UK, 239 (Active: 181); France, 935 (Active: 710); Germany, 270 (Active 241); Canada, 55 (Active 42); Italy, 113 (Active: 93); Japan, 215 (Active: 194); Russian Federation, 35 (Active: 22).
BRICS: Brazil, 400 (Active: 302); Russian Federation, 35 (Active: 22); India, 155 (Active: 88); China, 209 (Active: 139); South Africa, 53 (Active: 46).

96   Georg Kell, 'The Global Compact: Selected Experiences and Reflections', 59 *Journal of Business Ethics* 69 (2005), p. 69.

97   Ursula A. Wynhoven, 'The Protect-Respect-Remedy Framework and the United Nations Global Compact', 9 *Santa Clara Journal of International Law* 81 (2011), pp. 87–89.

make for an interesting combination. Together, they may meet with a greater degree of success in bridging the corporate accountability gap.

## The Draft Norms on the Responsibilities of Transnational Corporations and Other Business Enterprises

The story of the Draft UN Norms on the Responsibilities of Transnational Corporations and Other Business Enterprises is in many ways similar to, and the continuation of, the story of the UN Code of Conduct. As seen, negotiations on the Code of Conduct were abandoned in 1992. Just like the Code, the Norms were meant to be non-voluntary and universal in scope. Just like the Code, they were abandoned due to a lack of state support at the United Nations.

In 1997, the UN Sub-Commission on the Promotion and Protection of Human Rights (hereinafter the Sub-Commission) entrusted one of its members, El-Hadji Guissé, with the task of preparing a document on the question of the relationship between the enjoyment of human rights and the working methods and activities of transnational corporations.[98] Upon receiving his report on the Impact of the Activities of Transnational Corporations on the Realization of Economic, Social and Cultural Rights,[99] the Commission decided to set up a working group to examine the working methods and activities of transnational corporations.[100] In 1999 the Sub-Commission asked another one of its members, Professor David Weissbrodt, to prepare a draft code of conduct for multinational corporations.[101] Several successive drafts were prepared, and feedback was requested from various stakeholders. In 2003, the Sub-Commission eventually approved the Norms and transmitted them to the Commission on Human Rights for approval.[102] Such approval never came.

The Draft Norms were ambitious for several reasons. First, as touched upon in Chapter 5, they rested on the controversial idea that companies had

98  UN Sub-Commission, E/CN.4/Sub.2/1997/50, 1997/11. The sub-commission was a subsidiary body of the now defunct UN Commission on Human Rights, which was replaced by the Human Rights Council in 2006.
99  UN Sub-Commission, Working Document on the Impact of the Activities of Transnational Corporations on the Realization of Economic, Social and Cultural Rights, UN Doc. E/CN.4/Sub.2/1998/6.
100 UN Sub-Commission, UN Doc. E/CN.4/Sub.2/1998/45 (20 August 1998).
101 Sub-Commission, Report of the Sessional Working Group on the Working Methods and Activities of Transnational Corporations on Its First Session, UN Doc. E/CN.4/Sub.2/1999/9, para. 32.
102 UN Sub-Commission, Resolution 2003/16, E/CN.4/Sub.2/2003/L.11, para. 1 and 2. The Norms are in UN Doc. E/CN.4/Sub.2/2003/12/Rev.2 (26 August 2003). For the detailed drafting history of the Norms, see David Weissbrodt and Muria Kruger, 'Norms on the Responsibilities of Transnational Corporations and Other Business Enterprises with Regard to Human Rights', 97 *American Journal of International Law* 901 (2003), pp. 904–907.

obligations under international human rights law. These obligations were meant to exist only within the company's 'sphere of influence' and this nebulous concept was defined with precision neither in the Norms themselves nor in their official commentary.[103] Second, unlike the UN Guiding Principles adopted in 2011, which state that companies must 'respect' human rights, the Norms imposed the same obligations on companies as on states with regard to human rights. This means that the private sector was expected not only to respect but also to 'promote, secure the fulfilment of, (…) ensure respect of and protect human rights'.[104] Third, the Norms applied primarily to transnational corporations, but also to all business enterprises. Admittedly, the reference to the sphere of influence meant that large multinational companies had a wider range of obligations than small domestic businesses due to the multinational companies' 'ability to influence markets, governments, stakeholders, and communities';[105] nevertheless, at least in theory, the Norms were addressed to millions of businesses around the world. Fourth, Article 12 called on companies to respect all human rights, civil and political as well as economic, social and cultural, including those that certain states themselves had not accepted. This led one author to note that

> the definitions, broadly worded, encompass norms with universal legal effect, norms with limited legal effect among nations ratifying provisions of particular agreements, and norms with no legal effect. Under the *Norms,* all of these norms will become legally effective as part of the *private law* of TNCs. What a neat trick![106]

The Norms contained a list of obligations with which companies had to comply in the areas of non-discrimination, the right to security, forced labour, children's rights, health and safety, adequate remuneration, collective bargaining and freedom of association, bribery, consumer protection and environmental protection. In that sense, the Norms were meant to be a restatement of international law, both customary and treaty-based, but addressed specifically to companies. However, despite this claim, the Norms were not merely a restatement of the law. In reality, they sought to widen the obligations deriving from international human rights law. This is a fifth

---

103 Commentary on the Norms on the Responsibilities of Transnational Corporations and Other Business Enterprises with Regard to Human Rights, UN Doc. E/CN.4/Sub.2/2003/38/Rev.2.

104 Article 1, Draft Norms.

105 David Weissbrodt and Muria Kruger, 'Norms on the Responsibilities of Transnational Corporations and Other Business Enterprises with Regard to Human Rights', 97 *American Journal of International Law* 901 (2003), p. 912.

106 Larry Catá Backer, 'Multinational Corporations, Transnational Law: The United Nations' Norms on the Responsibilities of Transnational Corporations as Harbinger of Corporate Responsibility in International Law', 37 *Columbia Human Rights Law Review* 287 (2006), p. 340.

reason why the Norms can be said to be ambitious. For example, Article 14 on environmental protection included the obligation to abide by the precautionary principle, the international legal status of which was unclear at the time.[107] Article 3 on the right to security stated that companies 'shall not engage *or benefit from*' international crimes and other violations. As discussed in Chapter 4, benefiting from crimes without further participation is not a crime under international law. This Article 3 departed clearly from positive international law.

Article 15 on the implementation of the Norms provides that companies shall 'adopt, disseminate and implement internal rules of operation in compliance with the Norms', and regularly report on them. They shall also incorporate the Norms in their contracts with contractors, subcontractors, suppliers, licensees, distributors or natural or other legal persons. This is similar to what the UN Guiding Principles provide. The Norms, however, go further. Article 16 provides that companies 'shall be subject to periodic monitoring and verification by United Nations, other international and national mechanisms already in existence or yet to be created, regarding application of the Norms' and that NGOs should have an input in the process, setting up what one author called a 'surveillance scheme'.[108] This raises issues around the legitimacy of NGOs, which can be any group of like-minded individuals, to get involved in such monitoring.[109]

Article 17 calls on states to strengthen their domestic legal framework to deal with corporate human rights violations. Although this is not explicit in the Norms themselves and in their official commentary, David Weissbrodt suggested in an article published shortly after the Sub-Commission's adoption of the Norms that this obligation extended to 'the activities of each company with a statutory seat in their country, under whose law it was incorporated or formed, where it has its central administration, where it has its principal place of business, or where it is doing business'.[110] In other words, he seemed to embrace the notion of extraterritorial monitoring of corporate activities, one of the key points of contention during the drafting of the UN Guiding Principles. Finally, Article 18 imposes an obligation on companies to provide reparation to 'those persons, entities and communities that have been adversely affected by failures to comply with these Norms'.

While the NGO community welcomed the Norms, and there was some

107 John Gerard Ruggie, 'Business and Human Rights: The Evolving International Agenda', 101 *American Journal of International Law* 819 (2007), p. 825.
108 Larry Catá Backer, 'Multinational Corporations, Transnational Law: The United Nation's Norms on the Responsibilities of Transnational Corporations as Harbinger of Corporate Responsibility in International Law', 37 *Columbia Human Rights Law Review* 287 (2006), p. 335.
109 Ibid, pp. 384–388.
110 David Weissbrodt and Muria Kruger, 'Norms on the Responsibilities of Transnational Corporations and Other Business Enterprises with Regard to Human Rights', 97 *American Journal of International Law* 901 (2003), p. 921.

limited support from the private sector,[111] the Commission on Human Rights, which was an inter-governmental body, never approved the Norms. By and large Western states, along with the private sector, opposed the Norms while developing states remained silent, with the notable exception of Cuba, which supported them.[112] The Norms did have a number of flaws and perhaps went too far, but probably did not deserve to be abandoned in the way they eventually were. In this regard, Kinley and Chambers' analysis of the matter is enlightening. Speaking of the criticisms against the norms, they asserted that

> [s]ome of these [criticisms], such as the apparent novelty of such a venture in international law, the imprecision of some of the language used and the concerns over divisions of responsibility, are, at least on their face understandable and even appealing, but none stand up to analysis. It is evident that a multi-faceted attack was used to obscure the true message, which is, quite simply, that business alliances, in the main, do not want TNCs to be held legally accountable for the human rights abuses that they may inflict or are complicit in, and that the Norms are seen as a first step towards such regulation.[113]

In 2004, the Commission adopted a decision in which it asserted that the Draft Norms had 'no legal standing'. In that same decision the Commission requested that the UN Office of the High Commissioner for Human Rights 'compile a report setting out the scope and legal status of current initiatives and standards relating to the responsibility of transnational corporations, and submit such a report to the Commission on Human Rights at its 61st session', which was scheduled for March 2005.[114] In its report, the Office summed up the arguments of the pro- and anti-Norms and recommended to the Commission of Human Rights 'to maintain the draft Norms among existing initiatives and standards on business and human rights, with a view to their further consideration'. In particular, it suggested that the Commission wait for the results of the Norms road-testing in which some companies were engaged at the time.[115]

---

111  Ibid., pp. 906–907.
112  Pini Pavel Miretski and Sascha-Dominik Bachmann, 'UN Norms on the Responsibility of Transnational Corporations and other Business Enterprises with Regard to Human Rights: A Requiem', 17 *Deakin Law Review* 5 (2012), pp. 31–32. See also David Kinley and Rachel Chambers, 'The UN Human Rights Norms for Corporations: The Private Implications of Public International Law', 6(3) *Human Rights Law Review* 447 (2006), pp. 457–459.
113  David Kinley and Rachel Chambers, 'The UN Human Rights Norms for Corporations: The Private Implications of Public International Law', 6(3) *Human Rights Law Review* 447 (2006), p. 491.
114  UN Commission on Human Rights, Decision 2004/116, 'Responsibilities of transnational corporations and related business enterprises with regard to human rights', 20 April 2004.
115  UN Doc. E/CN.4/2005/91, p. 18.

Upon receiving this report, the Commission adopted a resolution in which it asked the UN Secretary-General to appoint a Special Representative on the issue of human rights and transnational corporations and other business enterprises with the view to clarify standards, and not to develop Norms or a Code or any regulatory instrument.[116] The appointee, Professor John Ruggie from Harvard University, wrote that when he started his mandate, human rights NGOs expected him to keep refining the Norms, or at least to use them as the basis of his work.[117] Meanwhile, business organisations 'insisted on precisely the opposite', and argued that there was 'no need for a new international framework'.[118] He could not rely on governmental support or guidance, either. In his book, Ruggie explains that the only piece of advice he received during one of his first meetings with governments in Geneva was: 'avoid a train wreck'.[119] The mandate did not start under the best auspices.

In this gloomy context, Ruggie prepared a report in the first months of his mandate in which he called for the Norms to be abandoned. In his words, 'the divisive debate' over them 'obscures rather than illuminates promising areas of consensus and cooperation among business, civil society, governments and international institutions with respect to human rights'.[120] Unsurprisingly, this 'deliberately undiplomatic language', in the words of Ruggie himself, prompted a reaction from one of the main architects of the Norms, David Weissbrodt.[121] While acknowledging that the new Special Representative's report contained a number of good ideas, Weissbrodt criticised it for embarking on 'an extremely negative and unproductive critique of the Norms – inspired, if not copied word for word, from the advocacy of the International Chamber of Commerce and the International Organization of Employers', two business organisations that had vigorously rejected the Norms.[122] Weissbrodt condemned the report's 'ridiculous and uncritical parroting of the arguments presented by the International Chamber of Commerce'[123] as counterproductive and unnecessary. It remains debatable

---

116 Commission on Human Rights, UN Doc. E/CN.4/2005/L.87, 15 April 2005.
117 John Gerard Ruggie, *Just Business*, New York and London: W. W. Norton and Company Ltd (2013), pp. xix–xx.
118 Ibid., p. xx.
119 Ibid.
120 Interim report of the Special Representative of the Secretary-General on the issue of human rights and transnational corporations and other business enterprises, UN Doc. E/CN.4/2006/97, 22 February 2006, para. 69. See also John Gerard Ruggie, 'Business and Human Rights: The Evolving International Agenda', 101 *American Journal of International Law* 819 (2007). Professor Ruggie's position to abandon the Norms was strongly criticised. See for example, David Kinley and Rachel Chambers, 'The UN Human Rights Norms for Corporations: The Private Implications of Public International Law', 6(3) *Human Rights Law Review* 447 (2006), p. 461.
121 John Gerard Ruggie, *Just Business*, New York and London: W. W. Norton and Company Ltd (2013), p. 54.
122 David Weissbrodt, 'UN Perspectives on "Business and Humanitarian and Human Rights Obligations"', 100 *American Society of International Law Proceedings* 129 (2006), p. 138.
123 Ibid., p. 139.

whether it was necessary to abandon the Norms in order to move the business and human rights agenda forward. While this bold decision may have been required, it could perhaps have been made more gracefully.

## The 'Protect, Respect and Remedy Framework' and the UN Guiding Principles on Business and Human Rights

The UN Guiding Principles are the latest business and human rights development within the United Nations and they can only be fully understood by placing them in their historical context. Following the failure of states to adopt the Code of Conduct developed in the 1970s and 1980s, two parallel routes were followed at the end of the 1990s. First, the UN sought to engage the private sector on issues of human rights, environmental protection and later corruption through the establishment of a platform for dialogue, the Global Compact. Second, within a sub-commission of the Commission on Human Rights, a small group of human rights experts and academics worked on the Draft Norms which in the end failed to attract governmental support. The Guiding Principles are the continuation of these initiatives and the elaboration of the Guiding Principles drew upon both of them in many ways.

This section intends to offer a narrative on the adoption of the Guiding Principles and their contents, bearing in mind that the present book has already covered a number of issues that are contained in, and/or were extensively discussed during the drafting process of, the UN Guiding Principles. These issues include the departure from the UN Norms; whether corporations have human rights obligations under international human rights law, and if so which rights are covered; whether international human rights law places obligations on states to monitor the overseas activities of companies domiciled in their territories; and the notion of sphere of influence. Hence, so as not to duplicate previous developments, this section mentions rather than thoroughly discusses the implications of some of these key issues.

The six-year mandate of the UN Secretary-General Special Representative has generated a great deal of attention and dozens of reports and comments by various stakeholders. These were usefully compiled by a London-based NGO, the Business and Human Rights Resource Centre, on their portal dedicated to the mandate. The portal constitutes a fantastic resource on business and human rights and was used extensively to draft this chapter.[124]

### *The Protect, Respect and Remedy Framework*

Professor Ruggie was appointed as the UN Secretary-General Special Representative (SGSR) on the issue of human rights and transnational

---

124 Business and Human Rights Resource Centre, Portal on the SGSR, www.business-human-rights.org/SpecialRepPortal/Home (last accessed 21 March 2016).

corporations and other business enterprises for an initial period of two years, during which he submitted two reports to the Commission on Human Rights, which later became the Human Rights Council. As mentioned above, in his first report he called for the UN Norms to be abandoned.[125] The second report, presented to the Council in 2007, is organised into five clusters of standards: the state duty to protect; corporate responsibility and accountability for international crimes; corporate responsibility for other human rights violations under international law; soft law mechanisms; and self-regulation. The report 'draws on some two-dozen research papers produced by or for the SRSG' as well as worldwide consultations.[126] It maps standards in these areas, but in the words of the SGSR himself, it is weak on the recommendations part. Therefore in this report he also asked the Human Rights Council to extend his mandate by one more year,[127] a request which was granted a few months later.[128]

In 2007 and 2008 the SGSR continued to hold consultations and to call for the participation of a wide range of stakeholders. In 2008 this resulted in the introduction of the 'Protect, Respect and Remedy' Framework in his report to the Human Rights Council.[129] The Framework emerged from the five clusters of standards of the 2007 report. It rests on three distinct but interrelated pillars: the state duty, under international human rights law, to *protect* against corporate human rights harm; the corporate responsibility to *respect* human rights, as a social expectation; and the right of victims to an effective *remedy*, whether judicial or non-judicial. The Framework bypasses the contentious issues related to the human rights obligations of businesses under international law, which had been so problematic at the time of the UN Norms, by suggesting that only states have such obligations. The word 'duty' in the phrase 'State duty to protect' was used to emphasise the idea of a legal obligation. By contrast, corporations only have a *responsibility* to respect human rights. The word 'responsibility' is therefore used in the non-legal sense. Moreover, businesses should respect human rights, which simply means 'do no harm'. Unlike the UN Norms, which called for businesses to 'promote, secure the fulfilment of (...) ensure respect of and protect human rights',[130] the Framework only speaks about doing no harm and abstaining

---

125 Interim report of the Special Representative of the Secretary-General on the issue of human rights and transnational corporations and other business enterprises, UN Doc. E/CN.4/2006/97, 22 February 2006.
126 Report of the Special Representative of the Secretary-General (SRSG) on the issue of human rights and transnational corporations and other business enterprises, A/HRC/4/035, 9 February 2007, para. 7.
127 Ibid., paras. 9 and 88.
128 John Gerard Ruggie, 'Business and Human Rights: The Evolving International Agenda', 101 *American Journal of International Law* 819 (2007), p. 838.
129 Report of the Special Representative of the Secretary-General on the issue of human rights and transnational corporations and other business enterprises, John Ruggie, A/HRC/8/5, 7 April 2008.
130 UN Norms, Article 1.

from committing human rights abuses – a much narrower scope of responsibility.[131]

The corporate responsibility to respect human rights 'is the basic expectation society has of business', and this responsibility is not grounded in international law.[132] This is not to say that businesses are not subjected to the domestic laws of the countries in which they operate. They are under a legal duty to respect such laws but the Framework takes the position that they do not have any additional legal duty to respect international human rights law, as only states have such duty. One author suggests that 'the elaboration of a corporate governance framework that is meant to apply concurrently with corporate obligations under the laws of the jurisdiction in which they operate is one of the greatest advancements of this framework'.[133] The argument is that the Norms were adding a layer of complexity by introducing the idea that corporations had human rights obligations under international law. By contrast, 'instead of suggesting further fragmentation of law at the transnational level, the framework is an attempt to build simultaneous public and private governance systems as well as coordinate, without integrating, their operations'.[134]

The Framework and the ensuing Guiding Principles rest on the idea of a polycentric governance where 'each governance system constitutes a complex cluster of its own'. Ruggie identified three separate systems: the system of public law and policy, the system of civil governance and the system of corporate governance.[135] He concluded that

> [i]n order to achieve better protection for individuals and communities against corporate-related human rights harm, each of these governance systems needs to be mobilized and pull in compatible directions.
>
> To foster that mobilization the Guiding Principles draw on the different discourses that reflect the respective social roles these governance systems play in regulating corporate conduct.[136]

Among the greatest strengths of the Framework and the Guiding Principles is that they allow for further discussion on each of the elements – the state duty

---

131  For a critique on equating the responsibility to respect with the do no harm principle, see David J. Karp, *Responsibility for Human Rights, Transnational Corporations in Imperfect States*, Cambridge: Cambridge University Press (2014), pp. 82–87.

132  Report of the Special Representative of the Secretary-General on the issue of human rights and transnational corporations and other business enterprises, John Ruggie, A/HRC/8/5, 7 April 2008, Para. 9.

133  Larry Catá Backer, 'On the Evolution of the United Nations' "Protect-Respect-Remedy" Project: The State, the Corporation and Human Rights in a Global Governance Context', 9 *Santa Clara Journal of International Law* 37 (2011), p. 43.

134  Ibid.

135  John Gerard Ruggie, *Just Business*, New York and London: W. W. Norton & Company Inc. (2013), p. xliii.

136  Ibid. p. xliv.

to protect, the corporate responsibility to respect and the responsibilities of both to provide remedies – without constantly having to go back and question progress made in any of the others. Hence, in the words of John Ruggie, the 'corporate responsibility to respect' pillar is about 'the independent social responsibilities of companies (…) in relation to human rights – where "independent" means that they exist irrespective of whether states are living up to their commitments.'[137] It is a social norm which exists independently of state duties and which, additionally, has acquired 'near-universal recognition'.[138]

While the SGSR's idea that businesses have no human rights obligations under international law is debatable, and arguably wrong when it comes to human rights violations amounting to international crimes, this position had the merits of allowing wider support for the Framework. The Human Rights Council unanimously welcomed the Framework and extended John Ruggie's mandate by three years, giving him the task of operationalising it. This constitutes a great achievement given that the Council's predecessor, the Commission on Human Rights, had clearly rejected the UN Norms.

### The Guiding Principles on Business and Human Rights

Consultations continued between 2008 and 2011 and in 2011 the SGSR presented the 'Guiding Principles on Business and Human Rights, implementing the "Protect, Respect, and Remedy" Framework'. The Human Rights Council unanimously endorsed the Guiding Principles on 16 June 2011, making a strong political statement.[139] The Council's endorsement of the Guiding Principles gives the corporate responsibility to respect enhanced legitimacy beyond a mere social expectation. While the process does not amount to the recognition of corporate human rights obligations under international law, it lifts the notion of corporate responsibility closer towards the legal sphere.[140]

The Guiding Principles are divided into three sections corresponding to each of the Framework's pillars: the state duty to protect (Guiding Principles 1–10), the corporate responsibility to respect (Guiding Principles 11–21) and the right of victims of corporate harm to access remedies (Guiding Principles 22–31). It is beyond the scope of this book to review each of the principles in detail. However, a few points deserve attention.

First, as mentioned earlier, Guiding Principle 1 makes clear that the state duty concerns the full range of human rights obligations, which means that states should 'prevent, investigate, punish and redress' corporate human

---

137  Ibid., p. 83.
138  Ibid., pp. 91–92.
139  UN Human Rights Council, 17/4 Human rights and transnational corporations and other business enterprises, A/HRC/RES/17/4, para. 1. See John Gerard Ruggie, *Just Business*, New York and London: W. W. Norton & Company Inc. (2013), pp. 120–121.
140  John Gerard Ruggie, *Just Business*, New York and London: W. W. Norton & Company Inc. (2013), p. 125.

rights abuses through 'effective policies, legislation, regulations and adjudication'. The scope of the state duty is wide. As John Ruggie put it, the state duty to protect is 'the bedrock of protection against corporate human rights abuse'.[141] By contrast, the corporate responsibility to respect simply means that corporations 'should avoid infringing on the human rights of others and should address adverse human rights impacts with which they are involved'.[142] While the corporate responsibility to respect is limited in terms of the range of measures that are expected from corporations, it concerns virtually all human rights, as emphasised in Guiding Principle 12. This constitutes one of the greatest achievements of the Guiding Principles and hopefully settles the debate about the kind of rights corporations should respect.

Second, Guiding Principle 2 asserts that 'States should set out clearly the expectation that all business enterprises domiciled in their territory and/or jurisdiction respect human rights throughout their operations'. Crucially, this does not amount to saying that international human rights treaties require states to regulate the overseas activities of corporations and to sanction companies that engage in human rights abuse in foreign countries. Many commentators have suggested that John Ruggie did not go far enough on this, as the law is rapidly evolving.[143] While the Guiding Principles do not create an obligation for states to monitor the overseas activities of corporations, the official commentary of this Principle emphasises that they are not prohibited from doing so and even encourages them to do it.[144] The range of measures that states may adopt to comply with this expectation is covered in Chapter 9 of this book.

Third, Guiding Principle 13 states that the corporate responsibility to respect requires businesses to avoid violating human rights and to seek to prevent or mitigate harm when it has already occurred. This can be achieved through the adoption of a policy commitment to respect human rights approved at the highest level in the company;[145] carrying out a due diligence process which 'should include assessing actual and potential human rights impacts, integrating and acting upon the findings, tracking responses, and communicating how impacts are addressed';[146] and the adoption of 'processes to enable the remediation of any adverse human rights impacts they cause or to which they contribute'.[147] It is therefore unambiguously

---

141  Ibid., p. 90.
142  Guiding Principle 11.
143  For a discussion on this see Nadia Bernaz, 'Enhancing Corporate Accountability for Human Rights Violations: Is Extraterritoriality the Magic Potion?', 117 *Journal of Business Ethics* 493 (2013), pp. 503–508.
144  Guiding Principles on Business and Human Rights: Implementing the United Nations 'Protect, Respect and Remedy' Framework, A/HRC/17/31, Official Commentary to GP 2.
145  Guiding Principles 15 and 16.
146  Guiding Principle 17.
147  Guiding Principle 15 and 22.

affirmed that the corporate responsibility to respect requires corporations to change the way they conduct their business and that in the human rights world, 'there is no equivalent to buying carbon offsets (...): philanthropic good deeds do not compensate for infringing on human rights'.[148]

Lastly, the Guiding Principles require states to have both judicial and non-judicial mechanisms in place to provide remedies to victims of corporate abuse 'when such abuses occur within their territory and/or jurisdiction'.[149] They should also facilitate non-state-based mechanisms,[150] while business enterprises should establish their own grievance mechanisms.[151] To clarify expectations, Guiding Principle 31 provides a list of 'effectiveness criteria for non-judicial grievance mechanisms'. Perhaps one of the greatest deficiencies of the Guiding Principles is that they do not set up their own enforcement or monitoring mechanism. Instead, enforcement is left in the hands of states and companies themselves.

Despite the inherent limitations highlighted in this section, the Protect, Respect and Remedy Framework and Guiding Principles are a positive development in the field of business and human rights, and they have the merit of providing a starting point from which to continue to address corporate human rights violations. When viewed in their historical context – the failure of both the Code of Conduct and the Norms and the adoption of the entirely voluntary Global Compact – they constitute a great achievement. A number of countries have started to adopt National Action Plans to implement the Guiding Principles.[152] Moreover, the Guiding Principles have prompted unprecedented convergence within the different soft law initiatives on business and human rights. The language of the Guiding Principles is used in the 2011 version of the OECD Guidelines on Multinational Enterprises,[153] in the 2012 version of the IFC Performance Standards[154] and in the 2011 EU Strategy on Corporate Social Responsibility.[155]

---

148 John Gerard Ruggie, *Just Business*, New York and London: W. W. Norton & Company Inc. (2013), p. 95.
149 Guiding Principle 25 and 26–27.
150 Guiding Principle 28.
151 Guiding Principle 29.
152 On this see the dedicated page of the Business and Human Rights Resource Centre: http://business-humanrights.org/en/un-guiding-principles/implementation-tools-examples/implementation-by-governments/by-type-of-initiative/national-action-plans (last accessed 12 April 2016). See also Damiano de Felice and Andreas Graf, 'The Potential of National Action Plans to Implement Human Rights Norms: An Early Assessment with Respect to the UN Guiding Principles on Business and Human Rights', 7 *Journal of Human Rights Practice* 40 (2015).
153 See below.
154 International Finance Corporation, Performance Standards on Environmental and Social Sustainability, 1 January 2012.
155 Communication from the Commission to the European Parliament, the Council, the European Economic and Social Committee and the Committee of the Regions, 'A renewed EU strategy 2011–14 for Corporate Social Responsibility', COM(2011) 681 final, 25 October 2011.

Crucially, most businesses and governments have accepted the Guiding Principles as an adequate basis for discussion.[156] While the NGOs' reactions to the Framework and the Guiding Principles have been much cooler, they now tend to use the Guiding Principles in their advocacy work while acknowledging their limitations and calling for more robust mechanisms.[157] John Ruggie himself has admitted that the Guiding Principles are only a starting point, 'a foundation for expanding the international human rights regime to encompass not only countries and individuals, but also companies'.[158]

As a follow-up to John Ruggie's mandate, the UN Human Rights Council created a working group on the issue of human rights and transnational corporations and other business enterprises consisting of five members.[159] Its role is to promote the Guiding Principles and to make recommendations for their implementation by governments and all relevant actors.[160]

The Guiding Principles aim to bridge the corporate accountability gap, but it is too early to say whether they will make a genuine impact on the lives of those most affected by corporate human rights violations. It will depend on the extent to which states and companies act upon them. The last part of this book covers the practical consequences of the state duty to protect human rights against corporate abuse. As seen in this section, the Guiding Principles' approach is to consider the corporate responsibility to respect human rights as a social and not a legal expectation. From a practical point of view, this means that it is left to companies themselves to act in order to implement the corporate responsibility to respect. This is the reason why the next chapter covers the issue of self-regulation of business.

## The OECD Guidelines for Multinational Enterprises

The Organisation for Economic Cooperation and Development (OECD) is an international organisation established in 1961. The ancestor of the

156 See International Organisation of Employers (IOE), the International Chamber of Commerce (ICC) and the Business and Industry Advisory Committee (BIAC) to the OECD, 'Joint Statement on Business & Human Rights to the United Nations Human Rights Council Geneva', 30 May 2011. See also Statements by governments at the Human Rights Council Session at which the Guiding Principles were endorsed, on the Business and Human Rights Resource Centre's website.

157 See for example Jens Martens, Global Policy Forum, 'Problematic Pragmatism. The Ruggie Report 2008: Background, Analysis and Perspectives', June 2008. See also Amnesty International, ESCR-Net, Human Rights Watch, International Commission of Jurists, International Federation for Human Rights (FIDH), Rights and Accountability in Development (RAID), 'Joint Civil Society Statement to the 17th Session of the Human Rights Council', 30 May 2011.

158 John Gerard Ruggie, *Just Business*, New York and London: W. W. Norton & Company Inc. (2013), p. 124.

159 UN Human Rights Council, Resolution in resolution A/HRC/17/4, 6 July 2011, para. 6.

160 For information on the Working Group, see its official webpage on the UN website, www.ohchr.org/EN/Issues/Business/Pages/WGHRandtransnationalcorporationsandoth erbusiness.aspx (last accessed 15 June 2016).

OECD, the Organisation for European Economic Cooperation (OEEC), was established in 1948 to manage the US-funded Marshall Plan for the reconstruction of Europe. The membership was initially composed only of Western, developed states, but has progressively come to include some emerging countries as well. However, the so-called BRICS countries (Brazil, Russia, India, China and South Africa) are not members of the OECD.[161]

In 1976, the OECD published the first version of their Guidelines for Multinational Enterprises (hereinafter 'the OECD Guidelines' or 'the Guidelines'). The Guidelines must be put in the context of the discussions on the UN Code of Conduct which were taking place at the same time. While the UN Code was eventually abandoned, the drafting process of the OECD Guidelines was successful. This may be because OECD countries constitute a relatively homogenous group of developed states. By contrast, as seen earlier, developing and developed countries disagreed a great deal about how to regulate transnational corporations, which eventually led to the Code's failure. Hence Daniel Plaine's suggestion that

> the United States opted for the negotiation of the OECD code first, rather than an OAS [Organisation of American States] or a U.N. code, on the implicit assumption that the standards for corporate conduct acceptable to most or all industrialized nations of the OECD would be far more palatable than those acceptable to the less developed countries in the U.N. or the OAS. In other words, the OECD was the most favorable forum available. The OECD agreements should constitute a common bargaining position of the industrialized countries in the progress of negotiations on codes of conduct in the U.N.[162]

This two-step plan did not succeed and while the OECD Guidelines were adopted and remain an important source of regulation for multinational corporations, they did not lead to prompt agreement at the international level, and the Code was never adopted.

The Guidelines are part of a package of documents annexed to a governmental Declaration on International Investment and International Enterprises.[163] Besides the Guidelines themselves, the package contains Decisions of the OECD Council on Inter-Governmental Consultation procedures on the Guidelines for Multinational Enterprises, on National Treatment and on International Investment Incentives and Disincentives. As with the UN Code of Conduct, it appears that the question of multinationals' impact

---

161 OECD Membership, OECD Website, www.oecd.org/about/membersandpartners/ (last accessed 15 June 2016).

162 Daniel J. Plaine, 'The OECD Guidelines for Multinational Enterprises', 11 *International Lawyer* 339 (1977), p. 340.

163 OECD, Declaration on International Investment and International Enterprises, 21 June 1976.

on human rights and the protection of the environment was seen at the time as inseparable from foreign direct investment as a whole.

The preamble to the Guidelines indicates that the Guidelines' aim is to 'encourage the positive contributions which multinational enterprises can make to economic and social progress and to minimise and resolve the difficulties to which their various operations may give rise'.[164] The preamble also highlights that the Guidelines are non-binding, non-legally enforceable voluntary recommendations addressed by states to multinational enterprises, and that the latter should first and foremost abide by the domestic law of the countries in which they operate.[165] Hence from the very first version of the Guidelines, which have been revised a number of times since their adoption, OECD member states embraced a non-binding, soft approach, leading to interrogations about whether or not enterprises should respect the Guidelines, and if so on what basis.

Discussing that version of the Guidelines in an article published in 1977 focusing on their practical implications for US companies, Daniel Plaine remarked that they 'cannot be ignored'.[166] He argued that, given the significant input of the business community in the negotiation of the Guidelines, it would be considered bad faith on its part to reject them, especially as they are part of a package that includes recommendations to governments which are to the advantage of multinational companies.[167] Moreover, 'it would hardly suit most companies to act in a manner blatantly inconsistent with what appears to be a consensus as to good corporate behavior'.[168] He pointed to instances where disregarding the Guidelines could backfire against US companies, when, for example, they seek help from the US government in investment disputes with a host state.[169] In sum, he concluded, the prospects of 'improving the battered images of our companies and of obtaining fairer treatment abroad should be well worth the obligations of complying with the Guidelines' standards of good conduct'.[170] His argument is similar to Ruggie's position on social expectations with regard to businesses' operations. Although it is not phrased in that way, it is clear that Plaine saw more in the Guidelines than a purely voluntary set of recommendations addressed to multinational companies. This goes to show once again that in the area of business and human rights, the traditional legal distinction between binding and non-binding instruments, as applicable to states, is ill suited to describe the complex mix of powers and interests at stake.

---

164 Preamble of the Guidelines, para. 2.
165 Ibid., para. 6–7.
166 Daniel J. Plaine, 'The OECD Guidelines for Multinational Enterprises', 11 *International Lawyer* 339 (1977), p. 343.
167 Ibid., p. 345.
168 Ibid., p. 344.
169 Ibid.
170 Ibid., pp. 345–346.

Compared to the more recent versions of the Guidelines, the 1976 version is relatively short and does not include any mention of 'human rights'. However, it does include references to issues such as social progress, protection of the environment, good relations with local communities and non-discrimination, as well as a chapter on 'employment and industrial relations' centred on labour rights.[171] Beyond that, the Guidelines provide guidance in a number of key areas, such as disclosure of information, competition, financing, taxation and science and technology, and a first chapter on 'General Policies'.

The Decision of the OECD Council on Inter-Governmental Consultation procedures on the Guidelines for Multinational Enterprises, which was part of the same package, entrusts the Committee on International Investment and Multinational Enterprises with the task to 'periodically or at the request of a Member country hold an exchange of views on matters related to the guidelines and the experience gained in their application'.[172] This was meant to give states the opportunity, among other things, to solve disputes related to the application of the Guidelines. The Decision also stated that it would be reviewed after three years.[173]

The 1979 review led to only one change to the Guidelines: the addition of a provision in paragraph 8 of the chapter on 'Employment and Industrial Relations'. The initial version required enterprises, during negotiations with representatives of employees, not to 'threaten to utilise a capacity to transfer the whole or part of an operating unit from the country concerned in order to influence unfairly those negotiations or to hinder the exercise of a right to organise'. In 1979 the paragraph was modified so as to also prohibit enterprises from threatening to 'transfer employees from the enterprises' component entities in other countries' in order to unfairly influence negotiations or the exercise of labour rights.[174]

The review report highlights the pioneering nature of the OECD work on the regulation of multinational enterprises and its influence on other systems. It also points to the similarities between the OECD Guidelines and other international initiatives such as the UN Code of Conduct and the ILO Declaration.[175] Clearly there was awareness among the OECD member states about the international context and the importance of the Guidelines within that context, as the only international, general text regulating multinational companies at the time.

171 General policies 2, 4 and 6, and Chapter 6.
172 Decision of the OECD Council on Inter-Governmental Consultation procedures on the Guidelines for Multinational Enterprises, para. 1 (1976).
173 Decision of the OECD Council on Inter-Governmental Consultation procedures on the Guidelines for Multinational Enterprises, para. 5.
174 OECD, 'International Investment and Multinational Enterprises, Review of the 1976 Declaration and Decisions', pp. 37–38.
175 OECD, 'International Investment and Multinational Enterprises, Review of the 1976 Declaration and Decisions', pp. 26–27.

The next review occurred in 1984 and resulted in paragraph 2 of the General Policies being modified to include 'consumer interests' as one of the member countries' aims to which multinational enterprises should give due consideration. Perhaps more importantly, it was on the occasion of this review that the Council of the OECD decided that

> Member governments shall set up National Contact Points for undertaking promotional activities, handling inquiries and for discussions with the parties concerned on all matters related to the Guidelines so that they can contribute to the solution of problems which may arise in this connection.[176]

As seen further below, the National Contact Points remain a key feature of the system set up by the OECD Guidelines.

In 1991, the next review process brought about the inclusion of a new chapter in the Guidelines, on the protection of the environment 'in response to the significant concerns that ha[d] developed in this area'.[177] The 1991 review emphasises a change in perceptions and attitudes towards multinational enterprises, and partly attributes this development to the Guidelines, the work of the OECD on direct investment and the National Contact Points.[178] While it is difficult to evaluate the extent to which the review's authors' perception on the role of the Guidelines was accurate, it is clear that by the beginning of the 1990s the opposition between developed and developing countries with regard to foreign direct investment had significantly reduced.

An OECD Report published in 1997 also points to the change of attitudes towards multinational enterprises, to the calmer relationships between developing and developed countries with regard to foreign investment and to the consistently moderate approach characterising the Guidelines and OECD work around them.[179] This may be seen as slightly ironic because at the same time negotiations for the adoption of the OECD-led Multilateral Agreement on Investment (MAI) were at an impasse, and they eventually failed in 1998 due to what had become irreconcilable positions between developing and developed countries. That being said, and as mentioned in Chapter 6, while states could not agree on a single text, they nevertheless encouraged foreign direct investment through the signature of hundreds of

---

176 OECD, 'The Guidelines for Multinational Enterprises, Second revised decision of the Council', May 1984, para. 1.
177 OECD, 'The OECD Declaration and Decisions on International Investment and Multinational Enterprises. 1991 Review', Paris: OECD (1992), pp. 38 and 52–54.
178 OECD, 'The OECD Declaration and Decisions on International Investment and Multinational Enterprises. 1991 Review', Paris: OECD (1992), pp. 39 and 41–42.
179 OECD, 'The OECD Guidelines for Multinational Enterprises', OCDE/GD(97)40, 24 March 1997, pp. 7–8.

Azeen
capitalis
elite

bilateral investment treaties, which goes to show that pacified relationships had indeed developed.

The 2000 version of the Guidelines introduced a reference to human rights in Chapter 2 on General Policies. OECD governments' acknowledgement of multinational corporations' potentially negative human rights impacts was an important step in the development of business and human rights as a distinct field of studies. A new paragraph 2 stated that 'enterprises should (...) respect the human rights of those affected by their activities consistent with the host government's international obligations and commitments'.[180] The official commentary of this provision reads as follows:

> While promoting and upholding human rights is primarily the responsibility of governments, where corporate conduct and human rights intersect enterprises do play a role, and thus MNEs are encouraged to respect human rights, not only in their dealings with employees, but also with respect to others affected by their activities, in a manner that is consistent with host governments' international obligations and commitments. The Universal Declaration of Human Rights and other human rights obligations of the government concerned are of particular relevance in this regard.[181]

Perhaps one can view OECD countries' recognition of the human rights impact of businesses and developing countries' growing support for foreign direct investment through the signature of bilateral investment treaties as two interconnected and mutually reinforcing developments, as if each side had taken a step towards the other.

The other important development in the 2000 version of the Guidelines is the introduction of a complaint mechanism against multinational enterprises to be administered by each state's National Contact Point, though the terms used are much less clear than those. As seen previously, the NCPs were introduced as part of the 1984 review of the Guidelines. Their role was to promote the Guidelines and facilitate discussions with the parties concerned – an imprecise and arguably weak mandate. The 2000 version includes 'procedural guidance' for NCPs on how to handle 'specific instances' during which NCPs can become involved in facilitating dialogue among parties. From a vague facilitator, each NCP hence comes to be in charge of running what can be described as an embryonic non-judicial, state-run dispute settlement mechanism. What is more, NCPs are required to 'make publicly available the result of these procedures'.[182]

180 OECD Guidelines, 2000 version.
181 OECD, Commentary on the OECD Guidelines for Multinational Enterprises, 2008, pp. 38–39. Although dated 2008, this version is the 2000 version.
182 OECD Guidelines, Procedural Guidance, 2000.

The 2000 amendments to the Guidelines were a significant step forward and undoubtedly raised the Guidelines' international profile. By interpreting the Guidelines and applying them to real situations, NCPs have played a key role in the development of business and human rights as a distinct field of study, advocacy and litigation. While it is beyond the scope of this book to delve into the rich and ever-growing body of 'caselaw' that NCPs around the world have produced since then, the interested reader is invited to browse the searchable database of these 'specific instances' available on the OECD website for an *aperçu* of the complaints and how NCPs have dealt with them.[183]

The latest review process led to the adoption of the 2011 version of the Guidelines. The changes introduced are substantial, and are summarised in a useful document issued by the OECD.[184] With regard to human rights, three changes must be highlighted. First, the reference, in paragraph 2 of Chapter II on general policies, to host countries' international human rights obligations and commitments was dropped. Multinational enterprises are now required to 'respect the internationally recognised human rights of those affected by their activities'. This means that this requirement exists irrespective of the scope of the host country's obligations and, crucially, irrespective of whether or not it is abiding by these obligations.   c l(- UNGPs

Second, an entirely new Chapter IV titled 'Human Rights' was introduced. The chapter's language is aligned with the UN Guiding Principles on Business and Human Rights. The OECD Guidelines now mention the state duty to protect human rights and the corporate responsibility to respect human rights, which means having a human rights policy, carrying out human rights due diligence and setting up remediation processes to address human rights violations. Such convergence in business and human rights standards constitutes an important development.

Third, the 2011 version of the Guidelines introduces important changes affecting NCPs. States adhering to the Guidelines are now required to 'make available human and financial resources to their National Contact Points so that they can effectively fulfil their responsibilities, taking into account internal budget priorities and practices.'[185] The Guidelines also provide that NCPs should be established in such a way as to enable them 'to operate in an impartial manner while maintaining an adequate level of accountability to the

---

183 The database is available at http://mneguidelines.oecd.org/database/ (last accessed 29 August 2014). For a discussion of the case, see OECD Watch, *Remedies Remain Rare* (2015); and John G. Ruggie and Tamaryn Nelson, 'Human Rights and the OECD Guidelines for Multinational Enterprises: Normative Innovations and Implementation Challenges', *Corporate Social Responsibility Initiative Working Paper No. 66*, Cambridge, MA: John F. Kennedy School of Government, Harvard University (2015).

184 OECD, 2011 Update of the OECD Guidelines for Multinational Enterprises, Comparative table of changes made to the 2000 text, 2012.

185 OECD, Amendment of the Decision of the Council on the OECD Guidelines for Multinational Enterprises.

adhering government'. Perhaps the greatest change of all for the purpose of this book is an increased focus on transparency in NCPs' treatment of specific instances. NCPs now have the obligation to give reasons as to why they wish to drop a 'case', and to issue a statement when no agreement between the parties can be reached. The statement may include reasons as to why no such agreement was reached, possibly because of a lack of cooperation on the part of the multinational enterprise. In practice, this means that a non-cooperative multinational enterprise accused of having violated human rights in the course of its operations may end up being named and shamed against its will and will not be able to prevent the NCP's report from being published. These changes have strengthened the NCP mechanism, which now has more teeth. This is all the more so because, while the Guidelines remain non-binding for multinational enterprises, the part of the Guidelines on National Contact Points is addressed to states and is binding them.

Both the procedural and substantive amendments introduced in 2011 contribute to viewing the OECD Guidelines as a key text for the international regulation of business in the human rights field. At the time of writing, the NCP-run specific instances' proceedings remain the closest thing there exists to an international mechanism to hold corporations accountable for human rights violations. Indeed, although NCPs are not international but domestic bodies, and although the Guidelines are not truly international in character since they emanate from the OECD and not an organisation with universal membership, NCPs interpret an international list of Guidelines and at least partly follow an internationally agreed procedure to deal with the 'cases' they are presented with. Although the OECD does not have universal membership, a total of forty-four countries have adhered to the Guidelines and are bound by the obligation to set up their own NCPs. These countries include the thirty-four OECD member states as well as ten non-member states.[186]

## Conclusion

In recent years international soft law initiatives have blossomed in the area of business and human rights. The UN Draft Code on Transnational Corporations and the UN Draft Norms on Business and Human Rights have both failed to attract governments' approval, but the UN Global Compact, the UN Guiding Principles and the OECD Guidelines succeeded in doing so and all constitute important developments. While they do not place binding legal obligations on businesses, these various initiatives seek to encourage businesses to at least respect human rights. The UN 'Protect, Respect and Remedy' Framework devised by John Ruggie and his team places the

---

186 These are Brazil, Argentina, Colombia, Egypt, Latvia, Lithuania, Morocco, Peru, Romania and Tunisia.

corporate responsibility to respect human rights in the realm of social expectations, as opposed to legal obligations. The UN Guiding Principles on Business and Human Rights – the initiative with the greatest potential so far – are also based on this premise. For lawyers, the notion of 'social expectation' may sound puzzling. Indeed, under any given domestic legal system, either a conduct is within the law or it is not, and in practice there is little room for non-strictly legal notions.

What, then, are the practical consequences of the assertion that society expects businesses to respect human rights? The cynical lawyer may answer that as long as a company acts within the domestic law applicable to its business, there will be no consequence for a company that does not respect human rights. Moreover, in countries where the legal framework is weak or where, as is often the case, law is poorly applied, a company may well be violating domestic law and still face no charge, lawsuit or fine. Ruggie has attempted to bridge this gap by introducing the notion of corporate human rights responsibility as a social expectation. As suggested in Chapter 5, it is argued here that this is a second-best option and that there is a strong argument to be made in favour of the recognition of corporate human rights obligations under international law, at least as far as certain human rights are concerned.

Whether we see the corporate responsibility to respect human rights as a legal obligation under international law or a mere social expectation, the fact remains that the initiatives reviewed in this section seek to induce change in how companies, especially multinational corporations, do business, and to make them more accountable. Even if the international legal framework on business and human rights was stronger, it would still be down to companies themselves to make the necessary behavioural changes needed for human rights to become embedded into their practices. In the same way that the reason why the majority of human beings will never kill anyone is not because the law prohibits it, but because they believe it is wrong and are capable of restraint, the fear of lawsuits is not the only reason why companies consciously choose to respect human rights. To a large extent the regulation of business in the area of business and human rights is self-imposed, and the next chapter focuses on the notion of self-regulation as well as other private modes of regulation in the business and human rights field, so as to complete the regulatory panorama.

# Bibliography

## *Books*

Karp, David J., *Responsibility for Human Rights, Transnational Corporations in Imperfect States*, Cambridge: Cambridge University Press (2014).
Ruggie, John G., *Just Business*, New York and London: W. W. Norton and Company Ltd (2013).

Tagi Sagafi-Nejad and John Dunning, *The UN and Transnational Corporations. From Code of Conduct to Global Compact*, Bloomington and Indianapolis: Indiana University Press (2008).

## Journal articles

Ball, George W., 'Cosmocorp: The Importance of Being Stateless', 2 *Columbia Journal of World Business* 25 (1967).

Bernaz, Nadia, 'Enhancing Corporate Accountability for Human Rights Violations: Is Extraterritoriality the Magic Potion?', 117 *Journal of Business Ethics* 493 (2013).

Blake, David H., 'International Labor and the Regulation of Multinational Corporations: Proposals and Prospects', 11 *San Diego Law Review* 179 (1973–1974).

Catá Backer, Larry, 'Multinational Corporations, Transnational Law: The United Nations' Norms on the Responsibilities of Transnational Corporations as Harbinger of Corporate Responsibility in International Law', 37 *Columbia Human Rights Law Review* 287 (2006).

Catá Backer, Larry, 'On the Evolution of the United Nations' 'Protect-Respect-Remedy' Project: The State, the Corporation and Human Rights in a Global Governance Context', 9 *Santa Clara Journal of International Law* 37 (2011).

Coonrod, Stephan 'The United Nations Code of Conduct for Transnational Corporations', 18 *Harvard International Law Journal* 273 (1977).

de Felice, Damiano and Graf, Andreas, 'The Potential of National Action Plans to Implement Human Rights Norms: an Early Assessment with Respect to the UN Guiding Principles on Business and Human Rights', 7 *Journal of Human Rights Practice* 40 (2015).

Deva, Surya, 'Global Compact: A Critique of the UN's "Public–Private" Partnership for Promoting Corporate Citizenship', 34 *Syracuse Journal of International Law and Commerce* 107 (2006–2007).

Ghafele, Roya, and Mercer, Angus, '"Not Starting in Sixth Gear": An Assessment of the UN Global Compact's Use of Soft Law as a Global Governance Structure for Corporate Social Responsibility', 17 *University of California Davis Journal of International Law and Policy* 41 (2010–2011).

Kell, Georg, 'The Global Compact: Selected Experiences and Reflections', 59 *Journal of Business Ethics* 69 (2005).

King, Betty, 'The U.N. Global Compact: Responsibility for Human Rights, Labor Relations, and the Environment in Developing Nations', 34 *Cornell International Law Journal* 481 (2001).

Kinley, David and Chambers, Rachel, 'The UN Human Rights Norms for Corporations: The Private Implications of Public International Law', 6(3) *Human Rights Law Review* 447 (2006).

Miretski, Pini Pavel and Bachmann, Sascha-Dominik, 'UN Norms on the Responsibility of Transnational Corporations and other Business Enterprises with Regard to Human Rights: a Requiem', 17 *Deakin Law Review* 5 (2012).

Oshionebo, Evaristus, 'The UN Global Compact and Accountability of Transnational Corporations: Separating Myth from Realities', 19 *Florida Journal of International Law* 1 2007.

Plaine, Daniel J., 'The OECD Guidelines for Multinational Enterprises', 11 *International Lawyer* 339 (1977).

Rubin, Seymour J, 'Harmonization of Rules: A Perspective on the UN Commission on Transnational Corporations', 8 *Law and Policy International in Business* 875 (1976).

Ruggie, John G., 'The Global Compact as a Learning Network', 7 *Journal of Corporate Citizenship* 371 (2001).

Ruggie, John G., 'Business and Human Rights: The Evolving International Agenda', 101 *American Journal of International Law* 819 (2007).

Sauvant, Karl P., 'The Negotiations of the United Nations Code of Conduct on Transnational Corporations Experience and Lessons Learned', 16 *The Journal of World Investment & Trade* 11 (2015).

Thérien, Jean-Philippe and Pouliot, Vincent, 'The Global Compact: Shifting the Politics of International Development?', 2 *Global Governance* 55 (2006).

Wang, Nian Tzu, 'The Design of an International Code of Conduct for Transnational Corporations', 10 *Journal of International Law and Economics* 319 (1975).

Weissbrodt, David and Kruger, Muria, 'Norms on the Responsibilities of Transnational Corporations and Other Business Enterprises with Regard to Human Rights', 97 *American Journal of International Law* 901 (2003).

Weissbrodt, David, 'UN Perspectives on "Business and Humanitarian and Human Rights Obligations"', 100 *American Society of International Law Proceedings* 129 (2006).

Wynhoven, Ursula A., 'The Protect-Respect-Remedy Framework and the United Nations Global Compact', 9 *Santa Clara Journal of International Law* 81 (2011).

*Book chapters*

Muchlinski, Peter, 'Attempts to extend the Accountability of Transnational Corporations: The Role of UNCTAD', *in* Menno T Kamminga and Saman Zia-Zarifi (eds) *Liability of Multinational Corporations under International Law*, The Hague, London, Boston: Kluwer Law International (2000), pp. 97–117.

*Official documents*

UN General Assembly Resolution 1803 (XVII) Permanent Sovereignty over natural resources, 14 December 1962.

Common Regime of Treatment of Foreign Capital and of Trademarks, Patents, Licenses, and Royalties (Decision 24) 10 ILM 152 (1971).

UN Department of Economic and Social Affairs, *World Economic Survey 1971, Current Economic Developments*, UN Doc. E/5144 (1972).

ECOSOC Resolution 1721 (LIII), 1972 in UN Doc. E/5209.

UN DESA, *Multinational Corporations in World Development*, UN Doc. ST/ECA/190 (1973).

UN General Assembly Resolution 3201 (S-VI) and 3202 (S-VI), 1 May 1974.

*The Impact of Multinational Corporations on the Development Process and on International Relations*, UN Doc. E/5500/Add.1 (Part I) (24 May 1974) 13 ILM. 800 (1974).

DESA, Summary of the Hearings Before the Group of Eminent Persons to Study the

Impact of Multinational Corporations on Development and on International Relations, UN Doc. ST/ESA/15 (1974).

UN General Assembly Resolution 3281 (XXIX) Charter of Economic Rights and Duties of States, 12 December 1974.

ECOSOC Resolution 1913 (LVII), December 1974.

ECOSOC Resolution 1908 (LVII), December 1974.

Commission on Transnational Corporations, Report on the First Session, E/5655 and Corr. 1; E/C.10/6 and Corr.1 and Add.1 (1975).

OECD, Declaration on International Investment and International Enterprises, 21 June 1976.

Decision of the OECD Council on Inter-Governmental Consultation procedures on the Guidelines for Multinational Enterprises (1976).

Transnational Corporations: Issues Involved in the Formulation of a Code of Conduct, UN Doc. E/C.10/17, 20 July 1976.

OECD, 'International Investment and Multinational Enterprises, Review of the 1976 Declaration and Decisions' (1979).

UN Document E/C.l0/1982/6, 5 June 1982, reprinted in 22 ILM 192 (1983).

OECD, 'The Guidelines for Multinational Enterprises, Second revised decision of the Council', May 1984.

OECD, 'The OECD Declaration and Decisions on International Investment and Multinational Enterprises. 1991 Review', Paris: OECD (1992).

OECD, 'The OECD Guidelines for Multinational Enterprises', OCDE/GD(97)40, 24 March 1997.

UN Sub-Commission, E/CN.4/Sub.2/1997/50 (1997).

UN Sub-Commission, UN Doc E/CN.4/Sub.2/1998/45 (1998).

South African Truth and Reconciliation Commission Report, Vol IV (1998).

UN Sub-Commission, Working Document on the Impact of the Activities of Transnational Corporations on the Realization of Economic, Social and Cultural Rights, UN Doc. E/CN.4/Sub.2/1998/6 (1998).

Press Release, Secretary-General, 'Secretary-General Proposes Global Compact on Human Rights, Labour, Environment, in Address to World Economic Forum in Davos', U.N. Doc. SG/SM/6881, 1 February 1999.

Sub-Commission, Report of the Sessional Working Group on the Working Methods and Activities of Transnational Corporations on Its First Session, UN Doc. E/CN.4/Sub.2/1999/9 (1999).

Ministerial Statement adopted by the Twenty-Fourth Annual Meeting of the Ministers of Foreign Affairs of the Group of 77 (2000), available at www.g77.org/doc/docs.html (last accessed 23 April 2016).

OECD Guidelines, Procedural Guidance, 2000.

OECD Guidelines, 2000 version.

UN Sub-Commission, Resolution 2003/16, E/CN.4/Sub.2/2003/L.11 (2003).

UN Doc. E/CN.4/Sub.2/2003/12/Rev.2 (2003).

Commentary on the Norms on the Responsibilities of Transnational Corporations and Other Business Enterprises with Regard to Human Rights, U.N. Doc. E/CN.4/Sub.2/2003/38/Rev.2 (2003).

UN Commission on Human Rights, Decision 2004/116, 'Responsibilities of transnational corporations and related business enterprises with regard to human rights (2004).

Report of the United Nations High Commissioner on Human Rights on the

Responsibilities of Transnational Corporations and Related Business Enterprises with Regard to Human Rights, UN Doc. E/CN.4/2005/91 (2005).

Human Rights and Transnational Corporations and Other Business Enterprises, UN Doc. E/CN.4/2005/L.87 (2005).

Interim report of the Special Representative of the Secretary-General on the issue of human rights and transnational corporations and other business enterprises, UN Doc. E/CN.4/2006/97 (2006).

Report of the Special Representative of the Secretary-General (SRSG) on the issue of human rights and transnational corporations and other business enterprises, A/HRC/4/035 (2007).

Report of the Special Representative of the Secretary-General on the issue of human rights and transnational corporations and other business enterprises, John Ruggie, A/HRC/8/5 (2008).

OECD, Commentary on the OECD Guidelines for Multinational Enterprises (2008).

UN Human Rights Council, Resolution 17/4 Human rights and transnational corporations and other business enterprises, A/HRC/RES/17/4 (2011).

Guiding Principles on Business and Human Rights: Implementing the United Nations 'Protect, Respect and Remedy' Framework, A/HRC/17/31 (2011)

Communication from the Commission to the European Parliament, the Council, the European Economic and Social Committee and the Committee of the Regions, 'A renewed EU strategy 2011-14 for Corporate Social Responsibility', COM(2011) 681 final, 25 October 2011.

International Finance Corporation, Performance Standards on Environmental and Social Sustainability, 1 January 2012.

### *Miscellaneous*

Amnesty International, ESCR-Net, Human Rights Watch, International Commission of Jurists, International Federation for Human Rights (FIDH), Rights and Accountability in Development (RAID), 'Joint Civil Society Statement to the 17th Session of the Human Rights Council', 30 May 2011.

Business and Human Rights Resource Centre, http://business-humanrights.org/ (last accessed 21 March 2016).

Global Compact website, www.unglobalcompact.org/ (last accessed 23 April 2016).

International Organisation of Employers (IOE), the International Chamber of Commerce (ICC) and the Business and Industry Advisory Committee (BIAC) to the OECD, 'Joint Statement on Business & Human Rights to the United Nations Human Rights Council Geneva', 30 May 2011.

Martens, Jens, Global Policy Forum, 'Problematic Pragmatism. The Ruggie Report 2008: Background, Analysis and Perspectives', June 2008.OECD, 2011, Update of the OECD Guidelines for Multinational Enterprises, Comparative table of changes made to the 2000 text (2012).

OECD website, www.oecd.org (last accessed 23 April 2016).

OECD Watch, *Remedies Remain Rare* (2015).

Ruggie, John G., and Nelson, Tamaryn, 'Human Rights and the OECD Guidelines for Multinational Enterprises: Normative Innovations and Implementation Challenges', *Corporate Social Responsibility Initiative Working Paper No. 66*, Cambridge, MA: John F. Kennedy School of Government, Harvard University (2015).

# 8 Private regulation in business and human rights

The previous chapter focused on public international regulation of businesses in the field of human rights. This regulation is public in nature in the sense that the initiatives presented all emanate from governments or inter-governmental organisations such as the United Nations. This is so even when the private sector was consulted during the elaboration of the standards, as was the case for the UN Guiding Principles on Business and Human Rights, or other standards such as ISO 26000.[1] Although this form of regulation does not formally bind businesses, it is addressed to them and it aims at enhancing their accountability, irrespective of the extent to which they are willing to be held to account.

By contrast, private and semi-private modes of regulation, which form the focus of this chapter, emanate from the private sector in the sense that the private sector is involved in the production of the standards and plays an active role in their enforcement. The very notion of private modes of regulation has generated some degree of controversy. As one group of authors have put it, 'for some, the idea of private regulatory power, particularly where it involves a degree of self-regulation, is tantamount to deregulation or an abdication of regulation'.[2] In response, these authors have argued that

---

1   The International Organization for Standardization, an inter-governmental organisation in charge of developing voluntary international standards in order to facilitate trade, adopted the International Guidance Standard on Organizational Social Responsibility (ISO 26000) in 2010. However, unlike ISO Standards, which are auditable and can give rise to certification (for a development on certification schemes, see below), ISO 26000 is not a management system standard. The Organization makes clear that ISO26000 'is not intended or appropriate for certification purposes or regulatory or contractual use' (ISO 26000, www.iso.org/iso/iso26000, last accessed 23 April 2016); rather, it is simply meant to provide companies with guidance on corporate social responsibility. On ISO26000 see Halina Ward, 'The ISO 26000 International Guidance Standard on Social Responsibility: Implications for Public Policy and Transnational Democracy', 2 *Theoretical Inquiries in Law* 665 (2011). See also John Gerard Ruggie, *Just Business*, New York and London: W. W. Norton & Company Inc. (2013), pp. 163–165.

2   Colin Scott, Fabrizio Cafaggi and Linda Senden, 'The Conceptual and Constitutional Challenge of Transnational Private Regulation', 38 *Journal of Law and Society* 1 (2011), p. 5.

it is not unreasonable to hypothesize that the combination of direct participation of market actors and the interdependence of such actors with both NGOs and governments within many TPRERs [Transnational Private Regulatory Regimes] has the potential to combine advantages both for effectiveness and legitimacy as compared with inter-governmental regimes.[3]

Despite disagreement over the notion itself, private regulation has flourished in recent years in areas as diverse as human rights, the protection of the environment and advertising.[4] As described by Tim Bartley,

standard setting and regulation are increasingly being accomplished through private means. This includes not only traditional programs of industry self-regulation but also systems of transnational private regulation, in which coalitions of nonstate actors codify, monitor, and in some cases certify firms' compliance with labor, environmental, human rights, or other standards of accountability. For instance, in the past two decades, controversies over sweatshops, child labor, tropical deforestation, and other issues have spurred the formation of dozens of nongovernmental certification associations.[5]

Many authors advance the weakness of public regulation at the international level as an explanation for the rise of so-called transnational private regulation. The argument goes that because international public regulation is weak and too general to be directly applicable to a particular sector, let alone a particular company, businesses resort to taking matters into their own hands and creating their own forms of regulation.[6] The main incentive for voluntarily regulating themselves is companies' concern over their reputation in the areas of human rights and the protection of the environment. Hence engaging in the production of private regulation is a way to mitigate reputational risks and eventually increase profits.[7] Beyond reputation, Santoro puts

---

3    Ibid., p. 19.

4    Ibid., p. 6.

5    Tim Bartley, 'Institutional Emergence in an Era of Globalization: The Rise of Transnational Private Regulation of Labor and Environmental Conditions', 113 *American Journal of Sociology* 297 (2007), pp. 297–298. See also Fabrizio Cafaggi, 'New Foundations of Transnational Private Regulation', 38 *Journal of Law and Society* 20 (2011), pp. 23 and 26–27.

6    Tim Bartley, 'Institutional Emergence in an Era of Globalization: The Rise of Transnational Private Regulation of Labor and Environmental Conditions', 113 *American Journal of Sociology* 297 (2007), p. 298.

7    For an analysis of the different factors at stake, see Jonathan C. Borck and Cary Coglianese, 'Beyond Compliance: Explaining Business Participation in Voluntary Environmental Programs', *in* Christine Parker and Vibeke Lehman Nielsen, *Explaining Compliance. Business Responses to Regulation*, Cheltenham (UK) and Northampton (MA, USA): Edward Elgar (2011), pp. 139–169.

forward two other reasons why companies might adopt human rights-oriented codes of conduct in the apparel sector:

> the sincere belief that corporate executives and their companies have a moral duty to address the sweatshop problem; and even in some cases a hard-headed calculation that, rather than imposing costs, doing good means doing well, i.e. honoring global labor rights will also help firms to maximize profits.[8]

In the same vein, speaking about different forms of environmental certification, which they call 'voluntary programmes', Potoski and Prakash argue that such programmes

> require participants to incur specific private costs to produce public goods. In return, participants receive benefits that are excluded from non- participants, thereby creating incentives to join the program. For firms, the benefits of membership over taking the same actions unilaterally are the excludable branding certification that allows members to publicize their (...) membership [to the program] and thus claim credit for their pro- environmental activities.[9]

While these authors are talking about environmental certification, the same incentives are arguably at play with regard to social certification such as SA8000, described below. These incentives also play a role in other forms of private regulation in the area of business and human rights, namely 'corporate self-regulatory initiatives' such as company-level and sector-level human rights policies and codes of conduct and 'voluntary monitoring initiatives' such as public–private partnerships and multi-stakeholder initiatives.[10] Different authors have different ways of categorising types of private regulation. Fabrizio Cafaggi, for example, proposes four models of regulation: industry-driven, NGO-led, expert-led and multi-stakeholder models.[11] Interestingly, he shows the importance, in each model, of the regulatory relationship structure, which includes the regulator, the regulated and 'the

---

8   Michael A. Santoro, 'Beyond Codes of Conduct and Monitoring: An Organizational Integrity Approach to Global Labor Practices', 25 *Human Rights Quarterly* 407 (2003), p. 409.

9   Matthew Potoski and Aseem Prakash, 'Green Clubs and Voluntary Governance: ISO 14001 and Firms' Regulatory Compliance', 49 *American Journal of Political Science* 235 (2005), p. 236.

10  The phrases 'corporate self-regulatory initiatives' and 'voluntary monitoring initiatives' are borrowed from Adelle Blackett, 'Global Governance, Legal Pluralism and the Decentered State: A Labor Law Critique of Codes of Corporate Conduct', 8 *Indiana Journal of Global Legal Studies* 401, (2000–2001), p. 401.

11  Fabrizio Cafaggi, 'New Foundations of Transnational Private Regulation', 38 *Journal of Law and Society* 20 (2011), pp. 31–38.

beneficiaries of the regulatory process, those who are supposed to benefit from compliance with the regulation and are harmed by their violations'.[12] For example, beneficiaries could be factory workers in the case of a labour rights code of conduct or communities affected by conflict in the case of the Kimberley Process Certification Scheme, the multi-stakeholder initiative aiming at eradicating the trade in conflict diamonds.

With this multifaceted context in mind, the following sections present the main features of self-regulatory initiatives and voluntary monitoring initiatives, as well as certification mechanisms in the area of business and human rights.

## Corporate self-regulatory initiatives: human rights policies and codes of conduct

As seen in Chapter 7, UN Guiding Principle 16 recommends that all business enterprises adopt a 'human rights policy'. When not paired with any external monitoring mechanism, codes of conduct and human rights policies represent the most basic form of self-regulation. The Business and Human Rights Resource Centre keeps a list of companies with human rights-oriented codes of conduct or human rights policies.[13] The list shows great diversity in the naming of these documents. For example, ArcelorMittal, Barclays, Chevron, Coca-Cola, Disney, Gap, GoldCorp, H&M, Marriott, Monsanto, Ritz-Carlton, Standard Chartered and Tesco have all opted for a 'Human Rights Policy' or a 'Human Rights (Policy) Statement', while British Airways, Chiquita, Colgate-Palmolive, Dell, Jujitsu, Glencore, Lego, Nokia, Panasonic, PepsiCo, Société Générale, Sony, Timberland and Volvo have favoured the 'Code of Conduct' phraseology. Declinations of phrases such as 'Ethics Policy', 'Code of Business Ethics' or 'Code of Corporate Ethics' are also popular choices made for instance by Alstom, Bouygues, Daewoo, Ericsson, Gucci and L'Oréal.

### *The early days of codes of conduct*

Companies did not wait for the adoption of the UN Guiding Principles before they engaged with the idea of human rights. In the United States, J.C. Penney was one of the first companies to formally adopt an ethical statement, at the beginning of the twentieth century. In 1913 James Cash Penney Jr., founder of the company, met with several of his business partners and together they agreed on what they called 'The Original Body of Doctrine', a set of principles guiding the company. These seven principles, also known as the 'Penney Idea', read as follows:

12   Ibid., p. 32.
13   Business and Human Rights Resource Centre, 'Company policy statement on human rights', http://business-humanrights.org/en/company-policy-statements-on-human-rights (last accessed 14 June 2016).

1. To serve the public, as nearly as we can, to its complete satisfaction; 2. To expect from the service we render a fair remuneration and not all the profit the traffic will bear; 3. To do all in our power to pack the customer's dollar full of value, quality, and satisfaction; 4. To continue to train ourselves and our associates so that the service we give will be more and more intelligently performed; 5. To improve constantly the human factor in our business; 6. To reward men and women in our organization through participation in what the business produces; 7. To test our every policy, method, and act in this wise: 'Does it square with what is right and just?'[14]

Although the phrase 'human rights' was unlikely to appear in a 1913 document, the values embodied in the principles have a certain human rights flavour, for example in the area of non-discrimination. Clearly, the adoption of such principles was more the exception than the rule at the time. It was not until the end of the twentieth century that the number of global companies adopting codes of conduct rose dramatically, undoubtedly to address their consumers' concerns. As one author noted,

The big wave in adopting codes of conduct (...) emerged as a response to consumer campaigns. Fearing that consumers might reject products made under poor conditions, major corporations, such as Levi Strauss, Reebok, Liz Claiborne, and later Nike, decided to address the labor standards problem. Levi Strauss was the first company to develop a comprehensive code of conduct in 1991. The significance of the Levi Strauss example was that it was the first code of conduct on labor practices for suppliers, which were independent business partners that supply a brand name with products or services. More and more firms committed themselves to ensuring consistent application of labor norms to workers, regardless of where they do business and whether they directly own the operation.[15]

These earlier codes adopted in the 1990s were a 'mixed bag'[16] in terms of content. At that time, the idea of linking business operations with human rights impact was radical and few companies were comfortable with taking the leap. Perhaps more than content, the scope of these new codes is their

14  Mary Elizabeth Curry, *Creating an American Institution. The Merchandising Genius of J.C. Penney*, New York and London: Garland Publishing Inc. (1993), p. 152. Interestingly, J.C. Penney's current Statement of Business Ethics still refers to these principles.
15  Anke Hassel, 'The Evolution of a Global Labor Governance Regime', 21 *Governance: An International Journal of Policy, Administration and Institutions* 231 (2008), p. 239.
16  Cynthia Estlund, 'Enforcement of Private Transnational Labor Regulation: A New Frontier in the Anti-Sweatshop Movement?', *in* Fabrizio Cafaggi (ed.), *Enforcement of Transnational Regulation. Ensuring Compliance in a Globalized World*, Cheltenham (UK) and Northampton (MA, USA): Edward Elgar (2012), p. 241.

most interesting feature. Early on, companies adopted codes that were meant to apply not only to the company and its subsidiaries but also, indirectly, to suppliers and sub-contractors, who were expected to follow the policy as well. The consequences of such policies can be far-reaching. Indeed,

> some of these private initiatives have been so extensive as to lead many firms either to cancel contracts or compel suppliers found to violate company guidelines to reform, to withdraw their operations from countries that violate labor rights norms, or to engage in constructive dialogue with suppliers and local officials.[17]

### Monitoring compliance with codes of conduct

It is difficult to assess codes of conduct and human rights policies' degree of effectiveness generally, because each company has its own code and processes. It seems as though a company doing its best to have its code of conduct enforced throughout its supply chain should be able to make a difference in the working conditions and lives of workers all the way down the supply chain. This might require external auditing, and in any event it does require internal processes to identify issues, address them and monitor progress. Monitoring the application of the code down the supply chain through auditing mechanisms is only one type of activity in which companies may engage, and research has shown that it is insufficient in itself to significantly improve working conditions.[18] This conclusion is reinforced by the existence of a growing business of audit fraud, in which suppliers use tricks, including tailor-made computer software, to fabricate false data so as to satisfy famous brands' auditing criteria and lie about the true working conditions in their factories.[19] Companies are therefore expected to do more than mere auditing, whether internal or external, and to have more elaborate policies in place, such as grievance mechanisms, as recommended in the UN Guiding Principles on Business and Human Rights. The necessity of embedding human rights policies in the daily operations of companies appears here with clarity. As Santoro notes,

> while codes of conduct and monitoring systems can help to uncover and assess the severity of human rights problems, they are not, in and of themselves, solutions to those problems. Just as financial accounting

17  Elisa Westfield, 'Globalization, Governance and Multinational Enterprise Responsibility: Corporate Codes of Conduct in the 21st Century', 42 *Virginia Journal of International Law* 1075 (2002), p. 1098.
18  See for example, Richard M. Locke, Fei Qin and Alberto Brause, 'Does Monitoring Improve Labor Standards? Lessons from Nike', 61 *Industrial and Labour Relations Review* 3 (2007–2008), pp. 20–21.
19  Ethical Trading Initiative, Auditing Working Conditions, www.ethicaltrade.org/issues/auditing-working-conditions (last accessed 23 April 2016).

can't generate profits, monitoring can't generate good behavior. In each case, the process can only tell you how well or poorly you are doing in achieving your financial or social objectives.[20]

In short, monitoring a code of conduct, however ambitious in its contents, will always be of limited efficiency if suppliers have strong financial incentives to cut corners in order to stay in business with, say, a multinational company in the apparel sector.[21] This leads to another important point, which is that by isolating the states' obligations from the responsibilities of businesses, the Guiding Principles leave the most complex problems untouched – those related to the political and legal contexts in which companies operate. In turn, codes of conduct tend to overlook the contexts in which they apply. Typically, CSR departments of Western multinational companies design codes of conduct which are to be applied in developing countries. These countries may face numerous regulatory challenges of their own due to under-development, poor governance and corruption. As one author contends,

> Codes of corporate conduct apply generally to the workers in companies with transnational involvement; few differentiate between individual countries or contemplate those countries' specificities. Tellingly, the differences between individual codes of corporate conduct seem more accurately to mirror the sensibilities of the various national audiences of consumers to whom the products are targeted, even at the risk that different MNEs that subcontract to the same local firm will seek to regulate the workers' conditions of employment differently. The regulatory link is the product, rather than the worker or the workplace.[22]

## Codes of conduct and consumer protection

In the end the main advantage of the codes may be that they help raise public awareness in developed countries regarding labour issues in developing countries. The fact that codes are common in the apparel industry, where 'brand-name loyalty is crucial',[23] reinforces the impression that the codes

---

20  Michael A. Santoro, 'Beyond Codes of Conduct and Monitoring: An Organizational Integrity Approach to Global Labor Practices', 25 *Human Rights Quarterly* 407 (2003), p. 410.

21  Cynthia Estlund, 'Enforcement of Private Transnational Labor Regulation: A New Frontier in the Anti-Sweatshop Movement?', *in* Fabrizio Cafaggi (ed.), *Enforcement of Transnational Regulation. Ensuring Compliance in a Globalized World*, Cheltenham (UK) and Northampton (MA, USA): Edward Elgar (2012), p. 246.

22  Adelle Blackett, 'Global Governance, Legal Pluralism and the Decentered State: A Labor Law Critique of Codes of Corporate Conduct', 8 *Indiana Journal of Global Legal Studies* 401, (2000–2001), p. 412.

23  Ibid., p. 425.

exist at least partly to satisfy Western customers. Private codes of conduct, by definition, can do nothing or very little to address the more structural issues that lead to violations of social rights and which remain first and foremost the responsibility of states. What is more, one of the risks associated with the development of corporate codes of conduct is that they focus attention away from the only actors who can genuinely address those structural problems – states – which could prove counterproductive in the long run.[24] Chapter 6 highlighted the danger of siloing the field of study of business and human rights away from other areas of international law. For example, one of the side effects of WTO agreements is that they encourage developing countries to keep wages low so as to maintain their competitive advantage. This limits states' capacity to adopt regulation that would be more protective of labour rights. Bearing in mind that this was only one example among a variety of others, it is clear that codes of conduct, even if their enforcement is externally audited, may be able to achieve only very little.

The nature, under domestic law, of codes of conduct and companies' public statements with regard to their human rights records remains an unsettled issue. In *Nike, Inc. v. Kasky* the US Supreme Court had the opportunity to decide whether Nike's statements that their labour practices were respectful of employees' human rights, while they knew this was not true, constituted violations of California's unfair trade practices and false advertising laws, or whether these statements constituted non-commercial speech, protected by the First Amendment to the US Constitution.[25] Eventually, the Court refused to make a decision on the merits and the parties – Marc Kasky, a consumer rights activist, and Nike – settled the case.[26] As more and more companies adopt human rights policies and codes of conduct following the adoption of the relatively consensual UN Guiding Principles on Business and Human Rights, more similar cases are expected to arise.[27]

---

24  Ibid., pp. 425–426 and 427–431. See also Cynthia Estlund, 'Enforcement of Private Transnational Labor Regulation: A New Frontier in the Anti-Sweatshop Movement?', *in* Fabrizio Cafaggi (ed.), *Enforcement of Transnational Regulation. Ensuring Compliance in a Globalized World*, Cheltenham (UK) and Northampton (MA, USA): Edward Elgar (2012), p. 249.

25  Among a vast literature on the case, see Tamara R. Piety, 'Grounding Nike: Exposing Nike's Quest for a Constitutional Right to Lie', 78 *Temple Law Review* 151 (2005).

26  Duncan Campbell, 'Nike's Big Ticking-off: How America's First Amendment on Free Speech Kept Accurate Corporate Reporting away from Company Spin', London: *The Guardian*, 17 November 2003, p. 25.

27  In 2013 several NGOs brought a case against Samsung before French courts using similar arguments. See Simon Mundy, 'Samsung Rejects Child Labour Allegations', London: *The Financial Times*, 27 February 2013. The case was rejected by a French court in January 2015, as reported in a blog published on the HEC School website in September 2015: Arnaud Van Waeyenberge, 'Les codes de conduite, nouvel outil juridique pour la protection des consommateurs', www.hec.fr/Knowledge/Environnement-des-Entreprises/Droit-Regulation-et-Institution/Les-codes-de-conduite-nouvel-outil-juridique-pour-la-protection-des-consommateurs (last accessed 21 March 2016).

*Sector initiatives and socially responsible investment*

As it stands, company-level codes of conduct are mere private modes of regulation, with a weak grip on complex human rights issues. Sector-level initiatives may be able to achieve more than individual company-level codes, especially when they are focused on certain aspects of the business, as opposed to being generally formulated, and are accompanied by reporting requirements. This is the case for example with the Equator Principles for project finance in the banking sector, which include social and environmental criteria. Adopted in 2003, the Equator Principles have supposedly levelled the playing field for participating banks, and have at least raised the sector's awareness of these issues, if nothing else. However, the Principles' monitoring system is imperfect and in practice monitoring is only done through the inherently limited NGOs' 'naming and shaming'.[28] In 1987 the chemical industry was one of the first sectors to agree on common standards through the Responsible Care Initiative, in an attempt to restore the industry's image after the Bhopal disaster.[29]

Another development of importance in the area of codes of conduct is the growing sector of socially responsible investing, which involves screening out companies that are deemed to engage in unethical business because of the nature of the business itself (e.g. tobacco companies) or because of the way a company conducts its business, irrespective of the sector.[30] In 2006 the United Nations launched the Principles for Responsible Investment.[31] Investors who sign up to the initiative, which is voluntary, commit to a set of principles and also commit to report annually on their progress. Rather than screening out, the initiative favours a policy of engagement with all companies. Because it involves the United Nations, a public actor, this initiative falls into the multi-stakeholder monitoring initiatives reviewed in the next section. Responsible investing is worth mentioning here, however, because beyond this UN initiative, it rests mainly on internal, purely private policies. Following their own codes of conduct, which may vary greatly, socially responsible investment companies, or managers of socially responsible funds, make their own socially responsible decisions and may decide to divest from certain companies due to what is considered inappropriate conduct. Publicly owned funds also engage in socially responsible investing. A prominent example of divestment includes the Church of England and the Norwegian

---

28   For a clear overview of the Principles, see Joshua A. Lance, 'Equator Principles III: A Hard Look at Soft Law', 17 *North Carolina Banking Institute* 175 (2013), p. 197.

29   Cynthia A. Williams, 'A Tale of Two Trajectories', 75 *Fordham Law Review* 1629 (2006–2007), p. 1640.

30   Although focused on environmental impact, the following article gives a good overview of the main aspects of responsible investing: Gail E. Henderson, 'Making Companies Environmentally Sustainable: The Limits of Responsible Investing', 13 *German Law Journal* 1412 (2012).

31   UN Principles for Responsible Investment, www.unpri.org/ (last accessed 23 April 2016).

Pension Funds' decisions to sell their stake in Vedanta Resources following concerns about the human rights impact of some of their operations in India.[32]

### The Sullivan Principles

Reverend Sullivan, an American civil rights activist dedicated to the fight against Apartheid, proposed the Sullivan Principles on Investment in South Africa in 1977 while the Apartheid regime was still in place in South Africa. There were originally six, and later seven, principles, all calling for equal treatment of whites and non-whites in South African workplaces operated by signatory US companies or their subsidiaries.[33] The Principles were in direct conflict with the segregationist racial policies then in force in South Africa. The self-stated long-term aim of the Sullivan Principles, beyond the immediate, modest effects on the working conditions of non-whites in certain companies, was to contribute to bringing down the Apartheid regime altogether. As Reverend Sullivan himself put it,

> The Statement of Principles and the programs developed in accordance with them provide a conduit through which companies with subsidiaries in South Africa may exercise moral leadership by using their resources, as one means among many, to work toward the peaceful elimination of apartheid and to improve the quality of life for South Africa's black and non-white population. I reason that if all multinational companies, led by U.S. companies, end discrimination in their plants and businesses, they will impart a remarkable, progressive influence on the country.[34]

In 1983, 147 companies had signed the Principles, which incurred reporting requirements.[35] The reporting system was innovative in many ways. Signatory companies themselves were to collect both quantitative and qualitative data, which was then evaluated by a supposedly independent consulting firm.[36] Crucially, at the time 'there existed no precedent for such an evaluation of corporate social responsibility'.[37] Thus, the Sullivan

---

32   Rhys Blakely, 'Church of England Sells Vedanta Stake over Records on Human Rights', London: *The Times*, 6 February 2010, p. 56.

33   The principles are reprinted in full in John Christopher Anderson, 'Respecting human Rights: Multinational Corporations Strike Out', 2 *University of Pennsylvania Journal of Labor and Employment Law* 463 (1999–2000), p. 477.

34   Reverend Leon Sullivan, 'Agents for Change: The Mobilization of Multinational Companies in South Africa', 15 *Law and Policy in International Business* 427 (1983), p. 430.

35   Ibid., p. 429. There were 200 in 1986; see Karen Paul, 'The Inadequacy of Sullivan Reporting', 57 *Business & Society Review* 61 (1986), p. 61.

36   D. Reid Weedon, Jr., 'The Evolution of Sullivan Principle Compliance', 57 *Business & Society Review* 56 (1986), pp. 57–58.

37   Ibid., p. 58.

Principles are an important milestone in the development of business and human rights as a field of study and, specifically, of reporting as a business and human rights tool to measure progress.

Yet despite the special place they hold in the field, the Sullivan Principles cannot be said to be without flaws. Some authors have criticised the Principles and the reporting system that was set up to monitor their implementation. For example, in 1986, Karen Paul contended that

> [t]he accuracy and objectivity, the consistency and reliability, and the validity and relevance of these reports are all open to question. Partly, these deficiencies may be due to the inherent difficulties of creating a reporting system in such an emotionally charged and politically explosive setting. But this fact itself should have made those responsible for the reports especially mindful of the need for reports that would be accurate, objective, consistent, reliable, valid, and relevant.[38]

Unsurprisingly, while the Principles achieved measurable results,[39] they did not bring about major change even at company level, let alone act as a catalyst for policy reform. The reality is that US, European and Japanese multinational companies operated in South Africa, taking advantage of, or at least being oblivious to, abhorrent racial policies. As claims were brought against a number of those companies for complicity in severe human rights violations, Chapter 9 of this book comes back to the liability of business for human rights violations at the time of Apartheid. For now, the enlightening words of Reverend Sullivan should suffice to illustrate the complexity of the task at hand:

> Whereas a few companies earnestly are trying to fulfill their social responsibilities in South Africa, too many are not exerting themselves enough to improve the conditions of blacks. Indeed, some are doing nothing much at all. Of the 147 companies that have signed the Principles, half of them are making good to fair progress, while the other half disgracefully are dragging their feet. Moreover, one half of the U.S. companies in South Africa, or almost 150 of them, have not even signed the Principles yet. These ignoble companies should withdraw from South Africa, for they have no moral justification for operating there.[40]

38  Karen Paul, 'The Inadequacy of Sullivan Reporting', 57 *Business & Society Review* 61 (1986), p. 62.

39  Reverend Leon Sullivan, 'Agents for Change: The Mobilization of Multinational Companies in South Africa', 15 *Law and Policy in International Business* 427 (1983), pp. 431–434. See also D. Reid Weedon, Jr., 'The Evolution of Sullivan Principle Compliance', 57 *Business & Society Review* 56 (1986), pp. 58–59.

40  Reverend Leon Sullivan, 'Agents for Change: The Mobilization of Multinational Companies in South Africa', 15 *Law and Policy in International Business* 427 (1983), pp. 434–435.

Beyond the fact that even signatory companies did not fully engage with the Principles, it was clear that even if they had been fully embraced, they could only have achieved so much in a country whose entire economic and social life relied on large-scale human rights violations.[41]

To some extent this comment is valid for all corporate self-regulatory initiatives. By remaining strictly within the system of corporate governance, and outside the system of public law, codes of conduct, even those accompanied by elaborate monitoring mechanisms, may induce change and encourage companies to respect human rights, but on their own they will always fail to address systemic social inequalities. Public and private modes of regulation must therefore go hand in hand if progress is to be made. With this in mind, perhaps the clearest contribution of the Sullivan Principles was that they served as a basis for the drafting of the Code of Conduct included in Section 207 of the US Comprehensive Anti-Apartheid Act of 1986.[42] Thus the norms included in the Sullivan Principles started their lives as purely private forms of regulation and later gained teeth, as well as public endorsement, through their inclusion in a piece of legislation. However, this exceptional fate is not that of the vast majority of codes of conduct, which remain an inherently limited mode of regulation.

### Voluntary monitoring initiatives: public–private partnerships and multi-stakeholder initiatives

In theory, initiatives that go beyond pure self-regulation by involving actors other than businesses at various stages, from the elaboration of standards to their enforcement, hold greater potential than codes of conduct and human rights policies. Voluntary monitoring initiatives seem to enjoy a higher degree of legitimacy, or accountability, than self-regulatory initiatives, especially when the former involve public actors such as states and international organisations.[43] Moreover, since more than one set of actors work towards the elaboration and implementation of these standards, the chances of businesses abiding by them are greater.

Giving an overview of voluntary monitoring initiatives in the area of business and human rights is not without difficulty given the multitude of different initiatives that have blossomed since the 1990s. A high degree of heterogeneity characterises these various initiatives. As Fabrizio Cafaggi noted,

---

41   Ibid., p. 438.
42   Comprehensive Anti-Apartheid Act of 1986, 2 U.S.C. 5001 (1988 & Supp. III 1991). See Jorge F. Perez-Lopez, 'Promoting International Respect for Worker Rights through Business Codes of Conduct', 17 *Fordham International Law Journal* 1 (1993–1994), pp. 26–29.
43   For a discussion on legitimacy and accountability of transnational private regulation see Deirdre Curtin and Linda Senden, 'Public Accountability of Transnational Private Regulation: Chimera or Reality?', 38 *Journal of Law and Society* 163 (2011).

even within multi-stakeholder organizations, there are differences dependent upon the distribution of power among the constituencies. In some, there is a leading constituency, shaping the choice of regulatory regime and its enforcement mechanisms while leaving the others some degree of control by voice or exit. In others, the power is distributed symmetrically, often producing a more principle-based regulation which is later specified at the stage of implementation.[44]

Given this context, any attempt to describe with precision all the different types of initiatives would be somewhat pointless, as each of them possesses unique features. One characteristic, however, deserves a mention: that of the presence or absence of a state actor among the participants in a given initiative. The initiatives which involve states include the Voluntary Principles on Security and Human Rights,[45] the Extractive Industries Transparency Initiative[46] and partnerships such as the ILO-led public–private partnership to combat child labour in the chocolate and cocoa industry, which brought together the ILO, the private sector and two countries, Ghana and Côte d'Ivoire.[47]

Among the prominent monitoring initiatives developed without state involvement are the Global Reporting Initiative (GRI),[48] the Fair Labor Association (FLA),[49] the Ethical Trading Initiative (ETI)[50] and the Global Network Initiative.[51] These initiatives all share a common feature: the active role of both the private sector and NGOs and/or trade unions. While the GRI, FLA and ETI are not limited to any given sector, the Global Network Initiative is specific to the information and communications technology sector. Companies have different reasons to voluntarily join these initiatives, among which reputational concerns feature prominently. For example, one author noted that four of the five companies that endorsed the GRI on its

---

44 Fabrizio Cafaggi, 'New Foundations of Transnational Private Regulation', 38 *Journal of Law and Society* 20 (2011), p. 35.
45 Voluntary Principles on Security and Human Rights, www.voluntaryprinciples.org/ (last accessed 23 April 2016).
46 Extractive Industries Transparency Initiative, http://eiti.org/ (last accessed 23 April 2016).
47 International Labour Organisation Factsheet, 'A partnership to combat child labour in the chocolate and cocoa industry'.
48 Global Reporting Initiative, www.globalreporting.org/ (last accessed 24 April 2016).
49 Fair Labor Association, www.fairlabor.org/ (last accessed 24 April 2016). See also Michael A. Santoro, 'Beyond Codes of Conduct and Monitoring: An Organizational Integrity Approach to Global Labor Practices', 25 *Human Rights Quarterly* 407 (2003), pp. 415–416.
50 Ethical Trading Initiative, www.ethicaltrade.org/ (last accessed 24 April 2016). See also Michael A. Santoro, 'Beyond Codes of Conduct and Monitoring: An Organizational Integrity Approach to Global Labor Practices', 25 *Human Rights Quarterly* 407 (2003), p. 416.
51 Global Network Initiative, http://globalnetworkinitiative.org/ (last accessed 24 April 2016).

launch date in 2002, namely Ford Motor Co., General Motors, Nike and Royal Dutch Shell, were all facing reputational and even legal risks at the time. In short, they all had 'pretty clear public relations reasons to want to be associated with a corporate accountability initiative'.[52]

It is difficult to assess each of these initiatives without engaging in research that would be outside the scope of this book, but one author's comment with regard to the enforcement difficulties they face deserves a mention. Speaking about the Fair Labor Association and the Ethical Trading Initiative, she notes that these multi-stakeholder initiatives

> represent the current state of the art in enforcement of private transnational labor regulation against lead firms [MNCs]. Yet these organizations' efforts to improve corporate accountability are in chronic conflict with their effort to gain voluntary corporate adherents. This tension constrains efforts to improve enforcement of these voluntary private regulatory undertakings, and may be the Achilles heel of private transnational regulation. The major multi-stakeholder organizations attempt to deal with the tension in part by maintaining tiers of participation with varying level of commitment; a firm may be able to sign onto a multi-stakeholder initiative by proclaiming an aspiration to improve performance and agreeing to report on progress toward meeting prescribed standards. That is not nothing, for even this can create soft pressure toward improving labor standards; but it is far from legal enforceability.[53]

While they fall short of legal enforceability as well, the next section shows that certification schemes in the area of business and human rights possibly represent the most elaborate form of private regulation in the field.

## Certification schemes

Certification is a process whereby a company, or a product, is recognised by a purportedly independent body as fulfilling certain criteria in areas such as environmental protection[54] and human rights. Perhaps the best known certification scheme in the latter area is the one run by Fairtrade International and its certification body FLO-CERT, which delivers the Fairtrade label to

52   Cynthia A. Williams, 'A Tale of Two Trajectories', 75 *Fordham Law Review* 1629 (2006–2007), p. 1643.

53   Cynthia Estlund, 'Enforcement of Private Transnational Labor Regulation: A New Frontier in the Anti-Sweatshop Movement?', *in* Fabrizio Cafaggi (ed.), *Enforcement of Transnational Regulation. Ensuring Compliance in a Globalized World*, Cheltenham (UK) and Northampton (MA, USA): Edward Elgar (2012), pp. 243–244.

54   See, for example, the Forest Stewardship Council certifications, www.fsc-uk.org/fsc-certificate-types.93.htm (last accessed 24 April 2016).

certain products produced in the global South. At the heart of the Fairtrade certification is the idea that local producers should be able to earn a decent living from their work. The fulfilling of labour rights also forms part of the certification process.[55] The link between the Fairtrade scheme and economic, social and cultural human rights is clear, even if the phrase 'human rights' does not feature prominently in the documents pertaining to the scheme. States are not involved in Fairtrade International, which is privately run.

Similarly, Social Accountability International (SAI) is a multi-stakeholder initiative independent from states. It has developed its own auditable standard, SA8000. Unlike FLO-CERT, SAI certifies companies, not products. It focuses on nine core elements: child labour, forced and compulsory labour, health and safety, freedom of association and right to collective bargaining, discrimination, disciplinary practices, working hours, remuneration and management systems. The last element means that 'facilities seeking to gain and maintain certification must go beyond simple compliance to integrate the standard into their management systems and practices'.[56]

These certification schemes are 'two of the oldest and most developed corporate social responsibility verification initiatives operating at an international level'.[57] Besides these, a final certification scheme which deserves mention in this book is the Kimberley Process Certification Scheme. Designed to eradicate the trade in 'conflict diamonds,' also known as 'blood diamonds' – which has proven to be a substantial source of funding for violent militias engaging in grave human rights violations, particularly in Africa – the Kimberley Process Certification Scheme is an ambitious multi-stakeholder initiative which brings together states, NGOs and the private sector, and was called for in a United Nations General Assembly resolution in 2000.[58] Despite the multi-stakeholder nature of the process as a whole, states (and the European Community) are the sole participants in the system. The original NGO participants, Global Witness and Partnership Africa Canada, as well as the industry body, the World Diamond Council, are simply observers. Their role is 'to monitor the effectiveness of the certification scheme' and 'to provide technical and administrative expertise',[59] but their powers are limited. Diamond-producing states are at the heart of the certification process since they are the ones in charge of delivering the 'conflict-free' certification to shipments of rough diamonds extracted from their territories. They perform this task

55  Fairtrade International, www.fairtrade.net/ (last accessed 24 April 2016).
56  Social Accountability International, 'SA8000 Standard', www.sa-intl.org/ (last accessed 24 April 2016).
57  Sasha Courville, 'Social Accountability Audits: Challenging or Defending Democratic Governance?', 25 *Law & Policy* 269 (2003), p. 277.
58  United Nations General Assembly, A/RES/55/56, 29 January 2001.
59  Kimberley Process, FAQ section, www.kimberleyprocess.com/en/faq (last accessed 24 April 2016).

domestically with little control from other participants and observers, which constitutes a major shortcoming.[60]

Global Witness had campaigned for the adoption of the scheme and continues to campaign for the scheme to be reformed, notably for the certification process to include human rights criteria. The only aspect the certification scheme covers is whether or not a particular shipment of diamonds has served to fund rebel groups. It does not cover labour rights and other human rights issues. While human rights were supposed to be at the heart of the scheme, Global Witness rightly notes that 'many participants in the scheme argue that human rights fall squarely outside the KP's remit'.[61] Moreover, the definition of the 'conflict diamond' as being a source of funding for rebel groups only is inherently flawed. Indeed, diamonds may serve to fund 'legitimate' governments' military activities, in the course of which similar human rights violations and international crimes may be committed.[62] The scheme does not cover this aspect.

Frustrated with what they viewed as the failure of the Kimberley Process to adequately address human rights violations, Global Witness left the scheme in 2011. Their Founding Director Charmian Gooch ended her statement with these telling words, which serve as an ideal conclusion not only to this short presentation of the Kimberley Process, but also to this chapter on private modes of regulation:

> We now have to recognise that this scheme, begun with so many good intentions, has done much that is useful but ultimately has failed to deliver. It has proved beyond doubt that voluntary schemes are not going to cut it in a multi-polar world where companies and countries compete for mineral resources.
>
> The Kimberley Process's refusal to evolve and address the clear links between diamonds, violence and tyranny has rendered it increasingly outdated. It is time for the diamond sector to start complying with international standards on minerals supply chain controls, including independent third party audits and regular public disclosure. Governments must show leadership by putting these standards into law.[63]

---

60  Jan Eric Wetzel, 'Targeted Economic Measures to Curb Armed Conflict? The Kimberley Process on the Trade of "Conflict Diamonds"', *in* Noëlle Quénivet and Shilan Shah-Davis (eds), *International Law and Armed Conflict. Challenges in the 21st Century*, The Hague: T.M.C. Asser Press (2010), pp. 175–176.

61  Global Witness, The Kimberley Process, www.globalwitness.org/campaigns/conflict/conflict-diamonds/kimberley-process.

62  Jan Eric Wetzel, 'Targeted Economic Measures to Curb Armed Conflict? The Kimberley Process on the Trade of 'Conflict Diamonds,'" *in* Noëlle Quénivet and Shilan Shah-Davis (eds), *International Law and Armed Conflict. Challenges in the 21st Century*, The Hague: T.M.C. Asser Press (2010), pp. 173–174.

63  Global Witness, 'Why we are leaving the Kimberley Process – a message from Global Witness Founding Director Charmian Gooch', 5 December 2011 (last accessed 24 April 2016).

## Conclusion

Private modes of regulation in the area of business and human rights are diverse and reflect stakeholders' creativity. These initiatives, however,

> exhibit built-in limitations; most do not address the role that governments must play in bridging governance gaps; they tend to be weak in terms of accountability provisions and remedy for harm; and by definition they involve only companies that voluntarily adopt such measures, in a form and at a pace of their own choosing.[64]

These initiatives may be able to achieve important results, especially in contexts where states are unable or unwilling to adopt and enforce legislation that would be protective of human rights. While holding corporations accountable for human rights violations through public law means is fraught with difficulties, as shown in the previous chapters in this Part, transnational private regulation provides a welcome – albeit limited – framework to engage with the private sector on human rights issues. As John Ruggie asserted, speaking about voluntary CSR initiatives,

> Like international law, they provide an essential building block in any overall strategy for adapting the human rights regime to provide more effective protection to individuals and communities against corporate-related human rights harm. But my research also indicated that they had significant and systematic limits, and therefore were not likely by themselves to bridge business and human rights governance gaps.[65]

In sum, to say that voluntary initiatives are useless in addressing human rights concerns would be an overstatement; to say that they are sufficient would be a lie. Business and human rights challenges may be of the kind that call for diversified ways to address them. This part has focused on one type of way: international law, international regulation and what the latter explicitly calls for, private modes of regulation. The next part of the book looks at a more solid way to embed human rights in business practice: domestic law.

## Bibliography

### Books

Curry, Mary Elizabeth, *Creating an American Institution. The Merchandising Genius of J.C. Penney*, New York and London: Garland Publishing Inc. (1993).

---

64  John Gerard Ruggie, *Just Business*, New York and London: W. W. Norton & Company Inc. (2013), p. xxviii.
65  Ibid., p. 77.

Ruggie, John Gerard, *Just Business*, New York and London: W. W. Norton & Company Inc. (2013).

## Journal articles

Anderson, John Christopher, 'Respecting Human Rights: Multinational Corporations Strike Out', 2 *University of Pennsylvania Journal of Labor and Employment Law* 463 (1999–2000).

Bartley, Tim, 'Institutional Emergence in an Era of Globalization: The Rise of Transnational Private Regulation of Labor and Environmental Conditions', 113 *American Journal of Sociology* 297 (2007).

Blackett, Adelle, 'Global Governance, Legal Pluralism and the Decentered State: A Labor Law Critique of Codes of Corporate Conduct', 8 *Indiana Journal of Global Legal Studies* 401 (2000–2001).

Cafaggi, Fabrizio, 'New Foundations of Transnational Private Regulation', 38 *Journal of Law and Society* 20 (2011).

Courville, Sasha, 'Social Accountability Audits: Challenging or Defending Democratic Governance?', 25 *Law & Policy* 269 (2003).

Curtin, Deirdre and Senden, Linda, 'Public Accountability of Transnational Private Regulation: Chimera or Reality?', 38 *Journal of Law and Society* 163 (2011).

Hassel, Anke, 'The Evolution of a Global Labor Governance Regime', 21 *Governance: an International Journal of Policy, Administration and Institutions* 231 (2008).

Henderson, Gail E., 'Making Companies Environmentally Sustainable: The Limits of Responsible Investing', 13 *German Law Journal* 1412 (2012).

Lance, Joshua A., 'Equator Principles III: A Hard Look at Soft Law', 17 *North Carolina Banking Institute* 175 (2013).

Locke, Richard M., Qin, Fei and Brause, Alberto, 'Does Monitoring Improve Labor Standards? Lessons from Nike', 61 *Industrial and Labour Relations Review* 3 (2007–2008).

Paul, Karen, 'The Inadequacy of Sullivan Reporting', 57 *Business & Society Review* 61 (1986).

Perez-Lopez, Jorge F., 'Promoting International Respect for Worker Rights through Business Codes of Conduct', 17 *Fordham International Law Journal* 1 (1993–1994).

Piety, Tamara R., 'Grounding Nike: Exposing Nike's Quest for a Constitutional Right to Lie', 78 *Temple Law Review* 151 (2005).

Potoski, Matthew and Prakash, Aseem, 'Green Clubs and Voluntary Governance: ISO 14001 and Firms' Regulatory Compliance', 49 *American Journal of Political Science* 235 (2005).

Reverend Sullivan, Leon, 'Agents for Change: The Mobilization of Multinational Companies in South Africa', 15 *Law and Policy in International Business* 427 (1983).

Santoro, Michael A., 'Beyond Codes of Conduct and Monitoring: An Organizational Integrity Approach to Global Labor Practices', 25 *Human Rights Quarterly* 407 (2003).

Scott, Colin, Cafaggi, Fabrizio, and Senden, Linda, 'The Conceptual and Constitutional Challenge of Transnational Private Regulation', 38 *Journal of Law and Society* 1 (2011).

Ward, Halina, 'The ISO 26000 International Guidance Standard on Social Responsibility: Implications for Public Policy and Transnational Democracy', 2 *Theoretical Inquiries in Law* 665 (2011).

Weedon, D. Reid Jr., 'The Evolution of Sullivan Principle Compliance', 57 *Business & Society Review* 56 (1986).

Westfield, Elisa, 'Globalization, Governance and Multinational Enterprise Responsibility: Corporate Codes of Conduct in the 21st Century', 42 *Virginia Journal of International Law* 1075 (2002).

Williams, Cynthia A., 'A Tale of Two Trajectories', 75 *Fordham Law Review* 1629 (2006–2007).

### Book chapters

Borck, Jonathan C. and Coglianese, Cary, 'Beyond Compliance: Explaining Business Participation in Voluntary Environmental Programs', *in* Christine Parker and Vibeke Lehman Nielsen (eds), *Explaining Compliance. Business Responses to Regulation*, Cheltenham (UK) and Northampton (MA, USA): Edward Elgar (2011), pp. 139–169.

Estlund, Cynthia, 'Enforcement of Private Transnational Labor Regulation: a New Frontier in the Anti-Sweatshop Movement?', *in* Fabrizio Cafaggi (ed.), *Enforcement of Transnational Regulation. Ensuring Compliance in a Globalized World*, Cheltenham (UK) and Northampton (MA, USA): Edward Elgar (2012), pp. 237–262.

Wetzel, Jan Eric, 'Targeted Economic Measures to Curb Armed Conflict? The Kimberley Process on the Trade of "Conflict Diamonds"', *in* Noëlle Quénivet and Shilan Shah-Davis (eds), *International Law and Armed Conflict. Challenges in the 21st Century*, The Hague: T.M.C. Asser Press (2010), pp. 161–181.

### Newspaper articles

Blakely, Rhys, 'Church of England Sells Vedanta Stake over Records on Human Rights', London: *The Times*, 6 February 2010, p. 56.

Campbell, Duncan, 'Nike's Big Ticking-off: How America's First Amendment on Free Speech Kept Accurate Corporate Reporting Away from Company Spin', London: *The Guardian*, 17 November 2003, p. 25.

Mundy, Simon, 'Samsung Rejects Child Labour Allegations', London: *The Financial Times*, 27 February 2013.

### Statutes

Comprehensive Anti-Apartheid Act of 1986, 2 U.S.C. 5001 (1988 & Supp. III 1991).

### Official documents

United Nations General Assembly Resolution, A/RES/55/56, 29 January 2001.

UN Principles for Responsible Investment, www.unpri.org/ (last accessed 23 April 2016).

## Websites

ISO 26000, www.iso.org/iso/iso26000 (last accessed 23 April 2016).

Ethical Trading Initiative, Auditing Working Conditions, www.ethicaltrade.org/issues/auditing-working-conditions (last accessed 23 April 2016).

Kimberley Process, www.kimberleyprocess.com/en/faq (last accessed 24 April 2016).

Voluntary Principles on Security and Human Rights, www.voluntaryprinciples.org/ (last accessed 23 April 2016).

Extractive Industries Transparency Initiative, http://eiti.org/ (last accessed 23 April 2016).

Global Reporting Initiative, www.globalreporting.org/ (last accessed 24 April 2016).

Fair Labor Association, www.fairlabor.org/ (last accessed 24 April 2016).

Ethical Trading Initiative, www.ethicaltrade.org/ (last accessed 24 April 2016).

Global Network Initiative, http://globalnetworkinitiative.org/ (last accessed 24 April 2016).

Forest Stewardship Council certifications, www.fsc-uk.org/en-uk/business-area/fsc-certificate-types (last accessed 24 April 2016).

Fairtrade International, www.fairtrade.net/ (last accessed 24 April 2016).

Social Accountability International, 'SA8000 Standard', www.sa-intl.org/ (last accessed 24 April 2016).

## Miscellaneous

Business and Human Rights Resource Centre, 'Company policy statement on human rights', http://business-humanrights.org/en/company-policy-statements-on-human-rights (last accessed 14 June 2016).

Global Witness, 'Why we are leaving the Kimberley Process - A message from Global Witness Founding Director Charmian Gooch', 5 December 2011, www.global-witness.org/en/archive/why-we-are-leaving-kimberley-process-message-global-witness-founding-director-charmian-gooch/ (last accessed 24 April 2016).

Global Witness, The Kimberley Process (2013), www.globalwitness.org/campaigns/conflict/conflict-diamonds/kimberley-process (last accessed 24 April 2016).

International Labour Organisation Factsheet, 'A partnership to combat child labour in the chocolate and cocoa industry', IVC/12/01/MAS[ILO_REF] (2015).

Van Waeyenberge, Arnaud, 'Les codes de conduite, nouvel outil juridique pour la protection des consommateurs' (2015), www.hec.fr/Knowledge/Environnement-des-Entreprises/Droit-Regulation-et-Institution/Les-codes-de-conduite-nouvel-outil-juridique-pour-la-protection-des-consommateurs (last accessed 21 March 2016).

# Part III

# Domestic law and policy

Embedding human rights in business
practice

By focusing on the international legal and policy frameworks, Part II has
highlighted some of the challenges to business' greater accountability for its
adverse human rights impact. Even if one is to consider that businesses have
human rights obligations under international law – a not-so-uncontroversial
position – the fact remains that enforcement mechanisms are lacking. Worse,
well-functioning mechanisms enforcing the narrow part of international law
that can unarguably be said to be directly applicable to corporations, such as
arbitral tribunals, imperfectly take human rights into consideration. The various soft law and private regulation initiatives that have blossomed in the field
of business and human rights since the 1970s also have their limitations.

Building on these observations, Part III focuses on domestic law and
policy in the area of business and human rights. Domestic regulation is
arguably more efficient to address corporate-related human rights violations
and to durably embed human rights in business practice. Positive changes at
the domestic level, however, have not occurred in a vacuum. Initiatives
discussed in Part II, such as the UN Guiding Principles on Business and
Human Rights, and more fundamentally the idea that businesses have
human rights responsibilities, have informed and prompted progress made in
the area at the domestic level. The UN Guiding Principles on Business and
Human Rights place on states the duty to protect against corporate abuse.
This can be achieved in two different ways: by shaping law and public policies so that they address the adverse human rights impact of businesses both
within and outside their territories (Chapter 9), and by providing judicial
remedies for victims of corporate human rights violations (Chapter 10).

# 9 Shaping law and public policies to address corporate human rights impact

Businesses, like other legal entities, are bound first and foremost by domestic law. As a general rule, whether a company is domiciled, has invested or is simply trading in a given country, it will be subject to the domestic law of that country. While states are under an obligation, under international human rights law, to protect potential victims from corporate human rights abuses, the type, depth and extent of the regulation of businesses can vary a great deal from one country to another. Moreover, one of the biggest obstacles to the effective prevention of businesses' human rights abuses is the fact that in many countries, especially developing countries, while the legal framework may be relatively sophisticated, rules are only partially enforced and corruption may distort their application.

In this context, this chapter cannot cover all aspects of the regulation of business in the human rights area by all governments around the world. Rather, it intends to present the various ways in which states may decide to shape their policies so as to fulfil their duty to protect human rights against corporate abuse, as required by the UN Guiding Principles on Business and Human Rights, but also by international human rights law generally.[1] As was the case with regard to the private regulation of companies,[2] states' public regulation of companies did not start with the adoption of the UN Guiding Principles. Employment law, environmental regulation, social reporting and procurement are among the various areas touching upon the field of business and human rights that states have been regulating for decades, well before the phrase 'business and human rights' was even coined. This chapter purports to review these policies through a business and human rights lens and to look at newer types of policy and regulation which states have adopted that fulfil their international legal obligation to protect human rights against corporate abuse, and contribute to bridging the corporate accountability gap.

UN Guiding Principle 2 on Business and Human Rights recommends that 'States should set out clearly the expectation that all business enterprises

---

1   See Chapter 7 for a discussion on the UN Guiding Principles on Business and Human Rights.
2   See Chapter 8 on private regulation.

domiciled in their territory and/or jurisdiction respect human rights throughout their operations'. This is meant to include business enterprises' overseas operations. With this in mind, this chapter is divided into two sections. The first section covers law and policies that are purely domestic, in the sense that they are meant to apply on the territory of the state that has adopted them, for the benefit of people who are present on that same territory. The second section covers law and policies that have extraterritorial implications, in the sense that although they apply on the territory of the state that has adopted them, they are for the benefit of people who live outside that territory, in a foreign country. Many of the policies discussed in the second section were adopted by the United States, or by US states, making this chapter rather US-centred. This is not to say that other countries have done nothing in this area. However, it seems as though the US has been at the forefront when it comes to the adoption of such policies, and that they have attracted a lot of media and scholarly attention.

## Domestic policies

Domestic regulation of business to address its adverse human rights impact predates the discussions on business and human rights at the international level. Various regulatory areas come to mind that could fit more or less squarely within a business and human rights framework. Among them are consumer protection, environmental regulation and occupational safety and health. Speaking about the early days of business regulation in the United States towards the end of the nineteenth century, one author contended that 'the classic justification for regulation was the argument that in some situations the public interest could be served only through governmental prescription, that in some instances a remedy could not be obtained through the workings of the marketplace'.[3] For example, the Interstate Commerce Act of 1887 and the Sherman Antitrust Act of 1890, 'landmark interventionist laws' in the United States, both intended at least partly to protect consumers' interests against the growing power of large corporations such as railway companies.[4]

---

3  Robert F. Himmelberg, 'Series Introduction', *in* Robert F. Himmelberg (ed.), *The Rise of Big Business and the Beginnings of Antitrust and Railroad Regulation (1870–1900)*, New York and London: Garland Publishing, Inc. (1994), p. viii.

4  Robert F. Himmelberg, 'Introduction', *in* Robert F. Himmelberg (ed.), *The Rise of Big Business and the Beginnings of Antitrust and Railroad Regulation (1870–1900)*, New York and London: Garland Publishing, Inc. (1994), p. xvii. Whether the Sherman Antitrust Act in particular was really intended to protect the public interest, as opposed to certain private interests, is in fact subject to controversy. On this see article by Thomas J. DiLorenzo, 'The Origins of Antitrust: An Interest-Group Perspective', (1985) reprinted *in* Robert F. Himmelberg (ed.), *The Rise of Big Business and the Beginnings of Antitrust and Railroad Regulation (1870–1900)*, New York and London: Garland Publishing, Inc. (1994).

Another area of importance is environmental regulation. In the United States, the Environmental Protection Agency (EPA) was created in 1970, following the public's growing interest in and concern regarding pollution issues.[5] Similar concerns led to the development of environmental regulation in other countries such as Spain[6] and Japan,[7] and to the first UN Conference on Human Environment in Stockholm in 1972. As is the case for other areas linked to business and human rights, regulation at the national level is needed. In the words of William Ruckelshaus, who served on the EPA for many years,

> You cannot leave most of these pollution problems to voluntary compliance. It will not work. It is a misunderstanding of the free enterprise system to suggest that somebody is voluntarily going to impose the cost on themselves which their competitors may or may not impose and then continue to seek to compete in the marketplace. They cannot do it. So the government has to provide a legislative, regulatory framework within which competition can take place.[8]

The link between human rights and the protection of the environment is clear. As was touched upon in Chapter 5, the European Court of Human Rights concluded that pollution constituted an unjustified interference with the applicant's right to a private and family life under Article 8 of the European Convention on Human Rights in its landmark case *López Ostra v Spain*.[9] In the African system of human rights protection, the African Charter of Human and Peoples' Rights includes the right to a general satisfactory environment.[10] Moreover, the case brought against Nigeria in relation to oil pollution in Ogoniland led the African Commission on Human and People's Rights to find Nigeria to be in violation of its obligations with regard to, among other rights, the right to health as guaranteed by the Charter.[11]

---

5   William D. Ruckelshaus, 'Environmental Protection: a Brief History of the Environmental Movement in American and the Implications Abroad', 15 *Environmental Law* 455 (1984–1985), pp. 455–457.

6   George Matthew Silvers, 'The Natural Environment in Spain: A Study of Environmental History, Legislation and Attitudes', 5 *Tulane Environmental Law Journal* 285 (1991–1992), p. 290.

7   Chao-chan Cheng, 'Comparative Study of the Formation and Development of Air and Water Pollution Control Laws in Taiwan and Japan', 3 *Pacific Rim Law and Policy Journal* S-43 (1993–1995), pp. S-57–58.

8   William D. Ruckelshaus, 'Environmental Protection: A Brief History of the Environmental Movement in American and the Implications Abroad', 15 *Environmental Law* 455 (1984–1985), p. 468.

9   ECtHR, *López Ostra v Spain* (1994).

10   African Charter on Human and People's Rights (1981), 21 ILM 58 (1982), Article 24.

11   African Commission on Human and People's Rights, 155/96: *Social and Economic Rights Action Center (SERAC) and Center for Economic and Social Rights (CESR) v Nigeria* (2001).

Perhaps the traditional regulatory area with the clearest link to business and human rights is labour or employment law and policies. This body of law regulates the relationship between businesses and their employees, and touches upon human rights such as freedom from discrimination, the right to unionise, the right to an adequate standard of living, the right to security and the right to health. As discussed in Chapter 3, while there is considerable debate about whether labour rights are human rights, they may be considered as such. In turn, employment law and policies that states choose to adopt fit into a business and human rights discussion.

Other areas of public policy also have a connection with business and human rights at the domestic level and may lead to enhanced corporate accountability, but have attracted much less attention. This is the case with public–private partnerships and government procurement with human rights criteria.[12] For example, in 2008, the Indian state of Uttar Pradesh introduced regulation which required bidding companies to have a certain percentage of members of lower castes in their workforce.[13] In a similar move, 'understanding how equalities and human rights principles and law apply to delivery of the particular service' is listed as one of the possible award criteria for service providers' tenders in the area of care and support services in Scotland.[14] The introduction of human rights-oriented criteria in areas that involve transferring public money to the private sector for the procurement of goods or services is a formidable tool in the hands of public authorities, and one which could have important practical repercussions if it were to be fully embraced. Moreover, it could have repercussions not only on the rights of individuals and groups living in the country where the regulation was adopted, but also on the situation of those living outside the country. This is the case when the procurement policy has extraterritorial implications. Examples of such policies are discussed in the next section, together with other policies with extraterritorial implications.

## Policies with extraterritorial implications

UN Guiding Principle 2 affirms that 'States should set out clearly the expectation that all business enterprises domiciled in their territory and/or jurisdiction respect human rights throughout their operations'. This Principle's official commentary mentions the adoption of 'domestic measures with extraterritorial implications' as one way in which this can be achieved. The commentary also contains examples of measures such as 'requirements on 'parent' companies to report on the global operations of

12    On this, see Claire Methven O'Brien, 'Essential Services, Public Procurement and Human Rights in Europe', University of Groningen Faculty of Law Research Paper No. 22/2015, 24 January 2015.
13    Naren Karunakaran, 'Bite the Caste Bullet', *Outlook Business*, 2 May 2009.
14    Scottish Government, 'Procurement of Care and Support Services', 2010, p. 61.

the entire enterprise (…) and performance standards required by institutions that support overseas investments.'[15] These measures should be distinguished from the exercise of direct extraterritorial jurisdiction by the courts of a given state, which is covered in the next chapter of this book.[16] For now, this section aims to critically present a selection of measures with extraterritorial implications in the area of business and human rights that states or public authorities have adopted.

## Early examples of measures with extraterritorial implications

In the 1970s, the idea that home states may influence the behaviour of 'their' multinational corporations' operations abroad so as to avoid adverse human rights and social impacts started to receive international attention. As seen in Chapter 7, this was a time when concerns regarding the activities of multi-national corporations in developing countries were mounting, and discussions around states' permanent sovereignty over their natural resources and the creation of a New International Economic Order were at their peak in the UN arena.

In 1972, reacting to the South African occupation of Namibia which led to a strike of African workers, the UN Security Council adopted Resolution 310, which called

> upon all States whose nationals and corporations are operating in Namibia (…) to use all available means to ensure that such nationals and corporations conform in their policies of hiring Namibian workers to the basic provisions of the Universal Declaration of Human Rights.[17]

Following the adoption of the Resolution, the UN Secretary-General invited states to report on the type of measures they had adopted to comply with it. In its answer to the Secretary-General, the United States acknowledged the presence of US businesses in Namibia and reported that it had sent the text of Resolution 310 and the text of the Universal Declaration of Human Rights to 'some 40 American business firms interested in Namibian affairs'. It added that 'the letter forwarding those documents (…) requested the cooperation of the companies in doing everything possible to ensure that any operations in Namibia in which they had an interest were fully consonant with the Declaration'.[18] Sending a letter can hardly be described as a

---

15 UN Doc. A/HRC/17/31, p. 7.
16 For an enlightening discussion of the various degrees of extraterritoriality, see Jennifer A. Zerk, *Extraterritorial Jurisdiction: Lessons for the Business and Human Rights Sphere from Six Regulatory Areas*, Corporate Social Responsibility Initiative Working Paper No. 59, Cambridge, MA: John F. Kennedy School of Government, Harvard University.
17 UN Security Council Resolution 310 (1972), para. 5.
18 Report by the Secretary-General on the Implementation of Security Council Resolution 301 (1972), S/10752, 31 July 1972, p. 14.

'measure', and the practical consequences of this are likely to have been limited, but the extraterritorial implication of the very fact of sending this letter is nevertheless clear. Indeed, what was sought here was the human rights protection of individuals and groups located outside the United States. This episode constitutes an early example of a domestic measure with extra-territorial implications in the area of business and human rights.

Two years later, the UN Group of Eminent Persons to Study the Role of Multinational Corporations on Development and on International Relations, the body that had recommended the negotiation of the UN Code of Conduct on Transnational Corporations as well as the creation of the dedicated UN Commission and UN Centre on Transnational Corporations,[19] also looked into the business and human rights aspects of the situation in Southern Africa. In the context of broader discussions on the adoption of the Code of Conduct on Transnational Corporations, the Group recommended that states do more to ensure that multinational corporations do not violate human rights while operating in developing countries, and explicitly asked states to adopt domes-tic measures with extraterritorial implications in the area of business and human rights. The 1974 Group's report reads as follows:

> Home country legislation should cover the prohibition of investment in countries upon which sanctions are imposed by the United Nations Security Council, for example, those which violate human rights and follow racist policies. (...)
>
> The Group recommends that home and host countries should ensure, through appropriate actions, that multinational corporations do not violate sanctions imposed by the United Nations Security Council, for example, on countries suppressing human rights and following racist policies.[20]

The report further states:

> [W]e support the idea that home countries, both individually and collec-tively, should insist upon the adherence by the multinational corporations under their jurisdiction to certain internationally accepted basic principles and standards, as conditions of their investment abroad, and should impose certain sanctions on corporations that disregard them.
>
> (...)
>
> The Group recommends that, through appropriate means, home countries prevent multinational corporations from going into countries where workers' rights are not respected, unless the affiliate obtains

19   See Chapter 7.
20   Group of Eminent Persons' final report, *The Impact of Multinational Corporations on the Development Process and on International Relations*, UN Doc. E/5500/Add.1 (Part I) (24 May 1974) 13 ILM. 800 (1974), pp. 828–829.

permission to apply internationally agreed labour standards, such as free collective bargaining, equal treatment of workers and humane labour relations.

The means at the disposal of home countries to that effect go from outright prohibition to the denial of tax credits for the taxes paid to host countries which violate human rights, to a ban on the entry into their own territory of the products produced in such countries, to the refusal of the benefit of investment insurance and guarantees.[21]

The reference to 'the refusal of investment insurance and guarantees' in the Group's report may have been prompted by the existence, since 1968, of a Swedish law making respect for certain labour rights a condition for government insurance for Swedish companies' foreign direct investment in developing countries.[22] The conditions introduced by the law concerned the areas of anti-discrimination, trade union activities, training, social security and social welfare.[23] They aimed at ensuring that Swedish companies did not violate the labour rights of host countries' workers, but a large degree of flexibility was allowed. The document listing the conditions read as follows:

The investor will be expected to conduct investigations and present plans on the above type of measures which are required according to the host country's laws, and to describe whatever additional measures he plans to take in favour of the foreign company's employees. On the basis of this information, negotiations between the applicant and EKN [Swedish Export Credits Guarantee Board] will determine what specific measures will be considered conditions for the guarantee.[24]

Moreover, the conditions were to be adapted depending on the type of industry and the local context.[25] The scheme appears not to have been a success. In an article published in 1979, one author deplored the ineffectiveness of the scheme and noted that 'no Swedish firm has ever used

---

21  Ibid., pp. 854–855.
22  The law is cited in Rudy J. Cerone, 'Regulation of the Labor Relations of Multinational Enterprises: A Comparative Analysis and a Proposal for NLRA Reform', 2 *Boston College International and Comparative Law Review* 371 (1979), p. 379, note 33, as 'Law of July 17, 1968, [1968] Sverges Forfattmingssamling [SFS] 447 (Swed.) (Social Conditions Attached to the Swedish Investment Guarantee Scheme).' However, the author of the present book has not been able to find this document. Instead, as Rudy J. Cerone also did, we used the translation provided in David H. Blake, 'International Labor and the Regulation of Multinational Corporations: Proposals and Prospects', 11 *San Diego Law Review* 179 (1973–1974), pp. 192–195.
23  'Social conditions attached to the Swedish Investment Guarantee Scheme', *in* David H. Blake, 'International Labor and the Regulation of Multinational Corporations: Proposals and Prospects', 11 *San Diego Law Review* 179 (1973–1974), pp. 192–195, paras. 5–10.
24  Ibid., para. 11.
25  Ibid., para. 12.

the insurance; they ignore the insurance program rather than meet its conditions'.[26] Despite this seeming lack of success, the social conditions attached to the Swedish Investment Guarantee Scheme as early as 1968 provide one of the first examples of a business and human rights policy taking the form of a measure with extraterritorial implications. Since then, other countries have followed suit in a variety of other areas.

## US local authorities and the fight against Apartheid in the 1970s and 1980s

The Apartheid regime in South Africa prompted reactions in the United States. In 1986 the US Congress adopted the Comprehensive Anti-Apartheid Act, overriding President Reagan's veto. Title III of the Act prohibited trade with South Africa for certain goods, as well as loans to the South African government. Overall, the Act aimed to 'prohibit loans to, other investments in, and certain other activities with respect to South Africa'.[27]

While the passage of this Act was an important step, it was not the only measure adopted by United States public authorities to show their disapproval of the Apartheid regime, and to seek to contribute to its fall. Rather, 'a formidable body of state and local anti-South Africa legislative and non-legislative measures' were adopted in the late 1970s and in the 1980s, which led some commentators to assert that 'never before ha[d] the United States witnessed such a plethora of non-federal legislation explicitly directed against a particular nation'.[28] US states, counties and cities adopted various

---

26  Rudy J. Cerone, 'Regulation of the Labor Relations of Multinational Enterprises: A Comparative Analysis and a Proposal for NLRA Reform', 2 *Boston College International and Comparative Law Review* 371 (1979), p. 379.

27  Comprehensive Anti-Apartheid Act of 1986, 2 U.S.C. 5001 (1988 & Supp. III 1991). On the Act, see Jeff Walker, 'Economic Sanctions: United States Sanctions Against South Africa - Comprehensive Anti- Apartheid Act of 1986', 28 *Harvard International Law Journal* 117 (1987).

28  Anton P. Pritchardt and Giorgio A. M. Radesich, *Divestment, Disinvestment, Divesture, Disengagement: A Survey of United States State and Local Anti-South African Legislation*, Faculty of Law, University of the Orange Free State, 1989, p. 5. See also Peter J. Spiro, 'State and Local Anti-South Africa Action as an Intrusion upon the Federal Power in Foreign Affairs', 2 *Virginia Law Review* 813 (1986), p. 815. Local anti-Apartheid measures are not the first occurrence of local authorities attempting to play a part in foreign policy, and also arguably to prompt regime change. In the 1960s a number of local authorities 'enacted ordinances intended to discourage local merchants from selling goods of Eastern European origin'. These so-called 'Communist Goods' ordinances either prohibited the sale of goods produced in communist countries, or subjected the sale of such goods to a costly licensing system and in some cases to the obligation to put up a sign in the store that read: 'Licensed to Sell Communist Imports'. See Richard B. Bilder, 'East–West Trade Boycotts: A Study in Private, Labor Union, State, and Local Interference with Foreign Policy', 118 *University of Pennsylvania Law Review* 841 (1970), pp. 841 and 882. See also 'Ordinances Restricting the Sale of "Communist Goods"', 65 *Columbia Law Review* 310 (1965).

measures, all aiming in the long run at ending the regime in South Africa. This fascinating episode of legal history is particularly relevant for the purpose of this book as it provides an opportunity to look at, review the difficulties created by, and discuss the overall efficacy of, a range of business and human rights measures with extraterritorial implications. In their survey of these measures, Pritchardt and Radesich classified them into four categories: divestment measures, investment prohibitions, deposit prohibitions and procurement (restriction) measures.[29]

Divestment could be partial or total. Partial, or conditional, divestment meant that a state, or public authority, would only keep securities in a given business entity doing business with South Africa if that business entity adhered to certain standards, usually the Sullivan Principles.[30] Partial divestment measures were 'the most popular form of Anti-South Africa action at state level'[31] and the type of measures favoured by Nobel Peace Prize winner Archbishop Desmond Tutu.[32] Total divestment measures aimed at removing all public assets from business entities doing business in South Africa. Investment prohibitions 'bar[red] the investment of new funds or assets in South Africa-related business entities or in South Africa generally'.[33] Deposit prohibitions 'generally exclude[d] a bank or financial institution from being designated as a depository for public bonds or monies'.[34] Finally, procurement (restriction) measures concerned:

---

29  Anton P. Pritchardt and Giorgio A. M. Radesich, *Divestment, Disinvestment, Divesture, Disengagement: A Survey of United States State and Local Anti-South African Legislation*, Faculty of Law, University of the Orange Free State, 1989, p. 9. The survey also provides useful definitions (pp. 7–8). Divestment (or divesture) 'usually refers to the act of an institutional investor's selling stock of American corporations doing business in or with South Africa'. Disinvestment 'refers to the act of United States corporations' closing or selling off their operations in South Africa and withdrawing what physical assets they can'. Although the terms divestment and disinvestment have different meanings, they tend to be used interchangeably.

30  On the Sullivan Principles, see Chapter 8.

31  Anton P. Pritchardt and Giorgio A. M. Radesich, *Divestment, Disinvestment, Divesture, Disengagement: A Survey of United States State and Local Anti-South African Legislation*, Faculty of Law, University of the Orange Free State, 1989, p. 9.

32  Mark Orkin, *Disinvestment, the Struggle and the Future. What Black South Africans Really Think*, Johannesburg: Ravan Press (1986), p. 7.

33  Anton P. Pritchardt and Giorgio A. M. Radesich, *Divestment, Disinvestment, Divesture, Disengagement: A Survey of United States State and Local Anti-South African Legislation*, Faculty of Law, University of the Orange Free State, 1989, p. 10. South Africa-related business entities are defined as follows: 'the South African relationship in the case of banks of financial institutions can be based on their making loans to South Africa, a South African business entity or a business entity doing business in or with South Africa. The South African relationship in the case of corporations can be based on their doing business in strategic products with South Africa or in South Africa'. 'Business entities can be divided into banks or financial institutions and corporations including their subsidiaries and affiliates.' Ibid., p. 9, footnotes 1 and 2.

34  Ibid., p. 10.

(1) bidding contracts (e.g. New York City);
(2) the purchase of South Africa-related goods and/or services (e.g. New York City);
(3) the purchase of goods and/or services of a business entity who deals with South Africa (e.g. New York City);
(4) the performance by artists with a South African connection (e.g. Newark, New Jersey).[35]

Pritchardt and Radesich then proceeded to map all state and local anti-Apartheid measures. The result of this exercise occupies almost 150 pages of their book and is therefore outside the scope of the present book.[36] Measures were taken in thirty-eight states and two territories (Washington DC and US Virgin Islands). In four states only local authorities adopted measures, not the state itself.[37] The various business and human rights measures with extra-territorial implications in South Africa that were adopted in the United States at that time raise two sets of questions with regard to their effectiveness on the one hand, and their conformity with the US Federal Constitution on the other. These questions are common when it comes to public policies with extraterritorial implications in the area of business and human rights.

There is little doubt that those championing a white-dominated South Africa did not support these measures, and that they had obvious reasons for holding such a view. They understood the risks associated with commercial and political isolation for the long-term sustainability of the regime. In this context, 'disinvestment thus offer[ed] powerful leverage, as a means of forcing the South African government to dismantle apartheid'.[38] In theory, then, these measures seemed to constitute a good way to contribute to the fall of the regime. Irrespective of the measures' effectiveness in bringing down the regime, some within the anti-Apartheid movement argued that they could be counterproductive and make the situation of non-white South Africans worse in the short run, and possibly in the long run as well. As one author put it,

> there is substantial disagreement among experts as well as laymen about the possible disadvantages. How costly will disinvestment be? Will

---

35  Ibid.
36  Ibid., pp. 11–159. They qualify the measures as being 'anti-South Africa'; rather, they were 'anti-Apartheid.' The states in which no measures were taken are Alabama, Alaska, Hawaii, Idaho, Kentucky, Mississippi, Montana, Nevada, New Mexico, South Dakota, Utah and Wyoming. Another source indicates that Hawaii did in fact adopt divestment legislation: see Eric Taylor, 'The History of Foreign Investment and Labor Law in South Africa and the Impact on Investment of the Labour Relations Act 66 of 1995', 9 *Transnational Law* 611 (1996), note 47, p. 620.
37  Arizona, Georgia, North Carolina and Texas.
38  Mark Orkin, *Disinvestment, the Struggle and the Future. What Black South Africans Really Think*, Johannesburg: Ravan Press (1986), p. 2.

blacks, who presumably can least afford it, have to bear the brunt? If so, are they willing to make the sacrifice?[39]

A survey conducted among non-white South Africans in 1985 revealed that by a short majority non-white South Africans supported disinvestment even if that came with a minor or even a substantial increase in unemployment.[40]

The core question of the survey was whether or not non-white South Africans supported disinvestment. With regard to this question, the author noted the fundamental distinction that had to be drawn between total and partial (conditional) disinvestment. He argued that questions regarding disinvestment should not be phrased in an either/or way, and that previous surveys which were based on such questions were therefore flawed. To him, the choice should not be between free investment and total disinvestment. Rather, it ought to be between free investment, total disinvestment and partial disinvestment. Giving participants three instead of two choices of answers in the survey, he found that 73 per cent of non-white South African supported disinvestment, either total (24 per cent) or partial (49 per cent). These results were in sharp contrast with other surveys conducted just the year before, which suggested that non-white South Africans were against disinvestment, thus fuelling the argument by Apartheid supporters that the measures adopted in the United States were elite-driven and disconnected from local realities.[41] While support for measures with extraterritorial implications on the part of the local population which they purport to protect is only one aspect of the evaluation of these measures, and such support is not a definite criterion when evaluating their effectiveness, it is an important element to be taken into consideration. This is all the more important because the opinions of end-receivers of measures with extraterritorial implications are rarely known. As the next sections show, the link between the measures and the population they purport to protect is often tenuous. Opinion polls among non-white South Africans and the heated discussions they triggered are therefore of particular interest because they contribute to linking the measures and the population more firmly than is usually the case.

Different views are held with regard to the effectiveness of these measures, and similar ones adopted by countries other than the United States, in bringing down the regime. On the one hand, it was said that 'many observers both inside and outside the country feel that these sanctions have been instrumental in inaugurating the political changes begun early in 1990 by South

39   Ibid.
40   Ibid., pp. 14–15.
41   Ibid., pp. 6–10. The results of the various surveys are usefully compared and contrasted in Meg Voorhes, *Black South African Views on Disinvestment*, Investor Responsibility Research Center Inc. (1986).

African State President F.W. De Klerk'.[42] In 1990, Dr Allan Boesak, a leader of the South African Council of Churches, contended that 'the single most important factor in changing the Government has been the sanctions'.[43] On the other hand, this view was not unanimously shared.[44] It would be beyond the scope of this book to try to determine with precision whether, or the extent to which, the measures with extraterritorial implications adopted by US public authorities contributed to bringing down the Apartheid regime. In any event, it is probably an unfeasible task. As one author noted in 1986,

> Although one can safely conclude that commercial and diplomatic relations between the United States and South Africa have recently suffered because of the state divestment and procurement actions, precise measurement of the ways and extent that these measures have contributed to this decline is impossible. Other factors have undoubtedly entered into the equation.[45]

In the end, those who truly wanted to see the end of Apartheid supported these measures, despite their being possibly in contravention of US constitutional law and principles, as discussed below. By contrast, those who supported the regime, such as the white South African business elite, criticised these measures. They were also criticised by those who wanted to do business in South Africa, essentially turning a blind eye to the country's racist policies. The latter category of people included some business elites in the West and their supporters in the political arena, principally within the US Republican party and the UK Conservative party.

While it is difficult to reach a definite conclusion on the question of whether, and if so to what extent, these measures contributed to bringing down the regime, one may look at their immediate consequences instead. These measures rest on a chain of causation-type idea. The idea was that by putting the South African government and South African businesses in a difficult position, they would have no choice but to reform themselves. Reform was the end goal, the final part of the chain. The antecedent goal up the chain was to put companies doing business in South Africa, especially those doing so without having adhered to schemes such as the Sullivan

---

42    Lynn Berat, 'Undoing and Redoing Business in South Africa: The Lifting of the Comprehensive Anti- Apartheid Act of 1986 and the Continuing Validity of State and Local Anti-Apartheid Legislation', 6 *Connecticut Journal of International Law* 7 (1990), p. 12.

43    James S. Henry, 'Even if Sanctions are Lifted, Few will Rush to South Africa', New York: *The New York Times*, 28 October 1990.

44    Anton P. Pritchardt and Giorgio A. M. Radesich, *Divestment, Disinvestment, Divesture, Disengagement: A Survey of United States State and Local Anti-South African Legislation*, Faculty of Law, University of the Orange Free State, 1989, pp. 164 and 166–168.

45    Peter J. Spiro, 'State and Local Anti-South Africa Action as an Intrusion upon the Federal Power in Foreign Affairs', 2 *Virginia Law Review* 813 (1986), p. 824.

Principles, in a difficult position so that they would be incentivised to change their behaviours, or stop dealing with South Africa altogether. With regard to that narrower goal, these measures undoubtedly met with some success. In 1990 *The New York Times* reported that United States direct investment in South Africa

> had increased from $490 million in 1966 to $2.6 billion in 1981. Since then, 214 of 324 United States companies have withdrawn, and investment has dropped now to $711 million, even lower than South Africa's direct investment in the United States.[46]

Admittedly, other factors, such as 'deteriorating economic and political conditions within South Africa', also played a role in this state of affairs, but

> at least two large firms (…) acknowledged city and state divestment activity as a major factor in their departure from South Africa, and business executives admit that mounting domestic pressure in the form of stock sales has increased doubts as to the advisability of continued South Africa operations. Many recognize the so-called 'hassle factor' of maintaining such a presence.[47]

Beyond the question of their effectiveness, the measures adopted by US local authorities raised constitutional concerns. This is an important point, and one which is likely to play a role with regard to other types of measures with extraterritorial implications adopted at local level in the United States.[48] Anti-Apartheid local measures were potentially in conflict with the 'Commerce Clause' of the US Constitution granting the US (federal) Congress the exclusive power to regulate foreign and interstate commerce, which implies that states cannot do so even in areas where Congress has not acted,[49] as well as with the principle embedded in Articles I and II of the Constitution that

---

46   James S. Henry, 'Even if Sanctions are Lifted, Few will Rush to South Africa', New York: *The New York Times*, 28 October 1990.
47   Peter J. Spiro, 'State and Local Anti-South Africa Action as an Intrusion upon the Federal Power in Foreign Affairs', 2 *Virginia Law Review* 813 (1986), p. 826.
48   See below the discussion about the constitutional challenges against the selective purchasing law regarding Burma.
49   US Constitution, Article I, Section 8, Clause III. This is known as the 'dormant commerce clause,' described as follows: the Commerce clause 'voids conflicting state actions. Concomitant to this affirmative power is Congress's implicit authority to restrain state governments from interfering with the flow of interstate commerce. Thus, when states enact divestment statutes affecting interstate commerce in an area or in a manner that does not directly conflict with a congressional act, the state act may nonetheless be unconstitutional if it offends the principle of free trade among the states.' Kevin P. Lewis, 'Dealing with South Africa: The Constitutionality of State and Local Divestment Legislation', 61 *Tulane Law Review* 469 (1987), pp. 475–476.

foreign policy is the responsibility of the federal government and not states, let alone infra-state entities. A third related argument could also be made, which rests on the doctrine of pre-emption.[50] The doctrine of pre-emption dictates that as a general rule, local laws are pre-empted by conflicting federal legislation. While initially there was no anti-Apartheid federal legislation, at that early time local measures could be said to be contrary to the policy of constructive engagement with South Africa which the Reagan administration had embraced, and which consisted precisely in not legislating.[51] In other words, this raised the question as to whether state action going against a federal policy of inaction, as opposed to federal law, could also be pre-empted. After the adoption of the federal Comprehensive Anti-Apartheid Act, more straightforward pre-emption arguments could be raised. Authors disagreed on both points.[52]

In a case involving a constitutional challenge brought against an ordinance adopted by the city of Baltimore and requesting city workers' pension funds to divest from companies doing business in South Africa, the Court of Appeals of Maryland rejected the pre-emption argument, holding instead that 'Congress had no intent to preempt'.[53] Moreover, the Court disagreed with the idea that the ordinance interfered with federal powers regarding foreign policy. In order to reach this conclusion they considered that the intent behind this measure

---

50   The three arguments, with relevant US Supreme Court caselaw, are examined in detail in Peter J. Spiro, 'State and Local Anti-South Africa Action as an Intrusion upon the Federal Power in Foreign Affairs', 2 *Virginia Law Review* 813 (1986).

51   Ibid., p. 828.

52   Ibid., p. 848. He further argued that

> Any legislation that purposefully undermines federal policy within the realm of foreign affairs should be struck down. Legislation inconsistent with constructive engagement has the potential to hamper greatly the federal plan for U.S.–South Africa relations. In the interests of maintaining the integrity of the federal policy, a court should find state divestment measures pre-empted (p. 849).

See also Christine Walsh, 'The Constitutionality of State and Local Governments' Response to Apartheid: Divestment Legislation', 13 *Fordham Urban Law Journal* 763 (1985), pp. 786–787. By contrast, Kevin P. Lewis argues that

> by refraining from using the dormant federal foreign affairs clause, the courts can avoid chilling the otherwise legitimate expressions of local governments without impairing Congress's right to preempt specific legislation that truly interferes with federal prerogatives. Considering the growing interest of the local citizen in matters formerly far removed from the concerns of the polis, there is much to be said for such an approach.

Kevin P. Lewis, 'Dealing with South Africa: The Constitutionality of State and Local Divestment Legislation', 61 *Tulane Law Review* 469 (1987), p. 517.

53   *Board of Trustees of the Employees Retirement Sys. Baltimore v. Mayor and City Council of Baltimore City*, 317 Md. 72, 562 A.2d 720 (Md. Ct. App. 1989), p. 743. See also Cynthia Golomb, 'Maryland Counters Apartheid: Board of Trustees v City of Baltimore', 14 *Maryland Journal of International Law and Trade* 251 (1990), p. 259.

was to ensure that the City's pension funds would not be invested in a manner that was morally offensive to many Baltimore residents and many beneficiaries of the pension funds. In addition (…), the effect of the Ordinances on South Africa (…) [was] only minimal and indirect.[54]

As such, they contended, there was no significant interference with federal powers. In other words, and interestingly for the purpose of this section, the Court considered that the extraterritorial implications of the ordinance were negligible and that perhaps the *raison d'être* of the measure was to satisfy local residents, not to improve the lives of those supposedly affected by the measure at the very end of the chain. Finally, the Court rejected the claimants' argument based on the commerce clause, and relied on the so-called market participation doctrine according to which local authorities may interfere with non-local commerce when they act as a market participant, as opposed to a market regulator.[55] Hence, 'just as a private merchant may elect not to do business in South Africa, so too may the City choose not to do business with a South African company'.[56]

## Public procurement

Public procurement policies are a powerful tool in the hand of states and local authorities seeking to influence the way businesses act abroad and may potentially impact on human rights. Some of the local anti-Apartheid legislation in the US included procurement aspects. Purely domestic procurement policies may also include human rights criteria.[57] This section, however, focuses on a range of public procurement policies with extraterritorial implications.

Human rights criteria vary in nature. The criteria may apply to the products being purchased. This implies some knowledge about supply chain processes and raises questions about how they can be evaluated. The criteria may apply to the company's human rights records irrespective of the product being purchased.[58] Again, this raises questions about the methods used to evaluate those records, and who is to do it. In more radical cases, human rights criteria may come down to looking at whether or not the company is

---

54  *Board of Trustees of the Employees Retirement Sys. Baltimore v. Mayor and City Council of Baltimore City*, 317 Md. 72, 562 A.2d 720 (Md. Ct. App. 1989), p. 746. See also Cynthia Golomb, 'Maryland Counters Apartheid: Board of Trustees v City of Baltimore', 14 *Maryland Journal of International Law and Trade* 251 (1990), pp. 260–261.

55  *Board of Trustees of the Employees Retirement Sys. Baltimore v. Mayor and City Council of Baltimore City*, 317 Md. 72, 562 A.2d 720 (Md. Ct. App. 1989), p. 753.

56  Cynthia Golomb, 'Maryland Counters Apartheid: Board of Trustees v City of Baltimore', 14 *Maryland Journal of International Law and Trade* 251 (1990), p. 261.

57  As seen above.

58  This is the approach favoured in the United Kingdom. See HM Government, 'Good Business: Implementing the UN Guiding Principles on Business and Human Rights', September 2013, pp. 9–10.

'doing business' in a country where human rights are routinely violated, as was the case for the anti-Apartheid measures. This implies passing a sweeping judgement about companies simply on the basis of their business presence in countries led by authoritarian governments. Examples of the latter kind of policy abound in the United States, at both state and infra-state levels. So-called 'selective purchasing laws' were popular in the 1990s. One commentator noted in 1999 that

> [a] number of selective purchasing laws have been enacted in the U.S. by state and city governments. Most prevent those state and city governments from dealing with companies doing business in Burma (Myanmar) because of the human rights situation in that country. The states with selective purchasing laws on Burma are Massachusetts and Vermont. Over 20 cities have enacted such laws on Burma, starting in 1995 with Berkeley (California), Madison (Wisconsin) and Santa Monica (California), and now including New York City, Los Angeles, Portland, San Francisco and Oakland. Several localities in Australia recently took a similar step. And Burma is not the only target: Berkeley, Oakland and Alameda County adopted selective purchasing laws on Nigeria during the period of military rule in that country, and Berkeley also targets companies doing business in Tibet if their operations have been criticised by the Tibetan government-in-exile.[59]

Among these measures with extraterritorial implications, the 'Act Regulating State Contracts with Companies Doing Business with or in Burma (Myanmar)' adopted in 1996 by the state of Massachusetts has attracted the most attention.[60] 'Doing business with Burma' was understood widely. Having operations in the country was enough to be affected by the law.[61] The law provided for the creation of a list of companies falling into that category and state authorities were not allowed to purchase goods or services from companies on the list, with a few exceptions, for instance if the purchase was 'essential'.[62] Massachusetts was forced to withdraw the Act following a US Supreme Court decision. Unlike the Court of Appeals of Maryland with regard to the Baltimore anti-Apartheid divestment ordinance, the US Supreme Court decided that federal legislation establishing sanctions against Burma pre-empted the Massachusetts Act.[63] Before its withdrawal, the Act

---

59    Christopher Avery, *Business and Human Rights at a Time of Change* (1999), chapter 2.8, http://198.170.85.29/Chapter2.htm#2.8.
60    1996 Mass. Acts 239, ch. 130.
61    Ibid., ch. 240.
62    Ibid., ch. 241.
63    *Crosby, Secretary of Administration and Finance of Massachusetts, et al. v National Foreign Trade Council* 530 U.S. 363. See above and *Board of Trustees of the Employees Retirement Sys. Baltimore v Mayor and City Council of Baltimore City*, 317 Md. 72, 562 A.2d 720 (Md. Ct. App. 1989).

remained in force for two years. In that short period of time, prominent companies such as Apple and Hewlett Packard pulled out of Burma to avoid appearing on the list. Many other companies, although unlikely to appear on the list, pulled out of Burma anyway in response to the growing boycott against them, presumably because of the publicity around the issue that the Act had generated.[64] As discussed in Chapter 6, the Act formed the basis of a claim before the World Trade Organisation Dispute Settlement Mechanism brought by Japan and the European Union against the United States, on behalf of their domestic companies affected by the Massachusetts Act. After the Act was withdrawn, the EU and Japan dropped the claim.[65]

In Europe, the European Commission has issued at least two important documents encouraging Member States to introduce human rights criteria in their public procurement policies: the 2010 Guide to Taking Account of Social Considerations in Public Procurement[66] and the 2011 Communication on Corporate Social Responsibility, which mentions 'the need to promote market reward for responsible business conduct, including through (...) public procurement'.[67] This holds great potential given that public procurement accounts for 17 per cent of the EU's GDP.[68] These documents are only recommendatory in nature. However, in February 2014 a new directive was adopted, which explicitly calls on Member States to

> take appropriate measures to ensure that in the performance of public contracts economic operators comply with applicable obligations in the fields of environmental social and labour law established by European Union law, national law, collective agreements or by the international environmental, social and labour provisions listed in Annex X.[69]

---

64  Mark B. Baker, 'Flying over the Judicial Hump: a Human Rights Drama featuring Burma, the Commonwealth of Massachusetts, the WTO and the Federal Courts', 32 *Law and Policy in International Business* 51 (2000), pp. 93–94.

65  United States—Measure Affecting Government Procurement, WT/DS 88 and DS 95, terminated on 11 February 2000.

66  European Commission, Guide to Taking Account of Social Considerations in Public Procurement, October 2010.

67  Final Communication from the Commission to the European Parliament, the Council, the European Economic and Social Committee and the Committee of the Regions, A renewed EU strategy 2011–14 for Corporate Social Responsibility, COM(2011) 681, 25 October 2011, p. 5.

68  European Commission, COM(2010) 546 final,6 October 2010, p. 16.

69  Directive 2014/24/EU of the European Parliament and of the Council of 26 February 2014 on public procurement and repealing Directive 2004/18/EC, Article 18(2). Annex X lists the following conventions: ILO Convention 87 on Freedom of Association and the Protection of the Right to Organise; ILO Convention 98 on the Right to Organise and Collective Bargaining; ILO Convention 29 on Forced Labour; ILO Convention 105 on the Abolition of Forced Labour; ILO Convention 138 on Minimum Age; ILO Convention 111 on Discrimination (Employment and Occupation); ILO Convention 100 on Equal Remuneration; ILO Convention 182 on Worst Forms of Child Labour; Vienna Convention for the protection of the Ozone Layer and its Montreal Protocol on substances

Many have highlighted the limitations of this directive from a human rights perspective.[70] It remains to be seen how this will translate in practice.

Including business and human rights requirements in procurement policies with extraterritorial implications is not without difficulties, and so far has not attracted the clearest support from public authorities around the world. To be fair, catch-all regulations such as the Massachusetts Act are probably not the best way to induce change and protect human rights. These measures end up preventing companies from doing business in certain countries rather than incentivising countries with poor human rights records to change so as to attract foreign investment again. As the experience with the Massachusetts Act has shown, selective purchasing laws primarily hit companies and their employees in the targeted country. Although it may be morally questionable for certain companies to make money while also providing funds to abusive regimes, the fundamental problem that these measures seek to address is the human rights violations suffered by the local population at the hands of their governments or other groups. Selective purchasing laws address the moral question and may bring comfort to some taxpayers in that respect, a point highlighted by the Court of Appeals of Maryland with regard to the anti-Apartheid ordinance adopted by the city of Baltimore.[71] Whether these measures have effects on the people they purport to protect, however, remains debatable. In sum, while these measures can be seen as being 'better than nothing', the link between them and the human rights violations may be too tenuous for the measures to truly prompt change.

### Export credit

As has been seen, linking governmental financial guarantees and insurance policies for foreign direct investment (FDI) to human rights requirements is not new; it already existed in Sweden at the end of the 1960s. Since then, the context has changed dramatically. Chapter 6 of this book covered the formidable growth of FDI in the past decades. As government-backed export credit has become essential for multinational companies, given the financial

that deplete the Ozone Layer; Basel Convention on the Control of Transboundary Movements of Hazardous Wastes and their Disposal (Basel Convention); Stockholm Convention on Persistent Organic Pollutants (Stockholm POPs Convention); Convention on the Prior Informed Consent Procedure for Certain Hazardous Chemicals and Pesticides in International Trade (UNEP/FAO) (The PIC Convention) Rotterdam, 10 September 1998 and its three regional Protocols.

70 Institute for Human Rights and Business, 'Protecting Rights by Purchasing Right: The Human Rights Provisions, Opportunities and Limitations Under the 2014 EU Public Procurement Directives' (2015).

71 *Board of Trustees of the Employees Retirement Sys. Baltimore v Mayor and City Council of Baltimore City*, 317 Md. 72, 562 A.2d 720 (Md. Ct. App. 1989), p. 746.

risks involved,[72] the growth in FDI has multiplied opportunities for states to adopt measures that aim at ensuring that public money is spent only for the benefit of human rights-abiding businesses, or at least on projects that will not result in human rights violations. In short, export finance, just like procurement, represents a powerful tool for states to influence how companies registered in their territories behave abroad.

At the international level, the Organisation for Economic Cooperation and Development (OECD) has developed guidelines to help states introduce eligibility criteria for export finance, initially in the areas of environmental protection and bribery. In 2012, the OECD Council adopted a Recommendation on environmental and social due diligence which refers to the UN Guiding Principles on Business and Human Rights and encourages states to take 'social impact' into consideration when assessing applications for officially supported export credits.[73] The head of the OECD export credit division noted in 2010 that both environmental protection and bribery

> were outside the traditional expertise of ECAs [Export Credit Agencies] and met considerable institutional resistance, based primarily on a historical lack of experience and uncertainty as to how to merge these issues within traditional export financing mandates and procedures.[74]

The adoption of the 2012 Recommendation, which explicitly refers to human rights, shows that the idea of introducing non-financial criteria is now shared by OECD countries, which still form the majority of capital-exporting countries. Incidentally, this trend mirrors actions in the area of project finance by international lenders such as the World Bank and the International Finance Corporation. Indeed, the Recommendation mentions both the IFC Performance Standards and the World Bank Safeguard Policies as benchmarks that states should use to assess applications at the domestic level.

Practically, states are encouraged to put each application in one of three categories. Category A projects are those that have 'the potential to have significant adverse environmental and/or social impacts, which are diverse, irreversible and/or unprecedented'.[75] Category B projects have potential

---

72   John Evans, 'Human Rights and Labour Standards: The Duty of Export Credit Agencies', *in* OECD, *Smart Rules for Fair Trade: 50 Years of Export Credits*, Paris: OECD Publishing (2010), p. 66.

73   OECD, Recommendation of the Council on Common Approaches for Officially Supported Export Credits and Environmental and Social Due Diligence, TAD/ECG(2012)5 28 June 2012; OECD Council Recommendation on Bribery and Officially Supported Export Credits, 18 December 2006. On this see Roel Nieuwenkamp, 'Evolving Expectations: The Role of Export Credit Agencies in Promoting and Exemplifying Responsible Business Practices' (2016), Institute of Human Rights and Business.

74   Steve Tvardek, 'Smart Rules for Fair Trade: Why Export Credit Matters', *in* OECD, *Smart Rules for Fair Trade: 50 Years of Export Credits*, Paris: OECD Publishing (2010), pp. 15–16.

environmental and social impacts that are 'less adverse than those of Category A projects. Typically, these impacts are few in number, site-specific, few if any are irreversible, and mitigation measures are more readily available'.[76] Finally, Category C projects have 'minimal or no potentially adverse environmental and/or social impacts'.[77] In their assessment, states are also asked to consider 'any statements or reports made publicly available by their National Contact Points (NCPs) at the conclusion of a specific instance procedure under the OECD Guidelines for Multinational Enterprises'.[78]

The UK government has announced that it supports the Recommendation and that UK Export Finance applies it in its daily work.[79] In 2010, an ambitious bill was defeated in the Canadian House of Commons by a vote of 140 to 134. The purpose of the C-300 Bill was 'to ensure that corporations engaged in mining, oil or gas activities and receiving support from the Government of Canada act in a manner consistent with international environmental best practices and with Canada's commitments to international human rights standards'.[80] The Bill provided for the creation of eligibility criteria for financial support from the Canadian government. To receive support, companies would have had to abide by the International Finance Corporation Performance Standards, the Voluntary Principles on Security and Human Rights, 'human rights provisions that ensure corporations operate in a manner that is consistent with international human rights standards' and 'any other standard consistent with international human rights standards'.[81] The defeat of the C-300 Bill shows that for some, the introduction of human rights requirements for the granting of export credit remains difficult to accept. Perhaps this is because of human rights requirements' high potential to protect the rights of vulnerable communities abroad. Indeed, unlike procurement policies with extraterritorial implications, in the area of export credit the link between the measure taken (granting funds) and the impact of business operations in the host country is much clearer. In sum, systematically linking credit to human rights records could make a significant difference in terms of human rights impact.

---

75  OECD, Recommendation of the Council on Common Approaches for Officially Supported Export Credits and Environmental and Social Due Diligence, TAD/ECG(2012)5 28 June 2012, para. 11.
76  Ibid.
77  Ibid.
78  OECD, Recommendation of the Council on Common Approaches for Officially Supported Export Credits and Environmental and Social Due Diligence, TAD/ECG(2012)5 28 June 2012, para. 15.
79  HM Government, 'Good Business: Implementing the UN Guiding Principles on Business and Human Rights', September 2013, p. 10.
80  Corporate Accountability of Mining, Oil and Gas Corporations in Developing Countries Act, C-300 Bill, Article 3.
81  Ibid., Article 5.

## Reporting and transparency requirements

Reporting is a final area in which much progress has been made in terms of encouraging corporate accountability in the area of human rights. Reporting is variably known as social disclosure, non-financial disclosure, extra-financial reporting, triple bottom line reporting, corporate social transparency and sustainability reporting.[82] Reporting may be entirely voluntary and fall within private modes of regulation, when for example companies join the Global Reporting Initiative mentioned in the previous chapter. However, states, as well as the European Union, have adopted legislation requiring companies to report regularly on their environmental, social and human rights performance.[83] In some states, stock exchanges have also introduced separate reporting requirements,[84] while the Hong Kong stock exchange has made human rights-oriented disclosure a precondition for extractive companies to be listed.[85] Reporting and transparency requirements fall within the larger category of measures with extraterritorial implications because companies are required to report and disclose information on their global operations, including their supply chains. For example, besides more general reporting requirements on human rights performance, both in Europe and in the United States, creative laws have been passed aiming to force companies to issue statements certifying that their supply chains are either 'slavery-free'[86]

82  Aaron A. Dhir, 'The Politics of Knowledge Dissemination: Corporate Reporting, Shareholder Voice, and Human Rights', 47 *Osgoode Hall Law Journal* 47 (2009), p. 50, note 9.

83  See for example UK Companies Act 2006 (Strategic Report and Directors' Report) Regulations 2013, specifically Chapter 414C(7)(b)(iii); and Directive 2014/95/EU of the European Parliament and of the Council, amending Directive 2013/34/EU as regards disclosure of non-financial and diversity information by certain large undertakings and groups, 22 October 2014. For an overview of different countries' requirements see Shift, 'Update to John Ruggie's Corporate Law Project: Human Rights Reporting Initiatives', November 2013. See also Damiano de Felice, 'Business and Human Rights Indicators to Measure the Corporate Responsibility to Respect: Challenges and Opportunities', 37 *Human Rights Quarterly* 511, pp. 544–545. In this article de Felice argues that 'A partial solution to the incompleteness and unreliability of self-reporting may come from recent and ongoing regulatory innovations that require corporate disclosure of sustainability information'.

84  Shift, 'Update to John Ruggie's Corporate Law Project: Human Rights Reporting Initiatives', November 2013.

85  On this see Nadia Bernaz, 'Enhancing Corporate Accountability for Human Rights Violations: Is Extraterritoriality the Magic Potion?', 117 *Journal of Business Ethics* 493 (2013), pp. 497–498.

86  California Transparency in Supply Chains Act of 2010, SB 657 (SB stands for Senate Bill); Section 54, UK Modern Slavery Act 2015, ch. 30. For a clear description of the relevant Section of the UK Modern Slavery Act, see Paul Henty and Simon Holdsworth, 'Big Businesses and Modern Slavery: What Your Organisation Should Be Doing', 4(4) *Compliance & Risk* 11. On the California Act, see Alexandra Prokopets, 'Trafficking in Information: Evaluating the Efficacy of the California Transparency in Supply Chains Act of 2010', 37 *Hastings International and Comparative Law Review* 351 (2014). See also

or 'conflict-free'.[87]

## Conclusion

This chapter has provided an overview of the various ways in which states and public authorities may positively influence how businesses registered in their territories operate so as to avoid negative human rights impacts and enhance corporate accountability. This influence may be with regard to the domestic operations of companies, and it may also extend to companies' operations abroad. In the latter case, the policies are said to have 'extraterritorial implications' in that they reach out outside the borders of the state itself.

This overview is by no means exhaustive and public creativity in the area should be further encouraged, as this is clearly part of the state duty to protect human rights outlined in the UN Guiding Principles on Business and Human Rights.[88] Another important aspect of the duty to protect is states' obligation to provide remedies, including judicial remedies, for victims of human rights violations. This is covered in the next chapter of this book.

pieces on proposed similar federal legislation in the United States: Sophia Eckert, 'The Business Transparency on Trafficking and Slavery Act: Fighting Forced Labor in Complex Global Supply Chains', 12 *Journal of International Business and Law* 383 (2013); Galit A. Sarfaty, 'Shining Light on Global Supply Chains', 56 *Harvard International Law Journal* 419 (2015). In February 2016 the Business and Human Rights Resource Centre reported that several lawsuits had been filed against companies using the full disclosures they had made in order to comply with the California Act. They noted the 'potentially perverse outcomes' of the Act and the 'need for full enforcement of the transparency requirements'. See Business and Human Rights Resource Centre, *In the Courtroom & Beyond: New Strategies to Overcome Inequality and Improve Access to Justice. Corporate Legal Accountability Annual Briefing*, February 2016, p. 5.

87  Section 1502, Dodd–Frank Wall Street Reform and Consumer Protection Act (Pub.L. 111–203). This provisions concerns 'conflict minerals' only and no other goods. Among a substantial literature on Section 1502, see Karen E. Woody, 'Conflict Minerals Legislation: the SEC's New Role as Diplomatic and Humanitarian Watchdog', 81 *Fordham Law Review* 1315 (2012–2013). She argues that the Act will do more harm than good in the Democratic Republic of the Congo (pp. 1345–1347). See also McKay S. Harline, 'Can We Make Them Obey: U.S. Reporting Companies, their Foreign Suppliers, and the Conflict Minerals Disclosure Requirement of Dodd-Frank', 35 *Northwestern Journal of International Law and Business* 439 (2014–2015). He concludes that 'until the international community demonstrates greater commitment to solving the conflict minerals trade, legislative schemes like § 1502 and the SEC conflict minerals rule will not succeed in ending the abuses they aim to prevent' (pp. 466–467).

88  For another public initiative not discussed here – the US Global Online Freedom Act – see John Gerard Ruggie, *Just Business*, New York and London: W. W. Norton & Company Inc. (2013), p. 15.

# Bibliography

## Books

Orkin, Mark, *Disinvestment, the Struggle and the Future. What Black South Africans Really Think*, Johannesburg: Ravan Press (1986).

Pritchardt, Anton P., Radesich, Giorgio A. M., *Divestment, Disinvestment, Divesture, Disengagement: A Survey of United States State and Local Anti-South African Legislation*, Faculty of Law, University of the Orange Free State, 1989.

Ruggie, John Gerard, *Just Business*, New York and London: W. W. Norton & Company Inc. (2013).

## Journal articles

Anonymous, 'Ordinances Restricting the Sale of "Communist Goods"', 65 *Columbia Law Review* 310 (1965).

Baker, Mark B., 'Flying over the Judicial Hump: A Human Rights Drama featuring Burma, the Commonwealth of Massachusetts, the WTO and the Federal Courts', 32 *Law and Policy in International Business* 51 (2000).

Berat, Lynn, 'Undoing and Redoing Business in South Africa: The Lifting of the Comprehensive Anti- Apartheid Act of 1986 and the Continuing Validity of State and Local Anti-Apartheid Legislation', 6 *Connecticut Journal of International Law* 7 (1990).

Bernaz, Nadia, 'Enhancing Corporate Accountability for Human Rights Violations: Is Extraterritoriality the Magic Potion?', 117 *Journal of Business Ethics* 493 (2013).

Bilder, Richard B., 'East–West Trade Boycotts: A Study in Private, Labor Union, State, and Local Interference with Foreign Policy', 118 *University of Pennsylvania Law Review* 841 (1970).

Blake, David H., 'International Labor and the Regulation of Multinational Corporations: Proposals and Prospects', 11 *San Diego Law Review* 179 (1973–1974).

Cerone, Rudy J., 'Regulation of the Labor Relations of Multinational Enterprises: A Comparative Analysis and a Proposal for NLRA Reform', 2 *Boston College International and Comparative Law Review* 371 (1979).

Cheng, Chao-chan, 'Comparative Study of the Formation and Development of Air and Water Pollution Control Laws in Taiwan and Japan', 3 *Pacific Rim Law and Policy Journal* S-43 (1993–1995).

de Felice, Damiano, 'Business and Human Rights Indicators to Measure the Corporate Responsibility to Respect: Challenges and Opportunities', 37 *Human Rights Quarterly* 511.

Dhir, Aaron A., 'The Politics of Knowledge Dissemination: Corporate Reporting, Shareholder Voice, and Human Rights', 47 *Osgoode Hall Law Journal* 47 (2009).

Eckert, Sophia, 'The Business Transparency on Trafficking and Slavery Act: Fighting Forced Labor in Complex Global Supply Chains', 12 *Journal of International Business and Law*, 383 (2013).

Golomb, Cynthia, 'Maryland Counters Apartheid: Board of Trustees v City of Baltimore', 14 *Maryland Journal of International Law and Trade* 251 (1990).

Harline, McKay S., 'Can We Make Them Obey: U.S. Reporting Companies, their

Foreign Suppliers, and the Conflict Minerals Disclosure Requirement of Dodd–Frank', 35 *Northwestern Journal of International Law and Business* 439 (2014–2015).

Henty, Paul, and Holdsworth, Simon, 'Big Businesses and Modern Slavery: What Your Organisation Should Be Doing', 4(4) *Compliance & Risk* 11.

Lewis, Kevin P., 'Dealing with South Africa: The Constitutionality of State and Local Divestment Legislation', 61 *Tulane Law Review* 469 (1987).

Prokopets, Alexandra, 'Trafficking in Information: Evaluating the Efficacy of the California Transparency in Supply Chains Act of 2010', 37 *Hastings International and Comparative Law Review* 351 (2014).

Ruckelshaus, William D., 'Environmental Protection: A Brief History of the Environmental Movement in American and the Implications Abroad', 15 *Environmental Law* 455 (1984–1985).

Sarfaty, Galit A., 'Shining Light on Global Supply Chains', 56 *Harvard International Law Journal*, 419 (2015).

Silvers, George Matthew, 'The Natural Environment in Spain: a Study of Environmental History, Legislation and Attitudes', 5 *Tulane Environmental Law Journal* 285 (1991–1992).

Spiro, Peter J., 'State and Local Anti-South Africa Action as an Intrusion upon the Federal Power in Foreign Affairs', 2 *Virginia Law Review* 813 (1986).

Taylor, Eric, 'The History of Foreign Investment and Labor Law in South Africa and the Impact on Investment of the Labour Relations Act 66 of 1995', 9 *Transnational Law* 611 (1996).

Walker, Jeff, 'Economic Sanctions: United States Sanctions Against South Africa – Comprehensive Anti-Apartheid Act of 1986', 28 *Harvard International Law Journal* 117 (1987).

Walsh, Christine, 'The Constitutionality of State and Local Governments' Response to Apartheid: Divestment Legislation', 13 *Fordham Urban Law Journal* 763 (1985).

Woody, Karen E., 'Conflict Minerals Legislation: the SEC's New Role as Diplomatic and Humanitarian Watchdog', 81 *Fordham Law Review* 1315 (2012–2013).

### Book chapters

DiLorenzo, Thomas J., 'The Origins of Antitrust: An Interest-Group Perspective', (1985) reprinted *in* Robert F. Himmelberg (ed.), *The Rise of Big Business and the Beginnings of Antitrust and Railroad Regulation (1870–1900)*, New York and London: Garland Publishing, Inc. (1994), pp. 63–80.

Himmelberg, Robert F., 'Series Introduction', *in* Robert F. Himmelberg (ed.), *The Rise of Big Business and the Beginnings of Antitrust and Railroad Regulation (1870–1900)*, New York and London: Garland Publishing, Inc. (1994), pp. vii–xiv.

Himmelberg, Robert F., 'Introduction', *in* Robert F. Himmelberg (ed.), *The Rise of Big Business and the Beginnings of Antitrust and Railroad Regulation (1870–1900)*, New York and London: Garland Publishing, Inc. (1994), pp. xv–xvi.

Evans, John, 'Human Rights and Labour Standards: The Duty of Export Credit Agencies', *in* OECD, *Smart Rules for Fair Trade: 50 Years of Export Credits*, Paris: OECD Publishing (2010), pp. 66–70.

Tvardek, Steve, 'Smart Rules for Fair Trade: Why Export Credit Matters', *in* OECD, *Smart Rules for Fair Trade: 50 Years of Export Credits*, Paris: OECD Publishing (2010), pp. 12–17.

## Statutes and bills

Constitution of the United States, Article I, Section 8, Clause 3 (1787).
Law of 17 July 1968, [1968] Sverges Forfattmingssamling [SFS] 447 (Swed.) (Social Conditions Attached to the Swedish Investment Guarantee Scheme).
Comprehensive Anti-Apartheid Act of 1986, 2 U.S.C. 5001 (1988 & Supp. III 1991).
1996 Mass. Acts 239, ch. 130.
Corporate Accountability of Mining, Oil and Gas Corporations in Developing Countries Act, C-300 Bill (2009).
Dodd–Frank Wall Street Reform and Consumer Protection Act (Pub.L. 111–203) (2010).
UK Companies Act 2006 (Strategic Report and Directors' Report) Regulations 2013.
California Transparency in Supply Chains Act of 2010, SB 657.
UK Modern Slavery Act 2015.

## Treaties

African Charter on Human and People's Rights (1981), 21 ILM 58 (1982).

## Cases

*Board of Trustees of the Employees Retirement Sys. Baltimore v. Mayor and City Council of Baltimore City*, 317 Md. 72, 562 A.2d 720 (Md. Ct. App. 1989).
*López Ostra v Spain*, [1995] 20 EHRR 277.
*Crosby, Secretary of Administration and Finance of Massachusetts, et al. V. National Foreign Trade Council* 530 U.S. 363 (2000).
United States—Measure Affecting Government Procurement, WT/DS 88 and DS 95, terminated on 11 February 2000.
African Commission on Human and People's Rights, 155/96: *Social and Economic Rights Action Center (SERAC) and Center for Economic and Social Rights (CESR) v Nigeria* (2001).

## Official documents

UN Security Council Resolution 310, Situation in Namibia (1972).
Report by the Secretary-General on the Implementation of Security Council Resolution 301 (1972), S/10752, 31 July 1972.
Group of Eminent Persons' final report, *The Impact of Multinational Corporations on the Development Process and on International Relations*, UN Doc. E/5500/Add.1 (Part I) (24 May 1974) 13 ILM. 800 (1974).
OECD Council Recommendation on Bribery and Officially Supported Export Credits, 18 December 2006.
European Commission, COM(2010) 546 final,6 October 2010.
Guiding Principles on Business and Human Rights: Implementing the United Nations Final Communication from the Commission to the European Parliament, the Council, the European Economic and Social Committee and the Committee of the Regions, A renewed EU strategy 2011-14 for Corporate Social Responsibility, COM(2011) 681, 25 October 2011.

'Protect, Respect and Remedy' Framework, UN Doc. A/HRC/17/31 (2011).

OECD, Recommendation of the Council on Common Approaches for Officially Supported Export Credits and Environmental and Social Due Diligence, TAD/ECG(2012)5 28 June 2012.

OECD, Recommendation of the Council on Common Approaches for Officially Supported Export Credits and Environmental and Social Due Diligence, TAD/ECG(2012)5 28 June 2012.

HM Government, 'Good Business: Implementing the UN Guiding Principles on Business and Human Rights', September 2013.

Directive 2014/24/EU of the European Parliament and of the Council of 26 February 2014 on public procurement and repealing Directive 2004/18/EC.

Directive 2014/95/EU of the European Parliament an of the Council, amending Directive 2013/34/EU as regards disclosure of non-financial and diversity information by certain large undertakings and groups, 22 October 2014.

## Miscellaneous

Avery, Christopher, *Business and Human Rights at a Time of Change* (1999), chapter 2.8, http://198.170.85.29/Chapter2.htm#2.8 (last accessed 15 June 2016).

Business and Human Rights Resource Centre, *In the Courtroom & Beyond: New Strategies to Overcome Inequality and Improve Access to Justice. Corporate Legal Accountability Annual Briefing*, February 2016.

European Commission, Guide to Taking Account of Social Considerations in Public Procurement, October 2010.

Institute for Human Rights and Business, 'Protecting Rights by Purchasing Right: The Human Rights Provisions, Opportunities and Limitations Under the 2014 EU Public Procurement Directives' (2015).

Methven O'Brien, Claire, 'Essential Services, Public Procurement and Human Rights in Europe', University of Groningen Faculty of Law Research Paper No. 22/2015, 24 January 2015.

Nieuwenkamp, Roel, 'Evolving Expectations: The Role of Export Credit Agencies in Promoting and Exemplifying Responsible Business Practices' (2016), Institute of Human Rights and Business.

Scottish Government, 'Procurement of Care and Support Services', 2010.

Shift, 'Update to John Ruggie's Corporate Law Project: Human Rights Reporting Initiatives', November 2013.

Voorhes, Meg, *Black South African Views on Disinvestment*, Investor Responsibility Research Center Inc. (1986).

Zerk, Jennifer A., *Extraterritorial Jurisdiction: Lessons for the Business and Human Rights Sphere from Six Regulatory Areas*, Corporate Social Responsibility Initiative Working Paper No. 59, Cambridge, MA: John F. Kennedy School of Government, Harvard University (2010).

## Newspaper and magazine articles

Henry, James S., 'Even if Sanctions are Lifted, Few will Rush to South Africa', New York: *The New York Times*, 28 October 1990.

Naren Karunakaran, 'Bite the Caste Bullet', *Outlook Business*, 2 May 2009.

# 10 Business and human rights litigation before domestic courts

## Progress and remaining obstacles

Business liability for human rights violations may be established in court in numerous ways. If the violations amount to criminal offences, companies or individual businesspeople may be prosecuted. Victims then tend to be relegated to a secondary role, although the *partie civile* status gives them a more prominent role in civil law than in common law countries.[1] Another route, which places victims at the heart of proceedings, is for them to bring a claim against the company in the hope of obtaining financial compensation as a civil remedy. Many of these civil claims are not explicitly labelled business and human rights claims but are personal injury claims or claims for compensation for property damages which have affected the livelihood of the claimants. The cause of action may derive from tort law, environmental law or other areas of law. Yet, there is a now a marked tendency to consider them as part of a growing body of business and human rights litigation, even if the actual causes of action may be named differently.

Whether the violation is remedied through the civil or criminal route depends on various legal considerations. Importantly, it also depends on the country in which it is being litigated. Criminal cases are more likely in continental Europe, while in the United States the emphasis is on civil litigation. Speaking about the Alien Tort Statute (ATS),[2] a federal statute which has come to play an essential role in business and human rights civil litigation in the United States, Kaeb and Scheffer note that

> [w]hile private party litigation plays an important role in American society as a vehicle for social change, civil litigation in most European legal systems is perceived as merely settling a private dispute in an individual case. But the European discomfort and reluctance to mimic the ATS in its structure are not indicative of a sentiment that corporations should be free from liability for their overseas involvement in violations of international law, which often amount to international crimes. Quite the opposite is true.

---

1   Vivian Grosswald Curran and David Sloss, 'Reviving Human Rights Litigation after Kiobel' 107 *American Journal of International Law* 858 (2013), p. 859.
2   28 U.S. Code § 1350.

The important transatlantic difference is that European jurisdictions rely primarily on criminal proceedings to right the wrongs at hand. This practice is in line with European legal culture where punishment and the expression of moral condemnation are in the public interest and, as such, are effectuated merely by the criminal process.[3]

Both criminal and civil cases are usually about redressing human rights violations committed in the country where the case is being heard. However, the circumstances that have given rise to most debates and legal difficulties are those in which the person or the company is being prosecuted, or the company is being sued, not in the country where the violations occurred but in the country where the suspected businessperson lives or is present, or the company is registered or is doing business. Typically, North American or European courts are dealing with these cases. The cases often involve a Western-based multinational company and a group of victims located in the developing world. These cases come before European or North American courts because of the perceived inadequacies of developing states' judicial systems, mainly underfunding, inertia, corruption and even more limited access to justice for vulnerable groups. For Western courts, taking on these

---

3    Caroline Kaeb and David Scheffer, 'The Paradox of Kiobel in Europe', 107 *American Journal of International Law* 852 (2013), p. 855. See also George P. Fletcher, *Tort Liability for Human Rights Abuses*, Oxford and Portland: Hart Publishing (2008). He argues that

> the preference for tort law over criminal law is largely an American story. As compared to jurists in Europe, Asia, and Latin America – indeed just about everywhere in the world – US human rights lawyers have many reasons to think 'tort' instead of 'crime'. Tort law is based on private incentives rather [than] the decisions of a governmental bureaucracy. This suits the American temperament for taking private action – even seeking private revenge – rather than relying on government bureaucracy [to] do it for them. (...) Europeans may say that the criminal sanction is the *ultima ratio*, the measure of last resort, but in fact they use it more often than do Americans to solve the problems of pollution and dangerous products, even minor problems of fraud and deceit. What makes the tort remedy so attractive in the United States? The answer is very simple – money. The combination of the jury system and the contingency fee means that tort awards are large and that tort lawyers can receive monetary rewards far in excess of their hourly fee. And let us not forget that we have in mind cases of malicious behaviour depriving others of their human rights: these inevitably invite punitive damage awards far in excess of compensatory damages. No country offers all these incentives to litigate in tort rather than sit and wait for the state to pay for a criminal prosecution. Of course, the lawyers must invest resources in the development of the case and they risk losing their stake, but, still, the opportunities are enticing. The lawyers can do well and do good for the world at the same time. The tort remedy – coupled with the jury system and contingency fee and punitive damages – create a powerful system of incentives for litigating human rights abuses (pp. 9–10).

See also Robert McCorquodale, 'Waving Not Drowning: Kiobel outside the United States', 107 *American Journal of International Law* 846 (2013), p. 849.

cases thus implies exercising some degree of extra-territorial jurisdiction – a rather controversial practice, as discussed below.[4]

This chapter does not purport to systematically address issues raised by business and human rights litigation in every country. This would be beyond the scope of the present book. Rather, it focuses on leading cases and uses them to introduce the main features of the two routes, criminal and civil, and the various legal obstacles that stand in the way of justice in selected jurisdictions where cases involving extra-territorial jurisdiction have gone through the judicial system. Arguably, all the cases discussed in this chapter had or have the potential to enhance accountability by holding some companies and individuals liable in court and, perhaps more importantly, by dissuading other companies and individuals from engaging in similar behaviour. The first section covers business and human rights civil litigation. The second section looks at criminal cases.

## Business and human rights civil claims

Both in and outside the United States, courts have had to deal with civil claims brought against multinational companies for their involvement in human rights violations. While none of these claims were explicitly labelled 'business and human rights', claimants were really seeking compensation for alleged violations of their rights. In the United States, leading business and human rights claims were brought under the Alien Tort Statute, a peculiar piece of legislation dating back from 1789. While the overall experience for plaintiffs using the Alien Tort Statute can hardly be described as successful, ATS litigation has attracted a lot of attention in the business and human rights field. However, as the ATS route has been riddled with obstacles, business and human rights litigation in other countries, particularly in Europe, has come to the fore. Interestingly, business and human rights litigation outside the United States raises issues that are similar, though not identical, to those raised in the United States.

---

4   Those cases have not exclusively come before European and American courts. See for example the conviction of Odebrecht, a Brazilian-headquartered multinational company, by a Brazilian court in September 2015. The company was accused of slave labour in its Angola operations related to the construction of a biofuel plant for Biocom, an Angolan company jointly owned by Odebrecht, Sonangol and Damer Indústria. As the Business and Human Rights Resource Centre noted, 'this case represents one of the first times a Brazilian company has been held liable for extraterritorial abuses, and thus sets an important precedent for Brazilian companies' accountability for their global operations'. See Business and Human Rights Resource Centre, *In the Courtroom & Beyond: New Strategies to Overcome Inequality and Improve Access to Justice. Corporate Legal Accountability Annual Briefing*, February 2016, p. 5.

### Alien Tort Statute litigation in the United States

This sub-section opens with a presentation of the main features of, and key cases brought under, the ATS. Next, it tackles a central question in business and human rights litigation: that of parent companies' liability for the acts of their foreign subsidiaries operating in developing states. It then provides an overview of the main jurisdictional and justiciability issues faced by claimants in ATS cases, including the *forum non conveniens* doctrine. Finally, it looks at the contours of complicity liability for corporations, and in particular at whether mere knowledge of the crimes of the principal are enough to incur civil liability under the ATS or whether a shared purpose, or even intent, is necessary.

### Main features and key cases

The Alien Tort Statute is part of the Judiciary Act establishing the federal judiciary and was adopted by the first United States Congress in 1789. The ATS is a concise piece of legislation that gives federal courts jurisdiction over certain claims. It consists of a single sentence and reads as follows: 'The district courts shall have original jurisdiction of any civil action by an alien for a tort only, committed in violation of the law of nations or a treaty of the United States.'[5] In other words, it opens US federal trial level courts to foreign nationals ('an alien'), for them to claim compensation for torts – that is, civil, non-contract-based wrongs – which are also violations of 'the law of nations or a treaty of the United States'. The 'law of nations' is how customary international law was referred to in the eighteenth century. The tort must therefore also be a violation of international law, either customary or emanating from an international treaty to which the United States is a party.[6] The origins of the Statute and precise intent of the framers of the ATS are unclear, but it is believed that what the framers had in mind at the time were offences such as 'violation of safe-conducts or passports, infringement of the rights of ambassadors and piracy'.[7]

The statute was essentially dormant until 1978, when two Paraguayan citizens brought a claim against a Paraguayan police officer who had entered the United States on a visitor's visa.[8] Dr Joel Filartiga and his daughter Dolly claimed that in Paraguay in 1976, Americo Norberto Pena-Irala, former

---

5    28 U.S. Code §1350.

6    In practice, the United States has attached reservations to the human rights treaties it has ratified so as to ensure that they are not self-executing (see Louis Henkin, 'U.S. Ratification of Human Rights Conventions: The Ghost of Senator Bricker', 89 *American Journal of International Law* 341 (1995), p. 348). This practice prevents the use of treaty provisions in ATS cases, where only violations of customary norms are being considered.

7    Anne-Marie Burley, 'The Alien Tort Statute and the Judiciary Act of 1789: A Badge of Honor', 3 *American Journal of International Law* 461 (1989), p. 469.

8    *Filartiga*, 630 F.2d 876 (June 30 1980).

Inspector General of Police in Asuncion, had kidnapped and tortured to death seventeen-year-old Joelito Filartiga, their son and brother.[9] The claim fit the requirements of the ATS. It was a civil action brought before the United States District Court for the Eastern District of New York, by aliens (non-US citizens), for a tort (wrongful death) which also happens to be a violation of customary international law (torture). The District Court, however, rejected the Filartigas' claims on the grounds that the 'law of nations' did not include the 'law which governs a state's treatment of its own citizens'[10] – a rather conservative, if not surprising, statement given the development of international human rights law since 1945.[11] On appeal, the United States Court of Appeals for the Second Circuit reversed the District Court's decision and found in favour of the plaintiffs. The decision closes on these powerful words:

> Among the rights universally proclaimed by all nations (…) is the right to be free of physical torture.
>
> Indeed, for purposes of civil liability, the torturer has become like the pirate and slave trader before him *hostis humani generis*, an enemy of all mankind.
>
> Our holding today, giving effect to a jurisdictional provision enacted by our First Congress, is a small but important step in the fulfillment of the ageless dream to free all people from brutal violence.

The next important decision for our purpose was rendered by the United States Court of Appeals for the Second Circuit in the *Kadic v Karadžic* case.[12] While previous ATS cases had been against state officials, or individuals who could be linked to state action, the Court decided in that case that the law of nations does not 'confine (…) its reach to state action'. 'Instead', they added, 'we hold that certain forms of conduct violate the law of nations whether undertaken by those acting under the auspices of a state or only as private individuals'.[13] By recognising that non-state actors such as individuals can violate the law of nations under certain circumstances, the Court of Appeals opened the door to future business and human rights litigation under the ATS.

Another claim of significance was brought in 1996 by a group of Burmese villagers. The claim was against Unocal, an energy company incorporated in California, for its alleged complicity in human rights abuses, particularly forced labour, committed by the Burmese regime in relation to a pipeline

---

9   Ibid., p. 878.
10  Ibib., p. 880.
11  See Chapter 5.
12  *Kadic and Doe v Karadžic*, 70 F.3d 232 (2d Cir. 1995).
13  Ibid., p. 239.

project in Burma.[14] While the parties eventually reached an out-of-court settlement, the case was about to go to trial at that point. This means that, for the first time, a federal court had recognised that corporations could violate international law. This claim started a series of ATS claims against corporate defendants for complicity liability.[15] By 2013, about 180 such claims had been filed.[16]

Notwithstanding this high number of claims, and what seemed like clear and established law, the idea that corporations, despite being non-state actors, may violate international law was explicitly rejected fifteen years later, also by the Court of Appeals for the Second Circuit, in the *Kiobel v Royal Dutch Petroleum* case.[17] Crucially, however, when *Kiobel* came before the US Supreme Court, *certiorari* was granted specifically to consider this uncertainty, but the Court did not address it in the end.[18] This could mean that the uncertainty in US courts over whether corporations may violate international law remains, but the most likely interpretation is that the Supreme Court considered the *Kiobel* decision of the Second Circuit to be an isolated one on that point. By ruling, for example, that 'mere corporate presence' was not enough to rebut the presumption against extraterritoriality, the Supreme Court implied *a contrario* that if a corporation was more than simply present, then a case could be heard under the ATS.[19] This point would make no sense if the Supreme Court's idea was that corporations could not violate international law. As one commentator noted, '[i]n effect, the Supreme Court's disposition leaves the Second Circuit as the outlier: every other court of appeals to address the issue has determined that corporations do not exist in an international law-free zone'.[20]

Another significant case in seeking to understand the mechanics of the ATS is *Sosa v Alvarez-Machain*, decided by the US Supreme Court in 2004. In that case, the Supreme Court elucidated the reference to the law of nations made in the ATS, and significantly limited its scope. The Court made clear that it should not be too restrictive and that it was not strictly bound

---

14  *Doe v Unocal*, 395 F.3d 932 (18 September 2002).

15  Robert C. Thompson, Anita Ramasastry and Mark B. Taylor, 'Translating Unocal: The Expanding Web of Liability for Business Entities Implicated in International Crimes', 40 *George Washington International Law Review* 841 (2008–2009), p. 842.

16  For a full list of ATS cases where at least one defendant is a corporate entity see Michael D. Goldhaber, 'Corporate Human Rights Litigation in Non-US Courts – A Comparative Scorecard', 3 *University of California Irvine Law Review* 127 (2013), Appendix A, pp. 137–149 (list compiled by Jonathan Drimmer).

17  *Kiobel v Royal Dutch Petroleum Co.*, 621 F.3d 111 (2d Cir. 2010), p. 145.

18  *Kiobel v Royal Dutch Petroleum Co.*, 133 S. Ct. 1659 (2013). This was 'most surprising', as noted by Ralph G. Steinhardt in 'Kiobel and the Weakening of Precedent: A Long Walk for a Short Drink', 107 *American Journal of International Law* 841 (2013), p. 844.

19  See below.

20  Ralph G. Steinhardt, '*Kiobel* and the Multiple Futures of Corporate Liability for Human Rights Violations', 28 *Maryland Journal of International Law* 1 (2013), p. 22.

by the international norms drafters of the Act had in mind in 1789.[21] However, they also held that the First Congress 'intended the ATS to furnish jurisdiction for a relatively modest set of actions alleging violations of the law of nations',[22] and that

> whatever the ultimate criteria for accepting a cause of action subject to jurisdiction under (...) [the ATS] (...) federal courts should not recognize private claims under federal common law for violations of any international law norm with less definite content and acceptance among civilized nations than the historical paradigms familiar when (...) [the ATS] was enacted.[23]

Having set this relatively high threshold, the Court concluded that arbitrary detention for a day – the act under scrutiny in that case – could not be considered on the same plane as piracy or crimes against ambassadors, which were probably on the minds of the drafters of the ATS in 1789. Hence it is not just any violation of an international norm (which is also a tort) that will allow a claim to be brought under the ATS. The decision therefore significantly restricted the type of claims that can be brought under the ATS.

### *Establishing liability of parent companies for the acts of their foreign subsidiaries*

Corporate structure is one of the main obstacles faced by plaintiffs when bringing a case against a corporation under the ATS. While a transnational corporation is a single economic entity, it is often composed of a multitude of subsidiaries, affiliates and partners all related to each other by complex legal links. As a leading academic in law and business notes:

> To the public and to economists, the multinational corporation is a single enterprise, 'the firm.' However, the law sees the multinational, such as British Petroleum with its tiers of sub-holding companies and more than 1,200 subsidiaries, as 1,200-odd separate independent entities. Under the traditional legal view, each of these intertwined segments of the British Petroleum enterprise is a separate juridical entity, with its own legal duties and liabilities separate and distinct from its parent corporation and affiliates under whose direction it is conducting its fragment of the common business being collectively conducted with the other members of the group. This is entity law. It is a legal conception

---

21  US Supreme Court, *Sosa v Alvarez-Machain*, 542 U.S. 692 (2004) reprinted in 43 ILM 1390 (2004), p. 1396.
22  Ibid, p. 1399.
23  Ibid., p. 1403.

that is manifestly anachronistic and bears no resemblance to the economic reality.[24]

Though possibly 'anachronistic', the concept of separate corporate juridical personality is deeply rooted in Western legal systems and derives from Roman law.[25] The practical consequences of this concept for corporate accountability for human rights violations are significant. Indeed, while US courts naturally have personal jurisdiction over US-based companies, it is more difficult to argue that they have jurisdiction over foreign companies, whether these are foreign subsidiaries of US parent companies or simply foreign parent companies.[26] Moreover, besides jurisdictional issues over foreign subsidiaries, claimants and human rights activists favour claims against parent companies because of better solvency levels, increased media and public opinion attention and, in turn, a higher potential deterrent effect.[27]

Corporate human rights violations are often committed by sub-entities of the parent company operating in foreign, developing countries, each of them legally separate from the parent. Because of the principle of separate legal personality, and as the US Supreme Court asserted in *United States v Bestfoods* (not an ATS case), '[i]t is a general principle of corporate law deeply "ingrained in our economic and legal systems" that a parent corporation (...) is not liable for the acts of its subsidiaries'.[28] This assertion stands in the way of claimants wishing to hold a parent company liable for the acts of its subsidiaries in business and human rights litigation.

There are, however, three possible ways around this principle. One is called 'piercing the corporate veil', and is only rarely used. In essence, a court will pierce the corporate veil, that is, overlook the strict separation between a parent and its subsidiary, if the parent is deemed to exercise an extremely high degree of control over the activities of the subsidiary. The doctrine will work only if in practice the degree of control is so high that the subsidiary has no separate identity of its own.[29] Accordingly in 2004, in the ATS case *Bowoto v Chevron*, Judge Susan Illston of the District Court of the Northern District of California considered that lead defendant Chevron Texaco Corp.

---

24  Philip I. Blumberg, 'Accountability of Multinational Corporations: The Barriers Presented by Concepts of the Corporate Juridical Entity', 24 *Hastings International and Comparative Law Review* 297 (2000–2001), p. 303.

25  Ibid., pp. 300–301.

26  The questions raised by jurisdiction over foreign companies are discussed below.

27  Michael Koebele, *Corporate Responsibility under the Alien Tort Statute, Enforcement of International Law through US Torts Law*, Leiden and Boston: Martinus Nijhoff Publishers (2009), p. 279.

28  *United States v Bestfoods*, 524 US 51 (1998), p. 61.

29  Philip I. Blumberg, 'Accountability of Multinational Corporations: The Barriers Presented by Concepts of the Corporate Juridical Entity', 24 *Hastings International and Comparative Law Review* 297 (2000–2001), pp. 304–307.

could not be held liable for the acts allegedly committed by its subsidiary, Chevron Nigeria Limited (CNL). She was guided by the concept of separate corporate juridical personality and considered that the conditions to pierce the corporate veil were not met.[30]

The second possibility is to consider that the subsidiary is acting as an agent of the parent company. Under this so-called agency theory of liability, just like a company might be liable for the acts of its employee through the mechanisms of vicarious liability, the parent company can be held liable for the acts of the subsidiary company as its agent. In *Bowoto v Chevron*, after careful consideration of the facts, Judge Illston concluded that 'the plaintiffs have presented sufficient facts from which a reasonable jury could find that an agency relationship existed and that CNL's alleged actions during the incidents at issue were within the scope of that agency relationship'.[31] Thus, while she refused to pierce the corporate veil, she embraced the agency principle.

A third theory of liability which can work in favour of claimants in ATS litigation for corporate human rights violations is the theory of enterprise liability. This theory rests on the idea that multinational companies are a single economic entity and should also be viewed as a single legal entity. While in direct contradiction with the sacrosanct principle of separate legal personality, it is said to focus 'on economic realities, rather than corporate formalities'.[32] It is unclear whether this principle can be applied in ATS litigation, and Judge Illston summarily dismissed it in *Bowoto v Chevron*.[33]

If they are unsuccessful in convincing federal courts that the acts of foreign subsidiaries can be attributed to the US parent company, claimants are then left with the option to sue the foreign subsidiary under the ATS. This option brings about a range of jurisdictional and justiciability issues, as do claims against foreign parent companies.

## Issues of jurisdiction and justiciability

As mentioned in this chapter's introduction, typical ATS cases against corporations for human rights violations concern acts committed outside the United States. Traditionally states only exercise their jurisdiction over acts committed within their own territories and avoid asserting jurisdiction over acts committed in another sovereign state's territory. However, due to the contents of the statute itself, ATS litigation has mainly been about acts committed abroad.[34] Until the 2013 *Kiobel v Royal Dutch Petroleum Co.*

30  *Bowoto v Chevron*, 312 F. Supp. 2d 1229 (N.D. Cal. 2004), p. 1247.
31  Ibid., p. 1246.
32  Ibid., p. 1237.
33  Ibid.
34  Paul L. Hoffman, 'Kiobel v. Royal Dutch Petroleum Co.: First Impressions', 52 *Columbia Journal of Transnational Law* 28 (2013–2014), pp. 29–30. See also Ralph G. Steinhardt, '*Kiobel* and the Multiple Futures of Corporate Liability for Human Rights Violations', 28 *Maryland Journal of International Law* 1 (2013), p. 10.

decision by the US Supreme Court, the situation was relatively clear. Under the ATS, US federal courts exercised their jurisdiction over violations of international law committed in the territories of foreign states. Such exercise was subject to well-established limitations: the *forum non conveniens*, political question, act of states and comity doctrines.[35]

Among the various obstacles faced by plaintiffs in business and human rights civil litigation under the ATS, the doctrine of *forum non conveniens* is one of the most difficult to bypass. The doctrine is discretionary in nature. This means that in a given case a court may decide not to proceed in order to let a foreign court, which is deemed a better forum, do so. It is a common law doctrine which stands in sharp contrast to the legal tradition in civil law countries where jurisdiction is exclusively a matter of law, and where discretion plays no role.[36] Under US law, in order to decide whether to take on the case, the court first has to check whether an alternative forum is available and adequate. If so, the court then proceeds to weigh the private interests of the parties and the public interest of the society of both possible forums in order to decide where the case would be better dealt with. *Forum non conveniens* is a critical doctrine which puts significant power in the hands of judges. They have generally used it to protect the American legal system from a flood of litigation and to avoid forum shopping.[37]

The case brought against Texaco in 1993 by a group of Ecuadorian plaintiffs provides an interesting example of the application of this doctrine. The claimants alleged that Texaco's large-scale dumping of toxic material and improper dealing with petroleum leakages had led to 'various physical injuries, including poisoning and the development of pre-cancerous growths'.[38] After various decisions by federal courts, the US Court of Appeals for the Second Circuit eventually dismissed the case on *forum non conveniens* grounds.[39] The Court held that Ecuadorian courts were available to examine the complaint.[40] This is not surprising as courts are available in most alternative forums, although a number of countries have adopted so-called 'retaliatory legislation' to prevent cases from proceeding in their own courts once a claim has been filed in US courts.[41] The adequacy part of the test is more delicate to handle as it implies passing judgements on the courts of foreign countries. This is especially sensitive where governments clearly

35  See Ralph G. Steinhardt, '*Kiobel* and the Multiple Futures of Corporate Liability for Human Rights Violations', 28 *Maryland Journal of International Law* 1 (2013), p. 10.
36  Michael Koebele, *Corporate Responsibility under the Alien Tort Statute, Enforcement of International Law through US Torts Law*, Leiden and Boston: Martinus Nijhoff Publishers (2009), p. 330.
37  Ibid., p. 325.
38  *Jota v Texaco, Inc.*, 157 F3d 153 (1998), p. 156.
39  *Aguinda v. Texaco, Inc.*, 303 F.3d 470 (2d Cir. 2002), p. 480.
40  Ibid., pp. 476–479.
41  Winston Anderson, 'Forum Non Conveniens Checkmated? – The Emergence of Retaliatory Legislation', 10 *Journal of Transnational Law and Policy* 183 (2000–2001), specifically p. 186 for a clear overview.

appear as the main perpetrators of the abuses in which corporations are alleged to be complicit.[42] The weighing exercise consists of examining the private and public interests at stake. However, no single interest is decisive. The starting point is the presumption in favour of the plaintiff's choice of forum. The presumption is stronger if the plaintiff is a citizen of the United States and less strong if he or she is an alien, which will always be the case in ATS litigation due to the very wording of the statute. United States residents who are not US citizens sit somewhere in between on that continuum. The residency and nationality of the defendant is also important. Other critical factors include the place where the events took place, access to evidence, availability of witnesses and the likelihood of enforcement of the US court's final decision in the country where the events occurred.[43] With regard to public interest considerations, US courts seek to avoid congesting the legal system and imposing undue jury obligations on American citizens. They may also consider that society at large, in the alternative forum, is primarily concerned with the case and deserves to see it litigated locally.[44] That said, in the *Wiwa v Royal Dutch Petroleum Co.* case, the Court of Appeal for the Second Circuit acknowledged that statutes such as the ATS can be seen 'as an expression of a federal policy interest in providing a legal system for various international human rights violations', and that therefore claims should not be lightly dismissed.[45]

Nonjusticiability concerns such as the act of state, political question and comity doctrines have played a role, albeit a modest one, in ATS litigation for corporate human rights abuse.[46] They are related though distinct doctrines that all have to do with the fact that the acts giving rise to ATS litigation are likely to have been committed on the territory of another state. Under the act of state doctrine, a court may decide not to adjudicate claims when it would imply judging the acts of a foreign, sovereign government. The doctrine was briefly considered and dismissed in *Filartiga*. Indeed, the Court of Appeals for the Second Circuit rejected the idea that 'action by a state official in violation of the Constitution and the laws of the Republic of Paraguay, and wholly unratified by that nation's government, could properly be characterized as an act of state'.[47] By contrast, in *Sarei v Rio Tinto*, Judge Morrow from the District Court for the Central District of California ruled that adjudicating the claim would necessarily involve reviewing Papua New Guinea's official acts. Thus it was barred by the act of state doctrine.[48]

---

42  Michael Koebele, *Corporate Responsibility under the Alien Tort Statute, Enforcement of International Law through US Torts Law*, Leiden and Boston: Martinus Nijhoff Publishers (2009), pp. 330–333.
43  Ibid., pp. 334–336.
44  Ibid., p. 337.
45  Ibid., p. 341.
46  For reasons behind this modest role, see ibid., pp. 355–356.
47  *Filartiga*, 630 F.2d 876 (1980), p. 889.
48  *Sarei v Rio Tinto PLC.*, 221 F. Supp.2d 1116 (C.D. Cal. 2002), p. 1193.

The political question doctrine allows a court to dismiss a claim if it feels that it raises issues that are of a political nature and ought to be addressed by the executive branch of government, rather than by the judiciary. It is particularly relevant in ATS cases because they might involve foreign policy aspects over which the US federal Constitution gives no power to the judiciary. As could be expected, it is a controversial doctrine, as the determination of what is strictly political and what can still be adjudicated is uneasy and dependent on the circumstances of the case and the personal inclination of the judges presented with the claim.[49] The political question doctrine served as one of the bases to dismiss the claim in the first instance in the ATS case *Sarei v Rio Tinto*, in which plaintiffs from the Island of Bougainville were engaged in a civil war with the government of Papua New Guinea over large-scale mining by Rio Tinto.[50]

Finally, courts may rely on the comity doctrine to dismiss a claim. Comity is an international legal concept which has to do with good relations among nations.[51] In short, US courts will not adjudicate a claim if doing so would be discourteous to a foreign country, as found by the judge of first instance in *Sarei v Rio Tinto*.[52] The type of relationship the US government has with the foreign government in question is likely to play an important role in how the doctrine is implemented in practice. As one commentator notes,

> [i]n some cases, such as the *apartheid* litigation, where both the South African and US governments protest the litigation, the 'foreign relations' argument for dismissal, whether based on deference to the Executive or on international comity toward the foreign government, may well be strong.
>
>     But in other cases – such as *Unocal,* where the foreign government was the murderous military dictatorship in Burma – the argument makes no sense.[53]

While nonjusticiability concerns had not been raised by the US federal executive branch during the first two decades of ATS litigation, things changed under the Bush Jr administration (2000–2008).[54] This administration

---

49  Michael Koebele, Corporate Responsibility under the Alien Tort Statute, Enforcement of International Law through US Torts Law, Leiden and Boston: Martinus Nijhoff Publishers (2009), pp. 349–353.
50  *Sarei v Rio Tinto PLC.*, 221 F. Supp.2d 1116 (C.D. Cal. 2002), pp. 1198–1199.
51  For a good overview of the doctrine, see Joel R. Paul, 'Comity in International Law', 32 *Harvard International Law Journal* 1 (1991).
52  *Sarei v Rio Tinto PLC.*, 221 F. Supp.2d 1116 (C.D. Cal. 2002), p. 1208.
53  Doug Cassel, 'Corporate Aiding and Abetting of Human Rights Violations: Confusion in the Courts, 6 *Northwestern University Journal of International Human Rights* 304 (2007–2008), p. 324.
54  However, in 1987, the Reagan administration did try to end a least one ATS case. See Anne-Marie Burley, 'The Alien Tort Statute and the Judiciary Act of 1789: A Badge of Honor', 3 *American Journal of International Law* 461 (1989), pp. 463 and 489.

attempted to torpedo ATS human rights litigation against corporations at early stages by presenting 'Statements of Interest', with success in the *Sarei* case.[55] Such attempts raised a great deal of criticism from commentators, who accused the administration of favouring their corporate friends to the detriment of victims of human rights violations.[56]

Despite criticism, these doctrines and the associated caselaw had the advantage of providing guidance to ATS litigants. As noted above, the 2013 Supreme Court decision in *Kiobel* somewhat 'throws that clarity out the window'.[57] Instead of relying on the doctrines or previous caselaw, the Court rejected the claim because they considered that the ATS did not give US courts jurisdiction over so-called foreign-cubed cases, that is, cases brought by foreign victims, against foreign defendants, for violations occurring in countries other than the United States. This presumption against extraterritoriality, they argued, can be rebutted if the claims 'touch and concern the territory of the United States' and 'do so with sufficient force to displace' it.[58] They added: '[c]orporations are often present in many countries, and it would reach too far to say that mere corporate presence suffices [to displace the presumption].'[59] They found that the presumption was not displaced with regard to the claim at hand as the defendant only had a limited presence in the United States. Surprisingly, they did not even consider the *forum non conveniens*, political question, act of states and comity doctrines. As lead counsel for the plaintiffs, Paul Hoffman, noted,

> It is unclear how the Kiobel majority views the relationship between the new presumption and existing limiting doctrines (e.g., forum non conveniens, political question, international comity) commonly litigated in ATS cases. Will the new Kiobel presumption become the last line of defense to ATS claims whenever the courts are dissatisfied with the results of the more traditional screening doctrines? Courts across the country will have to develop methods to interpret the new presumption. The most important observation in analyzing Kiobel may be the impossibility of predicting the presumption's future application.[60]

55  On this strategy, not limited to corporate cases, see Beth Stephens, 'Upsetting Checks and Balances: The Bush Administration's Efforts To Limit Human Rights Litigation', 7 *Harvard Human Rights Journal* 169 (2004). See also Brian C. Free, 'Awaiting Doe v Exxon Mobil Corp.: Advocating the Cautious Use of Executive Opinions in Alien Tort Claims Act Litigation', 12 *Pacific Rim Law & Policy Journal* 467 (2003).
56  See for example 'Oily Diplomacy', Editorial, *New York Times*, 9 August 2002.
57  Ralph G. Steinhardt, '*Kiobel* and the Multiple Futures of Corporate Liability for Human Rights Violations', 28 *Maryland Journal of International Law* 1 (2013), p. 10.
58  *Kiobel v Royal Dutch Petroleum Co.*, 133 S. Ct. 1659 (2013), p. 1669.
59  Ibid.
60  Paul L. Hoffman, 'Kiobel v. Royal Dutch Petroleum Co.: First Impressions', 52 *Columbia Journal of Transnational Law* 28 (2013–2014), p. 41.

This decision is all the more puzzling because many other ATS cases – including the *Sosa* case, decided by the Supreme Court itself – were foreign-cubed. Reconciling *Sosa* and *Kiobel* therefore seems difficult. Paul Hoffman considered that this would be nonetheless 'feasible'. Soon after the decision came out, he optimistically argued that *Kiobel* was limited to a narrow set of facts and that the decision should not be interpreted as a bar on all ATS claims arising from acts committed abroad.[61] For example, the hope was that *Kiobel* would not bar future claims brought against US defendants, as the Supreme Court remained silent on the issue. The post-*Kiobel* caselaw goes in both directions.

Just a few months after the *Kiobel* decision, the Court of Appeals for the Second Circuit considered that *Kiobel* did bar claims arising from acts committed abroad, not only by foreign defendants, but also by US defendants ('foreign-squared' cases).[62] Lower courts adopted similar reasonings in other cases.[63] Arguably, these courts read *Kiobel* too strictly by concluding that it provided a clear basis to dismiss the claims. All the Supreme Court said was that a mere corporate presence would not be enough to displace the presumption against extraterritoriality in ATS cases. However, it did not explicitly say that corporate citizenship, as opposed to presence, would not be enough to displace it. In other words, under *Kiobel*, the presumption could be displaced in a claim against a US company.[64] This is the conclusion reached by the Court of Appeals for the Fourth Circuit in 2014. In the ATS case *Al Shimari v CACI*, brought against an American corporation for acts of torture in the infamous Abu Ghraib prison in Iraq, the Court asserted that the claim touched and concerned the territory of the United States 'with sufficient force to displace the presumption' against extraterritoriality.[65] Hence, *Kiobel* may place US corporations at a disadvantage compared to their foreign competitors, who apparently cannot be sued under the ATS. That said, it is difficult to imagine US corporations publicly complaining about this, as it would essentially amount to them asserting that they should be allowed to engage in gross human rights violations.[66]

---

61  Ibid., pp. 39–40.
62  *Balintulo v Daimler AG*, 727 F.3d 174 (2d Cir. 2013).
63  For a list see case analysis of *Balintulo* in 27 *Harvard Law Review* 1493 (2013–2014), note 39, p. 1497.
64  Ibid., p. 1498.
65  *Al Shimari v CACI*, United States Court of Appeals for the Fourth Circuit, No. 13-1937 (30 June 2014).
66  For a discussion on this see Anupam Chander, 'Unshackling Foreign Corporations: Kiobel's Unexpected Legacy', 107 *American Journal of International Law* 829 (2013). See also John Gerard Ruggie, *Just Business*, New York and London: W. W. Norton & Company Inc. (2013), p. 199. For an analysis of the *Kiobel* test and how it has been applied by lower courts, see Ranon Altman, 'Extraterritorial Application of the Alien Tort Statute After Kiobel', 24 *University of Miami Business Law Review* 111 (2016), pp. 127–138.

*Corporate complicity liability: aiding and abetting human rights violations*

The involvement, and ensuing liability, of corporate entities in human rights violations is often indirect in nature. This is because of the strict definition given to the phrase 'law of nations' in *Sosa*. As seen, *Sosa* significantly limited the scope of the law of nations in ATS litigation. Hence for a claim to fall under the ATS, what is required is a violation of a norm of international law of the same nature, and enjoying the same level of acceptance, as the prohibition of piracy did in 1789. It is primarily states, or entities who possess some state-like characteristics such as rebel groups, who engage in violations of norms of that nature. This means that direct liability of a corporation under the ATS – although theoretically possible, and as alleged for example by the Ecuadorian claimants in the pre-*Sosa* case *Aguinda v Texaco*[67] – is unlikely.[68]

The most likely scenario is for a multinational company, or one of its subsidiaries, to get involved in violations committed by other actors, states or rebel groups. Under criminal law, this mode of indirect liability is called complicity, or aiding and abetting.[69] Although the phrase is primarily used in criminal law, 'aiding and abetting' liability has come to be used in ATS litigation against corporations, that is, in civil claims, not criminal proceedings. One possible explanation for this is that although it sits within the realm of civil remedies, the ATS 'must follow the contours both of tort law and of international criminal law in order to become (...) an effective instrument for correcting human rights abuses'.[70]

Establishing complicity liability requires proof of an act or omission by the company (the material element or *actus reus*), proof of the necessary state of mind (the mental element or *mens rea*) and sufficient proximity.[71] The mental element is particularly contentious. The issue is whether a knowledge, purpose or intent test ought to be used to establish liability. Because the ATS requires a violation of international law, it seems logical to use the standard required under international law. Unfortunately, this standard is unclear.[72] As

---

67 *Aguinda v Texaco, Inc.*, 303 F.3d 470 (2d Cir. 2002).

68 Alan O. Sykes, 'Corporate Liability for Extraterritorial Torts Under the Alien Tort Statute and Beyond: An Economic Analysis', 100 *Georgetown Law Journal* 2161 (2011–2012), p. 2170.

69 A third way in which a corporation can violate international law is when it is acting under the colour of state authority. As Sykes put it, 'a number of ATS suits have alleged that even though corporate agents are the primary wrongdoers, a degree of state involvement or support effectively makes the wrongdoing into "state action"' (ibid.).

70 George P. Fletcher, *Tort Liability for Human Rights Abuses*, Oxford and Portland: Hart Publishing (2008), p. 163.

71 International Commission of Jurists, *Report of the ICJ Expert Legal Panel on Corporate Complicity in International Crimes*, Vol. 1, pp. 8–26.

72 Moreover, under international law, the standard is for criminal aiding and abetting, since there is no recognition of civil aiding and abetting. See Alan O. Sykes, 'Corporate Liability for Extraterritorial Torts Under the Alien Tort Statute and Beyond: An Economic Analysis', 100 *Georgetown Law Journal* 2161 (2011–2012), p. 2171.

discussed in Chapter 4, there is uncertainty around which test was used in post-Second World War cases against German industrialists. Some post-Second World War cases lean towards the knowledge test, but not all of them are clear on the matter. In 1998, the International Criminal Tribunal for Rwanda (ICTR) adopted a mere knowledge test in the *Akayesu* judgment.[73] The International Criminal Tribunal for the Former Yugoslavia (ICTY) followed suit a few months later in the *Furundzija* judgment.[74] By contrast, the International Criminal Court (ICC)'s statute provides that

> a person shall be criminally responsible (…) if that person [f]or the purpose of facilitating the commission of such a crime, aids, abets, or otherwise assists in its commission or its attempted commission, including providing the means for its commission.[75]

This so-called purpose standard is meant to be a compromise between knowledge and intent, and is thought to be more stringent than mere knowledge, but less so than intent.[76] To complicate things further, the subsequent provision in the ICC Statute, which deals with an individual's contribution to a crime committed by a group of persons, seems to provide that mere knowledge of the intention of the group is enough to be held criminally responsible. This last point, however, is a disputed one.[77]

In sum, it would be an overstatement to say that the test for complicity liability under international criminal law is clearly a purpose test. While the purpose test emerges from Article 25(3)(c) of the ICC Statute, Article 25(3)(d) and case law from international tribunals lean towards a mere knowledge test. For some authors, this is evidence that under customary international law, the valid test is the knowledge test.[78] In other words, complicity liability for international crimes should emerge when, besides actions and omissions and proximity, the defendant has knowledge of the crimes committed by the principal perpetrator. The defendant does not need to have acted 'for the purpose of facilitating' the crimes, let alone with intent to facilitate the crimes. Professor Cassel concludes as follows:

73   *Akayesu*, Case No. ICTR-96-4-T, Trial Chamber, Judgement, para. 545.
74   *Furundzija*, Case No. IT-95-17/1-T, Trial Chamber, Judgment, para. 249.
75   Statute of the International Criminal Court, 2187 UNTS 90, Article 25(3)(c).
76   For a discussion on the *travaux* and on the likely meaning of 'purpose', see Doug Cassel, 'Corporate Aiding and Abetting of Human Rights Violations: Confusion in the Courts', 6 *Northwestern University Journal of International Human Rights* 304 (2007–2008), pp. 310–315.
77   See discussion on Article 25(3)(d) in ibid., p. 313 and Andrea Reggio, 'Aiding and Abetting In International Criminal Law: The Responsibility of Corporate Agents And Businessmen For "Trading With The Enemy" of Mankind', 5 *International Criminal Law Review* 623 (2005), pp. 646–647.
78   Doug Cassel, 'Corporate Aiding and Abetting of Human Rights Violations: Confusion in the Courts', 6 *Northwestern University Journal of International Human Rights* 304 (2007–2008), p. 315.

Moreover, even if a stricter interpretation of customary law might be required for ATS law in the US (…), leading to the adoption of the more stringent standard of ICC Statute article 25(3)(c) – that the aider and abettor must do so for the 'purpose' of facilitating a crime – such purpose need not be exclusive or primary. One who knowingly sells gas to the gas chamber operator for the primary purpose of profit may be inferred to have a secondary purpose of killing people, so that he can keep selling more gas to kill more people. Such a merchant of death aids and abets the principal murderers. Neither the ICC Statute nor any other source of international law should be interpreted otherwise.[79]

While international law leans towards the knowledge test, US courts have not always viewed matters in the same way and, at the time of writing, it is uncertain whether the ATS requires a knowledge or a purpose test for corporate complicity liability. In its controversial judgment in *Presbytarian Church of Sudan v Talisman*, the Court of Appeals for the Second Circuit embraced a purpose test, and argued that this was the applicable standard under international law:

> [A]pplying international law, we hold that the *mens rea* standard for aiding and abetting liability in ATS actions is purpose rather than knowledge alone. Even if there is a sufficient international consensus for imposing liability on individuals who *purposefully* aid and abet a violation of international law (…), no such consensus exists for imposing liability on individuals who *knowingly* (but not purposefully) aid and abet a violation of international law. (…) Only a purpose standard (…) has the requisite 'acceptance among civilized nations' for application in an action under the ATS. (…) Therefore, in reviewing the district court's grant of summary judgment to Talisman, we must test plaintiffs' evidence to see if it supports an inference that Talisman acted with the 'purpose' to advance the Government's human rights abuses.[80]

Applying the purpose test to the facts of the case, the Court of Appeals for the Second Circuit concluded that there was insufficient evidence supporting the position 'that Talisman acted with the purpose to advance violations of international humanitarian law'.[81] It is not hard to see that if this standard was to be upheld in all ATS cases, this could bring ATS litigation against corporations to an end. Most companies do not act with the purpose to advance violations. Rather, they can become complicit by providing governments with some material help, with knowledge of the consequences.

---

79   Ibid.
80   *Presbyterian Church of Sudan v. Talisman Energy Corp.*, 582 F.3d 244 (2d Cir. 2009), pp. 259–260.
81   Ibid., p. 264.

Requiring a shared purpose is unrealistic and ill-adapted to the concept of civil liability. As one author puts it,

> the criminal standard is pitched to individuals for whom these fine grada-tions between knowing and intending make a difference. In the context of corporate tort liability the most we can hope for is common knowl-edge that corporate activity will have the effect of facilitation of the criminal activity. (…) In the case of tortious wrongdoing it should be sufficient that the corporate defendant actually contributes to the result with the knowledge that its actions are likely to have contributed to that end.[82]

The difference between the knowledge and the purpose standards extends beyond academic debate, and choosing the latter over the former can effec-tively deprive ATS claimants of a remedy. For example, in the *Talisman* case, the Court acknowledged that the company 'helped build all-weather roads and improved airports, notwithstanding awareness that this infrastructure might be used for attacks on civilians'.[83] Yet they noted that since 'the proper test of liability is purpose (not knowledge), all this evidence of knowledge (…) cuts against Talisman's liability'.[84]

Thankfully for ATS claimants, not all Courts of Appeal agree with the Second Circuit. In 2011, in a case against oil giant Exxon Mobil, the DC Circuit rejected the conclusion reached in *Talisman* with regard to the purpose standard. They considered it to be 'flawed' and endorsed the knowl-edge standard.[85] In December 2013, the Court of Appeals for the Ninth Circuit also seems to have endorsed the knowledge standard, although the decision is not entirely clear on this point.[86] It therefore is an understatement to say that there is confusion in the courts on this point. Unless and until the US Supreme Court, or the US Congress, clarifies the matter, it is likely to remain as such.

### Business and human rights civil litigation outside the United States

The *Talisman* and *Kiobel* decisions and the ensuing uncertainties about the ATS route prompted renewed reflection on legal remedies outside the United States, where claims are not dependent on a perhaps dated, and in any event convoluted, piece of legislation. In Europe, business and human

---

82  George P. Fletcher, *Tort Liability for Human Rights Abuses*, Oxford and Portland: Hart Publishing (2008), p. 168.
83  *Presbyterian Church of Sudan v. Talisman Energy Corp.*, 582 F.3d 244 (2d Cir. 2009), p. 262.
84  Ibid.
85  *Doe VIII v. Exxon Mobil Corp.*, 654 F.3d 11 (D.C. Circ. 2011), p. 42. See also p. 50.
86  *Doe v Nestlé*, 738 F.3d 1048 (9th Cir. 2013).

rights civil litigation may be gaining momentum thanks to clear jurisdictional principles under EU law and promising jurisprudential and statutory developments in the area of parent company liability. Important developments in this regard have also occurred in Canada. That said, despite a relatively positive environment, the European legal framework is not without shortcomings.

First, EU law provides that the law applicable to civil claims is the law of the country where the damage (that is, the human rights violation) occurred. In practice, this means that pecuniary damages awarded are much lower than in the United States, where the law is particularly generous towards winning plaintiffs. Other characteristics of the law of most European countries, such as the absence of collective redress mechanisms, are also problematic, as discussed below. Second, litigation in this area is based on tort law. While there may be a human rights dimension to the claims, they are essentially personal injury claims, and international human rights law is not even mentioned in the proceedings. This is less empowering for victims than, for example, an ATS claim in which, by virtue of the wording of the statute, a precise violation of international (human rights) law must be identified. Hence in the United States, one may unambiguously talk about business and human rights litigation. This is not as clear in Europe.

### 'Brussels I' Regulation, civil universal jurisdiction and the doctrine of forum necessitatis

The European Union has developed a range of legal instruments aimed at providing certainty in the way in which courts of EU Member States approach questions of conflicts of laws and of jurisdiction such that forum shopping is reduced and uniformity increased. The so-called 'Brussels I' regulation is of particular relevance for the purpose of this book.[87] The regulation creates a framework detailing the exercise of jurisdiction in civil and commercial matters when the defendant, including a corporate defendant, is domiciled in a Member State. Under Article 4(1), 'persons domiciled in a Member State shall, whatever their nationality, be sued in the courts of that Member State'.[88] Crucially, this is so irrespective of the country in which the damage occurred and irrespective of the state of nationality and/or domicile of the claimants, which could well be a developing, non-EU member state. In short, a company domiciled in a Member State will be unable to resist a claim of jurisdiction. This means that the doctrine of *forum non conveniens*, a clear obstacle to jurisdiction in ATS cases in the United States, is not

---

87  Initially, this was Council Regulation (EC) 44/2001 of 22 December 2000 on jurisdiction and the recognition and enforcement of judgments in civil and commercial matters. It has now been recast and the new regulation is Regulation (EU) No 1215/2012 of 20 December 2012 on jurisdiction and the recognition and enforcement of judgments in civil and commercial matters (recast).

88  Regulation (EU) No 1215/2012 of 20 December 2012, Article 4(1).

applicable in EU Member States as long as the corporate defendant is domiciled in an EU country. The European Court of Justice confirmed this in 2005.[89]

What is more, and beyond the Brussels I regulation, the European Commission now considers that there exists a principle of civil universal jurisdiction under international law. This point was at the heart of the *amicus curiae* brief that the Commission submitted to the US Supreme Court in the *Kiobel* case.[90] Universal jurisdiction is one of the possible bases for jurisdiction recognised by international law. It is traditionally limited to criminal matters. It rests on the idea that certain crimes are so egregious that any country in the world may, and in some cases must, prosecute them even if the crimes have not occurred on the territory of the country in question, and neither the victims nor the alleged offender are nationals of that country. As the Commission argued in its brief, criminal universal jurisdiction is well established under international law. While conceding that civil universal jurisdiction is less established, the Commission put forward the idea that

> the assertion of universal civil jurisdiction is consistent with international law if confined by the limits in place for universal criminal jurisdiction. Accordingly, an ATS action based on universal jurisdiction should operate solely to provide civil remedies to the victims of repugnant criminal acts of universal concern.[91]

In other words, the Commission is not arguing in favour of a free-standing notion of civil universal jurisdiction, which would probably amount to stretching the concept too far. Instead, it is arguing in favour of universal civil jurisdiction for victims of violations of human rights, which would also attract universal criminal jurisdiction. In doing so, it is relying on arguments developed by litigators a few years before:

> It could be said (...) that though embryonic, state practice endorsing the exercise of universal civil jurisdiction as a permissive customary norm is beginning to emerge. It might be more accurate to characterize these developments, however, as an increasing recognition that the well-accepted modern rationale for exercising universal jurisdiction to impose criminal penalties also justifies exercising it to provide civil remedies. That is, rather than looking solely or primarily for separate and independent evidence of an emerging principle of universal civil jurisdiction,

89  ECJ, Case C-281/02 *Owusu v Jackson* [2005] 2 WLR 942, para. 46. The case was referring to the previous text in force with regard to these matters, the 1968 Brussels Convention.

90  Supplemental Brief of the European Commission on Behalf of the European Union in Support of Neither Party, *Kiobel v Royal Dutch Petroleum Co.*, 133 S.Ct. 1659 (2013) (No. 10–1491).

91  Ibid., pp. 17–18.

we might be better served by considering whether our existing understanding of universal jurisdiction encompasses a civil dimension and, if so, its appropriate scope and limits.[92]

In any event, the US Supreme Court did not embrace 'this purported international trend' in the *Kiobel* decision.[93] Hence, while this may well be an emerging trend, the idea of universal civil jurisdiction has not reached universal recognition yet.

Another development of interest in that area of the law is the emergence of the notion of *forum necessitatis*. Under this doctrine, the lack of an available or appropriate forum may lead courts to accept a case even when the usual conditions for the exercise of jurisdiction may not all be met. As one author notes,

> [*Forum necessitatis*] is thus the mirror image of *forum non conveniens*, which allows defendants to establish that a court should not hear a claim, despite the tests for jurisdiction being met, based on a range of discretionary factors. While the doctrines operate on similar principles, forum non conveniens gives defendants an extra chance to kill a case, whereas forum of necessity gives plaintiffs an extra chance to save it.[94]

When applying this doctrine, certain states consider that it must be impossible for the claimant to bring a claim in a different country, while others are more flexible and consider that jurisdiction should be exercised simply when it would be unreasonable for the claimant to bring their claim elsewhere.[95]

---

92  Donald Francis Donovan and Anthea Roberts, 'The Emerging Recognition of Universal Civil Jurisdiction', 100 *American Journal of International Law* 142 (2006), p. 153.

93  Julian G. Ku, 'Kiobel and the Surprising Death of Universal Jurisdiction under the Alien Tort Statute', 107 *American Journal of International Law* 835 (2013), p. 838.

94  Michael D. Goldhaber, 'Corporate Human Rights Litigation in Non-US. Courts – A Comparative Scorecard', 3 *University of California Irvine Law Review* 127 (2013), p. 135.

95  See Arnaud Nuyts, 'Study on Residual Jurisdiction' (Review of the Member States' Rules concerning the 'Residual Jurisdiction' of their courts in Civil and Commercial Matters pursuant to the Brussels I and II Regulations), Service Contract with the European Union, JLS/C4/2005/07-30-CE)0040309/00-37, General report (final version dated 3 September 2007). For an example see the Canadian case of *Van Breda v Village Resorts*, 2010 ONCA 84, [2010] 316 D.L.R. 4th 201 (Can. Ont. CA.) in which the Ontario Court of Appeal recognised the notion of forum of necessity, a recognition that the Canadian Supreme Court did not question (*Club Resorts Ltd. v Van Breda*, 2012 SCC 17, [2012] 1 S.C.R. 572). On this see Michael D. Goldhaber, 'Corporate Human Rights Litigation in Non-US Courts – A Comparative Scorecard', 3 *University of California Irvine Law Review* 127 (2013), pp. 135–136. For an example before Dutch courts, see *El-Hojouj v. Unnamed Libyan Officials*, Arrondissementsrechtbank Den Haag, Mar. 21, 2012, Case No.400882/HA ZA 11-2252 (ECLI:NL:RBSGR:2012:BV9748), mentioned *in* Nicola Jägers, Katinka Jesse and Jonathan Verschuuren, 'The Future of Corporate Liability for Extraterritorial Human Rights Abuses: the Dutch Case against Shell', *American Journal of International Law Unbound* (web exclusive) (January 2014), pp. e-39–40.

The doctrine is far from having reached universal acceptance, but it is never-theless interesting to note that indeed outside the United States the trend seems to be towards an enhanced exercise of civil jurisdiction, rather than a limited one. Another area in which significant developments have occurred in EU Member States is that of parent company liability.

*Parent company liability*

As has been seen, the powerful yet possibly anachronistic concept of separate corporate legal personality often stands in the way of holding parent compa-nies liable for the acts of their foreign subsidiaries. However, in the United Kingdom, courts have developed ways to hold parent companies liable for damages caused to employees of their subsidiaries. In *Lubbe v Cape plc*, a claim brought by South African asbestos workers that was eventually settled, the House of Lords considered the possibility that a parent company may owe a duty of care to employees of its subsidiary, but did not clearly resolve the issue.[96]

In 2012, in a groundbreaking case brought by David Chandler, a former employee of Cape Building Products Limited – a subsidiary of Cape plc – the Court of Appeal bypassed the principle of separate legal personality by recog-nising that a parent company may owe a duty of care to employees of its subsidiary.[97] David Chandler had developed asbestosis after having been exposed to asbestos for a few years while working for Cape Building Products Limited, a company that had since ceased to exist. Although the subsidiary was not foreign-based, the reasoning applied rested not on nationality but on whether or not a duty of care had arisen. In other words, there is no reason why the principle established in *Chandler* may not be applied in a case involv-ing a British parent company and a foreign subsidiary, provided that 'appropriate circumstances' are present. For the Court of Appeal,

> [t]hose circumstances include a situation where, as in the present case, (1) the businesses of the parent and subsidiary are in a relevant respect the same; (2) the parent has, or ought to have, superior knowledge on some relevant aspect of health and safety in the particular industry; (3) the subsidiary's system of work is unsafe as the parent company knew, or ought to have known; and (4) the parent knew or ought to have fore-seen that the subsidiary or its employees would rely on its using that superior knowledge for the employees' protection. For the purposes of (4) it is not necessary to show that the parent is in the practice of inter-vening in the health and safety policies of the subsidiary. The court will look at the relationship between the companies more widely. The court

96   *Lubbe v Cape Plc* [2000] UKHL 4.
97   *Chandler v Cape PLC*, No. [2012] EWCA Civ 525.

may find that element (4) is established where the evidence shows that the parent has a practice of intervening in the trading operations of the subsidiary, for example production and funding issues.[98]

The Court made clear that it was not piercing the corporate veil, that the parent company and the subsidiary remained separate entities and that there was 'no imposition or assumption of responsibility by reason only that a company is the parent company of another company'.[99] Yet, in practice, the effects of its decision are similar to those of piercing the veil in the sense that a parent company can be held liable for damage caused to what is legally speaking a third party, the employee of a separate legal entity, the subsidiary.[100]

Though of great importance for the purpose of this book, the principle established in *Chandler* is limited to the health and safety of employees and would most likely not apply in cases such as those brought under the ATS in the United States, where victims were usually not employees but third parties. Indeed, for a duty of care to arise, a well-established three-fold test of foreseeability, proximity and fairness must be passed.[101] Logically, this is much more likely to be the case with regard to employees, especially when it comes to the second and third elements of the test.

Going further, Dutch courts have accepted the possibility of a parent company owing a duty of care to victims who are not employees but who are nevertheless affected by their subsidiary's action or inaction. In 2013, in *Akpan*, the District Court of The Hague held that Royal Dutch Shell (RDS)'s subsidiary company, Shell Petroleum Development Company of Nigeria (SPDC), was liable for the damage incurred by the claimant due to oil spills. The Court dismissed the claim against the parent company because under Nigerian law, which they had to apply pursuant to the so-called Rome II EU regulation,[102] 'parent companies like RDS in general have no obligation (…) to prevent their (sub-)subsidiaries such as SPDC from inflicting damage on others through their business operations'.[103] In other words, as one commentator put it, 'had Nigerian tort law been different on this point of law, the parent company would have been in more trouble'.[104] Two years

---

98 Ibid., para. 80.

99 Ibid., para. 69.

100 On the case, see Robert McCorquodale, 'Waving Not Drowning: Kiobel outside the United States', 107 *American Journal of International Law* 846 (2013), p. 848.

101 *Caparo Industries plc v Dickman* [1990] UKHL 2.

102 See below.

103 District Court of The Hague, *Akpan and Milieudefensie v Royal Dutch Shell Plc and Shell Petroleum Development Company of Nigeria*, No. 337050/HA ZA 09-1580, para. 4.26 (30 January 2013). Available in English on Milieudefensie's website, www.milieudefensie.nl/publicaties/bezwaren-uitspraken/final-judgment-akpan-vs-shell-oil-spill-ikot-ada-udo/at_download/file (last accessed 15 June 2016).

104 Evelyne Schmid, 'A Glass at Least Half Full: The Dutch Court Ruling on Akpan v Royal Dutch Shell/Shell Nigeria', *Rights as Usual* (26 February 2013), http://rightsasusual.com/?p=265 (last accessed 25 April 2016).

later, the Dutch court of appeals overturned the District Court decision and held that Royal Dutch Shell could be held liable for the oil spills of its subsidiary.[105] Thus, under Dutch law, the principle that parent companies can be held liable for their subsidiaries' actions is established.[106]

In 2012, the French Supreme Court (*Cour de Cassation*) held a parent company – French oil giant Total – criminally liable for the acts of one of its subsidiaries, after the parent company had voluntarily taken responsibility with regard to the oversight of ship safety.[107] This decision had to do with the wreck of an oil tanker, the Erika, and the ensuing catastrophic oil spill along the French Atlantic coast. Though a criminal and not a civil matter, this decision is nevertheless important for the purpose of our examination of parent company liability. Building upon this promising decision, a group of parliamentarians introduced a bill before the French Parliament aiming to establish the legal responsibility of the parent company for the acts of its subsidiaries and its suppliers and sub-contractors if claimants could establish that the parent company had not done enough to prevent damages.[108] In March 2015 the French *Assemblée Nationale* adopted the bill,[109] but the French *Sénat* rejected it in November of the same year.[110] While the bill could still become law, at the time of writing its future is uncertain.

*The problem of applicable law*

As seen in the *Akpan* case, one of the issues that stands in the way of victims of corporate human rights violations getting justice in Europe is that European law provides that the law applicable to a dispute shall be the law

---

105 'Dutch Appeals Court Says Shell May Be Held Liable for Oil Spills in Nigeria', *The Guardian*, 18 December 2015.

106 For discussions on this, see Nicola Jägers, Katinka Jesse and Jonathan Verschuuren, 'The Future of Corporate Liability for Extraterritorial Human Rights Abuses: The Dutch Case against Shell', *American Journal of International Law Unbound* (web exclusive) (January 2014), p. e-41. See also Robert McCorquodale, 'Waving Not Drowning: Kiobel outside the United States', 107 *American Journal of International Law* 846 (2013), p. 850. Both pieces were published before the Court of Appeals decision.

107 French Cour de Cassation, arrêt Erika, No 3439, 25 September 2012, www.courdecassation.fr/IMG///Crim_arret3439_20120925.pdf (last accessed 15 June 2016). For an interesting commentary on this decision (in French) see Emmanuel Daoud, Clarisse Le Corre, 'L'évolution de la responsabilité pénale des entreprises', *Droit de l'environnement*, No 205 (2012) pp. 286. See also BBC News, 'France Upholds Total Verdict over Erika Oil Spill', 25 September 2012, www.bbc.co.uk/news/world-europe-19712798 (last accessed 15 June 2016).

108 Assemblée nationale, Proposition de loi relative au devoir de vigilance des sociétés mères et des entreprises donneuses d'ordre, No 1519 and No 1524, 6 November 2013.

109 Assemblée nationale, Proposition de loi relative au devoir de vigilance des sociétés mères et des entreprises donneuses d'ordre, adoptée par l'Assemblée Nationale en première lecture, 30 mars 2015.

110 Sénat, Proposition de loi relative au devoir de vigilance des sociétés mères et des entreprises donneuses d'ordre, 18 novembre 2015.

of the country where the damage occurred. Article 4(1) of the so-called 'Rome II' regulation provides as a general rule that

> the law applicable to a non-contractual obligation arising out of a tort/delict shall be the law of the country in which the damage occurs irrespective of the country in which the event giving rise to the damage occurred and irrespective of the country or countries in which the indirect consequences of that event occur.[111]

In *Akpan*, this meant the lower court placed no blame on the parent company because Nigerian law does not provide for parent companies' duty of care. While this can create obstacles for the claimant, it must firstly be acknowledged that making the law of the country where the damage occurred the law applicable to a dispute is, by and large, logical. If a particular conduct is not tortious in a given country, it really should not entail liability. Moreover, the general rule set out in Rome II effectively allows claimants to bypass one of the problems posed by the Alien Tort Statute in the United States. Alien Tort Statute litigation can be blamed for encouraging a Western country to impose its own laws on the rest of the world, and particularly poor, developing countries. While this is done in the name of human rights, it is nevertheless not without negative implications, at least from a political point of view.[112] The Rome II regulation, by providing that the host state law will apply, appears more respectful of the host state's sovereignty, or at least of its political choices. However, the downside of applying the law of the host state to a dispute, as opposed to, for example, the law of the forum, is that this can get in the way of holding parent companies accountable for their actions, as in the lower court decision in *Akpan*. That said, even in European countries, the principle of parent company liability is still not well entrenched and that particular point, though central in *Akpan*, is probably not the most significant. A more problematic consequence of Rome II is the measure of damages, which can be significantly lower in developing countries than in Europe.[113]

---

111 Regulation (EC) No 864/2007 on the Law Applicable to Non-Contractual Obligations.
112 On this see for example, V. Rock Grundman, 'The New Imperialism: The Extraterritorial Application of United States Law', 14 *The International Lawyer* 257 (1980); P. M. Roth, 'Reasonable Extraterritoriality: Correcting the Balance of Interests', 41 *International and Comparative Law Quarterly* 245 (1992); Ugo Mattei and Jeffrey Lena, 'US Jurisdiction over Conflicts Arising outside of the United States: Some Hegemonic Implications', 24 *Hastings International & Comparative Law Review* 381 (2000–2001); Austen L. Parrish, 'Reclaiming International Law from Extraterritoriality', 93 *Minnesota Law Review* 815 (2008–2009), especially Section III on 'The Extraterritoriality Threat'. See also Robert McCorquodale, 'Waving Not Drowning: Kiobel outside the United States', 107 *American Journal of International Law* 846 (2013), p. 847.
113 Michael D. Goldhaber, 'Corporate Human Rights Litigation in Non-US Courts – A Comparative Scorecard', 3 *University of California Irvine Law Review* 127 (2013), p. 132.

Despite the general rule set out in Article 4(1), the Rome II regime allows some degree of flexibility, which could prove central in business and human rights litigation. Article 26 provides that 'the application of a provision of the law of any country specified in this Regulation may be refused only if such application is manifestly incompatible with the public policy (*ordre public*) of the forum'.[114] Paragraph 32 of the preamble cites a legal provision 'which would have the effect of causing (…) punitive damages of an excessive nature to be awarded' as an example of a provision which a court may choose to ignore on grounds of public policy.[115] In such circumstances, then, the Regulation allows a court to apply the law of the forum, brushing aside the general rule of Article 4(1). Some have argued that the courts of European countries should also be allowed to ignore the law of the state where the damage occurred when applying it would lead to leaving human rights violations unredressed.[116] If a court in Europe were to refuse to apply the law of the state where the damage occurred because that would entail leaving victims of corporate abuse with no remedy, this would constitute an important development in business and human rights civil litigation. But '[t]o date, the applicability of this exception has not been authoritatively confirmed'.[117]

Beyond the specifics of Rome II, some features of the law of European states make business and human rights civil litigation difficult and less likely in Europe than in the United States. First, damages are much lower in Europe than in the United States. Punitive damages are non-existent in most European countries.[118] Other obstacles to obtaining justice in European courts for victims of corporate human rights violations by European multinational companies operating in developing countries include the absence of a conditional fee system, which means that an unsuccessful claimant has to pay the respondent's legal fees.[119] Finally, collective redress mechanisms such as class actions, which are particularly helpful for large-scale human rights violations, remain underdeveloped in Europe.[120]

---

114 Regulation (EC) No 864/2007 on the Law Applicable to Non-Contractual Obligations, Article 26.
115 Ibid., Preamble.
116 As the House of Lords envisaged in *Kuwait Airways Corp. v Iraq Airways Co.*, [2002] 2 A.C. 883, para. 18.
117 Gwynne Skinner, Robert McCorquodale and Olivier De Schutter, 'The Third Pillar: Access to Judicial Remedies for Human Rights Violations by Transnational Business' (2013), p. 8.
118 Some limited exceptions include England and Wales, Ireland and Cyprus. See Lotte Meurkens, 'The Punitive Damages Debate in Continental Europe: Food for Thought', *Maastricht European Private Law Institute Working Paper No 2014/01*, p. 10.
119 For more detail on this, country by country, see Gwynne Skinner, Robert McCorquodale and Olivier De Schutter, 'The Third Pillar: Access to Judicial Remedies for Human Rights Violations by Transnational Business' (2013), pp. 51–53.
120 Ibid., pp. 57–59.

*Tort litigation versus human rights litigation*

One of the striking features of business and human rights civil litigation in Europe, as opposed to the United States, is the fact that in Europe claims are based on tort law. In the vast majority of cases, the phrase 'human rights' is not even used in the course of the proceedings, let alone in the claim itself. As one author remarks, 'the label "tort" is a pale understatement when applied to the horrors inflicted upon victims and survivors of human rights abuses'.[121] Although the cases can be seen through a human rights lens, they are not really human rights cases as such. This is an important, symbolic point, which can be seen as disempowering for victims. Arguably, a successful human rights claim, leading to the recognition that one's rights were violated, is much more satisfying than an award for damages based on some obscure health and safety regulation. A human rights case is also more likely to be showcased for advocacy purposes and to induce changes in the practices of companies beyond the respondent.[122] Thus in the long run, human rights litigation may prove more effective at durably embedding human rights in business practice than mere non-contractual, civil litigation, even if they essentially look at the same facts.

On the positive side, thanks to the absence of references to international human rights law, civil litigation in the area of business and human rights tends to be more flexible in Europe than in the United States. The wording of the ATS, which expressly refers to the law of nations – coupled with the US Supreme Court's restrictive interpretation of the phrase in *Sosa* – means that only serious human rights violations can be redressed via the ATS and that business and human rights litigators have sometimes got lost in thorny issues such as whether corporations can even violate human rights under international law. Such discussions are less likely to occur when litigation remains centred on the tort of negligence or health and safety issues. When, however, a court in Europe is faced with 'proper' business and human rights litigation, questions similar to those arising in the United States will arise. For example, asked to determine whether a private company can violate international humanitarian law, the French Court of Appeal of Versailles gave a negative answer. The Court contended that private companies are not subjects of international law and therefore are not bound by it, thereby adopting a conservative reading of public international law.[123]

---

121  Beth Stephens, 'Conceptualizing Violence Under International Law: Do Tort Remedies Fit the Crime?', 60 *Albany Law Review* 579 (1997), p. 603.

122  Robert McCorquodale, 'Waving Not Drowning: Kiobel outside the United States', 107 *American Journal of International Law* 846 (2013), p. 851.

123  For a detailed discussion on whether private companies are subjects of international law, see Chapter 5. For a review of the French case, as well as a link to the decision (in French) see Valentina Azarov, 'Backtracking on Responsibility: French Court Absolves Veolia for Unlawful Railway Construction in Occupied Territory', *Rights as Usual* (1 May 2013), http://rightsasusual.com/?p=414 (last accessed 25 April 2016).

In that context, perhaps the main difference between Europe and the United States when it comes to judicial remedies in the area of business and human rights is the tendency in the United States to rely on civil litigation, while recourse to criminal law is more likely in Europe.[124]

## Prosecuting business and human rights violations

Establishing corporate criminal liability for human rights violations, especially those committed in a country different from the forum, raises three main types of issues – jurisdiction and prosecutorial discretion; whether corporate or individual liability, or both, should arise; and complicity liability – all of which have already been touched upon in this book. Hence the present section is relatively brief.

### *Jurisdictional issues and prosecutorial discretion*

As seen in the previous section, issues of jurisdiction are central when it comes to business and human rights civil litigation. This is because many cases are examined by courts located outside the country in which the violations occurred. Typically, North American and European courts examine violations committed in developing countries. As a result, numerous claims end in the early stages due to courts' lack of jurisdiction over them. Jurisdiction is also an important aspect of business and human rights criminal prosecutions.

In certain European countries, such as the Netherlands and France (and unlike the United Kingdom), the law allows prosecutions to be carried out for acts committed outside the territory, but with some limitations. Speaking specifically about Belgium, Germany and France, authors have noted that '[u]nder the traditional approach, continental European countries applied their criminal law extraterritorially, but their law did not reach foreign-cubed cases because various requirements of nationality and nexus restricted extraterritorial jurisdiction'.[125] As a reminder, foreign-cubed cases are cases involving a foreign defendant and foreign victims of violations committed in a foreign country. In these three countries, criminal proceedings may be initiated by victims themselves, as *parties civiles*, though under the control of public prosecution services, which are more or less willing to pursue such cases. As an additional obstacle, in France, unlike in Belgium and Germany, defendants currently need to have their 'habitual residency' on the French territory to be targeted by prosecutions for crimes falling under the jurisdiction of the International Criminal Court. A bill introduced in 2012 and

---

124 This is discussed at length in Caroline Kaeb and David Scheffer, 'The Paradox of Kiobel in Europe', 107 *American Journal of International Law* 852 (2013), p. 855.
125 Vivian Grosswald Curran and David Sloss, 'Reviving Human Rights Litigation after Kiobel' 107 *American Journal of International Law* 858 (2013), p. 859.

adopted by the Senate in 2013 aims to remove this condition. At the time of writing, the bill was still being examined by the lower chamber of the French Parliament.[126]

Despite a relatively victim-friendly environment, prosecutions of business and human rights violations have been rare. In practice, public prosecutors have been reluctant to pursue investigations.[127] The case against Lima Holding BV in the Netherlands provides a case in point. Lima Holding BV is the parent company of Riwal, a company involved in the construction of the separation wall in occupied Palestinian territory – a wall considered unlawful by the International Court of Justice in 2004.[128] The *parties civiles* brought a case against the company for complicity with war crimes and crimes against humanity. Among other reasons to dismiss the case, the Dutch Public Prosecutor's Office invoked its complexity and the probable lack of cooperation from Israeli authorities.[129] Such factors are likely to be present in most if not all business and human rights cases. To take another example, in France, the ongoing case against French software company Amesys for complicity with torture remains open thanks to the tenacity of an investigating judge who rescued it.[130] The company allegedly provided the Gaddafi regime with software designed for law enforcement which the regime used to track political opponents, who were later arrested and tortured.

## Corporate versus individual liability

As discussed in Chapter 5, in the context of the negotiations for the adoption of the Statute of the International Criminal Court, prosecuting business and human rights violations may consist of prosecuting a legal person – the company allegedly responsible for the violations – and/or one or several natural persons – the business executives who were in charge. Some countries have been reluctant to recognise the notion of corporate criminal

126 Proposition de loi tendant à modifier l'article 689-11 du code de procédure pénale relatif à la compétence territoriale du juge français concernant les infractions visées par le statut de la Cour pénale internationale, n° 753, déposée le 6 septembre 2012, www.senat.fr/leg/tas12-101.html (last accessed 15 June 2016).
127 Business and Human Rights Resource Centre, *Annual Briefing on Corporate Legal Accountability* (November 2013) p. 5.
128 *Legal Consequences of the Construction of a Wall in the Occupied Palestinian Territory*, Advisory Opinion, ICJ Reports 2004, para. 167.
129 See the letter sent by the Public Prosecutor's Office, *in* Valentina Azarov, 'Investigative or Political Barriers? Dutch Prosecutor Dismisses Criminal Complicity Case Against Riwal', *Rights as Usual* (29 May 2013), http://rightsasusual.appspot.com/?p=543 (last accessed 15 June 2016).
130 Fédération des Ligues des Droits de l'Homme (FIDH), 'Amesys Case: The investigation Chamber Green Lights the Investigative Proceedings on the Sale of Surveillance Equipment by Amesys to the Khadafi Regime', (2013), www.fidh.org/en/region/north-africa-middle-east/libya/Amesys-Case-The-Investigation-12752 (last accessed 15 June 2016).

liability and are more comfortable with prosecuting individuals.[131] Despite traditional resistance, in Europe, harmonisation on this point is underway and corporate liability is increasingly accepted on an area-by-area basis.[132] Those who are suspicious of the notion of corporate criminal liability argue that only individuals can commit crimes, and that recognising corporate liability may lead to shielding those really responsible for the crimes. As asserted by the International Military Tribunal at Nuremberg: 'Crimes against international law are committed by men, not by abstract entities, and only by punishing individuals who commit such crimes can the provisions of international law be enforced.'[133] The Tribunal was addressing the argument put forward by the defendants that only states can violate international law and that individuals should not be put on trial by an international tribunal. Using a similar line of reasoning, it can be argued that the notion of corporate liability diverts attention away from the 'real' criminals, who can only be human beings, and that corporate liability encourages impunity. Such argument, however, is easily dismissed because recognising corporate criminal liability does not stand in the way of individuals being prosecuted as well. It does not have to be one or the other; rather, both the company and selected individuals can be prosecuted.[134] Perhaps more convincing are concerns around collective punishment and consequences on third parties such as employees when a company is being prosecuted.

In practice, whether to prosecute companies themselves or the individuals working for the companies has proved to be a complex question, and the two approaches sometimes get blurred, as became clear during the post-Second World War prosecutions of industrialists covered in detail in Chapter 4. For example, in the *I.G. Farben* judgment, the tribunal remarked that

---

131 Germany is said to be one of these countries, though a closer look shows a more nuanced picture. Markus D. Dubber notes:

> The general take on corporate criminal liability in Germany is that it does not exist, could not exist, and – not surprisingly – did not exist, and not necessarily in this order. Those who look a little more closely at German legal history notice, however, that the story is not quite so simple, because corporate criminal liability did exist in Germany at some point. The more sophisticated story, then, is that German corporate criminal liability, although it may have existed at some point, no longer does.

Markus D. Dubber, 'The Comparative History and Theory of Corporate Criminal Liability', 16 *New Criminal Law Review* 203 (2013), p. 204.

132 See for example, in the area of human trafficking, Council Framework Decision 2002/629/JHA, art. 6(2), 2002 O.J. (L 203) 1.

133 International Military Tribunal (Nuremberg), Judgement and Sentences (1 October 1946) *reprinted in* 41 *American Journal of International Law* 172 (1947), p. 221.

134 As was the case for example in the controversial criminal trial held in the Democratic Republic of the Congo against, among other defendants, three employees of the company Anvil Mining Congo and against the company itself. See the judgment on the website of the Asser Institute: www.internationalcrimesdatabase.org/Case/766 (last accessed 15 June 2016).

[w]hile the Farben organization, as a corporation, is not charged under the indictment with committing a crime and is not the subject of prosecution in this case, it is the theory of the prosecution that the defendants individually and collectively used the Farben organization as an instrument by and through which they committed the crimes enumerated in the indictment.[135]

Thus, to some extent, the approach used during some of these trials was institutional. Companies as well as directors and managers were targeted 'even if corporate liability formally was not at stake'.[136] The fact that the prosecution traced 'responsibility on different levels of decision making instead of targeting only the head office' shows that they had adopted such a global approach.[137] The *Krupp* trial, for example, was partly 'about Krupp's corporate identity'.[138] In short, it was felt at the time that even though the cases were against individual businessmen, corporate and individual liability could not really be separated. Arguably, in order to fully expose the crimes, both forms of liability must be available.

While concerns about the notion of corporate criminal liability and how it could potentially encourage impunity, and even lead to collective punishment, are respectable, it is contended here that the advantages of recognising the notion of corporate criminal liability outweigh those concerns. Not only would such recognition address the accountability gap, but it also could be more efficient in the long run than the prosecution of individuals for business and human rights violations. First, public opinions and consumers know companies and brands, but not necessarily individual executives. Thus for advocacy purposes, targeting companies makes more sense. Second, prosecution of individuals is selective and does not always allow one to draw an accurate picture of a given corporate culture.[139] Ultimately, one of the goals of business and human rights litigation is to embed human rights in corporate practices. Punishment is important, but contributing to greater corporate accountability in general, outside a specific case, is even more important. Singling out companies (together with certain individuals when relevant) may help draw more attention to certain practices. For example, if

---

135 Trials of War Criminals Before the Nuernberg Military Tribunals Under Control Council Law No 10, vol. VIII 'The I.G. Farben Case', Washington: United States Government Printing Office (1952), p. 1108.
136 Kim C. Priemel, 'Tales of Totalitarianism: Conflicting Narratives in the Industrialist Cases at Nuremberg', *in* Kim C. Priemel and Alexa Stiller (eds), *Reassessing the Nuremberg Military Tribunals: Transitional Justice, Trial Narratives, and Historiography*, New York, Oxford: Berghahn Books (2012), p. 170.
137 Ibid.
138 Ibid., p. 173.
139 Tara L. Van Ho, 'Transnational Civil and Criminal Litigation', *in* Sabine Michalowski (ed.), *Corporate Accountability in the Context of Transitional Justice*, Abingdon: Routledge (2013), p. 57.

the charge against French software company Amesys for complicity with torture was upheld, it could open a wider debate on the ethical aspects of certain businesses.

Finally, companies typically have more assets than individuals. Corporate entities may be asked to pay more significant amounts in fines than individuals. Although criminal prosecutions are not about monetary compensation for a damage (civil lawsuits are), fines resulting from a successful prosecution can be used for reparation purposes.

### Establishing complicity liability under criminal law

As was covered in the previous section on civil litigation, one characteristic of the involvement of the business world (companies and individuals alike) in human rights violations is the fact that businesses are often complicit in their commission, rather than being the main perpetrators. Especially in the criminal law area, corporate liability for human rights violations is usually a form of complicity liability. An important difference between complicity liability for the purposes of getting compensated after a civil lawsuit and that for the purposes of establishing guilt in a criminal trial is the standard of persuasion required to establish each of them. This difference is striking in common law countries, such as the United States, the United Kingdom and Commonwealth countries. In such countries, civil claimants have to provide a 'preponderance of evidence' to back their claims. Another way to phrase this is to say that claimants need to prove their cases on the 'balance of probabilities'. Both standards can be summed up as requiring claimants to prove it is 'more likely than not' that they have a valid claim against the defendant. By contrast, in criminal proceedings in these countries, the defendant's guilt must be proved 'beyond a reasonable doubt', which is a very high standard. In civil law countries which follow the continental European model, the difference between civil and criminal law on this point is less salient. As one author puts it:

> In most civil law jurisdictions, (...) there is a common, but not universal, assumption that the standard of persuasion is the same for civil and criminal proceedings. The plaintiff in a civil case, as well as the prosecutor in a criminal case, must provide sufficient proof to convince the trier of fact of the truth of the facts at issue on the particular occasion. This is phrased in France and elsewhere as a requirement that the trier of fact have an 'intime conviction,' an inner, personal, subjective conviction or belief in the truth of the facts at issue.[140]

140 Richard W. Wright, 'Proving Facts: Belief versus Probability', 79 (2009), Scholarly Commons @ IIT Chicago-Kent College of Law, http://scholarship.kentlaw.iit.edu/fac_schol/709 (last accessed 15 June 2016), p. 80.

That said, while there can be a difference in *how* facts must be proved (the standard of persuasion), the types of facts that must be proved to establish liability, and the uncertainties around their contours, are similar in countries adhering to both legal traditions. As shown in Chapter 4 and in the previous section on civil litigation in the present chapter, debates around whether the knowledge, intent or purpose tests should be used for the purpose of establishing complicity liability are as central in criminal as in civil proceedings.

In the *Van Anraat* case, the defendant was found guilty of complicity with war crimes simply because it was found that he knew perfectly well what the consequences of his acts would be. This is a Dutch criminal case against a businessman accused of complicity with genocide and with war crimes for having sold certain chemicals used in the fabrication of mustard gas to the Saddam Hussein regime in Iraq. In 2007, the Court of Appeal of The Hague established that Frans Van Anraat had sold the chemicals, and that these particular batches of chemicals were used to make weapons that were later used to commit war crimes (material element). The Court also established that he knew the chemicals were going to Iraq, as opposed to a different destination, and that they would be used to make weapons, as opposed to dyes. He also knew of the political situation in Iraq and of the brutality of the regime. Thus, they concluded, he knew it was likely that the weapons would be used to commit war crimes (mental element).[141] This case is one of the very few contemporary criminal cases in the area of business and human rights that involves human rights violations in a developing country and a European businessperson.[142]

## Conclusion

This chapter has focused on business and human rights litigation for the purpose of establishing civil or criminal liability for (complicity in) human rights violations. However, there exist other forms of business and human rights litigation, which do not focus on establishing liability. *Kasky v Nike*, discussed in Chapter 8 and argued before United States courts, provides an interesting example of such litigation. The claimant, a consumer activist, sued Nike under California's Unfair Competition Law and False Advertising Law. The California Supreme Court found in favour of the claimant and the US Supreme Court declined to hear the case, which was eventually settled.[143]

---

141 *Van Anraat*, paras 12 and. 11.16, available in English at: www.asser.nl/upload/documents/DomCLIC/Docs/NLP/Netherlands/vanAnraat_Appeal_Judgment_09-05-2007_EN.pdf (last accessed 16 June 2016).

142 See also the case against Guus Kouwenhoven in the Netherlands, which is still ongoing at the time of writing. See www.haguejusticeportal.net/index.php?id=6412 (last accessed 25 April 2016).

143 Among a vast literature on the case, see Tamara R. Piety, 'Grounding Nike: Exposing Nike's Quest for a Constitutional Right to Lie', 78 *Temple Law Review* 151 (2005).

A similar case against Samsung France was brought before French courts in 2013.[144]

Such cases shed light on corporate human rights records. These cases are not about establishing liability for or redressing human rights violations as such; nevertheless, they are business and human rights cases in the wider sense. By exposing certain corporate practices, these cases help raise awareness and are important for advocacy purposes. The goal of all business and human rights litigation should be to help change corporate practices and contribute to embedding human rights into such practices. With this in mind, even unsuccessful cases are important. As one author notes,

> a price tag [cannot] be put on the human rights consciousness raised by the alien tort cases that were brought against corporations. Hearts and minds were won in both the street and the boardroom. New and perhaps more effective legal strategies to promote corporate accountability were inspired and cross-fertilized.[145]

As seen in this chapter, business and human rights litigation for the purposes of establishing liability for human rights violations committed overseas by Western multinational companies faces numerous obstacles at the moment. This is especially the case in the United States, where the Alien Tort Statute route may be closing. Yet this is not the end of the story. For example, 'in important respects, the winds are changing in Europe'.[146] Also, and more importantly, it is hoped that these battles will increasingly be fought in the courts of host states.

As a final note, it appears clearly that business and human rights civil litigation is an uncertain route to justice for victims of corporate human rights violations. Even those who do manage to win their case may never receive any form of compensation. Despite this troubling reality, Professor Steinhardt reminds us why human rights cases are still worth fighting for:

> Now we might ask, what is the value of such huge awards when there is a decent possibility that no money will actually change hands? To this, I can only reply with an anecdote from *In re Estate of Ferdinand Marcos, Human Rights Litigation* – the first full-blown human rights trial under the ATS. With Paul Hoffman, I was honored to represent a number of survivors of human rights abuses in the Philippines, and a multi-million dollar judgment was awarded. When told that there was a good chance

---

144 Simon Mundy, 'Samsung Rejects Child Labour Allegations', London: *The Financial Times*, 27 February 2013.
145 Michael D. Goldhaber, 'Corporate Human Rights Litigation in Non-US Courts – A Comparative Scorecard', 3 *University of California Irvine Law Review* 127 (2013), p. 129.
146 Caroline Kaeb and David Scheffer, 'The Paradox of Kiobel in Europe', 107 *American Journal of International Law* 852 (2013), p. 857.

of never seeing a dime of this award, this survivor of almost inconceivable abuse said something that I have not forgotten in twenty years, and that is, 'That's okay, it's enough to be believed.' *It is enough to be believed.*[147]

# Bibliography

## Books

Fletcher, George P., *Tort Liability for Human Rights Abuses*, Oxford and Portland: Hart Publishing (2008).

Koebele, Michael, *Corporate Responsibility under the Alien Tort Statute, Enforcement of International Law through US Torts Law*, Leiden and Boston: Martinus Nijhoff Publishers (2009).

Ruggie, John Gerard, *Just Business*, New York and London: W. W. Norton & Company Inc. (2013).

## Journal articles

Altman, Ranon, 'Extraterritorial Application of the Alien Tort Statute After Kiobel', 24 *University of Miami Business Law Review* 111 (2016).

Anderson, Winston, 'Forum Non Conveniens Checkmated? – The Emergence of Retaliatory Legislation', 10 *Journal of Transnational Law and Policy* 183 (2000–2001).

Anonymous, Case analysis of *Balintulo*, 27 *Harvard Law Review* 1493 (2013–2014).

Blumberg, Philip I., 'Accountability of Multinational Corporations: The Barriers Presented by Concepts of the Corporate Juridical Entity', 24 *Hastings International and Comparative Law Review* 297 (2000–2001).

Burley, Anne-Marie, 'The Alien Tort Statute and the Judiciary Act of 1789: A Badge of Honor', 3 *American Journal of International Law* 461 (1989).

Cassel, Doug, 'Corporate Aiding and Abetting of Human Rights Violations: Confusion in the Courts, 6 *Northwestern University Journal of International Human Rights* 304 (2007–2008).

Chander, Anupam, 'Unshackling Foreign Corporations: Kiobel's Unexpected Legacy', 107 *American Journal of International Law* 829 (2013).

Daoud, Emmanuel and Le Corre, Clarisse, 'L'évolution de la responsabilité pénale des entreprises', *Droit de l'environnement*, No 205 (2012).

Donovan, Donald Francis and Roberts, Anthea, 'The Emerging Recognition of Universal Civil Jurisdiction', 100 *American Journal of International Law* 142 (2006).

Dubber, Markus D., 'The Comparative History and Theory of Corporate Criminal Liability', 16 *New Criminal Law Review* 203 (2013).

---

147 Ralph G. Steinhardt, '*Kiobel* and the Multiple Futures of Corporate Liability for Human Rights Violations', 28 *Maryland Journal of International Law* 1 (2013), p. 4. Emphasis in the original.

Free, Brian C., 'Awaiting Doe v Exxon Mobil Corp.: Advocating the Cautious Use of Executive Opinions in Alien Tort Claims Act Litigation', 12 *Pacific Rim Law & Policy Journal* 467 (2003).

Goldhaber, Michael D., 'Corporate Human Rights Litigation in Non-US. Courts – A Comparative Scorecard', 3 *University of California Irvine Law Review* 127 (2013).

Grosswald Curran, Vivian and Sloss, David, 'Reviving Human Rights Litigation after Kiobel' 107 *American Journal of International Law* 858 (2013).

Grundman, V. Rock, 'The New Imperialism: The Extraterritorial Application of United States Law', 14 *The International Lawyer* 257 (1980).

Henkin, Louis, 'U.S. Ratification of Human Rights Conventions: The Ghost of Senator Bricker', 89 *American Journal of International Law* 341 (1995).

Hoffman, Paul L., 'Kiobel v. Royal Dutch Petroleum Co.: First Impressions', 52 *Columbia Journal of Transnational Law* 28 (2013–2014).

Jägers, Nicola, Jesse, Katinka and Verschuuren, Jonathan 'The Future of Corporate Liability for Extraterritorial Human Rights Abuses: The Dutch Case against Shell', *American Journal of International Law Unbound* (web exclusive) (January 2014).

Kaeb, Caroline and Scheffer, David, 'The Paradox of Kiobel in Europe', 107 *American Journal of International Law* 852 (2013).

Ku, Julian G., 'Kiobel and the Surprising Death of Universal Jurisdiction under the Alien Tort Statute', 107 *American Journal of International Law* 835 (2013).

Mattei, Ugo and Lena, Jeffrey, 'US Jurisdiction over Conflicts Arising outside of the United States: Some Hegemonic Implications', 24 *Hastings International & Comparative Law Review* 381 (2000–2001).

McCorquodale, Robert, 'Waving Not Drowning: Kiobel outside the United States', 107 *American Journal of International Law* 846 (2013).

Parrish, Austen L., 'Reclaiming International Law from Extraterritoriality', 93 *Minnesota Law Review* 815 (2008–2009).

Paul, Joel R., 'Comity in International Law', 32 *Harvard International Law Journal* 1 (1991).

Piety, Tamara R., 'Grounding Nike: Exposing Nike's Quest for a Constitutional Right to Lie', 78 *Temple Law Review* 151 (2005).

Reggio, Andrea, 'Aiding and Abetting In International Criminal Law: The Responsibility of Corporate Agents And Businessmen For "Trading With The Enemy" of Mankind', 5 *International Criminal Law Review* 623 (2005).

Roth, P. M., 'Reasonable Extraterritoriality: Correcting the Balance of Interests', 41 *International and Comparative Law Quarterly* 245 (1992).

Steinhardt, Ralph G., 'Kiobel and the Weakening of Precedent: A Long Walk for a Short Drink', 107 *American Journal of International Law* 841 (2013).

Steinhardt, Ralph G., '*Kiobel* and the Multiple Futures of Corporate Liability for Human Rights Violations', 28 *Maryland Journal of International Law* 1 (2013).

Stephens, Beth, 'Upsetting Checks and Balances: The Bush Administration's Efforts To Limit Human Rights Litigation', 7 *Harvard Human Rights Journal* 169 (2004).

Stephens, Beth, 'Conceptualizing Violence under International Law: Do Tort Remedies Fit the Crime?', 60 *Albany Law Review* 579 (1997).

Sykes, Alan O., 'Corporate Liability for Extraterritorial Torts Under the Alien Tort Statute and Beyond: An Economic Analysis', 100 *Georgetown Law Journal* 2161 (2011–2012).

Thompson, Robert C., Ramasastry, Anita and Taylor, Mark B., 'Translating Unocal: the Expanding Web of Liability for Business Entities Implicated in International Crimes', 40 *George Washington International Law Review* 841 (2008–2009).

## Book chapters

Priemel, Kim C., 'Tales of Totalitarianism: Conflicting Narratives in the Industrialist Cases at Nuremberg', *in* Kim C. Priemel and Alexa Stiller (eds), *Reassessing the Nuremberg Military Tribunals: Transitional Justice, Trial Narratives, and Historiography*, New York, Oxford: Berghahn Books (2012), pp. 161–193.
Van Ho, Tara L., 'Transnational Civil and Criminal Litigation', *in* Sabine Michalowski (ed.), *Corporate Accountability in the Context of Transitional Justice*, Abingdon: Routledge (2013), pp. 52–72.

## Newspaper articles

'Oily Diplomacy', Editorial, *New York Times*, 9 August 2002.
Mundy, Simon, 'Samsung Rejects Child Labour Allegations', London: *The Financial Times*, 27 February 2013.
'Dutch Appeals Court Says Shell May Be Held Liable for Oil Spills in Nigeria', *The Guardian*, 18 December 2015.

## Statutes

28 U.S. Code § 1350.

## Treaties

Statute of the International Criminal Court (1998), 2187 UNTS 90.

## Official documents

Council Regulation (EC) 44/2001 of 22 December 2000 on jurisdiction and the recognition and enforcement of judgments in civil and commercial matters.
Council Framework Decision 2002/629/JHA, art. 6(2), 2002 O.J. (L 203) 1.
Regulation (EC) No 864/2007 on the Law Applicable to Non-Contractual Obligations.
Regulation (EU) No 1215/2012 of 20 December 2012 on jurisdiction and the recognition and enforcement of judgments in civil and commercial matters (recast).
Proposition de loi de tendant à modifier l'article 689-11 du code de procédure pénale relatif à la compétence territoriale du juge français concernant les infractions visées par le statut de la Cour pénale internationale, n° 753, déposée le 6 septembre 2012, www.senat.fr/leg/tas12-101.html (last accessed 14 June 2016).
Assemblée nationale, Proposition de loi relative au devoir de vigilance des sociétés mères et des entreprises donneuses d'ordre, No 1519 and No 1524, 6 November 2013.

Assemblée nationale, Proposition de loi relative au devoir de vigilance des sociétés mères et des entreprises donneuses d'ordre, adoptée par l'Assemblée Nationale en première lecture, 30 mars 2015.

Sénat, Proposition de loi relative au devoir de vigilance des sociétés mères et des entreprises donneuses d'ordre, 18 novembre 2015.

## Cases and opinions

International Military Tribunal (Nuremberg), Judgement and Sentences (1 October 1946) *reprinted in* 41 *American Journal of International Law* 172 (1947).

Trials of War Criminals Before the Nuernberg Military Tribunals Under Control Council Law No 10, vol. VIII 'The I.G. Farben Case', Washington: United States Government Printing Office (1952).

*Filartiga*, 630 F.2d 876 (1980).

*Caparo Industries plc v Dickman* [1990] UKHL 2.

*Kadic and Doe v Karadžic*, 70 F.3d 232 (2d Cir. 1995).

*Jota v Texaco, Inc.*, 157 F3d 153 (1998).

*Akayesu*, Case No. ICTR-96-4-T, Trial Chamber, Judgement (1998).

*Furundzija*, Case No. IT-95-17/1-T, Trial Chamber, Judgement (1998).

*United States v Bestfoods*, 524 US 51 (1998).

*Lubbe v Cape Plc* [2000] UKHL 4.

*Aguinda v Texaco, Inc.*, 303 F.3d 470 (2d Cir. 2002).

*Kuwait Airways Corp. v Iraq Airways Co.*, [2002] 2 A.C. 883.

*Doe v Unocal*, 395 F.3d 932 (2002).

*Sarei v Rio Tinto PLC.*, 221 F. Supp.2d 1116 (C.D. Cal. 2002).

*Legal Consequences of the Construction of a Wall in the Occupied Palestinian Territory*, Advisory Opinion, ICJ Reports 2004.

*Sosa v Alvarez-Machain*, 542 U.S. 692 (2004).

*Bowoto v Chevron*, 312 F. Supp. 2d 1229 (N.D. Cal. 2004).

ECJ, Case C-281/02 *Owusu v Jackson* [2005] 2 WLR 942.

Court of Appeal of The Hague, *Van Anraat* (2007), available on the Asser Institute's website: www.asser.nl/upload/documents/DomCLIC/Docs/NLP/Netherlands/vanAnraat_Appeal_Judgment_09-05-2007_EN.pdf (last accessed 25 April 2016).

Cour militaire du Katanga, arrêt *Kilwa* (2007), available on the Asser Institute's website. www.asser.nl/upload/documents/DomCLIC/Docs/NLP/DRC/Kilwa_Arret_All_28-6-2007.pdf (last accessed 25 April 2016).

*Presbyterian Church of Sudan v Talisman Energy Corp.*, 582 F.3d 244 (2d Cir. 2009).

*Van Breda v Village Resorts*, 2010 ONCA 84, [2010] 316 D.L.R. 4th 201 (Can. Ont. CA.)

*Kiobel v Royal Dutch Petroleum Co.*, 621 F.3d 111 (2d Cir. 2010).

*Doe VIII v Exxon Mobil Corp.*, 654 F.3d 11 (D.C. Circ. 2011).

*Club Resorts Ltd. v Van Breda*, 2012 SCC 17, [2012] 1 S.C.R. 572.

*El-Hojouj v Unnamed Libyan Officials*, Arrondissementsrechtbank Den Haag, Mar. 21, 2012, Case No.400882/HA ZA 11-2252 (ECLI:NL:RBSGR:2012:BV9748).

French Cour de Cassation, arrêt Erika, No 3439, 25 September 2012, www.courde-cassation.fr/IMG///Crim_arret3439_20120925.pdf.

*Chandler v Cape PLC*, No. [2012] EWCA Civ 525.

*Doe v Nestlé*, 738 F.3d 1048 (9th Cir. 2013).

District Court of The Hague, *Akpan and Milieudefensie v Royal Dutch Shell Plc and Shell Petroleum Development Company of Nigeria*, No. 337050/IIA ZA 09-1580 (30 January 2013).

*Kiobel v Royal Dutch Petroleum Co.*, 133 S. Ct. 1659 (2013).

*Balintulo v Daimler AG*, 727 F.3d 174 (2d Cir. 2013).

*Al Shimari v CACI*, United States Court of Appeals for the Fourth Circuit, No. 13-1937 (30 June 2014).

## Miscellaneous

Azarov, Valentina, 'Backtracking on Responsibility: French Court Absolves Veolia for Unlawful Railway Construction in Occupied Territory', *Rights as Usual* (2013), http://rightsasusual.com/?p=414 (last accessed 25 April 2016).

BBC News, 'France Upholds Total Verdict over Erika Oil Spill', 25 September 2012, www.bbc.co.uk/news/world-europe-19712798.

Business and Human Rights Resource Centre, *In the Courtroom & Beyond: New Strategies to Overcome Inequality and Improve Access to Justice. Corporate Legal Accountability Annual Briefing*, February 2016.

Business and Human Rights Resource Centre, *Annual Briefing on Corporate Legal Accountability* (November 2013).

Fédération des Ligues des Droits de l'Homme (FIDH), 'Amesys Case: The investigation Chamber Green Lights the Investigative Proceedings on the Sale of Surveillance Equipment by Amesys to the Khadafi Regime', (2013), www.fidh.org/spip.php?page=article_pdf&id_article=12752.

International Commission of Jurists, *Report of the ICJ Expert Legal Panel on Corporate Complicity in International Crimes*, Vol. 1 (2008).

Meurkens, Lotte, 'The Punitive Damages Debate in Continental Europe: Food for Thought', *Maastricht European Private Law Institute Working Paper No 2014/01* (2014).

Nuyts, Arnaud, 'Study on Residual Jurisdiction' (Review of the Member States' Rules concerning the 'Residual Jurisdiction' of their courts in Civil and Commercial Matters pursuant to the Brussels I and II Regulations), Service Contract with the European Union, JLS/C4/2005/07-30-CE)0040309/00-37, General report (final version dated 3 September 2007).

Schmid, Evelyne, 'A Glass at Least Half Full: The Dutch Court Ruling on Akpan v Royal Dutch Shell/Shell Nigeria', *Rights as Usual* (2013), http://rightsasusual.com/?p=265 (last accessed 25 April 2016).

Skinner, Gwynne, McCorquodale, Robert and De Schutter, Olivier, 'The Third Pillar: Access to Judicial Remedies for Human Rights Violations by Transnational Business' (2013).

Special page on the prosecution of Guus Kouwenhoven in the Netherlands, www.haguejusticeportal.net/index.php?id=6412 (last accessed 25 April 2016).

Supplemental Brief of the European Commission on Behalf of the European Union in Support of Neither Party, *Kiobel v. Royal Dutch Petroleum Co.*, 133 S.Ct. 1659 (2013) (No. 10-1491).

Wright, Richard W., 'Proving Facts: Belief versus Probability', 79 (2009), Scholarly Commons @ IIT Chicago-Kent College of Law, http://scholarship.kentlaw.iit.edu/fac_schol/709.

# 11 The future of business and human rights

The interplay between business and human rights is not new, but the development of business and human rights as a distinct field, albeit a multifaceted one, is relatively recent. Part of the task at hand for those who work in this field is to frame existing and diverse areas of focus, such as health and safety in supply chains, social and environmental risk assessments, corporate codes of conduct, international human rights obligations of non-state actors, non-financial reporting requirements under domestic law and policy space for states hosting foreign direct investments, as business and human rights issues. These areas of focus may previously have been viewed as unrelated but looking at them through a business and human rights lens reveals that they are in fact all part of the same field of study and practice, which rests on two simple ideas. First, business entities should refrain from violating human rights. Second, if they do end up violating human rights, victims must be provided with a remedy. In essence, this is all this field is about: preventing and addressing human rights violations by the business sector.

Adopting a legal perspective, this book has presented the various ways in which this dual undertaking has been and could be further carried out in the future. These are the development of international law, both hard and soft; private regulation; government regulation; advocacy work, for example through naming and shaming; and, occasionally, litigation. Each of these routes has its advantages and its shortcomings and cannot, in itself, be enough to cover such a wide range of potential violations. As former UN Secretary-General Special Representative on Business and Human Rights Professor John Ruggie put it, what is needed is a 'smart mix' of measures.[1] This is all the more so because there is no single reason why corporations violate human rights. A look at both historical and contemporary business

---

1   Addendum to the Report of the UN Special Representative, 'Human Rights and Corporate Law: Trends and Observations from a Crossnational Study Conducted by the Special Representative', UN Doc. A/HRC/17/31/Add.2 (2011), para. 206. On this occasion he was only talking about the various measures states can adopt. However, his comment can be extended to all forms of regulation meant to prevent and address corporate human rights violations.

and human rights violations shows that numerous factors can be at play: opportunism, ignorance, weak governance, poor law enforcement, corruption, an overly competitive market, lack of management leadership and, though admittedly rarely, genuine wickedness.

One of the most prominent developments in the field has been the growing importance of international regulation. The United Nations and the OECD have developed soft law standards and the adoption of a business and human rights international treaty, the contents of which remain unclear, is on the UN Human Rights Council's agenda.[2] When it comes to the proposed treaty, managing expectations is essential. Even if the negotiations for its adoption are successful and a treaty does enter into force, having a binding business and human rights treaty will not, in itself, prevent business and human rights violations. A treaty would be an important milestone, but it cannot and should not be the only way to address business and human rights issues.[3]

The *raison d'être* of a business corporation is to generate profits. How to reconcile profit-making and respect for sometimes contradictory human rights standards, especially in areas where respect for the rule of law is not prevalent, is one of the key questions raised by the field of business and human rights. In passing, it is worth noting that this is not a question which has recently emerged. Although obviously not on the same scale, the moral dilemmas of seventeenth-century slave traders were similar in nature to the dilemmas faced by twenty-first-century managers of mining projects when it appears that such projects will violate the rights of local communities. These business and human rights dilemmas are real and intricate. This book did not purport to provide elusive ready-made solutions to address them. Rather, it has provided the background, outlining the complexity of the field so that business executives and policy-makers, in turn, can make informed decisions.

Change in corporate behaviour towards increased respect for human rights is likely to come from increased corporate accountability in the area of human rights. More individuals and business entities need to own the issues. Such accountability could take the form of legal liability. At the domestic level, a growing number of lawsuits and criminal prosecutions targeting corporations or corporate executives for their role in the commission of human rights violations in developing countries are taking place in Western countries, but these lawsuits and prosecutions, however prominent, represent a drop in the ocean. For business and human rights ideals to gain traction, other accountability mechanisms are needed, ranging from state-based non-judicial

---

2    UN Human Rights Council, Elaboration of an international legally binding instrument on transnational corporations and other business enterprises with respect to human rights, A/HRC/26/L.22/Rev.1 (25 June 2014).

3    For a discussion on the pros and cons of the treaty, see the special page of the Business and Human Rights Resource Centre, http://business-humanrights.org/en/binding-treaty (last accessed 25 April 2016).

mechanisms such as the OECD National Contact Points to internal dispute settlement mechanisms, following a given company's human rights policy. The role of self- or private regulation in enhancing accountability should not be ignored, either. Admittedly, self-regulation mechanisms such as codes of conduct can at times be pointless. Similarly, assuming that business and human rights violations can be prevented and addressed solely by engaging in dialogue with corporations is naïve.[4] However, a strategy of systematic antagonism towards large multinational corporations is likely to produce limited results.

Outside a legal framework, corporate cultures can be changed through the exercise of leadership at the highest corporate levels and by the rise of virtuous coalitions of corporations by sectors; 'holy alliance[s]' of the kind that French doctor and activist Louis René Villermé was proposing as early as 1840, though with limited hope of seeing them materialising.[5] Employees, trade unions, NGOs, governments and international organisations can also play their part in ensuring that businesses respect human rights. To achieve this ambitious goal, knowledge is key. It is with this in mind that this book was written.

## Bibliography

### *Books*

Villermé, Louis René, *Tableau de l'état physique et moral des ouvriers employés dans les Manufactures de Coton, de Laine, et de Soie*, Paris: Jules Renouard et Cie, Vol. II (1840).

### *Journal articles*

de Felice, Damiano, 'Banks and Human Rights Due Diligence: a Critical Analysis of the Thun Group's Discussion Paper on the UN Guiding Principles on Business and Human Rights;, 19 *The International Journal of Human Rights* 319 (2015).
Oshionebo, Evaristus, 'The UN Global Compact and Accountability of Transnational Corporations: Separating Myth from Realities', 19 *Florida Journal of International Law* 1 2007.

---

4    On this see Evaristus Oshionebo, 'The UN Global Compact and Accountability of Transnational Corporations: Separating Myth from Realities', 19 *Florida Journal of International Law* 1 2007, pp. 20–21.

5    Louis René Villermé, *Tableau de l'état physique et moral des ouvriers employés dans les Manufactures de Coton, de Laine, et de Soie*, Paris: Jules Renouard et Cie, Vol. II (1840), p. 93. See Chapter 3. See also, for the banking sector, the initiative of the Thun Group. On this, see Damiano de Felice, 'Banks and Human Rights Due Diligence: a Critical Analysis of the Thun Group's Discussion Paper on the UN Guiding Principles on Business and Human Rights', 19 *The International Journal of Human Rights* 319 (2015).

## Official documents

Addendum to the Report of the UN Special Representative, "Human Rights and Corporate Law: Trends and Observations from a Crossnational Study Conducted by the Special Representative", UN Doc. A/HRC/17/31/Add.2 (2011).

Human Rights Council, Elaboration of an international legally binding instrument on transnational corporations and other business enterprises with respect to human rights, A/HRC/26/L.22/Rev.1 (2014).

## Miscellaneous

Special page on the binding treaty, Business and Human Rights Resource Centre, http://business-humanrights.org/en/binding-treaty (last accessed 25 April 2016).

# Index